The Oxford American Book of Great Music Writing

The
OXFORD
★★★ AMERICAN ★★★
Book of Great
Music Writing

★ ★ ★

Edited *by*
Marc Smirnoff
Foreword *by*
Van Dyke Parks

The University of Arkansas Press
Fayetteville
2008

ISBN-10: 1-55728-887-9
ISBN-13: 978-1-55728-887-5

12   11   10   09   08   5   4   3   2   1

Designer: Marshall McKinney

⊗ The paper used in this publication meets the minimum requirements
of the American National Standard for Permanence of Paper for Printed
Library Materials Z39.48–1984.

LIBRARY OF CONGRESS CATALOGING-IN-PUBLICATION DATA

The Oxford American book of great music writing / edited by Marc
    Smirnoff ; foreword by Van Dyke Parks.
        p.   cm.
    Includes bibliographical references.
    ISBN 978-1-55728-887-5 (cloth : alk. paper)
    1. Popular music—Southern States—History and criticism.
  I. Smirnoff, Marc. II. Oxford American.
    ML3477.O94   2008
    781.640975—dc22
                                        2008026298

Rhythm and harmony find their way
in the inward places of the soul.

—PLATO

Contents

Acknowledgments

If the phrase "it takes a village" weren't copyrighted, we'd use it here. First and foremost, we thank the writers and artists—including the ones deserving inclusion in this book, but not here simply because of space limitations. We thank *all* of them, not only for their mountain-moving talent, but for their soul-stirring generosity. For example, most of the contributors to this book donated their fees back to *The Oxford American* (our small, nonprofit magazine recently suffered a hard-hitting embezzlement). That touches us deeply. So, yes, first and foremost, we thank our writers and artists, past and present (and future). They are beautiful, lovely, magnetic creatures, without whom. . . . We also thank the musicians who inspired our Southern Music issues, and these pieces, and, again, without whom. . . . We thank President Lu Hardin for his vision and good faith, which made it possible for us to call the University of Central Arkansas (UCA) and Conway, Arkansas, our beloved home, without whom and without which. . . .

We thank current *OA* staffers (Carol Ann, Ray, Paul, Kish, Jessi, Beri, Micah, Bre, Meazle, Matt, Kathleen, Jimmy, Wythe, Cristen) and past staffers. Y'all kick behind! And without y'all. . . . We thank the eagle-eyed and ultra-talented Project Leader of this book: Katherine "Daisy" Whitworth, without whom. . . . We thank irrepressible Bre Schrader and her amazing Team of UCA Students for their immense contributions—Chase Bridges, Sean Cavender, Traci Goodson, Rachel Gunter, Kelly Helfrich, Cheryl Killough, Kerry Krell, Mike McCuan, Madi Morgan, Julie Storing, Nathan Turbeville, Bonnie Ward, Scott Wray, and Letia Wyatt—without whom. . . . We thank our sublime readers for their enthusiastic support of *OA* music coverage. We also thank our readers for—let's be frank—our very existence, without which. . . . We thank the astute publishing team at the

University of Arkansas Press (and Marshall, our oh-so-smooth designer) for wanting to do this book. . . . We thank an earlier benefactor, John Grisham, for making it possible for us to get this far, without whom. . . . (For the record: Though John grew up in the town of Black Oak, Arkansas, he was not, contrary to persistent rumor, the original drummer in the band of that name.) We thank our wise Board of Directors (Lu, Warwick, Rex, Bill, and Alan), our donors, our advertisers and retailers, and everyone else along the way who believed in *The Oxford American* and in one fashion or another encouraged us, probably much more than they realized. . . .

Because we've been blessed, there is no way to name everyone here but without them, we were, and we are, nothing. *We mean every word of this.*

Finally, the editor would like to insert a personal acknowledgment: To his fellow staffers, past and present, for everything. To his father who told him: Find something in life that you love doing and do it. And to C.A.F., J.E.P., J.B., and J.H.: For their constancy.

Foreword

Greek to Me
by Van Dyke Parks

1 April 2008

Mathematician-Philosopher Pythagoras was born and raised in the country, but he hit the road early. He hit Memphis (the Egyptian one), Cairo (not Illinois), and even met the Pharaoh (though not Sam the Sham). In short, Pythagoras was as global as one could be. He met all the Who that were Who in those days (sixth century B.C.) because he was a giant with Charisma, Warmth, and Charm galore. Star qualities.

They were quieter times for sure. You could hear yourself think. Pythagoras dug music the most, so he took time to design the Octave and the Fifth. He figured it all out: How we would sing to the Gods and each other by codifying the modes. Some modes were rosy ("Onward Christian Soldiers," Ionian). Some were blue ("My Yiddishe Mama," Aeolian, now the modified Hungarian minor).

Rules governed modal use and gave music its traction and purpose. One such rule, introduced by Rome, that decreed the tritone leap taboo ("Diabolus in Musica"), was unlocked only after many medieval ghosts had been exorcized from the mind of Western man. Enlightenment of that sort was the direct result of movable print. Yet, I digress.

One day, Pythagoras, now enrobed with his students at the Acropolis, paused among the temples on that sacred hill. As Zephyrs gently caressed them, each structure shuddered with a barely audible tone. The students heard these tones, which Pythagoras named "fundamentals." Thus, modal music, fit to please the ear of some God or another, was born.

Just one Greek made up all that we call Music! Such a brainstorm could only have been generated in a time when you could hear yourself. Think of it! Someone invented Music. This musical-history anecdote would be lost entirely on a rock audience attending Yanni's recent gig at the Acropolis. Doubtless, it's safe here.

It would take a millennium for attorneys and accountants to learn how to cook the books. About the time these camp followers perfected their racket through the legal Ebonics in recording contracts, I'd gotten my ears wrapped around canned music. Actually, my first memory of canned music was in 1948: Spike Jones's phenomenal "William Tell Overture." His sonorities had a profound effect on my future.

Shortly thereafter, they started pumping the power of song into New York elevators to beef up the urban audio environment. I was there. I got my Muzak memories in Otis Elevators. It was in one such elevator that my own Uncle Sam introduced me to his boss. Uncle Sam placed advertising for the music behemoth RCA. His boss was David Sarnoff, "The General." (Sarnoff liked folks to call him "The General.") Before "The General" came up with the idea of broadcasting music on commercial radio, most Americans' musical entertainment was some hard-backboned hymnal, in hand but once a week, or an occasional holiday parade.

We rode up with that man.

Below, on the ground outside at Rockefeller Center, a monument to a gilded Prometheus reminded us who had stolen the flame from the hearth of Zeus and brought fire to mortal mankind. Inside the spacious elevator, all was mellow. Hardwood and mahogany. Our ascent was faintly scored with a narcotic string arrangement. Just as I recognized it as a version of "The Song From *Moulin Rouge*," it dawned on me: *They're telling us what to think and feel.* I was ten years old, a naturally skeptical age. But I'd read Orwell. I knew one thing for sure: Things were getting louder.

Before we hit his floor, "The General" asked Uncle Sam what kind of music appealed to him, and by what means did he hear it. Uncle Sam admitted to classical music, Fats Waller, some Duchin and Shearing, but added that he didn't have a record player.

My Uncle Sam must have been some good ad-man for "The General," for it wasn't long after that "The General" sent him hundreds and hundreds of records, the entire Red Seal catalog in fact, to his home in Long Island. It spoke volumes that "The General" also included a competitor's state-of-the-art record player, a Magnavox.

That was back in 1953, the year Elvis took his first acetate home ("My Happiness") to his mother, as a belated birthday present. He would shake things up. Like the Psalmist David before him, he'd take on giants.

Elvis made a blip on our national radar. Many of the artists featured here did not. To read on is to Discover America.

Rage Against the Machine

by Marc Smirnoff

For those of us who love music—a figure estimated at 90% of the world's population—the field of music journalism can seem more like a swamp than a field; one innocent misstep and you're up to your neck in smelly muck.

A profound disconnect is often at play between music journalism—with its focus on frivolous side issues like money, celebrity, controversy, and image—and the reasons people love music.

Of the possibility of excellence in music writing, however, there is no limit. Lester Bangs single-handedly decimated any possible theory of limits. (As did others.) (With his other hand, Bangs held the door open to the ecstasies that attend pop-music absorption.)

So let's not blame the medium of writing itself for the disconnect. Like music, writing is a power, and the centuries have proven that first-rate criticism—of books, paintings, food, drama, ideas, people, etc.—*deepens* our engagement. Such nonfiction (or journalism or criticism—they blur) proclaims an almost holy fondness for its subject, even when (or especially when) howling in agony or anger from the rooftop. The best of this writing is eventually accepted as art.

You may now want to skip ahead to the pieces that bejewel this collection because I am about to rant. My ranting will come across as petty, bitter, and small-minded. But I won't be able to stop (that's part of being small-minded).

For the generally deplorable state of contemporary music writing, I blame *Rolling Stone.*

When *Rolling Stone* debuted in 1967, the hippie counterculture was in full bloom. Sure, hippies were prone to thick-skulled excess, but *somebody* had to stand up to the rigid and potentially soul-tampering forces that persisted back then in the U.S.A. (knee-jerk conformity, knee-jerk militarism, knee-jerk racism....).

Flower Power eventually triumphed in the Cultural War; first, though, the longhairs took a beating. Here's how, in the 1960s, William F. Buckley, Jr., saw the Beatles: They "are not merely awful [but] I would consider it sacrilegious to say anything less than that they are godawful. They are so unbelievably horrible, so appallingly unmusical, so dogmatically insensitive to the magic of the art, that they qualify as crowned heads of antimusic." *

So, yes, another perspective was needed—the old thinking did not go far enough. By swooping in to engage a previously untapped youth demographic, *Rolling Stone* became part of something large. And with power on their side, the editors and the on-fire writers could spark their young readership to go that extra step, to venture into the world as dragon-slayers and do-gooders.

So much was possible.

In the first issue, the editor and founder asserted that *Rolling Stone* would be "not just about music but also about the things and attitudes that the music embraces."

Unfortunately, it came to pass that to *Rolling Stone*'s editor and founder, music often "embraces" crapola.

Among the celebrities who have adorned the cover of *Rolling Stone*, the so-called U.S. music industry bible: The cast of *Friends*, Pamela Anderson, David Spade, Jar Jar Binks, Orlando Bloom, Princess Caroline of Monaco (well, at least her parties *rocked*), Laura Dern, Dana Carvey, Matt LeBlanc (solo), Jennifer Aniston (solo), Katie Holmes, the Olsen Twins.

Now, for fun, let's consider musicians who haven't yet appeared on a *Rolling Stone* cover: The Kinks, Allen Toussaint, Big Star, the Sex Pistols, King Sunny Ade, Charles Wright, Candi Staton, Greg Brown, Karen Dalton, Jerry Lee Lewis, Howlin' Wolf, Van Dyke Parks, Moondog, Daniel Johnston, Joanna Newsom, Little Richard, Wilco....

In the beginning, though, music was central to *Rolling Stone*'s crusade, just as it was to their public.

By using just about everything, including brains and passion, to explore "godawful" pop music, early *Rolling Stone* spoke directly to the unclean millions.

---

*I actually admired the late Mr. Buckley, deeply. When, for our 2000 Music Issue, I asked him to comment about his old critique of the Beatles, he said, with inevitable Buckley dignity, "I was simply wrong."

It turned us on. It forged community. It explained the mystic meanings of sound, harmony, and groove. . . .

But if power, good or otherwise, corrupts, then it's not surprising that at some point—and I don't know when exactly—the '70s? the '80s?—*Rolling Stone* bought into the flashy, cheap, soul-sucking baubles of: fame, partying, Hollywood gossip, TV shows, and other ephemeral crazes. In the 1950s and '60s, hipsters acknowledged that pop subjects could intertwine and influence one another. But each was regarded as *distinct*. Now, thanks to *Rolling Stone*, we had a clusterf**k. Suddenly, vapid TV programs drew more coverage than wildly artistic pop-music achievements. To *Rolling Stone*, there was no difference between Matt LeBlanc and Bob Dylan.

Yet the Old Guard media hasn't stopped hyping the magazine. As late as 2002, *The Guardian* of London called it "The U.S. music industry bible." That same year, a *Salon* critic wrote that *Rolling Stone*'s "name (and its very typeface) still has a resonance with readers like me."

In an editorial for *The Oxford American*'s second annual Southern Music Issue, I mocked a 1997 *Rolling Stone* article about RZA of the rap group Wu-Tang Clan. The Clan was touring—or "riding shotgun"—with Rage Against the Machine, the pop metal group. When *Rolling Stone* asked RZA, "So you're into stuff like the Zapatistas cause?" the rapper replied, "Say that again?"

What followed was a superhuman effort to uphold a hip veneer, because, as we all know, nothing's more important than a hip veneer.

> *Rolling Stone*: They're the rebel farmers in southern Mexico that [Rage Against the Machine] sings about.
>
> RZA: Ok, right. I've never heard of that.
>
> *Rolling Stone*: Maybe it's unfair to ask you about Rage's lyrics. I'm sure they wouldn't understand a lot of yours . . . so let's talk about your lyrics. . . .

Rolling Stone then quoted lines from Wu-Tang Clan songs for RZA to translate.

> *Rolling Stone*: How about this one: "Bigger dick sex enigma, pistol fertilize your stigma/Stink box, order from Pink Dot"?
>
> RZA: That's all slang. "Bigger dick sex enigma"—that's bragging about my shit. "Fertilize your stigma"—the pistol is going to fertilize your stigma, your pussy. Your stink box is your pussy. I say "Pink Dot" [an L.A. convenience store] 'cause I'm in L.A. I've got some pussy, I'm going to order up some food from Pink Dot. . . .

Heavy. There's more:

> *Rolling Stone*: You have two kids?

RZA: I don't even know how many babies I got.

Rolling Stone: You must know. Wouldn't all their mothers be hitting you up for money?

RZA: That's what the money I make is for anyway. I don't like to talk about babies. Say if I've got five babies with five women—I'm working for them. I'm not working for me.

RZA began, finally, to flesh himself out when he described an excruciating childhood. ("There were fires and floods, and getting evicted. Damn we were poor, too—and you're getting shot at, and you're getting robbed for 35 cents going to the corner store. That's why I ain't motivated by the same things that motivate other people.")

In the end, it was *Rolling Stone*'s exploitation that was especially nauseating, even more nauseating than RZA. Next to the headline 100% AGGRESSION, RZA appeared on the cover with the guy from Rage. Inside, a photo of eight snarling Wu-Tangers, two of them holding their crotches, illustrated the piece. In short, *Rolling Stone* refused to connect the misogynistic dots, as if only a square could, or should, give any thought to the future lives of five babies and five mothers.

Another example of exploitation: A September 13, 2001 issue of *Rolling Stone* revealed, in a concert review, that feisty Patti Smith had "spat out her own enemies list, which included MTV, VH1 and this magazine for turning 'the young into consumers.'" That self-same issue's cover featured a barely post-adolescent Britney Spears in a tight jungle-theme bikini and the words: DON'T TREAT ME LIKE A LITTLE GIRL.

Look, I know my criticisms are hurtful. I know many of the kind, perceptive contributors in this book have written or worked, or work, for *Rolling Stone*. I also know that, at times, or, perhaps frequently, *Rolling Stone* runs good war reporting, good political writing, and—dare I say it?—good music writing. (A cynic would contend that the twenty or so pages allocated to serious writing in modern-day *Rolling Stone* is a diversionary tactic.)

Rolling Stone pushes what somebody I know calls The Cult of the New, the almost infantile preoccupation with whatever is HOT or POPULAR or BLATANTLY SUPERFICIAL. Luckily, The Cult of the New, despite the brain-swishing urgency of its WHO'S HOT/WHO'S NOT headlines, is nothing but a media-concocted mirage; one, thank God, we can pass through.

The truth is, people don't consume HOT NEWNESS at the expense of *everything* else. I learned this from my younger days clerking at bookstores. We sold a lot of bestsellers but not just bestsellers. In fact, when you counted up the generally older volumes bought by individuals using individualized radar systems, you saw that, collectively, those older titles generated the majority of sales.

Somebody goes into a bookstore and scoops up a creepy Highsmith or a collection of Welty heart-twisters. Somebody goes into a record store for an early Lucinda Williams or a genre-bending Kinks album. These (comparatively) untrendy purchases happen all the time.

Want proof? Examine your own behavior. You read old books, you listen to old music, you watch old movies.

Let's call this "the love factor." We'll extend ourselves to watch a movie, or listen to a record, or read a book if we think there's a chance we might "love" something about it, *regardless of the year when said artifact was created.*

Of course, we don't necessarily use the word "love" when facing entertainment options. It's more like: "This could be interesting. . . . Hmm. . . . I liked that other Anthony Mann movie. . . . Maybe this one is all right. . . ." But it amounts to the same thing: being open to, or even keen on, falling in love with an aesthetic experience. (Yes, yes, a lot of new stuff has legitimate appeal. But so does a lot of old stuff. That's all I'm saying. But it's also why The Cult of the New can't be trusted. The Cult lies.)

I've chosen this circuitous—okay, longwinded—route to confess that the first *Oxford American* Southern Music Issue, which came out in 1996, was, in part, conceived as the Anti-*Rolling Stone.* We wanted a music issue that we ourselves clamored to read, that wasn't afraid of examining artists who weren't trendy or famous or even necessarily alive, but whose artistry could still reward the good listener. We wanted a music issue that, rather than kowtowing to the marketplace or focus groups, paid tribute to how music seeps into us.

If this fantasy magazine of ours decided to profile contemporary talent, we wanted meaning, not facile PR blather. And if it shadowed the Famous—after all, who would want to ignore Elvis or Ray or Dolly?—we simply needed discoveries, not the repeat button.

Essentially, death to clichés is what we craved and that brings us to the matter of prose. What better homage to music than prose that is also musical and supple and daring? So we wished for that, too.

In short, we sought a forum for the kind of music writing that tried, perhaps foolishly, to tap into the cosmos, much as the music we love does.

The notion that music coverage is a natural fit for a "Southern Magazine of Good Writing" also spurred us on: *The Oxford American,* after all, springs from the region that birthed America's favorite musical genres—blues, country, jazz, rock & roll, rockabilly, zydeco, r&b, "folk" gospel, Cajun, bluegrass, etc.

It's a funny thing about the South. Yes, we've endured or caused a tragic, painful, horrific history. But even in the midst of the worst times, people of all shades somehow found a way to make music—uncanny music, music that contributed not only to American culture, but to world culture, to world souls.

Such, then, were some of the spirits that flickered about as we set out to create an annual Southern Music Issue. Thankfully, a smart audience welcomed our approach. And now, in commemoration of ten years of hearty, ambitious, devout Music issues, we take sincere pleasure in presenting to you, the hearty, ambitious, devout music fan, some mesmerizing pieces from our past.

For two reasons, we are bold enough to say this book delivers "Great Music Writing."

1. We think the writing we've collected for you *is* Great Music Writing. We'll throw down the gauntlet on that point. (I do, however, wish this book bulged with three or four times as many pages. Other favorites of mine—and there are a lot—are absent here simply because we lacked space. I miss their company already.**)

2. Whether we are technically right or wrong in saying this book consists of "Great Music Writing"—that's actually your call—we do believe in the concept, nay, the *necessity* of Great Music Writing—*of Great Music Writing or Bust.* We say: Don't do it, don't read it, if it ain't at least *trying* to be great.

The subject deserves nothing less.

**If this book hits deep with you, but you don't yet subscribe to *The Oxford American*, the magazine that made an initial home for these glorious vagabonds—and I like to think that some of these pieces could've been published *nowhere* else—please become an *OA* subscriber. That would be a very helpful, very concrete way of encouraging the kind of writing that is herein presented. Thank you! (www.oxfordamericanmag.com)

Blues

Falling Into Place

A MUSIC WRITER LOOKS BACK by Peter Guralnick

I could act as if I don't really know how it happened, but it wouldn't be true. I know exactly how I got to this place, whether for good or ill, and I can't pretend otherwise.

I wanted to be a writer. Not a rock writer—there was no such thing. I wanted to write novels and stories. And so I did—and occasionally still do. When I was fifteen, I first read *The Paris Review* interview with Ernest Hemingway in which he spoke of his working methods, and I took note of the fact that he set himself a quota of at least so many words a day. With as much self-doubt as temerity, I did the same, committing myself to the idea that should inspiration ever deign to visit, I was not going to be absent from my post. And so I began a daily vigil that has persisted more or less over the last forty years.

When I was around fifteen, too, I fell in love with the blues: Lightnin' Hopkins and Big Bill Broonzy, Leadbelly and Muddy Waters, Howlin' Wolf and Blind Willie McTell. I lived it, breathed it, absorbed it by osmosis, fantasized it—don't ask me why. It was like the writing of Italo Svevo or Henry Green: It just turned me around in a way that I am no more inclined to quantify or explain today than I was then. But I never dreamt of writing about it. There was nowhere to write about it *in*. And besides, I'm not sure I could have imagined a way to truly evoke just what I was feeling at the time. *Experience, don't analyze,* my inner voice whispered. Though that didn't stop my friend Bob Smith and me from scrutinizing liner notes, poring over the one book we knew to exist on the subject (Sam Charters's *The Country Blues*), and talking about the blues—*all the time.* It was almost as if by the time we saw our first bluesman, Lightnin' Hopkins, live and in person in the spring of 1961, we had created a virtual world that ignored the complexities of the real one. All of a sudden we were forced to adjust to the idea that there were actual people who made the music, subject to neither our preconceptions nor fantasies and, of course, far more interesting than either.

I won't bore you with all the mundane details of my awakening to that music and that world. Everyone has a similar story. Suffice it to say that I almost literally held my breath every time I went to see any one of the great bluesmen in those days, for fear that all of this beauty, all of this wit, all of this gloriously undifferentiated reality might somehow disappear as suddenly as it had first manifested itself in my life.

I was perfectly happy as a mere acolyte, expanding my world to the soul and gospel shows that came through town, when a series of related events conspired to rob me of my innocence. First I stumbled upon the English blues magazines *Blues Unlimited* and *Blues World* in 1964 and 1965. I started writing to the editors of both and, inspired by the recognition that there were others out there like me, began to file reports on shows I attended. It was this sense of a larger community, as hungry as I for insights and information, that led me to approach the great Mississippi bluesman Skip James in the summer of 1965. There could have been no more unlikely interviewer than I, and certainly no one burdened with a greater degree of self-consciousness, but I had witnessed Skip's astonishing performance at Newport the previous summer, just after his rediscovery in a Tunica, Mississippi, hospital and his even more astonishing reclamation of the weird, almost unearthly sound that characterized his remote 1931 recordings. So I presented myself as best I could, asked questions at whose obviousness I winced even as they were being greeted with a kind of courtly gravity by the person to whom they were addressed, and persisted in this exercise in self-abasement because, I told myself, greatness such as this would not pass my way again.

That was my entire motivation. I wanted to tell the world something of the inimitable nature of Skip James's music, I wanted to proclaim Muddy Waters's and Bo Diddley's genius, I wanted to find some way to describe the transcendent drama of the rhythm-and-blues revues that I had witnessed, featuring breathtaking performances by such virtuosic entertainers as Solomon Burke, Otis Redding, Joe Tex, and Jackie Wilson—frequently on the same bill. When in 1966 an underground music press began to emerge, first with the appearance of *Crawdaddy! The Magazine of Rock 'n' Roll,* Paul Williams's utopian embrace of the revolution, then, in the same year, with the arrival of *Boston After Dark,* "Boston's Only Complete Entertainment Weekly," and finally, in 1967, with *Rolling Stone,* my course was set. In each case someone at the paper knew of my love for the blues (and who within the sound of my voice could *fail* to be aware of it?) and asked if I would like to write about the music. I never saw it as a life decision (I had no intention of abandoning my novels and short stories), but I never hesitated, either. How could I refuse the opportunity to tell people about this music that I thought was so great? How could I turn down the chance simply to put some of those names down on paper?

Muddy Waters, Howlin' Wolf, James Brown, Solomon Burke, Robert Pete Williams, Jerry Lee Lewis, Bo Diddley, Elvis Presley, Chuck Berry, and Buddy Guy—these were among the first stories I wrote, some of them no longer than one hundred and fifty to two hundred words. They were intended to *sell*—not a product but an unarticulated belief, a belief in the intrinsic worth of American vernacular culture. Even writing these names down today evokes some of the same secret thrill, but it could never fully suggest the tenor of a time when merely to name was to validate, when so much of this music was not simply ignored but reviled in the mainstream press. To be able to write in my perfectly serious, if not altogether unself-conscious way, of James Brown's "brilliant sense of theatrics," his "genius for showmanship," and the "passionate conviction" with which he transformed his show into something like a religious ritual, to proclaim Solomon Burke an artist "whose every song seems to [possess] the underlying conviction that somehow or other by his investment of emotion he might alter the world's course," to describe Muddy Waters as the creator of a seminal style whose songs were our contemporary classics, to speak of the "existential acts" with which Elvis "helped to liberate a generation"—these were my own intentional acts of subversion, by which I was clearly attempting to undermine ingrained cultural prejudices and, no doubt, declare my own.

The more I wrote, of course, the more I found the need to seek out a vocabulary that could suggest something of the experience that I found so compelling. Writing about music is, as more than one dismissive wag has pointed out, a little like dancing about architecture, and for someone almost entirely lacking in musical training or knowledge, it is even more so. What I was trying to capture, though, I realized from the start, was the *feeling*, not the technique. I was not trying to provide deconstructive analysis of the swoops and glissandos that went into the first few bars of Aretha Franklin's "I Never Loved a Man (The Way I Loved You)" any more than I would have attempted to break down the sentence structure of Henry Green's *Pack My Bag;* what I was interested in was exhortatory writing, writing that would bring the reader to the same appreciation of the subject that I felt, that would in a sense mimic the same emotions not just that I experienced but that I believed the musician put into the music in the first place. Just how ambivalent I was about this whole enterprise can be gleaned from the opening paragraph of the epilogue to my first book. "I consider this chapter a swan song," I wrote in 1971, "not only to the book but to my whole brief critical career. Next time you see me I hope I will be my younger, less self-conscious and critical self. It would be nice to just sit back and listen to the music again without a notebook always poised or the next interviewing question always in the back of your mind."

Well, perhaps it's unnecessary to admit, but, save for an interlude, that never really happened. After writing another novel, two years later I was back, lured by the siren song of Bobby "Blue" Bland and Waylon Jennings. My moment of abject self-recognition in fact came while I was writing the Bobby "Blue" Bland story, spending my time shuttling back and forth between teaching classics at Boston University and hanging out at the somewhat seedy soul club downtown where Bobby was playing a weeklong engagement. My teaching job was running out, and I thought I'd better look for a new one, so I arranged for an interview at a nearby prep school, where I met with the head of the English department and talked about some of my favorite books, like *Tristram Shandy* and Thomas Pynchon's *V*. That night Bobby's bandleader, Mel Jackson, called a horn rehearsal for after the show, and I sat around for an hour or two as the lights were turned up, the club emptied out, and all of its tawdry glitter was unmasked. Finally, it became obvious that the rehearsal was never going to happen. Bobby had gone back to the hotel, the horn players had drifted off to various unspecified assignations, and in the end Mel Jackson just shrugged and walked up the stairs to the deserted street.

I was exhausted and, no doubt, frustrated, too. But I realized in that moment that I would rather sit around in this club watching all the transactions that were taking place and waiting for an event that was not going to occur than spend a lifetime teaching English in a muted, well-bred, academic setting. And so my fate was sealed. It involved an admission I had never wanted to make: that I was drawn not just to the music but to the life. I had discovered what Murray Kempton called the lure of "going around." That was twenty-five years ago, and since then I have never really tried to escape.

I don't mean to suggest in any way that my experience has been without pitfalls or regrets—but it has been enormous fun. To meet and write about my heroes, diverse and unreconstructed figures all, has been as exciting an adventure as anything I could ever have imagined as a kid, except maybe playing big-league baseball. As far as the pitfalls go, they are, I suppose, just the pitfalls of life: As soon as you start out doing *some*thing, you can no longer do everything. As soon as you set words down on paper (the moment in fact that you embark upon any kind of real-life adventure), you have to let go of the dream of perfection; you are forced inevitably to make do with reality.

The reality that anyone who writes about music (or film, or literature) has to make do with is: How do you sustain enthusiasm, how do you avoid repetition, how do you keep from tangling up in the web of your own words and ideas? Maybe that's the dilemma of writing in general—or just of life. I know that early on I stumbled upon a strategy that seemed to accommodate both my strengths and weaknesses. I started writing about people primarily, presenting the music within the context of their backgrounds, their aspirations, their cultural traditions. That helped solve a number of problems. It allowed me to seek a colloquial language suited to each subject and better suited, I thought, to the subject as a whole than generational enthusiasm (the "groovy/far out/awesome" syndrome) or academic pretension. It allowed me, in other words, to *reflect* the music without trying to dissect it, something for which I was neither prepared nor in which I believed. It also gave me a fresh path to pursue every time I started a new project, since each artist stakes out his own territory, every artist has his or her own story to tell, no matter how it may connect with a common tradition or fuse in certain elemental ways with that of others. But the pursuit of endless byways can carry with it its own price, as any writer, as anyone who appreciates the digressive and the strange, inevitably finds. You listen to music for a living, and you no longer hear with the ears of the teenager who once discovered it. You pursue your curiosity, and it tends to carry you further and further afield, until the question arises: How do you get back to the place you once were? How do you rekindle that simple enthusiasm for the music, the ardor I sought to describe in that same 1971 epilogue to my first book as "an emotional experience which I could not deny. It expressed for me a sense of sharp release and a feeling of almost savage joy"?

The short answer is that you can't—at least not without assuming a kind of disingenuousness as embarrassing as any other transparent attempt to deny age or experience. But in another sense, who knows what disingenuousness I was capable of even at fifteen, when I first discovered the music, or at twenty-seven, when I wrote those words? I'm not convinced we are ever wholly ingenuous. But whether we are or not, what other hope is there except in surrender, whatever indignities surrender may entail? So in the end that is my advice: Surrender to the music. That is what I trust the underlying message of my writing to be. Surrender to Muddy Waters. Surrender to Solomon Burke. Surrender to Sam Cooke and Bob Dylan and Sleepy LaBeef and the Mighty Clouds of Joy. We are all just looking to get lost.

Leadbelly

ANOTHER WORLD by Robert Gordon

───

You are sitting next to strangers, on a city bus, or maybe in a doctor's waiting room. The space is close and would be claustrophobic, but you begin to overhear conversation—a riveting tale, an old man's life, a world away from your own. The one you thought was his son next to him, or his niece on his other side, are strangers, and this man is talking not to them but to everyone; and unlike the crazed rants from which polite folk avert their eyes, his story holds the room rapt.

Such is the effect of *Leadbelly's Last Sessions, Part One,* a revelation of another world in song. I have been listening to my copy for more than twenty years, and I continue to learn from it—not only about Leadbelly's life and American song but also about musical arrangements and production and about my own life and what I don't know.

This album is no *Sgt. Pepper's,* no hi-tech layering of sound. In fact, it could hardly be more lo-fi. It is only Leadbelly and his wife, Martha, singing—no instruments. They're not even in a recording studio but in a New York apartment; a friend, jazz scholar Frederic Ramsey, Jr., had invited them to dinner, after which a discussion about recording led to retrieving a tape deck from the closet. We hear dishes being cleared, beer bottles being opened. Then, Leadbelly sings 'em as he thinks of 'em, moving from early-twentieth-century field holler to contemporary protest song. There are gospel and Army songs, pop tunes, and plenty of blues. Over the course of an hour, Leadbelly sings more than thirty. Some get introductions, others flit past.

I had a hard time finding my way into this record when I bought it as a teenager in the mid-'70s. ALL USED LPS $1.88 read the store's banner out front. I knew nothing of Leadbelly but what the cover photo told me: he was black and old. The LP was also old (I was buying the 1962 reissue of the 1953 original release), on thick vinyl, and made of heavier paper stock than the glossy Boston and Kiss albums that overflowed from other bins.

Instead of opening with the hook of a great pop hit, *Leadbelly's Last Sessions* begins with muffled conversation and hard-to-understand words, making us eavesdroppers. Once the singing finally begins (no guitar, no piano, no harmonica whipped out from anyone's pocket), it's a far cry from the push and pull of teenage amour:

> I was standing in the bottom
> Working mud up to my knees
> I was working for the captain
> And he's so hard to please.

I remember reeling around when I heard him sing "Miss Liza Jane." We'd sung that in kindergarten. Then: "Jimmy crack corn and I don't care . . . ," then "Bet on Stewball, he might win win win." I recognized "Bring Me a Little Water Silvy" from a Belafonte record my family played on car trips, and just before the first side ended, I got a roots-rock surprise. There was a hard-rock radio hit at the time by some group, Ramjam perhaps, called "Black Betty," and here it was again, just Leadbelly's voice and his handclapping—one clap per measure, smacking like a bullwhip:

> Black Betty had a baby
> Bam ba lam
> Little thing went crazy
> Bam ba lam.

The link across time hooked me. I still didn't like Ramjam's version, but I no longer laughed when I heard it. I returned to Leadbelly less hesitantly.

After one tune, Ramsey says, "That's an old, old song, isn't it?"

"Way back," says Leadbelly, "way back."

"They made a record of it recently," says Ramsey.

"Mm . . . hmm," responds Leadbelly, "but not like that they didn't."

Born in Texas in 1888 to former slaves, Huddie "Leadbelly" Ledbetter served time in a Texas penitentiary for murder. A composer of such facility, he wrote a song for the visiting governor, which won him a pardon. After serving time again in Louisiana's Angola prison on a second murder charge, he entered the employment of John Lomax, a song collector from Texas. Lomax assumed management of his career, making Leadbelly his manservant.

This distant world has its own language. The heat beats down so relentlessly on chain-gang convicts, they take it personally and name the sun:

> Go down old Hannah
> Please don't rise no more
> And if you do rise in the morning
> Set this world on fire.

The song is slow and heavy, a tempo for the long haul. Ramsey says, "That's the first time I've heard you sing that many verses."

"Oh well," says Leadbelly, "you can just make 'em right on up."

Periodically throughout the evening we hear Leadbelly pause or slow in his singing, groping for a rhyme or idea. Once, he makes "anywhere" rhyme with "car."

He sings a series of field hollers, wherein individual words are dragged over many notes. His bass tones are thick and humid like summer. As important as the words are to one alone in the field ("I don't know you/What have I done?"), the sound of the voice is supreme, the calling forth of the rumbling from deep within, cajoling it from the pit of the soul through the belly and along the gullet before it flies from the throat to the open sky and Hannah above, where its dissipation is so vast as to make the plaint totally ineffective. The sun won't feel that rumble, no matter how deep I go. The futility builds belief in the process, in the making of the sounds, in the emotion with which they are vested. *Forget Hannah, if she don't hear my plea, at least I'll feel better having made it.*

Leadbelly pauses after these hollers to speak a few quiet sentences in his deep voice to Ramsey: "I be around home sometimes and do that one. My baby, she says, 'What's the matter, you sick or something?' When you get the blues feeling, I be washing dishes, keep her from having to wash 'em. I love to wash dishes. . . . Well, I know you got it running and you want something else, let me see what I can give you," and without hesitation, as much for himself as for the listener who has been left on the floorboards, he cannonballs into the excitement of "Rock Island Line." The power of a train as a means out of a bad place, a promise not of freedom but of escape, is overwhelming.

Not until well into the evening do we hear from Leadbelly's wife. During "Ship of Zion," Martha joins in, the additional voice giving new dimension to the material. Their voices were made for blending; even when their harmonies are off, they are on. She contributes to the next song, then she returns several times, but like a sitar or a studio effect, she's on only enough cuts to make us want more.

Much later and a couple verses into an old Army song, Leadbelly says, "That's the part you can catch; come in there." Obligingly, like a weary soldier, she joins him on the chorus. "That's pretty good, your coming in there," he drawls, and continues. After the fourth verse, when she again adds her mournful harmony, he interjects, like a dope fiend who's taken a good hit, "Oh good God, it's killer."

> The biscuits that they give you
> They say they're mighty fine
> But one jumped off the table
> Knocked down a pal of mine.

They do a few more, her voice turning the bread to cake, and after the last one, Leadbelly speaks the closing flourish: "Wow!"

The interjections that he sprinkles throughout the album are as integral as the music. They are about timing, mood, and effect, like horn lines in a soul song. Between verses of one holler, Leadbelly creates whip sounds, the captive's cry, and the captain's gleeful retort—in the same breath. The contrast, the ease of delivery, and the way these asides make the lyrics stand out have helped me understand how much more complex songs come together from various elements.

His protest songs reach to the same authority as his gospel:

> If the Negro was good enough to fight
> Why can't we get a little equal rights? . . .
>
> One thing folks should realize
> Six feet of dirt makes us all the same size
>
> Well, God made us all and in Him we trust
> Nobody in this world is better than us.

That song leads right back into the next:

> We're in the same boat brother
> We're in the same boat brother
>
> And if you shake one end
> You're gonna rock the other.

He drags the second "same" like a trombone's blue note, at once gleeful and woefully sad. There's also handclapping, which, after the lack of accompaniment, is thunderous.

Leadbelly may attend church and may join in a protest song, but he's never far from the street. In "Mistreating Mama," each verse is a short story, the next line building on the previous one, so that a song that begins (belted out like Ethel Merman), "Mama, Papa's got the blues" leads to:

Don't bother me
I'm as mean as can be
I'm like the butcher coming down the street
I'll cut you all to pieces
Like I would a piece of meat.

The songs blend together, trancelike, conveying their meanings by mood rather than lyrics. The occasional discussion, at a lower volume, becomes the soft part of the symphony, preparing us for an explosion of song. And like the melody of hushed violins, when Leadbelly's quiet discussion is investigated, it reveals its complexity. It took years of listening before I distinguished an argument between tracks. A conversation is silenced by the sudden presence of Martha's thin voice, sounding a beautiful weariness:

I'm thinking of a friend
Whom I used to know
Who wandered and suffered
In this world below
I—

But she stops short and says, "I forgot."
Leadbelly: "Go ahead and sing something. Christ. You started."
The song returns to Martha's mind, and she continues her elegy.

What are they doing in heaven today
Where sins and sorrows are all done away.

She makes it through the chorus once before Leadbelly interjects, "That's good, let loose on that thing, sing it, let yourself on go." She forges ahead, and he quiets.

There was someone who was poor
And suffered in pain—

"Let loose," Leadbelly says, no longer playing the between-line turnarounds but sabotaging her song, the only one she leads. She *tsks* her tongue and says, "I wish you would leave me alone."
"Sing it, honey, you done all right now."
"I can't. If you talking—"
"All right, I'll lay low. But you were doing good, come on, what's the matter with you?"
"I'll sing later," she says.

"Don't pay me no mind. Just think about what you're doing."

"I can't! I'm trying to listen to you. How I'm gonna—"

"Don't listen to me, you're singing. Somebody says something to me and I'm singing, I don't listen to 'em. You watch and see if I don't."

"You do it all the time."

She quiets, and everyone quiets. "Just pour it right on there," says Leadbelly as if nothing's happened, as if he's not, like the butcher in "Mistreating Mama," mean as he can be. "That was a good piece. Special, too."

With the next-to-last track, Leadbelly changes his tone, launching into a sermonette built around the repetition of the phrase "in the world." Purposely disjointed and mumbled, only occasional words are decipherable ("I met an old man . . . a different type of man from our world . . . I walked into a bar . . . in the world and asked for a drink in the world . . .") until the ending, which is stated clearly: "We all got to get peace together because we're in the world together." It's Leadbelly producing the record, giving a final meditation, a closing convocation. "I'm sleepy now," he says, "I want to go home. I'm going to have to go home."

But there's still a hot coal on his fire, and ever the professional, he knows to leave 'em singing, so he makes the thought into a song. "I Want to Go Home" sounds made-up on the spot, and it is light and fun, but its plea for freedom, refracted through the evening's material, evokes the captivity of the slave.

The quiet that follows the record's completion is huge, and puzzling. The initial distance from the artist has completely disappeared. It's not as though we were sucked in close but, rather, crawled willingly, song by song, nearer my God to thee, and his sudden absence leaves us wanting. Here we are, after all, in the world we know, far from this other place we couldn't invent, yet that drips from our being, so recently immersed in it.

This album is a testament to the nature of song, how lyrics and music live, how they can resonate on such a deep level to a man born just after the Civil War and to a man born a century later during Vietnam. This album spreads itself across a life, with some songs belonging to childhood, some to adolescence, and many yet to reveal themselves. Leadbelly's studio recordings fail to capture the personality that makes this night so eternal. The ease of the situation draws him out, and he seems to sing for the sake of the song, not for his own personal gain. The living was hard, but the art is fun.

Leadbelly's Last Sessions is now available on CD through Smithsonian Folkways. The CD set contains four discs, and I know I'll enjoy the other three when I get to them (and get over the invasiveness of the guitar). But my exploration of *Part One*, with its continued revelations, always draws me, and when it concludes, nothing else will do.

Bessie Smith

ANY WOMAN'S BLUES by Carol Ann Fitzgerald

A few years ago, a woman I had a soulful connection with nearly charmed me into changing my sexual allegiance. Later, on mid-winter trips to the Los Angeles area, she would play Bessie Smith on a boom box while rubbing my back and neck. I had injured myself in yoga class—Iyengar, known for its strict, lengthy poses—while trying to get over a boy. I would slip away from my magazine job and trod ten blocks south for a forty-five-minute class; no one at work even noticed my absences.

The woman who nearly charmed me had musical taste that was much more educated and interesting than my own. I attributed it to the fact that she worked in newspapers, the ultimate reality enhancer. She was one of those women who seems a few inches taller than she actually is. She mailed me cassette tapes filled with tunes that I had never heard—by Aaron Copland, Lucinda Williams, Scott Joplin, and Bessie Smith. Bessie didn't captivate me right away; the gritty reproduction sounded so removed from the actual voice that it was as if the pen had run out of ink. I couldn't hear *her* grit at first. All I heard were plangent tones, a slowpoke rhythm, and homespun pith.

On my last trip to California, I came down with an exhausting case of the flu. My heart had not healed in five months, which seemed an eternity. Balancing on my head in yoga I had twisted or snapped something in my neck. The doctor gave me painkillers—Tylenol with codeine—and, doped up, I took off dreamy days from work and watched the curtains blow in my sixth-floor walk-up. By the time I got to California, I had tapered off the painkillers—though I missed their comforting blur—and she drove up to LAX to pick me up and then we spent a rainy week driving along the coast to Monterey, where we visited the aquarium and gaped at the giant jellyfish. The jellyfish were spectacular—and it was not just because I was giving in to seduction—the undulations and flutter, the watery shape-shifting so obviously reminiscent of women.

Because I was sick, I slept while she rubbed my back in motel beds. Her hands clenched and declenched, just shy of hurting. We burned candles that smelled like pumpkin pie. Bessie was on repeat. My friend kept playing the CD over and over because it conveyed a message she wanted me to hear. Maybe it would convince me that women are better than any other thing. We cut the trip short and drove southward, where it was warmer.

Long before microphones and amps and digital equipment, Bessie made her first recording with the Columbia Graphophone Company in 1923. The technology at that time confounds me; how a voice hollered into a funnel—sheer sonic vibrations—converted into grooves on soft black wax. The recording—*Down Hearted Blues*—was an immediate success. She'd been born dirt-poor in Tennessee—in a shack, like Elvis, like other blues magicians. There were seven siblings, and shortages of everything—food, love, floor space. She was musical from the get-go. Her pops, a Baptist preacher, died when she was preverbal; her mother died when she was eight. In those days, death was not as malleable as it is now. Bad things couldn't be mended and held off. Her grouchy older sister Viola raised her. Big brother Clarence was a musical prodigy, too. From an early age, she was performing at minstrel and tent shows and on the vaudeville circuit. Slavery had ended just thirty-one years before her birth and it still stained everything. A natural entertainer, she danced and changed costumes—feathery boas, beaded gowns and hats. But of course we don't get that—her devilish humor, her bowl-sized grin—on the recordings. We just get her clear, rippling vocalization, and the simple background instruments—usually at most a piano, a cornet, a trombone. The effect on a listener is physical—like a voice thrown with exceptional aim, the sound lands somewhere inside the high parts of your lungs and stretches languorously. Even if you don't see her earlier photos, in which her eyes and mouth seem to gasp with joy, you hear a certain exuberance. This is what I find arresting when I listen to old blues: by expressing pain and suffering, the cloud is lifted. It is like dreams and bad relationships, how they dissipate when you start bemoaning them to friends.

The word *languor* epitomizes something Bessian. Maybe it's the South, its drawl rendered in melodic form. Imagine life before air conditioners and widespread plumbing, its adagio tempo. On tour, Bessie traveled in her own Pullman car, roomy enough to transport all of her troupe.

She liked fur coats—a white ermine, in particular—and diamonds. She carried corn liquor in her purse. She could lie as quick as any woman. In light of her own sexual appetites, her jealousy was extreme.

She didn't invent anything, does anyone?, except perhaps her own stage presence. Her style of blues was built on other melodies—by the great W.C. Handy and Tin Pan Alley songwriters—as well as the evolving forms of jazz. Also in her alluvial voice: the gravity of old spirituals. Musically speaking, if you want an equation: She linked the past (rural blues) and the future (citified syncopation, jumpy and thrilling as a series of one-night stands).

My friend's hands were on my back but my heart was still broken from a boy. He thought I was certifiable; I thought his loner tendencies cut me off. After a yoga class, I came upon him at the elevator slipping his phone number to a supple brunette in a leotard. My friend's love is constant. Her hands say: I won't run away from you, I will make you feel good and understood for the rest of your life.

That first recording, which was actually an audition with Columbia, sold nearly eight hundred thousand copies in six months. Instant coronation: "The Empress of the Blues." In 1924, she became the highest-paid black performer in the country. In 1925, she met and recorded with Louis Armstrong ("St. Louis Blues" was one of the happy results; Bessie later starred in a short film version based on the song). As rich as she got, she always carried thousands of dollar bills under her clothes, and if you needed change for a hundred—like Louis Armstrong once did—she whipped out the dollar bills like some sort of cartoon character. She was nearly six feet tall and over two hundred pounds and in the photos her hands look enormous, like oversized heads of lettuce. Onstage, they say, she was *resplendent*. Less kind critics called her portly, and one even called her fat.

Her temper, when it flared up, was lethal. Here are just a few of the folks Bessie tussled with:

- A guy who stabbed her in the stomach—she chased him down before collapsing.
- A gal with a switchblade in a Baltimore nightclub—B. roughed her up.
- Her niece Ruby—for fooling around with B.'s main squeeze, Eggie,

a handsome male dancer. (B. didn't stay mad at anyone for long and soon reconciled with R.)

- Herself: Threw her own body down a flight of stairs to convince her ever-suspicious hubby that she'd been hit by a car (he fell for it. Where B. really was: a two-day tryst).
- The chorus girl who fooled around with her husband—she pushed the tart off the train.
- The showgirl who, in a fit of envy, chopped up Ruby's expensive new shoes, a gift from B.—B. knocked the girl's teeth out.
- The Ku Klux Klan, whom she reportedly cussed at and scared off in Concord, North Carolina.
- Gertrude Saunders, her hubby's paramour, whom she dragged through the mud and pummeled and bloodied.

But unleashed emotions—whether blissful or malefic—tend to ignite corresponding reactions. Like early American musics, human behavior may be founded on the call-and-response technique. Once the "honeymoon" ended, Bessie's husband took to beating her for certain behaviors. You hear about violence in the lyrics she herself composed:

It's all about a man who always kicks and dogs me aroun'

And when I try to kill him, that's when my love for him come down

This woman, my newspaper friend, has shapely biceps and muscled thighs. Her strength is an implicit guarantee that she will never run from my bad side. This is how people can slink into your life: Acceptance. She traveled across the country in a bus after the World Trade Center attacks. Downtown, where I lived, smoke, and an incense of burned hair, lingered. The air possessed an almost attractive sepia tint, like we were immersed in antique photographs. People on sidewalks wearing surgical masks. My friend held my hand. She had just turned forty. She doubted that any man could ever comprehend my intricacies. Certainly not that idiot who was stringing me along. I had called his cell phone hundreds of times while he went to tango class and the boxing ring and private Spanish lessons in Central Park. He had his own personal Shiatsu masseuse.

Though Bessie's lyrics usually wash about me incomprehensibly, I sometimes find myself listening exclusively to the text.

I'd rather he would hit me,

than jump right up and quit me

Happiness, it never lasts a day, my heart is almost breaking while I say

A good man is hard to find, you always get the other kind

*Just when you think that he is your pal, you look for him and find him fooling
'round some other gal*

Then you rave, you even crave to see him laying in his grave

Inspired by Bessie's song, Flannery O'Connor constructed her devastating short story of a maddening old woman and an equally maddening misfit. About which Flannery said: "This story . . . certainly calls up a good deal of the South's mythic background, and it should elicit from you a degree of pity and terror, even though its way of being serious is a comic one."

When a woman straddles the abyss while keenly aware of absurdity, her powers are unmatched. People say that men tell jokes and women tell stories. They say women forget punchlines. Men perform and women spectate. Science has proven that women's laughter—on average an octave higher than men's—is acoustically akin to song. Bessie's sense of humor is a great big tunnel through which her powerful voice pours.

Some of the musicians who revered her: Billie Holiday, Frank Sinatra, Nina Simone. Janis Joplin was convinced—it was the '60s—that she *was* Bessie Smith reincarnated. Quote: Bessie "showed me the air and taught me how to fill it."

Here are some of her early titles:

Down Hearted Blues, Gulf Coast Blues, Oh Daddy Blues, Bleeding Hearted Blues, Lady Luck Blues, Yodeling Blues, Midnight Blues, Jail-House Blues, Graveyard Dream Blues, Sam Jones Blues, Cemetery Blues, Far Away Blues, Any Woman's Blues, Chicago Bound Blues, Frosty Morning Blues, Haunted House Blues, Eavesdropper's Blues, Easy Come, Easy Go Blues, Sorrowful Blues, Hateful Blues, Boweavil Blues, Rocking Chair Blues.

(These titles are from *Volume 1* of *The Complete Recordings*.)

(Who, I wonder, is Sam Jones?)

Here are some later titles from *Volume 4*:

Empty Bed Blues, Washwoman's Blues, Poor Man's Blues, Wasted Life Blues, Dirty No-Gooder's Blues, Blue Spirit Blues, Worn Out Papa Blues, Blue Blues, Shipwreck Blues.

If you just read the titles in her discography, you will definitely start to feel lousy.

She played with Louis Armstrong, Benny Goodman. Louis's cornet—perky, modest, richly toned—is a perfect echo of Bessie's wood-grained voice. Some critics assert that her voice approximates the horn. It is possible to speculate that her gift was like a spirit around which she just had to pucker up and blow.

She drank excessively, preferring home-brewed concoctions to more refined, factory-sealed substances. She was rambunctious. If you read any of the accounts of her life (Chris Albertson's masterful, highly readable *Bessie* is the definitive source), you'll ascertain that she had one of those love/hate connections with Jack Gee, her second husband (the first one died), a petty, pompous scoundrel. Though he roughed her up, he seems more like a kept man than a king lording over her. Sure, while she was touring he'd frequently bust in on her—his fists hungry for contact—but she devised an excellent system of clever escapes, not to mention expert silencing of her close allies. On at least two occasions, she dispatched him, at his request, to a spa in Hot Springs, Arkansas, to soothe his nerves. If he wanted money (he had no job to speak of), he was obliged to ask her sister, the mean one, for whatever amount Bessie felt comfortable with. Guilt sometimes drove her to buy him baubles, including a 1926 custom-built Cadillac.

Pugnacious is a word that crops up frequently when you start to explore the legend of Bessie Smith. Not long after she became huge (and her rags-to-riches velocity was staggering), she moved to my own hometown, Philadelphia. At some point, possibly posthumously, she was dubbed "Philadelphia's favorite daughter." I remember a rare family trip to South Philly to bestow Christmas gifts on the housemaid who'd raised us until she retired and how she hushed us to hear a song on the radio. She said that, like Bessie Smith, she came up from the South and made a home in Philly. If you want my story, she said, listen to this music. I had no idea who Bessie Smith was and her music didn't make a dent on me. It may have been that year that our maid lost her daughter in a horrific car accident that decapitated her. It was the detail in that story—the decapitation—that made us all ache.

Gimme a pigfoot and a bottle of beer, Bessie wallers, but it doesn't sound sloppy or crass. Despite the stories about her appetites and foul mouth, she sounds classy. The singer of her songs wasn't: aggressive, meek, corny, skinny, obese, horny, frigid. But neither did she toe any line of moderation. She was merely herself. They say she had an appetite for chitterlings and that when she was touring she would cook up batches in the boardinghouse and feed the entire supporting cast (chorus girls, magicians, jugglers, etc.) and even the prop boys.

I don't know smack about phrasing, chords, and pitch, but the sound Bessie makes is of exquisite accuracy. One-syllable words become sentences, paragraphs. The vowels luxuriate.

Langston Hughes said: "Let the blare of Negro jazz bands and the bellowing voice of Bessie Smith penetrate the closed ears of the colored near-intellectuals. . . ."

James Baldwin, a great admirer, remembered "playing her till I fell asleep."

When it comes to music, we project what we most crave onto its makers. When we listen to certain tunes—and play them for our friends—we are making a statement of who we are or who we want to be. Like Hughes and Baldwin, Bessie was black, brazen, and her sexual preferences, at the very least, aroused speculation.

At the end of her career, when the popularity of blues had faded, she updated her act, choosing swing tunes and transforming her outfits (formerly, feathered headgear and hoopskirts) to sleek evening gowns. Very few of her songs were sexual. (One of the exceptions: *I need a little sugar in my bowl, I need a little hot dog on my roll. . . . What's the matter, hard papa, come on, and save you mama's soul.*)

They say her excessive drinking, and the course of American history itself, the Great Depression, for example, contributed to Bessie's demise. Plus, vaudeville theaters were giving way to talking pictures. Most folks thought she was washed up for good. The blues were so *over!*

The income she gained from Columbia for more than two hundred recordings: $28,575. After she died, two of the people she left behind (Jack Gee, from whom she was estranged at the time, and "Snooks," a boy she had informally adopted) brought an unsuccessful lawsuit against Columbia for 1) not paying her for some of the songs she recorded, which they later released and made money off of, and for 2) leaving her royalty clauses blank. These were punishable offenses, but Jack Gee and Snooks were not decreed legitimate recipients.

If you are, like me, somewhere near the fifty-yard line of your life, and you are unmarried, then her romantic escapades—a series of trials and errors—might make sense. But if you try to imagine the conventions that marked the early part of the twentieth century—even during the giddy '20s—then they astound.

After she dumped young Eggie, she became involved with a fetching chorus girl, Lillian Simpson (who once tried to gas herself to death after fighting with Bessie).

But despite an occasional snarl, her voice usually surrounds you gently. Life is all about suffering, of course, but even that suffering can be squeezed for a little earthy humor and acceptance. I remember two black girls in my private-school class. We were very nice and polite—and even grateful—to them. But there was always a divide. They rode the suburban train from Center City to the Bryn Mawr train station. I sensed a momentary pause every time I spoke with them. Stacey was the tall, robustly figured one. When she laughed, which was frequently, the guffaws splashed on and on. I can still remember decades later the way it erupted from her and married up the place. She brought a Bessie Smith record to music class (I brought Fleetwood Mac because I loved Stevie Nicks's long hair). I remember not listening, staring out the window, bored by the *past*. I was in love with my English teacher. I was a virgin.

Decades later, in a car at night on Highway 61 near Clarksdale, Mississippi, on the same road she was killed on, I was fighting with a new boyfriend. Something about a girl he'd been flirting with. He taunted me: Are you really *angry*. Despite the grammar, there was no question mark. I ignored him. The CD we were listening to was a compilation of classic jazz women. He wasn't keen on her. She sure is operatic, he said. I knew him well enough to know that operatic and shrill were very close on his sonic scale of disturbing sounds. I saw his fingers tapping on the wheel and this time he queried me—Are you really angry?—and his tone was softer, placating. Because when Bessie sings, you will feel the mood lifting. Or at least that's what I feel. It doesn't matter about her biography and her proclivities and her untimely end. Music makes you not care.

> *Once I lived the life of a millionaire spending my money I didn't care*
>
> *I carried my friends out for a good time buying bootleg liquor, champagne
>   and wine*
>
> *Then I began to fall so low I didn't have a friend and no place to go*
>
> *mmmmmmm when you're down and out*
> *mmmmmm not one penny*
> *and my friends, I haven't any*

When Bessie hums—those *m*'s bumping up like shoreline surf—she really breaks through the tinny recordings. It is clear that her voice doesn't need words at all. This is the lesson of those titles: The words really aren't all that important. She could have simply hummed her two hundred songs and people still would have snatched up her records and played them until they wore out. There is meat in her voice. Things aren't prettied up nor are they melodramatized. This woman knew naughty. Those *m*'s pouring out like purrs.

The thing about Bessie is that she doesn't play the victim. There's muttering in the lyrics, minor complaints, sure, but there's also sly resolve, spry intonations. Despite the primitive recordings, her articulation is clean and precise. In music and in life, Bessie knew exactly how to get her way.

At the Monterey Aquarium, my woman friend took a photo of me in front of the giant jellyfish tank. My mouth is parted, the camera's focus directly on my lips, my face colored clammy blue from underwater lights, and all around my head are transparent, plasmic forms. They look like silk panties, hiding and revealing at once. I remember feeling breathless. I thought perhaps my whole life would change because of this trip. I was open to anything. The jellyfish room had muted lighting and the tanks stretched up to the ceiling and of course we didn't have to say the obvious, that this womblike setting contained soft, vaginal entities that could alter you. I liked thinking of myself as a lesbian. It made me feel strong. Like all those blues singers she introduced me to. She kept repeating to me: Bessie is from Philadelphia, too. Though as it turned out Bessie was from Chattanooga. Her lover, Richard Morgan (uncle of vibraphonist Lionel Hampton), was driving that fatal night. It was way past midnight. A truck had stopped on the narrow shoulder and they plowed into the back of it. Morgan didn't get a scratch. Her arm was ripped out of the socket. A white doctor was driving by and stopped. The sun came up. Someone called for an ambulance: The doctor didn't want to bloody his car, they said. Rumors spread. Morgan withered away after Bessie died. He hardly spoke, his body shrank. He might as well have perished, too.

I have been on this road a number of times, but it is eerie to be on it listening to Bessie and to be told that this is where she died. Her career was rebounding, they say, because she figured out how to channel her classic blues into something more stylish, more au courant. She was in her early forties. Everything new gets old, so you adapt. She wound up loving a man. Her voice, even when she was young, had maturity. It didn't need to gush and weep because it had already been there and back. She wasn't about ego and sizzling emotion. She knew that sometimes restraint can be anything but.

Bessie had: a round head, plump cheeks, a gorgeous smile, and a charisma quite different than that of sleek Billie H. and dangerous, glamorous Josephine B., who received a thousand marriage proposals in a single year.

They say she inspired empathy. The warm tones shift and stir like some sort of rich batter in a mixing bowl. The notes cling and blend. Her voice is incongruous—raw *and* polished. Like fancy china and silver on a picnic table.

But she possessed that temper, or perhaps it possessed her. What I hear in her music is the tension of holding back versus wanting to roar (she didn't care for white people, they say, and she didn't care for people putting on "dicty" airs, black or white, and it is rumored that she beat up Carl Van Vechten's effusive wife—a dainty ex-ballerina—at his swank Midtown apartment). After Bessie, and because of Bessie, other female singers would rage. Think of all those girls gone sour: Chrissie Hynde, Courtney Love, Janis Joplin. Bessie's voice may have been more rough than smooth—but rough is relative to the era you inhabit—and, in her case, the rough lay over the smooth rather than vice versa. She knew how to work within her maximum power zone—her "peak" range—and even though her voice would extend and bend notes, the volume stays consistent. She's husky but melodic. She growls but doesn't shrill. My new boyfriend looks at me pointedly while we are driving in the dark on that Clarksdale road. Why is it that girls have to shrill? he asks. The world would be a much easier place if girls didn't shrill, he adds. Though I am used to him trying to get my goat, it is harder for me to admit when he's right. All around us, the alluvial flats. Cypress trees stick up out of the swamp as if half-buried by a flood. She sings of floods, too—she was prescient. *Backwater blues done call me to pack my things and go,* she sang, and three months later, in 1927, the Mississippi River swelled up, levees burst, the flood was epic. She had a woman's intuition *and* she was Southern. Since I've been South, I've changed. Not only my musical tastes, but also my outlook and expression: I don't have to shout to get people's attention. In New York, you have to shout. In Philly, a little less so.

Dicty is one of those words that you sometimes find in archives and because it is so beguiling—and onomatopoetic—you wonder about racial overtones: Used in conversation, will it evoke something horrible that my Northern roots aren't aware of?

When I visit the Philadelphia Art Museum, where my mother is a tour guide, I usually find myself taking in Duchamp's *Bride Stripped Bare by Her Bachelors, Even (The Large Glass)*. On their own terms, the oddly connected shapes in the fractured glass surprise me. But a little history gets you in on the humor: a Dada rush as unintelligible joy: anything can be anything. Not to mention the skyline of the city in the window behind Duchamp's window that became Bessie's Yankee home.

> *There's nineteen men livin' in my neighborhood*
>
> *Eighteen of them are fools and the one ain't no doggone good*

I came as close to succumbing to my woman friend as I suppose I can come. I can't deny the attraction that was there. My senses as electric and throbbing as those jellyfish. On the last day I spent with her, we were hanging laundry in the yard behind her pretty bungalow. The sky a heartbreaking blue like you'll only see in Southern California. White sheets were flapping all around us—it was like a scene in a movie. Her hair was the color of honey. The flu was still in me, but it was lessening. A chopper flew overhead and we looked at each other while every sound on earth was drowned out. Then it faded and Bessie's voice came rolling out the living room window. Philadelphia, California, Mississippi, Arkansas: This woman's voice connects them all. If you listen to her music, the songs will weave together intricately, as if there is some larger purpose than creating a series of hits. I wanted that trip, that setting, that situation to be the transformative one—the one where the epiphany to beat all epiphanies would swoop me up—but that happened later and at the time I didn't even notice it. I was too busy in my pricey Chelsea apartment taping up fifty cardboard boxes with books and packing my clothing—bell-bottom jeans and wedge sandals, most of which I would never wear again—and schlepping garbage bags down six steep tenement flights to the trash. The whole building was enclosed in tall metal spikes. You needed a key for everything, trash cans, laundry room, inner stairwells.

And just like that, I was living in the South. If we do indeed have souls—as many women and some men seem to think—mine was turning down the volume. Think of a loudspeaker broadcasting your inner voice: In New York City, circa 2005, your everyday voice may wind up at, say, nine on a scale of ten; but in undiscovered Arkansas, you may find it subsides to a middling four or five. I was closing in on Bessie's age when she was at her peak. The upwardly thirties, to be precise. If she's somewhere in the universe, I think she's not complaining about the duration of her odyssey because—doggone it—she had a good time. How many of us get to share our easy inner rhythms and wry spirits with the tone-deaf planet? My California friend was musical, too; she played guitar when she wasn't rubbing my back, and she sang along in a thin, sweet, embarrassed voice. Music—like food, like sex—connects us. It can cause nostalgia and sometimes regrets. Technology is miraculous. New York is bustling—around the chasm on Wall Street. If Bessie had survived the car crash, they say her arm would have been amputated. Even so, I imagine she would have continued to sing.

Country

Jimmy Martin

TRUE ADVENTURES WITH THE KING OF BLUEGRASS
by Tom Piazza

It's pitch-dark and cold and I'm sitting in my car at the top of a driveway on a small hill outside Nashville, trying to decide what to do. In an hour and a half, the Grand Ole Opry starts, and I'm supposed to attend with the King of Bluegrass himself— or, rather, the King-in-Exile, the sixty-nine-year-old Black Sheep of the Great Dysfunctional Family of Country Music—Jimmy Martin, veteran of Bill Monroe's early-1950s Blue Grass Boys and one-time Decca recording star in his own right. Inside the nearby house, which is totally dark, Jimmy Martin is submerged in some advanced state of inebriation, waiting for me. Outside my car, two of Martin's hunting dogs are howling their heads off in the cold, black night air in a frenzy of bloodlust.

I've hit the horn a few times, but no lights have gone on, no doors have opened. The Dodge van and the Ford pickup are there, with the coon-hunting bumper stickers (WHEN THE TAILGATE DROPS, THE BULLSHIT STOPS), as is the midnight-blue 1985 Lincoln stretch limousine in which we took his garbage to the town incinerator yesterday, so I know he didn't run out on me. Finally, I tentatively open my door to see if I can make it to the house, but one of the dogs comes peeling around the front bumper and I close it again, fast. I decide to pull out and call him from the gas station on the corner of Old Hickory Boulevard.

It's kind of beautiful out here, actually. Hermitage is an eastern suburb of Nashville about fifteen minutes out Interstate 40 from downtown. Rolling hills, shopping centers, subdivisions, plus the usual swelling of motels and fast-food joints around the highway interchange, like an infection around a puncture wound. The main attraction is President Andrew Jackson's house, the Hermitage, where historically minded Nashville tourists can go for a couple hours' respite from the Eternal Twang.

I have always wanted to meet Jimmy Martin. I heard that he was a difficult person, but I don't know if anything could have prepared me for the last two days. But you may not even know who Jimmy Martin is, so first things first. . . .

One night in 1949, a completely unknown, twenty-two-year-old singer-guitarist from Sneedville, Tennessee, walked up to Bill Monroe backstage at the Grand Ole Opry and asked if he could sing him a song. Monroe agreed, and before an hour had passed he invited the young man on the road with his band, the Blue Grass Boys. At that time, Monroe and his mandolin had already pioneered the sound that would become known as bluegrass, a form of country music reaching back to earlier mountain styles and adding an emphasis on instrumental precision and virtuosity. Monroe's two most famous sidemen of the 1940s, the guitarist-singer Lester Flatt and the banjoist Earl Scruggs, were as important in many ways to the music's development as Monroe; when they left the Blue Grass Boys, in 1948, they were stars in their own right.

Martin's arrival brought another element into the group; his high, strong voice, stronger than Lester Flatt's, gave a new edge to the vocal blend, and his aggressive guitar added a stronger push to the rhythm as well. His early-1950s recordings with Monroe, including "Uncle Pen," "River of Death," and "The Little Girl and the Dreadful Snake," are classics. After five years with Monroe, Martin went on his own, first teaming up with the very young Osborne Brothers and then forming his own group. The 1957–1961 incarnation of the Sunny Mountain Boys, as he called them, with the mandolinist Paul Williams and the banjo prodigy J.D. Crowe, is widely regarded as one of the greatest bands in bluegrass history.

Martin had a string of hits in the late 1950s and early '60s, including "Ocean of Diamonds," "Sophronie," the truck-driving anthem "Widow Maker," "You Don't Know My Mind," and his signature tune, "Sunny Side of the Mountain." Martin's vocals—high, plaintive, and lonesome—wrung every bit of meaning and feeling out of the lyrics. Like many country performers, he was capable of astonishing sentimentality, musical crocodile tears, like his duet with his young daughter on "Daddy, Will Santa Claus Ever Have to Die?" But at his best his phrasing, the impact of the urgency behind his long, held notes, could be staggering.

Although his early recordings are considered bluegrass classics, to my ears he seemed to take more chances and gain in expressiveness as he got older. In 1973 he received a gold record, along with Roy Acuff, Doc Watson, Merle Travis, and Maybelle Carter, for his contribution to the Nitty Gritty Dirt Band's first *Will the Circle Be Unbroken* album; his performances are arguably the best thing about that record.

Despite all this, Martin has remained a kind of shadowy figure, with much less of a public profile than some of his bluegrass peers, like Ralph Stanley, or the Osborne Brothers. He is seen in Rachel Liebling's excellent 1991 bluegrass documentary film *High Lonesome*, but the glimpses are only tantalizing. In some ways, Martin doesn't fit into the categories that have evolved in the country-music world. He is too raw for the commercial and slick Nashville establishment and in a way too unapologetically country in the old sense—mixing sentiment and showmanship with George Jones– and Hank Williams–style barroom heartbreak—for the folk-revival types to whom bluegrass was, and is, essentially folk music. On top of that, the King of Bluegrass, as he called himself, had a reputation as a heavy drinker and a volatile personality. As I asked around, I began to realize that Nashville insiders traded Martin stories back and forth the way 1960s Washington insiders used to tell Lyndon Johnson stories.

Still, his obscurity was hard for me to fathom. When I got into bluegrass, after twenty-five years of listening to jazz, Martin seemed, and still seems, to be the greatest. On heartbreak songs he could tell it like it is, with no posing, only pure truth. . . .

> Tomorrow's just another day to worry—
> To wake up, my dear, and I wonder why
> Must a sea of heartache slowly drown me?
> Why can't I steal away somewhere and die?

He sang to the hilt, as if the full weight of a human life hung on every line. His phrasing was alive with expressive turns, his voice breaking at times, or falling off a note he had held just long enough. His nasal, reedy tones reached back all the way to country music's deepest Scotch-Irish roots; at its highest and lonesomest, his voice conveyed the near-madness and absolutism of bagpipes in full cry. The only comparison in my experience was to the keening sound of certain jazz players, the altoist Jackie McLean or, especially, the tenor giant John Coltrane. Why, I always wondered, wasn't he everybody's favorite?

I did some digging and got his phone number and in early October of last year called to try and set up an interview. From the first he was guarded, even suspicious, and it was clear that he was in no rush to have me visit. His voice was unmistakable from his records—high, nasal, and deep country—and he spoke loud and in italics much of the time. After some confusion over my name (*"Tom T. Hall?"*), he gave a series of grunted, grudging responses to my initial comments about why I was calling. When I told him he was my favorite bluegrass singer he shifted gears a little, thanking me, and saying, "I can't *tell* you how many thousands of people have told me that over the years. When did you want to come up and see me?" I suggested a date in November, and he began hedging, saying that he would be spending a lot of time out of town coon hunting. We agreed that I'd call him in a week or two to see how his plans were shaping up.

A week and a half later I called him again to try and zero in on a date. It was immediately obvious not only that he didn't remember our previous conversation ("Tom T. *WHAT?*"), but that he was drunk. I started explaining that I wanted to write a piece on him, but he cut me off in mid-sentence.

"*Whut,*" he began, dramatically, "is *in* this . . ." another dramatic pause, "for *Jimmy Martin?*" His speech was heavy and over-deliberate, rather than slurred.

Before I could answer, he broke in and said, "Pub*lic*ity?"

"Well, yeah—" I began.

"I mean," he said, "what kind . . . of *money* . . . is in it?"

"Well," I began, again, realizing that he probably hadn't had a lot of magazine articles done on him lately, "magazines don't really do that. They don't pay the subjects of—" and here he broke in again.

"*You're* . . ." he said, "telling *me* . . . what *magazines* do?"

Uh-oh, I thought.

"I've had *all kinds* of write-ups," he went on, cranking up, his voice suddenly seething with a weirdly intimate rage. "I'm the *KING OF BLUEGRASS,* and *you're* . . . telling *me* . . . what *magazines* do?"

I wasn't sure what I was supposed to say to this, so I kept quiet.

"I'm just saying," he went on, picking up a little speed now, as if there were a response expected of me that he could see I was going to be too dim to get, so he was going to have to lob me the serve one more time, "is there gonna be a *few dollars* in it for Jimmy Martin to buy himself a *fifth* of *whiskey?*"

This, I began to sense, was some kind of test. Feeling my way, I said, "I tell you what . . . if you want to do the interview . . . I'll bring you the fifth of whiskey *myself.*"

"*ALL right!*" he hollered, sounding hugely pleased. "*COME 'n' see me.* When you wanna come up?"

I suggested a date in mid-November, and he said it would be fine. Then he said, "Listen . . . I gotta go. I got a black girl here tryin' to talk to me. You know what . . . every white girl I ever went with, she got a *home* offa me. Now I'm gonna see about a *black* one and tell the others to *kiss my ass.* How does *that* sound to you?"

I said it made sense, and he said, "Good. Call me closer to the time," then he hung up and I sat at my desk, shaking my head. After that call I had a pang of misgiving about the whole idea, as if I might be getting myself into something I'd prefer to stay out of, but I was too curious to give up. Boy, I thought, whatever you do, don't forget that whiskey.

Over the next month we talked two more times. The first time, he sounded sober and friendly, even asking me one or two questions about myself. He had a happy memory of New Orleans, where I live ("I played down there when Johnny Horton had his hit on 'Battle of New Orleans.' We played 'Ocean of Diamonds' and 'Sophronie' and tore his ass to pieces."), and we were able to settle on November 20, a Wednesday, for me to come up, but there was only one hitch. What I had to do, he said, was call the weather report for Richmond, Indiana, that week and see what the temperature was going to be. If it was going to be in the thirties up there, it would be too cold to go coon hunting and I could come see him in Nashville. But if it was going to be in the forties or fifties, then I might as well stay home because he'd be in Indiana, hunting. I had no intention of calling the weather report in Indiana; I decided to just call Martin again a few days beforehand.

On November 17, the Sunday before I was to go up, I called him to confirm, and he was the old Jimmy again; he grumbled, chafed ("Now, that's *how* many days you're taking up?"), but I finally got him to agree that I would drive up on Wednesday, we would visit on Thursday, and then we could take it from there. Thursday, right? Yep. Okay. See you then. Hang up.

That's it. I was going.

The drive from New Orleans took ten hours. As soon as I arrived at the Holiday Inn in Hermitage that Wednesday night, I called Martin.

"Oh, hell," he said, gloomily. "I was fixing to spend tomorrow rabbit hunting. But I guess I'll spend it with you. . . ." He sounded like a teenager forced to bring his kid brother along on a date. We agreed that I'd come over at ten in the morning; he gave me directions to his house, and that was it.

Thursday dawned gray and raw; yellow leaves blew around the motel parking lot. I had breakfast and ran through some of the things I wanted to ask Martin, but I was already realizing that the questions I wanted to ask him weren't really the point of this trip. Whatever I was looking for, I probably wouldn't find by asking him a bunch of questions. But it was a place to start, at least.

His house, it turned out, was closer than I realized, and five minutes before ten A.M., I pulled up to the big iron gates he had described, at the foot of a long blacktop driveway leading up to a large, ochre-colored ranch house on several hilly acres of land. At the top of the driveway I could see a figure moving. I made my way up the driveway and parked in some mud off to the right, the only paved spots being taken up by a couple of vans and a long, midnight-blue stretch limousine, the rear license plate of which read KING JM. Across the lip of the limo's trunk, yellow and orange letters spelled out the title of his best-known hit, SUNNY SIDE OF THE MOUNTAIN. The moving figure was, of course, Martin, attended by two dogs that bayed lustily at my approach. Martin didn't stop what he was doing or register my arrival in any way; by the time I opened the door of my car he had disappeared into the limo, and as I got out his taillights squeezed bright and the limo started to back up.

I grabbed my stuff and approached the limo, the tinted driver's-side window rolled down halfway, and there was Jimmy Martin looking up at me, unsmiling, suspicion in his red and slightly watery eyes, his head as big as a large ham and very jowlly, with long gray sideburns and thin gray hair combed straight back and left a little bit long by the collar of his black nylon windbreaker.

"Leave your bags in your car," he said. "I gotta do an errand here; you can come with me."

By the time I climbed into his passenger seat, Martin was trying to maneuver the limo into a five-point U-turn so that he could get it out of his driveway. He worked the gear shift, which was on the steering column, with dogged concentration and without saying a word. The hood was as big as a queen-sized bed. On the first leg of the turn the limo stalled, and Martin cursed and restarted it with effort. The car stalled twice more before he got it through the turn; at one point he spun the wheels and they splattered mud all over my car, which was about twenty feet behind the limo. Finally, the turn was completed, and we coasted down the driveway with the engine gurgling uncertainly, and out onto the road.

Once we were underway, I tried a few conversation openers, but it was like trying to play tennis in the sand. It took three long minutes, driving at about fifteen miles an hour, to get to our destination just off the main road: the back of a one-story brick building where somebody was busy throwing wood and other garbage into an incinerator.

"Wait here," Martin said, getting out and slamming the door. For the first time I turned and looked in the back area of the limo, which was upholstered in blue velvet, but not very well cared for, littered with scraps of paper and junk. In the middle of the back seat were two giant bags of garbage and a broken crutch. Martin opened the back door, grabbed the garbage, and closed it again. I watched him bring it over to the guy; they stood around talking, inaudibly to me, for about five minutes while I sat in the front seat.

When they were finished, Martin got back in without any explanation, and we headed back to the house, with the limo stalling only once more.

The dogs were really whooping it up when we arrived, and Martin hollered at them as we got out and they skulked away quietly. At the end of the driveway stood a big STOP sign, with stick-on letters added, reading BAD DOG WILL BITE TAIL. I grabbed my bags out of my car and followed Martin inside.

We walked under a carport and through a storm door into an unheated den, where the floor was piled with boxes of cassettes, CDs, an upright bass, sound equipment, and other stuff. I followed him up a few steps, through a door and past a daybed where a collection of mesh caps of all sorts was displayed, then through another door into a vestibule with a bathroom and a bedroom off of it, which led directly into the kitchen. It was obviously a bachelor's house: Clothes were set out to dry on a chair by the heater, and at the Formica kitchen table space would have had to be cleared amid papers, mail-order catalogs, letters, and empty cassette cases to make room for a second person to eat. I unpacked my cassette recorder and notebook while Martin wordlessly looked through some mail, but before we got started I was going to give him the whiskey I had promised him.

I had put some thought into the choice, actually. I had initially bought him a bottle of Knob Creek, a very good Kentucky bourbon. But after I bought it I wondered if there wouldn't be some state loyalty involved in Martin's whiskey preference. He had begun life in Tennessee, after all, and had spent the last twenty-five years living there. Tennessee was the home of the Grand Ole Opry, etc., etc., and for all I knew some kind of horrible blood rivalry might exist between Tennessee and Kentucky. So I went back to the liquor store and picked up a bottle of Gentleman Jack as well, to cover the Tennessee base.

Now I reminded him of the conversation, made a little speech about the rationale for my choice, during which he looked blankly at the bottles, then I handed the bottles to him, feeling proud of myself.

"I drink Seagram's 7," he said. Then he walked across the kitchen, stashed the bottles in a cabinet, and that was that.

The interview started slowly. We discussed a few things perfunctorily for a while (Do you have a favorite country singer? "George Jones." Why? " 'Cause he's the best."). He also said he liked Hank Williams, Roy Acuff, Ernest Tubb, Bill Monroe, Lester Flatt and Earl Scruggs, and Marty Stuart. His favorite guitarists were Chet Atkins and Doc Watson. Not Merle Travis? I asked. "Well, yeah, I would have to say Merle Travis. Put Merle Travis in there. . . ."

Before long, though, he steered the conversation to what turned out to be his preoccupation: the fact that he has never been invited to join the Grand Ole Opry. His exclusion clearly causes him pain; he has various theories about why he has been passed by, but he has not given up hope of being asked. He produced letters from a number of people in and out of the music business who sang his praises and expressed wonder that he wasn't on it. It is obviously the great frustration of his life. To grasp why, one has to realize that to someone of Martin's generation, who grew up listening to it on the radio, the Opry *was* country music. All the greatest stars were on it; it was the pinnacle of exposure and prestige. Being on the Opry was tantamount to being in a family; being asked to join was the final seal of approval on a performer, an entrance into a pantheon that included all of one's heroes—Hank Williams, Roy Acuff, Bill Monroe, Ernest Tubb, and on and on. Martin has been lobbying for his inclusion for years, and we talked about the question for a good while before I could lead him on to other things.

Once we got past the topic, he relaxed a little and actually started to be fun company. He has a good sense of humor, which balances out his tendency to talk about how rough he's had it. He really started to warm up when he talked about hunting. A perfect day, he said, is one on which he can "get my beagle dogs and take 'em out and run 'em and just enjoy their voices." It turns out that he has named most of his hunting dogs after other country singers. "My beagle dogs," he said, "are named George Jones, Earl Scruggs, Little Tater Dickens, and Marty Stuart. My coon dogs are Tom T. Hall, Turbo, Cas Walker, Cas Walker Jr. . . ."

"Turbo?" I said.

"He's named after that motor in them hot rods; we say his voice sounds like Number Five just went by." Martin then did an eerily realistic dog bark—guttural at first, then quickly louder and tapering off, like a loud car passing really fast. "I go out huntin' sometimes with Marty Stuart [referring now to the man, not his canine namesake]. Earl Scruggs just called the other day; he just had a quadruple bypass operation. Little Jimmy Dickens goes hunting rabbits with me. Ain't nothin' no better than a rabbit fried in a skillet, good and brown, and make gravy in the skillet, then make you some biscuits, then you can just tell Kroger's what to do with their steaks." At this, he laughed a beautiful, infectious laugh.

"Country music," he said, "what makes it is, you're singing by the way you've had to live. And if you had a hard life to live, then you sing a hard life song. Then you turn around and sing about how good you wish it *could* have been. When I sing, whether it's recording or at a show, or just sittin' down here with you, I give it all I got from the heart. And if it'd be something sad in there, I've *hit* that sad road. 'Cause I used to be barefooted, no shoes on my feet, had no dad when I was four years old, nobody to give me a dollar to go to a show. Had to walk five miles to town to see a show. We'd get one pair of shoes when it frosted, and time it got warmin' up your toes was walkin' out of 'em. You wore 'em day and night and everywhere you went.

"In writin' songs," he went on, "you gotta have something good to write *about*. You can't just sit down and say I'm just absolutely gonna write a song out of nowhere—and that's just about the way the song sounds. It has to *hit* you."

Referring to a recent song he had written, he said, "*That* song started and I'm sittin' on the damn *commode*—all reared back and I start in to write that thing. And I've heard a lot of people say that's where it *started*, on the commode. Well, I'll tell you, the best place to read the newspaper, get you a glass and sit on the goddamn commode and read and read and read and enjoy it better'n anything in the world." Again he laughed and laughed at this. He was so out front with everything, and I decided I really liked him, even if he was hard to deal with.

I asked him if he had a favorite time in his life. He thought for a second and said, "I was glad that Bill Monroe hired me, but sometimes that was rough there. Traveling six in a car, with the bass tied on top, used to sleep on each other's shoulders, that was the pillow, worked seven days a week, seven nights. . . . I guess for enjoyment, when I had Paul Williams and J.D. Crowe with me, on *The Louisiana Hayride*, and in Wheeling, West Virginia. We could really sing it, really pick it; we had it down just right. J.D. Crowe was fourteen years old. I learned him how to sing baritone and how to tone his voice in with mine. Paul, too. We slept in the same house and could rehearse and get it down like we wanted to.

"Seems like that's when I liked to sing, and . . . we'd ride along in the cars and sing our songs and enjoy it, get it to soundin' good. In those days everybody liked to sing, and liked to hear that harmony, liked to get it better so they could make more money. Playin' in them little bars for five dollars a night and tips. And sayin',

'Oh, God, please help me get good enough to get out of here.' And *mean* that. Now the boys meet me at the festivals backstage, we show up—'Are you in tune?' 'Yeah, let me see if we are'—go on, do the show, and go off. . . . It just ain't as good as it was then. And I hate to say this, but it never *will* be, because it's run different. Most of the bands don't even travel in the same car and come to the shows together. They come with their girlfriends, or their wives, or whatsoever, so it's a girlfriend deal, it's not a professional deal. And it shouldn't be like that; business should be *business*. If you're gonna make a living at it.

"They're payin' big money, though," he said, with a tinge of bitterness audible now. "But there's little rehearsin'. *No* rehearsin', to tell you the truth. My band don't know what it is to rehearse. If they get out there the night before I do, or stay a night after, they might jam out there and play everything in the world, but there's no rehearsin'. Nothin' *serious*. You can't go into a job just laughin' and having fun and expect to show what you're doing. If you're driving a bulldozer, you're liable to run over something. You got to have your mind down to the *business*. And I've been told this many times: 'You just take your music too serious.' I don't see how you could be too serious about somethin' that's gonna feed your family and make you a living the rest of your life. I don't see as you could *get* too serious about that." At my expression of surprise, Martin said, "The man who said that couldn't *pick*. A man that don't wanta get serious about somethin', he don't wanta get *good*. Am I right?" He was, of course, right, but the pressure behind the way he said it spoke of some buried frustration, a sense of injustice, of not being sufficiently recognized for his own abilities while standards were falling apart all around him. . . .

As I was thinking this, he looked at me and said, "But the biggest thing I have been asked by the public is, 'Why ain't you on the Grand Ole Opry? Why can't we hear you on the Grand Ole Opry?' I just laugh back and say, 'Well, I guess I just ain't good enough.'"

He showed me a photo of a plaque commemorating his induction into the International Bluegrass Music Association Hall of Honor, which he was very proud of. Then we started to wind down. We had gotten along well, after all, and I liked him. He was opinionated as hell, cranky, and overbearing, but he was honest and had a great sense of gusto for life, and real passion about his music. He was himself, nothing else, and that alone is hard to come by. Still, I felt we had only scratched the surface, and I wanted to see him in some other context if possible, get a feeling for how he related to other people. He said he enjoyed our conversation, and we talked about getting together again later in the weekend, since I was staying in Nashville until Sunday.

At one point, I mentioned that I was going to try and get to see the Grand Ole Opry, and he cautioned me to get my ticket quick if I didn't have one already. Then he suggested that we might go together.

"Really?" I said.

Sure, he said, they all knew him backstage, and we could just go inside that way.

I didn't want to scare him off by seeming too excited about the idea, but it was perfect. He asked me to check and see who was going to be on the Opry, which runs on Friday and Saturday nights, and we agreed to talk about it the next day.

On my way out, walking through the den, Martin gave me two of his cassettes out of a couple of big cardboard boxes, and sold me two more at ten dollars apiece. Then he pointed out a selection of mesh caps in various colors, emblazoned with a JIMMY MARTIN—KING OF BLUEGRASS logo. I chose one in burgundy with gold lettering, which I thought was a bargain at five dollars. Now I had the rest of the day to look around Nashville.

Roughly speaking, Nashville today is at least two towns. First, and best, is downtown, where you can find the old Ryman Auditorium (home of the Grand Ole Opry until its move to suburban Opryland in 1974), the original Ernest Tubb Record Shop (where they used to have the post-Opry broadcasts on Saturday nights after the crowds left the Ryman), Tootsie's Orchid Lounge, and other landmarks. Downtown is the province of the ghosts who make country music something worth thinking about seriously—Hank Williams, Roy Acuff, Lefty Frizzell, and on and on. It attracts the hipper tourists, and musicians with a sense of tradition, as well as quite a few aging, struggling characters in denim, Western shirts, and cowboy boots.

Just west of downtown lies Music Row, the heart and soul, if you can call it a soul, of New Nashville, where you find the big music publishers, record companies, ASCAP headquarters, the Country Music Hall of Fame, and gift shops owned by Barbara Mandrell, George Jones, and other luminaries. Music Row can be a little rough on you if you think country music is still about deep, soulful expression from the hills and honky-tonks. The Country Music Hall of Fame, for example, is a lot of fun for anybody with an interest in country music, full of great artifacts and video installations. But most of the Hall's visitors waltz past the rare Hank Williams photos and Uncle Dave Macon videos vacant-eyed and clueless, in order to gape at the Reba McEntire and Garth Brooks exhibits. Well, there's nothing wrong with that, but it is a clue to the sensibility of the New Nashville's bread-and-butter constituency.

Music Row contains no shadowy cubbyholes full of interesting stuff, the way old downtown does. The senior citizens who get off of the tour buses in matching warm-up suits don't want shadowy and interesting; they want bright and aggressively heartwarming. They graze happily among the T-shirts and souvenir spoon rests and coffee mugs at Barbara Mandrell's store, where a Christmas-sale sign reads: SPECIAL: NATIVITIES 25% OFF, which just about says it all, and at the George Jones Gift Shop, where rows and rows of glass display shelves under bright fluorescent lights are crammed with frilly dolls, little ceramic figurines, souvenir spoons, salt and pepper shakers, coffee mugs reading I'M NOT GROUCHY—I'M CONSTIPATED. . . .

All of which, I thought, helps explain why Jimmy Martin might be anathema to New Nashville. Imagine the souvenir-spoon crowd listening to him sing "Steal Away Somewhere and Die." Not likely. Yet all the garishness and bad taste is no aberration; it's part of the fiber of the world that country music serves. You can't really separate one from the other, any more than you can just forget about Martin performances like "I'd Rather Have America" and "Daddy, Will Santa Claus Ever Have to Die?"

That night I had dinner with a friend, a well-known songwriter and performer who has lived in Nashville for almost thirty years and was part of the so-called New Breed of younger figures who shook up the town in the late 1960s. My friend is actually something of a connoisseur of Jimmy Martin stories, and he added a few to my stockpile, including one about a trip, involving Martin and a couple other musicians, to see Clint Eastwood's movie *Unforgiven*. At one point in the movie, a small country shack came on the screen, and Martin supposedly stood up at his seat and hollered, "That shack there is just like the one Jimmy Martin grew up in, back in Sneedville, Tennessee, that y'all been asking me about, folks." Everybody in the theater turned around wondering what the hell was going on, while Martin's companions sank low into their seats.

After we laughed about this, my friend continued, "But, at the same time, I'll never forget once we were having this benefit concert for a local band who had had an accident on the road and needed money. The whole bluegrass community had rallied to their support and held a benefit concert, which Jimmy hadn't been invited to appear on. Late in the evening, though, he showed up backstage anyway, real quiet, with a big jar, like a Mason jar, full of coins and bills. He had had a show earlier that night and he had collected all that money from his audience himself, and he wanted to contribute it. It wasn't a showy thing at all; he just gave it and left quietly.

"Another time," my friend went on, "the son of some dear mutual friends of Jimmy's and mine had died under extremely tragic circumstances, and one of the visitors during the worst of this episode was Jimmy. He walked in and he had obviously been crying beforehand. He had some little plaster statue he had bought for them, maybe it was a Madonna, and as soon as he got in, he just let it all out, crying and saying how sorry he was that it had happened and how much he loved them. . . ." My friend stopped talking for a moment, and I realized he was trying to keep from crying himself. "He only stayed for about five minutes," he went on. "But of all the visits during those days, that's the one that was maybe the most moving."

He kind of shook his head. I could relate; even in the short time I had spent with Martin, I could see those disproportions—the deep loneliness and the huge ego, the self-assertion and the sensitivity and the defensiveness. When I mentioned the possibility that I might go to the Opry with Martin, my friend looked at me and raised his eyebrows. "If there's any chance of doing that," he said, "don't miss it. Something interesting will happen."

"I know," I said. "That's what I'm afraid of."

That was last night. Earlier today, Martin and I talked on the phone and he said he wanted to go; he told me to get dressed up ("Not like what you come to see me in yesterday") and meet him at his house at six o'clock. My first stab at doing that, ten minutes ago, was unsuccessful, and I had to call him from the gas station to get him to let me in. From the sound of his voice, he's in no shape to go anywhere, but he insists he wants to go.

Now, as I pull up to his house again, I finally see him, in my headlights, struggling to open the screen door, and I turn my lights and motor off. He's yelling at the dogs, and they quiet down. I get out of the car, but he has already disappeared back into the house. I follow, groping my way through his den in the dark.

The only light on in the house appears to be the overhead one in the kitchen. As I enter the room, Martin is sitting down in his chair at the kitchen table. He's wearing his blue jumpsuit, and his eyes are unfocused.

"I'm higher than a Georgia . . . kite," he says. "I know what they'll say . . . 'Jimmy Martin's been drinkin' again' . . . but I don't owe them anything." He looks up at me. "Do I?"

I can see his eyes pull into focus. "Where's your Jimmy Martin cap?" he says, squinting at me.

"I left it back at the hotel," I say. His eyes narrow into slits. "I can borrow one of yours," I offer, "if you want me to wear one."

"You got one of your own, didn't you?"

"You said on the phone you wanted me to get a little dressed up, so—"

"So it's fuck Jimmy Martin."

Silence.

"Listen," he says, steadying himself with his forearm on the table. "If I give you the keys to the limo . . . will you drive? Can you drive the limo?"

The *limo*?

"Jimmy," I say, "why don't we just take my car—"

"*NO!*" he says, his voice rising. "We're takin' the *limo*, with 'Sunny Side of the Mountain' along the back and everything. They'll recognize it. They *know* me. Can you drive it?"

"Why don't we—"

"*We're takin' the limo*," he says. "We can drive right inside. Whoever says hello says hello." He stands up, unsteadily. "Me and you are goin' to the Opry," he says. "Did you get you a drink?"

"No," I say.

"Well, go and git you one. Right there."

"Where, Jimmy?"

"*In the cabinet,*" he says. I find the cabinet he's indicating, and inside it the bottle of Knob Creek I gave him yesterday, with about an inch and a half of bourbon left in it.

"Me and you are goin' to the Opry," he says, shuffling past me and leaving the room. "Don't drink too much."

I'm standing here and I don't know what to do. I'm almost overwhelmed by a feeling of not wanting to be here. The single overhead light, this chaos, the malevolent magnetic field he generates. I want to get out. But at the same time, it's *Jimmy Martin. . . .*

Now I hear a grunting sound coming from a small room off the kitchen. I say, "Are you okay, Jimmy?"

"Come see what I'm doin'."

I walk back to the garage end of the kitchen and look in the doorway to where he is, and it's his bedroom, small, barely enough room for the double bed on which Martin is sitting, utterly transformed. His hair is neat and he is wearing black slacks, a fire-engine-red shirt buttoned at the neck, and white leather boots with little multi-colored jewels sewn on.

"Wait a minute, now," he says. He gets a black Western jacket out of the closet and puts it on, then a clip-on tie, white leather with little tassels at the bottom. "All right, hold on," he says, and from a chair in the corner he grabs a white straw cowboy hat with feathers arranged as a hat band.

"How do I look?" he says, now presenting himself to me. "Huh?"

"You look great," I tell him. I'm not lying. Getting dressed up for these guys is a form of warfare, total plumage warfare, and Martin hasn't been a pro for forty-eight years for nothing.

It is not quite 6:30 by the time we leave the house. The night outside is cold, cloudless, and moonless. Just outside the carport, the limo is a long, sleek, indistinct presence in the darkness. Opening the driver's door is a small project in itself; the seat is cold through my slacks, and when I pull the door shut it closes like the lid of a tomb. Martin is next to me in the passenger seat.

I turn the ignition and the limo grumbles to life while I fish around for the lights. The rear window, way back there, is about the size and shape of a business envelope, so I lower my window to look out behind. I slide her into reverse, a hard shift, and ease off the brake.

"Cut her back and to the right as hard as you kin," Martin says. "Cut her."

I'm cutting her and hoping I'm not going to hit the tree that I know is back there. When I get what I think is far enough back, I shift into drive and it stalls out immediately.

"Oh boy," Martin says. "Go ahead and start her up again."

I start her, pull her into gear, and move forward until the front bumper is almost against the Dodge van's rear bumper, where it stalls again. My own car is sitting halfway under the carport, boxed in now by the limo, and I look at it nostalgically in the headlights. I try to start the limo again; Martin is saying, "Cut the lights! Cut the lights!"

I cut the lights and try again quickly, but it won't even turn over.

"We done it now," Martin says.

I try to get it going another time or two, but the limo is dead. "Son of a bitch," Martin says, opening the passenger door. "Crack the hood."

Martin disappears into the house. I get out and open the gigantic hood; I can hear the dogs moving back and forth somewhere in the darkness. My car is completely blocked in by the dead limousine.

Now Martin reappears; he's carrying something about the size of a shoebox, and trailing a long, heavy-duty orange extension cord. He hands me the plug from the box and the end of an extension cord.

"Plug this in there," he says.

The end of the extension cord seems like it's been melted, and the plug tines won't fit into it easily. I'm struggling with the fit, and I feel it start to slide in when I'm blinded by a bright shower of sparks in my face. I drop the cord and the plug on the ground and stand there trying to get my sight back.

"Which one of these is red?" I hear him asking me. I blink my eyes a few times; he's holding out the charger clamps. I squint, but it's hard to see them; it's too dark. . . .

"Can't you tell which one these is red?" he says.

I look at him for a second. I breathe slowly through my nose. "Why don't you turn on a light?" I say.

He heads off someplace again, and I try the plug again and get it in this time. Martin comes back and gets the clamps attached, and I go and turn the ignition and it zooms to life. While it is charging, Martin tells me to get the jumper cables out of his Ford pickup and throw them in the back of the limo. He disconnects the clamps and puts the charger away and we get back into the limo, and I maneuver it through its turn, and we head out, slowly, down the driveway and out onto the road. I'm trying to breathe nice and slowly.

"Me and you are goin' to the Grand Ole Opry," he says now. "And your name is *what?*"

"Tom Piazza," I say.

"Tom," he repeats, as if going over a set of difficult instructions. "And you're doin' a article."

"Right."

"Okay."

We pull onto I-40 West, heading toward Nashville. We need to get to Briley Parkway and go north to Opryland. Outside the car, the Tennessee hills pass in the dark like huge, slumbering animals. I'm holding the limo steady right around fifty and most cars are passing me, but that's okay. I'm in no hurry. This is an island of tranquility here. God only knows what's going to happen when we get to the Opry. I know Martin has feuds with various members of the Opry; he's not crazy about the Osborne Brothers, and I've heard that he especially has a problem with Ricky Skaggs, one of the younger generation of bluegrass stars. Evidently Skaggs was a guest on Martin's latest CD and wouldn't sing the tenor part that Martin wanted him to sing because it was too high. Martin feels that Skaggs's refusal was a form of attempted sabotage, motivated by professional jealousy, although Skaggs, of course, is the one with the spot on the Opry.

Now Briley Parkway comes up, with the sign for Opryland, and this is the last definite turn I know; from here on I have to rely on Martin. I take the exit and follow the curve along to the right.

"Do I look all right?" he asks.

I tell him he looks great.

"When we go down here, I want you to be close to me now, and everything," he says.

"I'll be right next to you the whole time," I say.

"Tell 'em who you are."

"Okay."

"You a magazine man—Tom, right?"

"Right."

Now, off to the left, Opryland appears, a city of lights in the darkness. Big tour buses pass us as we make our way along in the right lane; the traffic is much denser now. We go under a bridge, exit, and curl up and back around over Briley Parkway, and there, ahead of us, are the gates to Opryland. I'm happy to be somewhere near civilization. I follow the line of traffic through the entrance. "When's the last time you came to the Opry?" I ask, breathing a little easier now that we've found the place.

"I can come down here anytime I *want* to," he says.

"Yeah," I say, "but when's the last time you did?"

"I'd say it's been about six months," he says. "But they'll know me well enough. They'll know me. Just walk in there with me. Your name's what?"

We're being funneled into Opryland, with giant tour buses looming outside the windows like ocean liners over a rowboat. "Boy, ain't that got it?" he says. Out the front windshield, spread all out before us, is a huge jungle of tiny, white Christmas lights among the trees of Opryland. "Ain't this Opryland? Huh?"

After a few wrong turns, we find a service road that takes us alongside Opryland to a place where the chain-link fence opens and a guard, bundled up and holding a clipboard, stands in the middle of the street under bright lights.

"Pull over here," Jimmy says. "Lower your window. Roll your *glass* down, now. Roll your glass on down. You need to talk to this guy right here. *Hold* it—"

We pull up to the guy and I say hi and he says, "Hi, y'all," and bends down to look in my window, at which point Jimmy yells out *"HEY!"* in a happy greeting, and the guy says, "Hey, Mr. Martin!" cheerfully, and Jimmy, looking across me out my window, hollers back, *"Mister Martin? Mister?* Just say *Jimmy.* . . . I'm goin' rabbit huntin' tomorrow. . . ."

A woman comes over, another guard, also bundled up and carrying a clipboard; she approaches, hollers, "Hi, Jimmy. You got you a driver now?," and Jimmy says, "Who is *this? Candy?"* "Yes," she answers, coquettishly, and Martin says, "Candy . . . I *love* you." "I love you, too," she answers. Jimmy says, "Can we just pull in over here some place?" and the guy says, "Just pull in the dock, over on the other side of the van," and Candy says, "Over on the other side of that van, there by the canopy in that second dock," and Jimmy says, "Just where I can get out of everybody's way," and they both smile and say, sure, go ahead, and as we start pulling away, Martin hollers, *"LOVE* you. *MERRY CHRISTMAS!"* As we pull away, I breathe deeply in relief; they knew him, they were happy to see him, he was on good terms with them, and I begin to think that the evening might smooth out after all. A tall, rangy looking guy in denim with a cowboy hat and carrying a guitar case is walking in front of the limo, toward the entrance in front of us, and I slow down a little. "I don't want to run over this guy with the guitar, here," I explain.

"Fuck 'im," Martin says.

I get the limo situated right next to a loading bay; before we get out Martin finds the bottle of Knob Creek, which he had been looking for, and we both take swigs, then we get out and head for the stage door.

Swarms of people mill around inside the brightly lit reception area, under the gaze of a security officer and a tough-looking middle-aged lady at the security desk; people are greeting each other, coming and going, musicians walking in with instrument cases, and the first impression is of a high school on the night of a big basketball game. The lady at the desk knows Jimmy and waves us in, and before ten seconds have gone by, he is saying, "Hey! Willie!" to a short guy with short, salt-and-pepper hair and a well-trimmed mustache. His name is Willie Ackerman, a drummer who played on a number of Jimmy's recordings in the 1960s. "I put the bass drum in bluegrass music," he says. "Good to meet you," I say. We mill along together for a few moments in the crowd and he and Martin exchange some small talk.

I am at the Grand Ole Opry, backstage. It feels, indeed, like a big night at the high school, down to the putty-colored metal lockers that line the hall, the dressing rooms off the hall, with people crowding in and spilling out into the general stream—laughter, snatches of jokes, and gossip overheard as you pass along—the halls even have the same dimensions of a high-school hall, crowded with people, men and women, men with very dyed-looking hair and rhinestone-studded suits and guitars around their shoulders; at one point I recognize Charlie Louvin, of the Louvin Brothers. I follow Jimmy, who is alternately oblivious and glad-handing people as if he's running for senator. He attracts a fair amount of attention, even here, where flamboyance is part of the recipe.

Eventually, we come to the dark, cave-like stage entrance, with heavy curtains going way up into the dark rigging above. The curtains at the front of the stage are closed, and I can hear the audience filing in out front. People in this area come and go with a more focused sense of purpose than out in the noisy halls; by the entrance to the area stand a guitarist and another young man and woman, harmonizing a bit. We walk into the bright, comfortable green room, just to the left of the stage entrance, and someone, a big man with stooped shoulders, comes over to Jimmy.

"Jimmy, how you doin' there?" he says, putting his arm around Martin and shaking his hand. "How's the old Hall of Fame member?"

"Well," Jimmy says, "I'm a Hall of Fame member, and the big booker ain't booked me *shit*."

Glancing at me a little embarrassedly, the other guy says, "Well, you never know; tomorrow's a brand-new day." We stand for a minute listening to the little group singing their song. "They're singing some bluegrass right over there," the man says. Martin grunts. This must be difficult for him being here, I think, like crashing a party. He seems to go in and out of his drunkenness; sometimes he's lucid, other times he has trouble putting a sentence together.

Now another man comes up and asks him, "Are you on the Opry tonight?"

Martin says, "No. They won't let me on it."

"Well, when are you going to get the hell on it?"

"Hey, Charlie," Martin says, grinning, "I can get out there and sing it and put it over!"

"I know it. I've seen you do it. Get out there and sing one."

Martin seems pleased by the encounter. He gets the two guys seated; he's going to tell them a joke. Two women are walking around a shopping mall, carrying heavy baskets full of all the stuff they bought. They get tired at one point and they sit down. After they've been sitting fifteen, twenty minutes, one of them says, "I tell you, I got to get up here; my rear end done plum went to sleep on me." The other one says, "I thought it did; I thought I heard it *snore* three or four times."

Great laughter at the joke. "Now you beat *that*, goddamn it," Martin says, triumphantly. We walk away, toward the stage area.

This is going okay, I think. He's seen some old friends, his ego's getting stroked, people seem to like having him around. Who knows?, I think. Maybe they will invite him to join after all.

We approach the small group that had been singing, and Jimmy stops. He says, "You're going to play on the Grand Ole Opry?"

"Yes, sir," the young man with the guitar says. He puts his hand out and says, "How are you doing, Mr. Martin?"

"What are you going to sing on it?" Jimmy asks.

"I'm playing with Ricky Skaggs," he says.

"Yeah?" Jimmy says.

"Yeah," the young man says. "Gonna play a little bluegrass tonight."

"A little bluegrass," Jimmy says.

"Yeah."

"Well," Jimmy begins, "he's about the *sorriest* fuckin' bluegrass you could ever hope to be on *with*, I'll tell you."

All three look at him, still smiling, but a little stunned; the woman says, "Ohhhh," as if he must be trying to make a good-humored joke that he has just taken a little too far, and the young man with the guitar, smiling even more broadly, says, "Well, bless your heart. . . ."

"Well," Martin says, even louder now, "I'm just telling you, he's about the sorriest bluegrass, and *tell him I said it.*"

"I'll do it," the young man says, smiling even more broadly, as Martin lumbers off.

I start off after Martin, who abruptly stops, turns around, and adds, "*Hey,* bring him over here and let *me* tell him that."

"He's back there!" the young man yells after us.

Now we're making our way along through the dark backstage area, and I'm thinking maybe I should just lead Martin out of here before something really bad happens. He's heading for another well-lit area, where some instruments—fiddles, banjos—are tuning up, sawing away, warming up. "Didn't I tell him?" Jimmy says to me, proudly. "Let's see if we can see anybody back here."

Now we enter a brightly lit, garage-like area, with musicians milling around, and a number of older men who look like a certain type you still see behind the scenes at prizefights—slit-eyed, white-shoed, pencil mustaches, sitting in chairs, watching everything. "Hello, Jimmy," someone says; a middle-aged man walking toward us, with a banjo, wearing a plaid sports shirt. "Good to see you, man," the man says, with genuine warmth. They shake hands. They make some small talk, mostly Jimmy talking about his hunting plans. The banjoist seems to know all about the hunting and the dogs. Then Jimmy tells him the joke about the two women. The banjoist laughs and laughs. Jimmy says, "I don't want you to *steal* this on me, now." Everything seems to be cool again.

Then Jimmy says, "Let's me, you, and Brewster do a tune." The banjoist calls the guitarist and singer Paul Brewster over. Across the room I see a big guy walk by, with a kind of combination crewcut and bouffant hairstyle, carrying a mandolin; it's Ricky Skaggs.

From my left side I suddenly hear Martin's voice, loud, hollering, "Is that the *BIGGEST ASSHOLE* in Nashville?"

Immediately the banjoist launches into a loud, unaccompanied solo, Earl

Scruggs–style, an old Bill Monroe–Lester Flatt tune from the late 1940s called "Will You Be Loving Another Man?" and it is beautiful, ringing, pure and uncut, and, his attention distracted like a bull's by a red cape, Martin begins singing the refrain, the banjoist and the guitarist joining in with the harmony, then Martin sings the first verse over just the banjo, his voice piercing and brilliant, then the refrain again, with the harmony, and the banjo comes in for a solo, so spangling and stinging and precise, the melody appearing out of a shower of rhythmic sequins and winking lights and now Martin comes in for another chorus, with the banjo underneath him telegraphing a constant commentary, goading and dancing around Martin's melody, and it's as if they have all levitated about six inches off the floor, pure exhilaration, and by far the best music I have heard during my time in Nashville.

When it's over, there is that lag of a few seconds that it always takes for reality to be sucked back into the vacuum where great music has been, and as reality returns, along with it strides Ricky Skaggs.

"Hey, Jimmy," he says, pleasantly, walking over to our little group, strumming his mandolin, perhaps a bit nervously. "How you doin'?"

"Okay," Martin says, making it sound, somehow, like a challenge. "How *you* doin'?"

"Okay," Strum, strum.

"Think you can still sing tenor to me?" Oh no, I think.

Skaggs laughs, strums a little more. "I don't know. If you don't get it too high for me."

"Ricky, it's left up to you," Martin says. "It's not left up to me. If you want to make a ass out of yourself and don't want to sing tenor with me, don't do it. *He* can sing tenor with me...." indicating Paul Brewster, who had been taking the high part in the song they had just sung.

"He sure can," Skaggs says, strumming, already regretting that he has come over. "He sings a good tenor to me."

"But *you* can't sing tenor to me," Martin persists. "You did with Ralph Stanley, didn't you?"

"I was sixteen then," Skaggs answers.

"He lost his balls, huh?" Martin says, to the few of us gathered around. "He lost his balls; he can't sing tenor with Jimmy no more."

Strum, strum.

"I can sing lead with any sumbitch who's ever sung...." Martin says.

"You sure can," Skaggs says.

"Huh?"

"You sure can," Skaggs says, no longer looking at Martin.

Not to be placated, Martin goes on, "You let me down."

"I couldn't sing it that high, Jimmy."

"You didn't *hurt* me," Martin says, "about making money. I made it."

"That's right, you sure did." Skaggs says. Then, wearing a Mona Lisa smile and nodding politely, he says, "Good to see you guys," and steps away.

Skaggs and his band rehearse a few numbers now, and Martin stands watching them, and they sound good, especially the banjoist and the lead guitar player, who is astounding. Jimmy stands listening, more or less unimpressed. At one point, a short man in a white cowboy hat and blue cowboy suit comes over and it turns out to be Little Jimmy Dickens, one of the legends of the Opry, and the two of them stand there with an arm around each other's shoulder watching Skaggs's band rehearse, and I'm glad Jimmy's found a port in the storm.

Now I kind of pull back and listen; I just want to enjoy being here a little bit. If Martin can survive being that much of a pain in the ass to someone, then he can probably weather just about anything. A while goes by, and then quicker movements begin to thread through the crowd, among the laughter and the picking, and someone calls out, "Five minutes till segment," and it's getting time for the Opry to start.

We move to the backstage area, the wings; the backup musicians are taking their places, and the backup singers are gathering around the mikes, the curtain is still closed, and the band hits a fast breakdown song, and before I know it the audience is visible, and cheering, and Porter Wagoner is leading things off, a gleaming white silhouette in front of the yawning cavern of the audience, a glowing nimbus around him and his bejeweled suit.

The first act on the bill is Little Jimmy Dickens himself, who hits the stage like a bomb going off, gyrating and singing "Take an Old Cold Tater and Wait," which has been his Opry signature tune since the 1950s; his guitar is almost as big as he is, and he shakes so much that he looks as if he's wrestling an alligator. After Dickens leaves the stage, to huge applause, Wagoner talks to the audience a little more then introduces Skeeter Davis, who sings her old hit "The End of the World." During each tune, the upcoming performers gather behind the curtain just off to the side of the stage to watch the act preceding them.

Everybody does one song apiece, eighty-year-old Bill Carlisle comes out and does an act combining singing and high-jumping, and it's a good variety show, but as I watch I can't help thinking that it's almost as if Jimmy Martin would be too strong a flavor to introduce into this stew, like uncorking corn liquor at a polite wine tasting. The performers appear one by one as if they are making cameo appearances in a movie about the Opry, and I can't see Martin fitting into it. Anyway, in his frustration he does everything he can to make sure he won't get on. He lashes out almost as if he's trying to give himself some sense that he's the one in control, that he's the one on the offensive, and not just sitting there helplessly. Whatever his reasons, he is doing exactly what he needs to do to keep himself off the Opry.

During Jimmy C. Newman's number, it occurs to me that Martin has been very quiet. He was talking to someone for a while, but now he is standing at the theater rope that demarks the small area of the wings where the performers are about to go on, and he has been standing there silently for quite a while. I look at him, and his gaze is fixed straight ahead, and I'm thinking something doesn't look right, maybe it is just the difficulty of watching the party going on around him, but I say, "Hey, Jimmy—everything okay?"

No answer; he keeps staring straight ahead.

"Jimmy—is everything all right?"

Now he turns his head just a little in my direction and squints as if to say, Hold on a minute, I'm thinking about something.

Then, nodding in the direction of a small group of people standing just off-stage behind the curtain, he says, "Go over there and tell Bill Anderson to come over here. I'm going to knock his ass right off him."

"What are you talking about?" I say.

"Will you just go over there and tell him to come here and we can go outside—"

"I'm not going to do that. Hold on a second—hey," I say, trying to get his attention. "What happened?" This is not cool; Anderson is one of the Opry's biggest stars and has been since the mid-1960s. What this is about I have no idea.

"He talked to me in a way I don't like to be talked to, and I'm going to knock his ass off. I'll go over there *myself*—" and he moves as if he is going to climb over the theater cord, and I grab his arm and say, "Hold on, man, what are you doing? You don't want to do this. *Hey* . . . Jimmy. . . ." People are starting to notice, now.

"I *will*," he says. "I'll knock him down right *here*—"

"Hold on, man," I say, under my breath, "You don't want to do this. Don't . . ." —here I have an inspiration—". . . don't *lower* yourself into that. The hell with Bill Anderson," I say, laying it on thick. "What does it matter what he says? Come on," I say, "let's get out of here, okay? I've seen enough. . . . I'm bushed. . . . Let's get out of here and have a drink."

It's too late, though; as I'm saying this, Bill Anderson walks past us with a couple of other men, not looking at us, heading toward the green room, and Martin lunges toward them. I step in front of him to hold him back, and as I do this I can tell that it is some kind of charade, because he doesn't struggle. As soon as the group passes, Martin hollers out to the people who have been watching, "He walked right *by* me. . . . If he hadn't a-been holdin' me *back* I woulda knocked his *ass* off," and meanwhile someone out on stage is singing about yet another Lonely Heartbreak, and it occurs to me that it will be a miracle if they ever even let Jimmy Martin set foot backstage again at the Opry after this, much less perform. Calling someone an asshole is one thing, but moving on someone in front of witnesses is another. I've got to get him out of here, and I say to him now, "Come on, let's get the hell out of here, screw Bill Anderson anyway," and he kind of nods.

But before I can pull him away he stands for a long moment looking out toward the stage, and the singer and the audience. Impatient to get him out before something worse happens, I, who have come to the Opry very late in the game, say, "Come on, Jimmy, let's go." Then Jimmy Martin, who might well be taking his last look at the biggest dream of his life, turns around and walks out.

I spent Saturday tooling around the city, buying CDs and souvenirs and just looking around, with the previous night looming in my mind like a weird nightmare. I called Martin in the afternoon; he had a hunting buddy over visiting him and he sounded rested and happy.

On Sunday morning I called again to say goodbye, and he volunteered to come down and meet me for breakfast at the Hardee's by the Holiday Inn. While I waited for him, I tried to think if there was anything I wanted to ask him that I hadn't already asked him, but there wasn't.

He arrived late—car trouble, of course—in the limo, and we had breakfast. Martin ordered fried chicken. We talked for a few minutes about different things, but what was most on Martin's mind was a set of videotapes of stars of the Grand Ole Opry he saw advertised on television and which he thought I should get. "All of 'em is on there," he said, "Rod Brasfield, Minnie Pearl, Roy Acuff, Uncle Dave Macon," and on and on, and he talked about each one lovingly, especially Brasfield, a comedian whom Martin called "the best thing ever to hit Nashville." Martin wasn't making a nominating speech for himself this morning; he was just thinking about the people who made him want to do what he has been doing for almost fifty years, with an enthusiasm that reached back to the little shoeless kid's awe and love for those voices coming out of the radio. "Get 'em," he says, "if you wanna see the real thing. The *real* thing," he said, with lots of meaning in the emphasis.

Eventually, it's time for me to go, and we head out into the bright morning. Before I go, though, he wants to tell me a joke. "There was this guy, said he could go around and talk to statues in town, and they'd talk back to him. So one day he walked up to this one, and, God, it was a big 'un, and he says, 'Old man statue, this is so-and-so.' The statue said, 'Yeah, glad to meet you.' So he says, 'Listen, what would be the first thing you would do if you could come alive for a hour?' And the statue answered him back, said, 'Shoot me *ten million pigeons*. . . .'" I don't know if he means this to be a little parable of our couple of days together—I doubt it— but it occurs to me that it works as such, and I laugh along with him.

Then Martin, in his blue jumpsuit, black nylon windbreaker, and dirty white mesh cap, gets into his limo, which starts up with a gurgling roar, and I watch and wave as he backs her out, wheels her around, and rides off into the distance up Old Hickory Boulevard in a midnight-blue blaze of country grandeur, the *KING OF BLUEGRASS* himself.

Early History

Blind Tom Wiggins

SLAVERY ONSTAGE by John Ryan Seawright

———

Thomas Greene Wiggins was born a few miles north of Columbus, Georgia, on May 25, 1849. He was the youngest child of Charity and Mingo Wiggins, slaves of Wiley Jones of Harris County. Jones had moved to Georgia's western frontier hoping to improve his fortunes, but in the fall of 1850 the sheriff advertised his property to be sold for the settlement of debts. The Wiggins family—two adults well past their physical prime with three small children, the youngest a blind infant—was not an attractive proposition for a slave buyer, and the family had little chance of surviving a sale intact. But shortly before the sale, Jones's neighbor, General James Bethune, agreed to buy the entire Wiggins family.

James Neil Bethune was born in Greene County, Georgia, in 1803, the son of a cotton planter. He graduated from the University of Georgia in 1823, studied law under Judge A.B. Longstreet, and moved to the new town of Columbus, where he established a lucrative law practice and bought a half-interest in the *Columbus Enquirer*, before becoming sole owner. In 1832, Bethune married Frances Gunby, the co-superintendent and music teacher of the Columbus Female Academy, a position she continued to hold after their marriage and the birth of their children.

Bethune commanded Georgia troops against the Creek Nation in 1836; he would be known as "General" for the rest of his life. As editor of the *Enquirer*, and later of the *Columbus Cornerstone*, General Bethune was a spokesman for the extreme pro-slavery and states' rights faction in Georgia politics. Unlike most wealthy Georgia professionals, however, he owned little land and few slaves. On buying the Wiggins family he put them to work as house servants and workers on the small farm that supplied the household.

The Wigginses and the Bethunes soon noticed that even apart from his blindness, Tom, the youngest Wiggins, was an unusual child. His slow development and odd physical movements led General Bethune to conclude that Tom was "idiotic" and to subject him to "obedience lessons."

Tom's only interest was in sound; he listened for hours to the little corn mill in the kitchen or to the rain in the gutter spouts. When he was two years old, he surprised General Bethune's son James by singing the exact words and melody to a song James had been singing a few minutes before. Not long after, Tom heard the Bethune daughters singing on the porch and joined them, singing first in unison, then in harmony. Later, after slipping into the parlor and playing several tunes that the Bethune girls had been practicing on the piano, Tom was made the household pet. General Bethune's oldest daughter, Mary, gave him piano lessons, and from then on he spent little time with his parents and brothers.

Tom learned any piece played for him with uncanny speed, and at age five he composed a piece of program music, "The Rainstorm," a keyboard imitation of a thunderstorm. The Bethune children began to exhibit Tom to their friends, and General Bethune installed a piano in his downtown office so Tom could entertain clients and town idlers. In the fall of 1857, General Bethune decided to end the free performances. He booked Columbus's Temperance Hall and advertised the appearance of the "eight-year-old genius without benefit of instruction, yet capable of performing the most difficult works by Beethoven, Mozart, Hertz, and others of equal reputation." The performance before a large and appreciative audience initiated three decades of nearly constant travel for Tom Wiggins. Following the success of the Columbus show, General Bethune took Tom across the state to Macon, Atlanta, and Athens, where John Christy of the *Southern Watchman* declared the performance "the most remarkable ever witnessed in the city, one that would put to blush many professors of music."

When this string of performances ended, General Bethune realized that Tom was potentially a more valuable investment than his own newspaper and law practice combined. Soon after the tour, however, Frances Bethune died, leaving seven children. Grief for his wife, his duty to his children, and his growing role in the debate over state and regional policy made it impossible for General Bethune to continue as a musical impresario. In 1859, he leased Tom to Perry Oliver of Savannah for three years in return for $15,000. An adult slave in Georgia in 1858 could be hired for less than two hundred dollars a year; General Bethune and Oliver had set Tom's value equal to that of the workforce of a large plantation.

A more accomplished showman than General Bethune, Perry Oliver soon learned to emphasize the more sensational aspects of Tom's talent. During his Charleston shows, Oliver began the practice of inviting local composers onstage to perform their unpublished works, which Tom would, without hesitation, reproduce perfectly. Oliver's publicity also emphasized such tours de force as Tom's ability to play two melodies simultaneously while singing a third, and his imitations on the piano of various natural and mechanical sounds.

On June 9, 1860, when Tom was eleven years old, he gave a private performance in Washington, D.C., for the first Japanese delegation to the U.S., and was reported to have given a command performance for President Buchanan. Shortly afterward, Tom appeared in Baltimore on June 18, a date chosen by Oliver to coincide with the Democratic National Convention. The Baltimore shows were well attended, and one drew more than a thousand black audience members. It was during this visit that H.J. Wiesel was hired by Oliver to come to Tom's hotel room and transcribe two dance tunes, "The Oliver Gallop" and "The Virginia Polka," that would be the first of Tom's many published compositions. Wiesel reported to curious reporters that Tom traveled with his own servant and a music teacher.

The Northern press had been publishing notices of Tom's performances since his appearance in New Orleans. Oliver was eager to take Tom through the North, despite the national crisis then deepening in the wake of Lincoln's election. In early 1861, Tom and Oliver arrived in New York on a steamer from Savannah. Tom gave an invitation-only recital at their hotel, and Oliver secured an agent and rented a hall. On January 19, Georgia seceded from the Union, and three days later New York police seized a shipment of guns en route to Savannah. Oliver, apprehensive that abolitionists would disrupt Tom's performances or even attempt to kidnap him, canceled the appearances and hastened South.

War had already broken out when Oliver took Tom to St. Louis in May. As federal troops battled state militia outside the city, Tom entertained his "decidedly fashionable" audience not only with a musical program but also with a verbatim recitation of a speech he had heard Stephen Douglas deliver, even re-creating Douglas's accent and intonation.

For the next four years, Tom would perform only within the Confederacy, and much of the income he generated would go to support its war effort. In February of 1862, he played an extended engagement in the Confederate capital, and the *Richmond Dispatch* reported that "there had not been such a mania among the people for hearing a musical celebrity (Jenny Lind not excepted)." Oliver took Tom on one more extended tour in the spring of 1862. Within weeks, New Orleans surrendered and Savannah was threatened by the capture of Fort Pulaski a few miles south of the city. The U.S. Navy was rapidly diminishing the number of venues open to Perry Oliver. Furthermore, Confederate money was rapidly decreasing in value, and more and more of it was expected to be directed toward the war. Oliver's golden days with Blind Tom were over. In October, he and General Bethune canceled the final year of their contract, and Tom returned to the General's direct control.

All of General Bethune's sons and sons-in-law were officers in the Confederate Army, and the General did his part for the cause by keeping up Tom's benefit performances across the steadily shrinking territory of the Confederacy.

On a tour of Alabama in the spring of 1864, Tom first performed what would become his best-known composition, "The Battle of Manassas." One of General Bethune's sons, in Columbus on furlough, had described the battle to the household, inspiring Tom to write a piece that blended "Dixie," "The Star-Spangled Banner," "La Marseillaise," and "The Girl I Left Behind Me" with the sounds of drums, fifes, cannons, hoofbeats, and the arrival of trains bringing reinforcements.

Northern interest in Blind Tom continued unabated during the war. In 1862, Rebecca Blaise Harding Davis published an article on Tom in *The Atlantic Monthly* that provoked harsh criticism from John Sullivan Dwight in his *Journal of Music*. Dwight expressed skepticism about Tom's ability to play long, complex pieces after a single hearing and objected strongly to Davis's description of Tom as a genius: "A mere morbid, brainless memory, a freak of idiotism, is not genius." He concluded by saying that Tom could have gained fame only in the "semi-barbarous" South. Among those responding to Dwight's article were a "Musical Lady," who considered it "an injustice to the Black race to let Tom pass as a musical phenomenon," and a "Spiritualist" from Boston, the first of many to ascribe Tom's abilities to supernatural agency.

Praise for Tom as a musician was almost inevitably qualified with the blunt word *idiot*. Tom's mental functions were not normal, but he was far from the untutored musical automaton portrayed in the press. He was able not only to reproduce but also to improvise and compose, and as in "The Battle of Manassas," he was clearly aware of the extra-musical significance of the popular music he incorporated into his compositions. The strongest case against Tom's "idiocy" is the musical instruction he received throughout his childhood and youth, instruction arranged by General Bethune and Oliver even as they promoted Tom as an untaught child of nature.

But Tom Wiggins's peculiarities were many. Onstage he assumed odd postures and made spasmodic gestures, and his facial muscles would often go slack as he hunched gracelessly over the piano. At the end of a piece he would lead the applause himself and introduce the next piece, always referring to himself in the third person. Out of the public eye, his behavior was likewise eccentric, governed by inflexible habits and vehement protests at deviations from routine. He ate with his hands and smelled all his food carefully for the least trace of butter, which he loathed. When not at the piano, he often repeated phrases over and over, and frequently dug and gouged violently at his eyes. In a time when classification of mental disorders did little more than differentiate between "idiots" and "maniacs," it is not surprising that Tom should have been labeled "idiotic." He plainly displayed all symptoms of a disorder that had no name until thirty-five years after his death: classical autistic syndrome. As Oliver Sacks first pointed out in his essay "Prodigies," Tom's idiosyncratic speech, intense and odd response to sensory stimulus, compulsive behavior, uncontrollable hand-flapping, strange postures, emotional detachment from his mother, eye-gouging, uncanny powers of recall and mimesis, and his one astonishing talent in stark contrast to his other mental faculties, all point unmistakably to autism.

America had never lacked for African-American classical performers. Before Tom, there had been the Negro Philharmonic Society of New Orleans (established 1830) and such composers as Victor McCarthy and Basil Bares of New Orleans and J.W. Postelwaite of St. Louis. But white audiences increasingly grew to neglect them in favor of "natural" African-American musicians who performed spirituals, banjo tunes, and white versions of "plantation melodies." While Tom could not have maintained his popularity for decades if he had not been an outstanding musician, it is equally true that his compositions and interpretations of the European classics were made palatable to his white audiences by the "idiocy" that confirmed for them his status as a "natural" musician.

On April 16, 1865, a week after Lee surrendered at Appomattox, federal forces entered Columbus, Georgia. General Bethune had already left the city with Tom for the home of one of Bethune's daughters in Florida. He returned a few weeks later and immediately set about maintaining his control over Tom in the new order of things called Reconstruction. The Freedmen's Bureau, created in March of 1865, was intended to oversee the slaves' transition into freedom and citizenship, but it also approved, witnessed, and enforced labor contracts that were often little more than new forms of slavery. The Bureau began operations in Georgia on May 20. Ten days later, General Bethune filed a contract with the Bureau between himself and Tom's parents, Mingo and Charity, "binding" Tom to him for five years. General Bethune was to take care of Tom and provide musical instruction. Mingo and Charity were to receive five hundred dollars a year and a house, and Tom was to receive twenty dollars a month and ten percent of General Bethune's profits from his performances.

In June, General Bethune, his two sons, and music teacher W.P. Howard headed North with the newly re-enslaved Tom to begin recouping the losses they had sustained during the war. After several weeks in Tennessee and Kentucky, Tom made his first Northern appearance in more than four years in New Albany, Indiana. The large crowds and extravagant newspaper coverage gave promise of further success, but after the third show General Bethune was served with a writ of habeas corpus filed by one Tabbs Gross, who claimed sole legal guardianship of Thomas Wiggins.

Tabbs Gross, thirty-five, was a former Kentucky slave who had bought his freedom before the war and moved to Cincinnati, where he prospered. Gross's big break came when he got hold of a discarded panoramic painting of scenes from *Uncle Tom's Cabin*. He packed up this unlikely treasure and headed for England, where he exhibited the panorama, returning to Cincinnati with a small fortune. A few years earlier, in 1863, Gross had conceived a plan to buy Tom Wiggins and his parents from General Bethune, bring them North to freedom, and manage Tom's career. Gross made an audacious journey deep into the Confederacy, located General Bethune, and made his offer. General Bethune wanted $20,000 in gold and a five-year half-interest in the profits, more than Gross was willing to pay. Gross returned to Ohio at the end of the war, again located General Bethune, and accepted his offer with a provision for payment in installments (Gross paid $1,000 down on the spot). Gross met General Bethune in Louisville, Kentucky, in June of 1865, with the second installment of $4,000. He was to take possession of Tom at this time, but General Bethune refused the payment and told Gross he had changed his mind. He gave Gross three hundred dollars of the down payment with a promissory note for the balance.

When Gross followed Bethune to Indiana and filed suit, the General, an experienced attorney, responded by leaving the state with Tom. Gross and his attorney caught up with Bethune in Cincinnati and again initiated proceedings against him, charging him with "unlawfully restraining Tom of his liberty." The trial, before Judge Woodruff of the Hamilton County probate court, attracted national attention. General Bethune argued that his contract with Charity and Mingo was valid and that he had always treated Tom well. He called many character witnesses attesting to his humane and Christian treatment of his slaves. General Bethune's counsel assailed Gross's character, accusing him of having operated a brothel. Gross's attorneys made a threefold attack on General Bethune's contract with Charity and Mingo, claiming that Georgia law made no provision for such "apprenticeships," that Georgia Law granted slave parents no power over their offspring, and that, at any rate, the document had been forced upon the Wiginses by intimidation and misrepresentation. Gross's attorneys deprecated General Bethune's paternal care, saying that he would have done no less for a valuable animal. They also contrasted the trivial sums allotted to Tom and his parents with the fortune General Bethune had already made from Tom.

The trial exposed tensions between Tom's parents and General Bethune. Isaac Turner, a black man, testified that Mingo Wiggins had told him of the bitterness he had long felt at Tom's status as the Bethunes' pet, since it had made Tom "disrespect him as a father." Turner asked Mingo whether any of his and Charity's other children had been made "pets," to which Mingo had replied, "Well, there's no money in them." Tom's own testimony was coherent, which greatly confused Judge Woodruff, whose opinion on Tom's competence changed from one day to the next, describing him by turns as "mentally incompetent," "sufficiently able to choose his own guardian," and "incapable of making decisions." Judge Woodruff finally upheld the legality of the Georgia contract and ruled in favor of General Bethune. The verdict prompted outrage in the Northern press, but it generated further interest in Tom and insured the success of his first tour of the North. In Philadelphia, the Bethunes arranged a private concert for a number of scientists, doctors, and professional musicians who examined and tested Tom on his ability to play difficult pieces after one hearing, identify pitches, and analyze complex chords.

Tom's Northern visit lasted until July 1866, when the Bethunes took him for one year to Great Britain and France. The European tour generated much praise for Tom and much money for the Bethunes. The Bethunes and Tom returned in the spring of 1867 to their new home, Elway Farm, near Warrenton, Virginia, a comfortable Southern setting close to several Northern cities and the fashionable resorts of Western Virginia. Tom toured continuously throughout the rest of the 1860s, earning several hundred thousand dollars (his few months in London alone had grossed over $100,000). Tom's indenture to General Bethune was to end on July 25, 1870, two months after his twenty-first birthday, but General Bethune had laid his plans carefully. His son John had little trouble getting a Virginia probate judge to declare Tom incompetent and name him (John) guardian. Mingo Wiggins had died by this time, but Charity was still living in Georgia. There is no record of her protesting the guardianship, and it is likely that she knew nothing about it until later. Her son was now in his third captivity under the Bethunes, whose annual net income from his performances and publishing was now conservatively estimated at more than $50,000 a year.

Not long after the change in guardianship, John Bethune decided to devote more time to his thoroughbred horses and handed Tom's management over to Thomas Warhurst, a professional theatrical manager. Tom's popularity—and the revenues—increased throughout the 1870s and early '80s. "Blind Tom," as he was billed, was one of the most famous performers of the day and one of the few who could command premium ticket prices. During that period, he played New Orleans nearly every Mardi Gras week, performed at the closing week of the 1876 Philadelphia Centennial Exhibition and the 1881 presidential inauguration festivities, and toured Canada and the West Coast. In 1875, John Bethune moved to New York City, where he and Tom took up residence at Elize Stutzbach's boardinghouse on St. Mark's Place in Greenwich Village. Tom was no longer a child prodigy; he had grown tall and, in his thirties, quite fat. General Bethune and Warhurst continued to dress him in a short "roundabout" jacket and tight pants until newspaper writers began to comment on his ludicrous appearance. Tom then began appearing in the voluminous black suit he would wear for the rest of his career.

In 1882, John Bethune, a bachelor for fifty years, married his New York landlady, Elize Stutzbach, a middle-aged divorcée. The marriage was not a happy one. In July of 1883, Elize initiated divorce proceedings on grounds of abandonment and nonsupport. Bethune responded with claims that Elize had refused to live with him, that she had married him for his money, and that they were in fact not married at all—her divorce from Mr. Stutzbach, according to Bethune, having never been final. The judge set a date for the divorce proceedings to be heard, and a $2,500 appearance bond for Bethune.

On February 16, 1884, John Bethune leaped to board a departing train at a Wilmington, Delaware, station, missed his footing, and was crushed to death. Elize Bethune hastened to Wilmington with her attorney, Albert Lerche, to claim her deceased husband's personal effects. She soon found that she could expect little more from Bethune's estate than the contents of his pockets. Shortly before his death, John Bethune had made a new will leaving his entire property to his father, the General, and expressly cutting off Elize Bethune "by reason of her gross misconduct since the alleged marriage." General Bethune lost no time in once more having Wiggins declared incompetent, not only in Virginia but also in Georgia, where Wiggins was making what would be his last visit to his native state.

On July 9, 1885, Charity Wiggins filed a petition in the U.S. Circuit Court of Alexandria, Virginia, seeking to release her son from the custody of General Bethune. Charity Wiggins had a genuine grievance against General Bethune, but the presence of Albert Lerche as her attorney clearly shows the hand of Elize Stutzbach Bethune in the proceedings. The case ground through the U.S. courts for nearly two years, and was bitterly contested by General Bethune, whose chances for keeping control of Wiggins looked good until the New York Supreme Court, with the approval of Tom's mother, appointed Elize Bethune to be his guardian. In March of 1887, a federal judge ordered General Bethune to relinquish custody of Tom and to pay $7,000. In the courtroom, Tom turned his back on his mother and said he wanted to remain with General Bethune, but he reluctantly agreed to go to New York. He and Charity spent the next few years together in Elize Bethune's home.

Elize Bethune had her revenge against her late husband's family, and she quickly sent Tom out on the road with a new manager to begin reaping the more tangible benefits of her victory. In 1889, she married her attorney, Albert Lerche. On May 31, 1889, three thousand people died when a dam broke above Johnstown, Pennsylvania. Several newspapers reported that Elize and Albert Lerche had identified the body of a black man found at Johnstown as Tom Wiggins, and had him buried.

In 1894, a reporter discovered that Tom Wiggins was still alive. Albert and Elize Lerche refused to be interviewed and shortly thereafter moved from New York to an isolated house in New Jersey's Navesink Highlands. It turned out that the Lerches had kept Tom in comfortable seclusion in their New York apartment while they battled several lawsuits stemming from Albert Lerche's somewhat shady law practice and their failure to pay the attorneys who had argued the custody case for them. It is likely they feared that the profits of any performances by Tom would be attached by their creditors, or that their treasure would be taken from them.

General Bethune died at the age of ninety-one in 1895, and Charity Wiggins in 1902 at one hundred and two. A few months before her death, she had told a reporter from the *Columbus Enquirer*, "They stole him from me. When I was in New York I signed away my rights. They won't let Thomas come to see me, and I am not allowed to see him." Tom did not return to Georgia for his mother's funeral. In 1904, Elize Lerche booked Tom into New York's Circle Theater, his first performance in nearly fifteen years. He made a few small tours of the Northeast in the next two years, then returned to seclusion in Hoboken, New Jersey, where Mrs. Lerche had lived since the disappearance of her husband.

Near the end of May of 1908, Tom fell to the floor while playing the piano. Elize Lerche helped him back onto the bench, but he could not continue; his upper right side had been paralyzed from a stroke. For several weeks, the distraught and frustrated Tom tried to play with his left hand alone. On the night of June 13, he rose from the piano in tears and said, "I'm done, all gone," took a few steps, and fell dead.

Tom Wiggins's death was reported by most of the country's major newspapers. His body was displayed briefly in a Manhattan funeral home and buried in the Evergreens Cemetery in Brooklyn, to the anger and disappointment of his brothers and sisters in Columbus.

Elize Bethune died in 1910 and was also buried in the Evergreens, in a plot with the Lohlein family, apparently her relatives. In 1938, Tom's grave was reopened and the body of Gustav Lohlein was buried in it. The cemetery records do not show that Tom's body was removed, but the records of Hoboken's Evergreen Cemetery show that at some time his body was buried there in an unmarked grave. In the 1930s, it was reported that Tom Wiggins's body had again been exhumed and re-buried in an unmarked grave six miles north of Columbus. Lack of documentation did not keep the state of Georgia from putting up a marker near the spot. Tom Wiggins's body remains as elusive in death as his mind and spirit were in life.

Emmett Miller

GET DOWN, MOSES by Nick Tosches

Emmett Miller died, forgotten and on the skids, in 1962. On his death certificate, in the space indicating the usual occupation of the deceased, it said simply: Entertainer.

And that, just as simply, is what he was: a blackface singer and comic who rose and fell in a time of twilight, in the mingling, falling darkness of the final days of minstrelsy and vaudeville. He was a son of the Deep South, born with the century, in 1900. The years of his glory were 1927, when he was the new and shining star of the fading Al G. Field Minstrels, the last of the big old-time minstrel companies, and 1928–29, when he made the Okeh recordings for which he is today remembered. And while in so many ways Emmett Miller was, and considered himself to be, simply an entertainer, these recordings, on which celebrated jazz musicians— the Dorsey brothers, Eddie Lang, Gene Krupa, and others—accompanied him under the veiling name of the Georgia Crackers, are a magic and a mystery unto themselves.

The music of Emmett Miller, as captured on these recordings, is as wondrous today as when he wrought it a world ago. Emanation and transcendence of the bloodlines of country and blues, jazz and pop, black and white, it stands unique: prophecy and summation, birth-cry and howl everlasting of the chimera of all that has come to be known as American music.

To say that he influenced Jimmie Rodgers, to say that without his 1925 and 1928 recordings of "Lovesick Blues," Hank Williams would have sung no

"Lovesick Blues," is to state only the obvious. The depths and elusiveness of his importance are oceanic.

He was, yes, simply an entertainer, but a musical Rosetta Stone as well, a key to how all before him that is lost to us, unrecorded and unseen, became transmuted into all that we know and hear today.

If minstrelsy is to be understood, it must be seen neither with myopic simplicity, as merely a racist relic (although, it was often crudely racist), nor as a textbook manifestation of ideology or psychology.

The songs and music of the minstrel shows, and of their smaller and shabbier counterparts, the medicine shows, were as important an influence on Southern black music, on what came to be called the blues, as on white Southern music, which came to be called country. Minstrelsy was the common blood, inspiration, and breeding ground of both these inchoate forms.

One example may prove illuminating. "I've Got a Gal for Ev'ry Day in the Week" was a ragtime "coon" song—as it was then called—composed in 1900, with lyrics by the Irish comic Pat Rooney and music by Harry von Tilzer. It emerged, metamorphosed into a country-blues song, in 1928, and was recorded for Victor as "My Monday Blues" by Jim Jackson, a Mississippi-born veteran of the medicine-show circuit who derived much from minstrelsy—who did as every performer, black or white, rural or urban, did: took from where he could. In 1944 the song reemerged, metamorphosed once again, as a fast-swinging blast of proto–rock & roll jive by Big Joe Turner, accompanied by boogie-woogie pianist Pete Johnson. The title of Turner's Decca recording, "I Got a Gal for Every Day in the Week," recalls the 1900 minstrel original, but Turner takes credit as the song's composer.

In the Petersburg, Virginia, *Farmer's Register* of April 1, 1838, one William B. Smith published an account of his experiences at a "beer dance" held by slaves on a neighboring plantation. He described their dancing, recorded bits of their song and speech, and concluded with the observation that "Virginia slaves were the happiest of the human race."

Not quite five years later, the Virginia Minstrels, the first professionally organized blackface group, made their debut at the Bowery Amphitheater in New York. Bills for the show announced "the novel, grotesque, original and surpassingly melodious Ethiopian Band entitled THE VIRGINIA MINSTRELS," and it was not long before all blackface performers came to be called minstrels.

It was with the Virginia Minstrels and their successors that blackface minstrelsy became the heart of nineteenth-century show business, the first emanation of a pervasive and purely American mass culture.

Blackface minstrelsy was born not of the South, but of the North, and its vision, though embraced by the South, was of the urban Northeast; and the popularity of blackface minstrelsy, perhaps America's first cultural export, was as great in England as at home.

Christy's Minstrels, the most famous of the New York shows, were active by May of 1844; there were also the Kentucky Minstrels, and the Ring and Parker Minstrels. In an 1846 article called "True American Singing," Walt Whitman professed a liking for a minstrel group called the Harmoneons: "Indeed, their negro singing altogether proves how shiningly golden talent can be spread over a subject generally considered 'low.'"

Whitman was a devotee of minstrelsy, of what he called "nigger songs." He wrote of minstrel bands, including Christy's Minstrels, for the *Brooklyn Star* and the *Brooklyn Daily Eagle;* he considered Stephen Foster's songs to be "our best work so far" in American music.

Stephen Foster, a white native of Pittsburgh, was the first American to make a living writing songs. What he knew of the South, he learned through minstrel shows—a job as a bookkeeper for his brother in Cincinnati in 1846 had brought him as far south as he had been—and his vision of the South, beginning with his *Songs of the Sable Harmonists* of 1848, in turn gave minstrelsy, and America, its most popular and abiding songs: "Oh! Susannah" (1847), "Camptown Races" (1850), "The Old Folks at Home" (1851), "Massa's in de Cold, Cold Ground" (1852), "My Old Kentucky Home" (1853), "Jeannie with the Light Brown Hair" (1854), and "Old Black Joe" (1860)—roughly a hundred and seventy-five of them. Foster's South, the South of minstrelsy, a South dreamt by the North, was a romance embraced by the South itself—the greatest nostalgia is that for what has never truly been.

As the music historian Charles Hamm has said of Foster's impact: "Never before, and rarely since, did any music come so close to being a shared experience for so many Americans." More than a century later, the songs of Stephen Foster still imbued the living spirit of American music: Ray Charles recorded "Swanee River Rock" for Atlantic in 1957; Jerry Lee Lewis recorded "Old Black Joe" for Sun in 1960; later in the '60s, Ornette Coleman wove shards of the same song into his concert performances.

Regard for Foster was shared by Abraham Lincoln, who also possessed a fondness for minstrelsy, and by Frederick Douglass, who had escaped from slavery in 1838, and who described Foster's songs as expressive of "the finest feelings of human nature."

It should be noted that Douglass had no such praise for minstrelsy, which he described in 1848 as "sporting over the miseries and misfortunes of an oppressed people." Those so engaged were "contemptible." He named the Virginia Minstrels, Christy's Minstrels, and the Ethiopian Serenaders as "the filthy scum of white society, who have stolen from us a complexion denied to them by nature, in which to make money, and pander to the corrupt taste of their white fellow citizens."

Douglass was moved to speak on the subject again in June of 1849, when he announced in his newspaper, *North Star,* the coming to Rochester of "Gavitt's Original Ethiopian Serenaders, said to be composed entirely of colored people." He deemed it as "something gained, when the colored man in any form can appear before a white audience; and we think that even this company, with industry, application, and a proper cultivation of their taste, may yet be instrumental in removing the prejudice against our race. But they must cease to exaggerate the exaggerations of our enemies; and represent the colored man rather as he is, than as Ethiopian Minstrels usually represent him to be."

By 1856 there were isolated instances of black minstrel shows in the Northeast—"we do not see why the genuine article should not succeed," reflected the *New York Clipper* of one such show in November of 1858. But it was not until 1865 that the first all-black minstrel group of endurance made its debut: the Georgia Minstrels, a band of ex-slaves organized in Macon, Georgia, by a white man named W.H. Lee. It became not uncommon for black troupes to distinguish themselves from their white counterparts by adopting the generic designation Georgia Minstrels. By the end of that year, there were at least three black troupes going by the name of the Georgia Minstrels, the best-known of them being Booker and Clayton's Georgia Minstrels.

After the Civil War, black men on the stage in blackface became plentiful. Sam Lucas, a black born to free parents in Ohio, attended Wilberforce University, worked as a barber, and served in the Union Army before entering minstrelsy in 1869. He sang many of his own songs, including "De Day I Was Sot Free," "My Dear Old Southern Home," and "Carve Dat Possum," certainly the most carnivorous of blackface songs:

> De possum meat am good to eat,
> Carve him to de heart.

Ike Simond (c. 1847–1905), "a banjo player comique" known as Old Slack, recalled in his *Reminiscence and Pocket History of the Colored Profession from 1865 to 1891* that Lucas once told him that "he would never black his face again, and as I have met him in nearly every city of the United States since that time I don't think he ever has." Lucas eventually became the first black performer to be cast in a starring moving-picture role, as Tom in the seventh filming of *Uncle Tom's Cabin,* a World Pictures five-reeler of 1914.

Billy Kersands was from New York. He danced, mimicked frogs and cows in his songs, and capped his sly performances as a babber-lipped buffoon by placing billiard balls or a cup and saucer in his mouth. (See the guy with the balls in his mouth on the cover of the Rolling Stones' *Exile on Main Street.*) He was the master of the "essence," the most famous of minstrelsy dances, born of the shuffle and progenitor of the soft shoe. He led his own troupe, Billy Kersands' Minstrels, and in the 1870s and 1880s was the highest-paid black entertainer of the day, as popular among blacks as among whites. He once told a fellow entertainer: "Son, if they hate me, I'm still whipping them, because I'm making them laugh."

Black men in blackface seem disreputable still in the eyes of history—misunderstood, neglected, regarded as an embarrassment. Today Kersands, like Lucas, is ignored by the five volumes of the *Encyclopedia of African-American Culture and History* (1966), and by the six volumes of *The African American Encyclopedia* (1993).

Not so for the apparently more respectable James A. Bland, one of whose compositions came to be embraced in 1940 as the state song of Virginia. Bland was born to a free family in Flushing, New York, and grew up in Washington, D.C., where his father was an examiner with the U.S. Patent Office. James attended Howard University before joining Haverly's Colored Minstrels, in which Lucas and Kersands also worked. He was later a featured member of Sprague's Georgia Minstrels, and became a sort of black Stephen Foster, composing minstrel classics such as "Carry Me Back to Old Virginny" (1878) and "Oh, Dem Golden Slippers" (1879). Like Stephen Foster before him, he died in poverty.

Bert Williams (1874–1922), an immigrant from Antigua who would become the most famous of black entertainers, entered minstrelsy in 1892, after attending Stanford University.

Shepherd Edmonds (1876–1957) from Memphis, and Sylvester Russell (c. 1865–1930) from New Jersey, were two noted black musicians who worked in the 1890s in the Al G. Field Minstrels. Russell went on to become a music and drama editor for *The Freeman*.

From one black troupe alone, the Mississippi-based Rabbit Foot Minstrels, would emerge the classic big-city blues singers Ma Rainey, Ida Cox, and Bessie Smith, as well as the rhythm-and-blues progenitor Louis Jordan. Rufus Thomas, whose "Bear Cat" of 1953 became the first hit on Sam Phillips's little Sun Records label, was a latter-day alumnus of the Rabbit Foot Minstrels, as was the blues artist Skip James. W.C. Handy, the so-called father of the blues, was a minstrel musician from 1896 to 1903. Country-blues singers who worked in blackface included Furry Lewis, Jim Jackson, and Big Joe Williams.

We deal here not only with the desire to prosper, or the universal human need for survival, but also with the mysteries of the psyche. The idea of blacks in blackface may at first glance seem to invite all manner of philosophical inquiry. But is the willingness of blacks to assume the mask of gross stereotype any more baffling or troubling than the universal tendency to masquerade? White Southerners still embrace and cultivate the theatrically defined stereotype of the good ol' boy. Italian Americans mimic the words and ways and assume the roles that Hollywood has created for them. The Irish stereotype in America would evaporate were it not for the devotion to role-playing that lends them the illusion of actuality. America, alone of nations, envisioned herself in terms of a dream. Nothing in this country is real; everyone is an actor. From long-tail blue to dashiki, from organ-grinder to the godfather, it is all a masquerade. If the halcyon lark of antebellum plantation life invented by minstrelsy was a sham, it was at least a sham that few performers took for reality. The same cannot be said of modern cultural shams such as the fantasy of African-American roots perceived in, say, Kwanzaa, a holiday invented in America in 1966, and perhaps not much closer than minstrelsy to the reality of any true African culture. Like the stereotypical posings of rap, Kwanzaa Kultur is an emanation not unlike minstrelsy. As always, it is the noble white man— Hallmark and the corporate media—who profits most.

Popular culture is often the product of who we are only in that it is the product of the lies, pretenses, and falsehoods that define us, and beneath which we hide and often, ultimately, lose the little truth from which we flee. Its meaning, insofar as it has any meaning at all, is essentially pathetic. In the case of the black man in blackface, it can at least be said that his motive was forthright, respectable, and pure: that is, money, the all-American, multicultural tradition of selling out. The same can be true of the professional good ol' boy, the Italian American, the Irishman, as long as they are faking it onstage, selling it to the suckers. It is when they bear the masquerade, the role, offstage—when the stage-walk and the stage-talk become the street-walk and the street-talk, when show business becomes the business of life—that they become truly frauds, with the fraud taken one step further by white audiences who in turn make it their own street-act. As far as I can tell, this was not the case generally with blacks who blacked up to make a buck. Offstage they lived apart from stereotype, which is more than can be said of many of the professional ethnic pretenders of today, be they white or black, singers or actors—or audience members.

Dan Emmett, the founder of the Virginia Minstrels, had gone on to join Bryant's Minstrels in 1858. A year later he introduced the song "Dixie." Though speculation regarding its true origin has been ceaseless, the song was copyrighted in his name as "I Wish I Was in Dixie's Land" in 1860. Attending a minstrel show not long before the election of that year, Abraham Lincoln heard "Dixie" for the first time, and he was so enraptured by it that he hollered out, "Let's have it again! Let's have it again!" As the war that followed neared its end, he advocated the song as one that the reunited nation could join in singing. If the founding of the first minstrel troupe had not rendered Dan Emmett the most celebrated and legendary of minstrels, "Dixie" surely did. It became the anthem of the South, and he its blackface Orpheus.

By the time of his death at eighty-nine in 1904 (the year Al Jolson began appearing in blackface), younger minstrels had taken to adopting the name of Emmett in tribute and for cachet. It was a practice that continued well into the decline of minstrelsy, and for a long time I thought that Emmett Miller's true identity might have been irrevocably lost to it.

Having seen the documents of his life, I now know that he was born Emmett Dewey Miller in Macon, Georgia, on February 2, 1900.

The fascination that black folk culture, real and imagined, held for whites ran deep in the homeland of Emmett Miller's youth. Joel Chandler Harris (1848–1908), from Eatonton, Georgia, worked at a number of Southern newspapers, including the *Macon Telegraph*, before joining the staff of the *Atlanta Constitution* in 1876. His "Uncle Remus" stories, which began to appear in the summer of 1879, depicted a rich and relatively authentic world of black dialect, folklore, and humor that in many ways represented a marked contrast, and in some ways was a literary parallel, to the ersatz black folksiness, quaint dialect, and racist burlesque of the minstrel shows. That is to say that the character of Uncle Remus was essentially, like the idyllic vision of minstrelsy, a figment of white fantasy—Harris saw Remus as having "nothing but pleasant memories of the discipline of slavery"—but the tales and fables of Br'er Rabbit that Harris told through Remus were the genuine stuff of black storytellers long before Harris.

If Macon can be said to have had a place in publishing, the journalist and author Harry Stillwell Edwards (1855–1938) and his publisher, the J.W. Burke Company, must be said to stand at the center of that place. Among Edwards's many books was *Eneas Africanus* (1919), a slim epistolary tale of "an old family Negro" who becomes separated from his owner in 1864 and finally finds his way back to his Georgia home after an eight-year journey through seven states, sheltered by kindly white folks along his winding way. He returns with a group of former slaves in tow, presenting them to his master: "I done brought you a whole bunch o' new Yallerhama, Burningham Niggers, Marse George! Some folks tell me dey is free, but I know dey b'long ter Marse George." The tale of this "vanishing type" is "dear to the hearts of the Southerners, young and old," says Edwards in his little preface. "Is the story true? Everybody says it is." So popular was *Eneas Africanus* that in 1920 the J.W. Burke Company offered it simultaneously in five editions, ranging in price from fifty cents for the paperback to two and a half dollars for the illustrated "ooze"-leather edition.

In Edwards's tale, the owner of Eneas is a man named Tommey. Is it mere coincidence that the errant slave in William Faulkner's *Go Down, Moses* bears the name of Tomey's Turl?

Macon was also the proud birthplace of the poet Sidney Lanier. But the tales of Chandler and Edwards held a place in the local cultural heart that the metaphysical conceits of Lanier did not reach. If Emmett Miller's cultural background is to be placed in a literary time-line, it is this: He was born in the year that *Uncle Remus's Magazine* came to be, and he began his journey from Macon in the year that the journey of *Eneas Africanus* took the town by gentle storm.

Miller made his first recording on Saturday, October 25, 1924, at the Okeh studio in New York City. Miller's debut was a version, with piano accompaniment by one Walter Rothrock, of Happy Lawson's 1921 "Any Time," which was Miller's signature song onstage. On November 7, he returned to the studio with Rothrock to record "The Pickaninny's Paradise," a 1918 song that had been introduced by the Courtney Sisters, and had been recorded by the Sterling Trio for Victor in early 1919. The song beckons a child to "Come lay your black, kinky head in a bed on a pillow of white," as the singer unveils his vision of heaven, where will be found "sweet molasses all around."

"The Pickaninny's Paradise" was written by the Tin Pan Alley team of Sam Ehrich and Nat Osborne. Ehrich, from New Orleans, was the song's lyricist; Osborne, a native of New York, wrote the music. "The Pickaninny's Paradise" was already something of an atavism, a throwback to an era of sentimental minstrel songs and sensibilities that the Jazz Age had rendered antiquated and passé. And yet the figure of the pickaninny clung not only to the fading world of minstrelsy. Eleven months after Miller's recording, Ethel Waters would record a "Pickaninny Blues" for Columbia. Like the "Pickaninny's Slumber Song" of 1919, "Pickaninny Blues" of 1920 was a lullaby in the vein of "The Pickaninny's Paradise."

Miller's first record makes it abundantly clear that he was already, in 1924, one of the strangest and most stunning of stylists ever to record. In an age when scat singing was coming to represent a stylistic avant-garde of sorts, Miller's debut represented an avant-garde of its own, an altogether otherworldly voice, a bizarre malarkey of the soul that seemed both a death-cry and a birth-cry: the last mutant mongrel emanation of old and dead and dying styles, the first mutant mongrel emanation of a style far more reckless and free than the cool of scat. The slurred arabesques, the yodel-like falsetto melisma: the attributes of Miller's brilliance as we know them are here, fluorescent and full.

These attributes are the driving force of "Any Time." Their presence is more spare in "The Pickaninny's Paradise," their effect stranger and more subtle. The song's description of heaven grows ever more ghastly as it unfolds. There is a sweetness in Miller's voice as he sings of this place where—so hideous an image— "every bird in the sky has diamond eyes"; a sweetness that is cheap, theatrical, exuberant, disarming at once—and then, as if to signal and savor the sudden ominous descent of those birds, those fugitives, in this trite and tawdry heaven, from the hell of Hieronymus Bosch, he completes the rhyme with a dire, careening howl that contorts the simple innocence of the word "nice" into a cry whose effect, saccharin and strychnine at once, is altogether unsettling: "Now, ain't that *niii-yiii-yiii-yiii-yice?*"

The suggestion is not that Miller designed it so, not that he knew from Hieronymus Bosch or felt toward this mawkish song other than warmly and well. To the contrary, this distasteful and perversely racist song may well reflect to some degree his taste; its grotesque bathos, his poetic sense. He was, after all, a man whose literary grasp very likely fell short of that Macon bestseller *Eneas Africanus*. No, the suggestion is that impulse and a galvanic sensitivity to certain words, certain lyrical and musical colors, conspired in him to articulate, as startling sound, ambiguities and conflations of feeling that were otherwise inexpressible; the suggestion is that beneath his conscious artfulness, beneath his showmanship, something hidden, unknown if not unfelt, was subconsciously at work.

I think, in this context, of George Jones as a modern example: a cipher, a blank, void of self-awareness or verbal expression, and yet a singer from whose invisible depths torrents of perception and emotion emerge with impossible eloquence. Like Jones, Miller often recorded songs that were mediocre or worse. It is as if the songs, the words, do not matter; as if the feeling in the voice addresses what the songs merely suggest, or as if the songs merely provide a subterfuge. None of which means that Miller was not, first and foremost, an entertainer. His concern was showmanship, not expression, not art or creativity or any of the pretenses that are the sucker's racket of today. Singing was not for him a way of dealing with his feelings; booze took care of that. But when he sang, something of brilliance sometimes emerged, something rare and true and imminent and wild, from beneath the counterfeit spontaneity and garish mannerisms of style.

The recordings for which Miller has come to be celebrated, made for Okeh with the Dorsey brothers and other well-known jazzmen working under the name of the Georgia Crackers, were the product of seven New York sessions spanning a period of fifteen months in 1928–29.

In the autumn of 1928, had a citizen found his way to the right Manhattan speakeasy, he might have encountered not only Emmett Miller but William Faulkner as well. It was in New York in October of this year that Faulkner, sojourning from Mississippi, completed *The Sound and the Fury*. Faulkner, it is said, was once thrown out of a speakeasy for singing "I Can't Give You Anything But Love," and this was the season of that song.

I like to think of the two of them meeting, the singer with the trick voice and the singing author of *The Sound and the Fury*, lost in the after-hours haze, two visionary sons of a dying South.

They both died in 1962, Faulkner and Miller, the one venerated, the other forgotten. The end, perhaps, of something. It was the year of Dee Dee Sharp and "Mashed Potato Time," of Little Eva and "The Loco-Motion." Bob Dylan was recording in New York, the Rolling Stones were coming into being in London.

Faulkner was no stranger to minstrelsy, jazz, or blackface comedy. Ford's Minstrels and W.C. Handy were as much a part of his youth as the canon of Western literature (which for him, as we have seen, may have included *Eneas*

Africanus as well as the *Aeneid*), and he himself was a singer both of "Carry Me Back to Old Virginny" and "I Can't Give You Anything But Love."

The Sound and the Fury of 1929, the Georgia Crackers recordings of 1928–29: They are strange and wonderful cries, no matter how disparate, of the same strange and wonderful day, of a dying South and of things to come. It is said that Faulkner played over and over again a record of "Rhapsody in Blue" as he churned out *Sanctuary*. Maybe the Georgia Crackers provided the background for something else. (I remember rummaging through Faulkner's house in Oxford, twenty-odd years ago, before it had been gussied up and given the full landmark treatment, and finding there, lying in a dusty corner, a 45-rpm copy of the 1950 RCA-Victor recording of "Rudolph the Red-Nosed Reindeer" by Spike Jones and His City Slickers.)

Emmett Miller ended up where he had begun, in Macon. He made his final tour, with a tawdry Southern circuit-show called *Dixiana*, in 1949. At this time, another Macon showman, an audacious singer of a different sort, was coming up. Richard Penniman, at eighteen, would make his first records, as Little Richard, for RCA-Victor in Atlanta in October 1951, twenty-four years to the month after Emmett Miller's triumphant entry into that city as the new star of the Al G. Field Minstrels. One of Richard's songs, "Miss Ann," would covertly celebrate the proprietress of Ann's Tic-Toc Club, a gay bar at 434 Cotton Avenue in Macon. Emmett at the time haunted the joints on Second Street.

Steve Sholes, the A&R executive who signed Richard, would sign Elvis Presley to Victor in 1955, and would arrange for Presley's appearances in 1956 on the Dorsey Brothers' CBS television program, *Stage Show*. And Elvis would sing Little Richard's "Tutti Frutti" on the Dorseys' show, just as Emmett twenty-eight years before, with the Dorseys behind him, had sung the songs of other black men. For the Dorseys, it soon would end. Tommy would die a few months later, in November of 1956. Jimmy would follow in 1957. But the strange and endless song whose waves they had sailed, the strange and gaudy medicine show of American culture, went on: the secrets of its history, its revelations, lost beneath its sound and fury, like the secrets and revelations of an ancient mystery cult, lost to the dust of time, that endure, untelling, beneath the endless veils of passing.

Rock & Roll/Pop

My Morning Jacket

A DESCENT INTO FANDOM by **William Bowers**

━━━━

An ominous ninety-nine-second rumble: Is that a looped growl? A funnel cloud in an echo chamber? Is somebody's work-truck underwater? What noisome thing is being wrought in the foul rag-and-bone shop of Kentucky? Keyboards and drums announce themselves teasingly, and build, mastered as if emerging from the disagreeable soundcloud. So beginneth my favorite album by my favorite rock band, My Morning Jacket's seventy-four-minute *At Dawn* (one hundred and eighteen if you count the bonus disc). The whole mess is organic and mechanized, tribal and industrial, ancient and futuristic, and when that rumble fades and frontman Jim James belts out the words "At daw-awwn," he sounds, well, predestined; his eruption is the messianic moment to which the intro's murk had been lumbering all along. Dawn is, of course, the prime context for a melodramatization of "potentiality," and James nails it, providing his listeners with the same anything-can-happen tingle one gets from a vacation bender, a breakup, a layoff, or sometimes just from being online. The song is secular gospel, and in this initial exclamation, James is invoking the Big Bang.

He goes on to embody an enemy's perspective, proclaiming, "All your life is obsceee-eene!" As someone burdened with guilt about preposterous American comfort, and as a fan of original sin, and of Kafka's heightened sense of fraudulence, and of Goethe's awareness that each of us is capable of committing every possible horror (Philip Larkin had a point with that whole "man hands on misery to man" thing, huh?), I am inclined to agree with the accuser. Yessirree, all my life, obscene: check.

James sings the line with a singular strain that hints that he, too, is tempted by teetotaling negation. But James is on a musical mission, and to him, the meaning of "obscene" probably goes to the word's roots, which would imply being "off stage," or out of sight, i.e. not in front of a microphone. Instead of surrendering to despair, though, James tells us how he handles the detractor: "That's when my knife rises/Their life ends/And my life starts again/Again .../Agceeeaeeein." I don't think what he's describing has anything to do with the standard exaltations of rebirth. He's dealing with the will to power, with Cain, with rock & roll.

It is—I can't believe I'm saying this, in a world full of mothers and children—the most inspiring song about murder I've ever heard. If it were playing at my house, and you were my guest, I'd position you by the stereo and stop just short of *forcing* you to listen. If you resisted, and yammered, I'd ask you to leave the room. If you then made too much noise in the kitchen, I might escort you to the front stoop, and plant you in a rocking chair beside the bottle-packed recycling bin. Your civil rights, the mosquitoes, and that cat-pee-smelling chemical with which the neighborhood spray truck tries to combat the mosquitoes would keep you company while I finished listening to the song in the respectful silence it deserved. Our juxtaposition would befit *At Dawn*, an album as rich on a night when friends are coming over as it is the nights when one would give anything to have friends coming over.

The excuse for my ridiculous behavior splits sweetly into matters of nature and nurture. Heredity: I descend from song obsessors who either made people listen along or neglected them for their neglect. Habitat: I was subject to their obsessions, interpolated as pop hostage and exile, and now I pass the savings onto my guests.

God love him, Dad turned our "living room"—intriguing what this phrase implies about a house's other rooms—into his "music room." He removed the standard furniture and filled the space with stereo equipment and album stacks. My sister and I were pretty much banned from this chamber, even though it was the only route to our bedrooms. So on a daily basis we'd have to hotfoot incognito, best we could, through an audiophile's danger zone. Sometimes Dad spread albums on the floor in flowcharts representing an ideally sequenced listening session. These arrangements looked like vinyl hopscotch to a kid. Once my sister pounced on a Lionel Richie record and was dispatched to Mom for discipline. Dad didn't beat us; that would have interrupted his reverie.

Dad's father, though, was worse, and still is. He also did away with the concept of a family-gathering forum and converted his parlor to an all-stereo layout, but in a much larger and older house. With a beautiful smile, he'd turn up the amplifiers and engineer cracks along the wall that fissured to reach the cathedral ceiling.

On some of my visits to his house, he doesn't speak to me or anyone accompanying me; he just blasts his stereos, playing one song per album, for an hour or so. After each song with that certain *it*, he barks, "That's got it!" He'll move from Junior Wells into some Van Halen into some Johnny Cash into some Herbie Hancock, etc. Music keeps this eighty-year-old young: He drives a vintage Mustang with fifteen-inch "booming" speakers; he has subdued, and pistol-whipped, would-be burglars; one Christmas he gave me a mix-tape consisting of selections by Paul Simon, Ween, and Bass Master Funk.

My older brother's music obsession was metal. Its clamor and celebration of communal deviance clashed with his quiet, insular nature, but he'd come out of his room to declare that Quiet Riot and Billy Squier and Judas Priest and Kiss and Twisted Sister were titans. He'd skulk around me, lupine, explaining what a virtue it was to play a tape until it wore out, until some part of it disintegrated. Then he'd skulk, lupine, into his (also off-limits) room, where, we later learned, he'd head-banged a hole into the wall behind his framed hologram poster of an eagle and a wolf atop jagged rocks.

All of these men were Christians, and I accompanied them to sermons during which we were told that we should eschew faith in worldly possessions. One church even hosted—pregnant gulp—album bonfires. I would dream of Christ showing up at our house, his brilliant purity difficult to behold against our redneck-rococo décor; he would proceed to overturn the house's music collections the same way that, in TV movies and Easter skits, he trashed the moneychangers' tables in the temple. A friend's Presbyterian mother told me that in heaven we'd listen to a beautiful choir all the time, and I couldn't believe that we would have no say in selecting the eternal soundtrack. I guess I was like a tribesman confused by the shiny watches and jewelry of the missionaries; I couldn't grasp the salvation-message because I wanted to grasp the *stuff*. Who cared to matriculate to an afterlife without one's record collection?

Though the logistics of divorce conspired to separate me at an early age from my father, brother, and grandfather, I too became a packrat of sound, "joining" my clan of man-children, and, I soon learned, a pervasive larger fraternity of collectors. For gift-exchanging holidays, we don't ask for CDs or box sets. We ask for big, ornate, customized CD cabinets. My genus of collector is very different from the hoarder of 78s who covets each rarity as an individual artifact. Nor does our ilk have much in common with the high-minded curators certain that their classical repository will sustain post-apocalyptic humanity's faith in itself. The separatist sophisticateurs who hole up with their mineral water, their flyswatters, their crossbows, and their Sun Ra discographies find my kind blasphemously indiscreet—for we are abstract, fetishizing quantity and variety. Our stockpiles are manifestations of an ownership virus, and there is something latently colonial about how we conceive of our collections as a vast domain. We forge and sever bonds via the burning of exceedingly cosmopolitan mix CDs that all but exclaim, "Look how indiscriminate my discriminating palate is!"

Many of us think we're better than those paraphernaliens who collect sports cards, Beanie Babies, *Star Wars* leavings, or those little porcelain boots, but we are wrong. Our fixed attachment to our stashes is obviously a type of compensation for some pointed lack. The dominant psychobabble on Grandpa is that because he had nothing during the Great Depression, he must define and protect himself by (or, burden himself with) surplus now. No matter what kind of sensitive aesthetes we obsessives think we are because we collect music (which, we'd argue with rectitude, is culturally superior to, say, collecting Nazi jewelry), we can be just as pathetically contentious and bullying as the next buff or self-elected aficionado. Our collections can be abysses: An hour can be spent packing seventeen hours' worth of music for a two-hour drive. My teeth can fall into disrepair, but my music shelves will be severely ordered and maintained.

With loving self-mockery John Cusack played one of us music-obsessives in the film of Nick Hornby's *High Fidelity,* a performance made more interesting by its being an extension of Cusack's role in *Say Anything.* In the climactic scene of that film Cusack woos the object of his affection by standing outside her widow in dramatic rain, hoisting a boom box blaring Peter Gabriel's "In Your Eyes." (The universal "awwws" this scene triggered are why *Entertainment Weekly* named the film "the number one Modern Romance of all time.") The moment is a sign that something profoundly transgressive has happened; the romantic tradition of Romeos and Cyranos who spoke in self-composed verse beneath their sweethearts' windows has been supplanted by a Lloyd Dobler merely pressing the PLAY button on a machine to unleash a supposedly passionate commodity he selected. In James Joyce's "The Dead," which is careful to include a reference to Romeo's "balcony scene," the doomed, weather-braving Michael Furey at least used his own voice to sing someone else's song to Gretta. Suddenly with Lloyd—a creation of lifetime music-geek Cameron Crowe—we are happy to let our albums communicate for us; the lazy courtier is a DJ who earns/expresses the same value as the song's performer. (Think of the scene in *24 Hour Party People* in which the Tony Wilson character points out that the club DJ receives the applause that bands used to get. Though some DJs actually do make art, in the majority of American clubs the DJ is praised merely for selecting the work of other people. This "privilege the messenger" ethic is unique to music; imagine a projectionist getting laid for his successful looping of a film. Such is the minor-league deification we obsessives seek to obtain as a perk.)

Enter My Morning Jacket, an amazingly multivalent five-piece originating and operating from Louisville, Lexington, and Shelbyville, Kentucky. To my veteran ears, the band was *everything*: The performances crystallized on their releases spanned disparate genres and synthesized the shopworn approaches of all the music I'd overheard growing up. But MMJ was still somehow strikingly original, as if Neil Young were dragging the Beach Boys across an abstract plane to have a cookout on a shipwreck. When considering their obvious influences and their disorienting freshness, I think of that complaint on a Forest Service comment card: "The places where trails do not exist are not well marked." And their Southern goulash covered a stately-to-shambolic spectrum that could please fans of Chet Atkins's protean virtuosity as well as fans of the Silver Jews' casually articulate slopcountry. My Morning Jacket's music cultivated in me an acute esteem. I became, for them, the music-obsessive equivalent of a junkie: a completist. The fool completist must have it all, and therefore spends a great amount of time and money hunting a band's every recorded and performed morsel, eventually spiraling off into a bootleg-archiving delirium. It's not pretty. Listservs, file-sharing sites, and eBay are our crackhouses, our venues-as-middlemen: I once sold a tour-only Songs:Ohia CD for $83 to another completist (who won the online auction against several similarly desperate obsessives), so that I could spend the money on an illegal compilation of rare My Morning Jacket material. My conundrums flounder outside the realm of good and evil: I've lain awake nights on tragically unchanged pillowcases, fretting over not being able to find a copy of the Louisville sampler on which MMJ covers "Take My Breath Away," Berlin's love theme from *Top Gun*. I had obviously sidestepped the designated saviors of my spiritual upbringing and (to bastardize William James) used music to fill the faith-hole. When pressed to explain my fanaticism for My Morning Jacket, or to argue the band's relevance, I pause: Like many a modern Southerner, I teem with fairly illogical aversions and often indefensible convictions. Just as my neighbor can't fathom anyone challenging his WHY AREN'T YOU SAVED? bumper sticker, I think: Who are these skeptics kidding? Is it not just plainly obvious that My Morning Jacket is the greatest band in the world?

No Guralnick-style approach will do: Though I want to ascribe a myth to the band ("While kayaking in Boulder, Colorado, James encountered Buddha. . . ."), they aren't dead. Sticking to band history seems ridiculous, since their legacy is just beginning; they're currently recording their major-label debut, and besides, they're younger than I am, damn them. In his contribution to the anthology *Rock Over the Edge: Transformations in Popular Music Culture*, R.J. Warren Zanes (himself an estimable star, as a member of the Del Fuegos) analyzes the subtexts of fandom, examining how fans fantasize about, and over-identify with, their musical heroes—Zanes seeks to add to that list of responses the possibility of "queer desire." Despite being at ease with recognizing Jude Law's fineness, and despite having formed a few My Morning Jacket–inspired best-friend supergroups with names like Trust Bucket, Falcon Stirrup, Birthmark Jones, and Commemorative Stoneware that only lasted one drunken night, I can safely say that no part of my loyalty to Jim James's sublime quintet involves wanting to lick him, or be him, or master him, or be mastered by him. I just enjoy hearing him make good on his musical gifts.

Any trial requiring my testimony would be wise to have me swear with my hand on a copy of *At Dawn*. Such allegiance—slightly aggravated, of course—breeds cretinism, and I have often become one of the band's chauvinists, despite the world's not needing another asshole. I scorn acquaintances who resist my missionary dotage. Believing that My Morning Jacket should always headline, I hold grudges against the acts for whom I've seen them open. When folks attempt to lump MMJ in subgenres such as alt-country or indie-pop, I am quick to assert that Jim James regards his troupe as a rock band, plain and simple. Still MMJ typically plays to "indie" crowds, made up of people who attend club performances with a churchgoer's regularity and emphasis on dress, though these shows are more democratized than church: The indie-faithful occasionally flock to concerts in order to critique, or even mock, the pulpiteers.

When they aren't trying to fake an ever-changing vernacular, the hipsters' anything-goes, endocannibalistic conversations will begin with greetings along the lines of, "Hey, has your bumper sticker freed Tibet yet?" Aware of the pressures that lead them to disdain sincere enthusiasm, I can sympathize with their retreat into irony. Their heads are busy with cultural minutiae, the result of survey-style education and commercial grooming; they are trying to keep straight Malcolm McLaren from Marshall McLuhan, and to sort the Cavity Creeps from the Flavor Crystals. The multiplicity of delights competing for their attention can impoverish their sense of the especial. But as Mark Dery wrote, "Irony is a leaky prophylactic against consumerism, conformity, and other social diseases spread by advertising." Though My Morning Jacket can indulge in some healthy stage badinage, and though I've seen Jim James use bizarre accessories to distance himself from the audience (hiding his face behind a stuffed buffalo head, draping himself in a tie-dyed muumuu), the band champions earnestness, a trait that distinguishes them from Louisville's killjoy, "post-rock" scene. The band's emotivity can trigger a hipster's nag reflex, and when less-dedicated fans begin their jabs, we overzealous MMJ disciples wince with the agony that drove Kierkegaard to call the burden of enduring glib criticism "the long martyrdom of being trampled to death by geese." The band even volleys with audience members moved to indulge in Ironist's Tourette's, the strange, indie variation on heckling: an urge to shout random phrases during hushes. (Jim James once announced, "This next one's called 'Jesus and God,' off our album *Desert Storm*," after a sozzled ticketholder yelled, between numbers, "Jesus and God!" and "Desert Storm!") Americans' freedom to carouse notwithstanding, the more garrulous the crowd gets, the more petulant we Nietzschean superfans get. When someone near me at a show called the band My Boring Racket, I was ready to throw down, but for the good sense of an accompanying female who pointed out the insufferable silliness of my would-be centurionship.

That said, My Morning Jacket concerts leave a majority of their attendees agog. The band grew out of Jim James's solo performances at sundry open-mikes, and he has honed a still-malleable stage mystique. Stout and wide-eyed, he veers from coming across as a spacey, barefoot, farm-bred ragamuffin to a fully cognizant, self-consciously sexy bandleader extraordinaire to an intimidating, head-banging, Flying-V-pummeling Black Sabbath and Slayer devotee to an intimate, approachable, crooning, hippie reification of John the Baptist. Bassist Two-Tone Tommy, resembling a lankier and more worried Nirvana-era Dave Grohl, seems to take his flail-or-chill cues from James. Guitarist (and cousin to James) Johnny Quaid, prone to playing his Gibson high above his head during intense passages, is a curious mix of Adonis and Gremlin, embodying the "ruggedly handsome" hero/villain of a thousand unfilmed screenplays. These three core members have been together five years. Keyboardist Danny Cash, distant kin to The Man in Black and a talented graphic designer whose look suggests a mellow greaser, joined before the recording of *At Dawn*. The band's third and seemingly permanent drummer, Patrick Hallahan, is James's childhood best bud—he's a giant guy with a wavy mop that suggests a grunge hybrid of a Louis XIV wig and the Cowardly Lion's mane. In this epoch of casting-call "bands" with prefabricated images, you'd be hard-pressed to summon a rollicking fivesome more hirsute and oleaginous than these mugs.

This assemblage of ponytails, wires, T-shirts, boots, and flip-flops has ruined at least one version of my life. See, I was in love with that aforementioned woman, the one who sparingly pointed out the lameness of my fascist fandom, and we'd bonded over the course of a half dozen My Morning Jacket concerts. She was the givingest and most creative woman I'd ever known, and MMJ's handling of romantic material can do wonders for a blossoming coupledom; James allowed us to imagine that our union was some uncanny heterosexual masterpiece, the way he portrays love as the validating and visceral miracle-burden that it can be when it, as the dialect-poet David Lee wrote, "sparkles like a diamond in a goat's ast."

MMJ songs were in the background during our abortive efforts to get wine stains off the ceiling with OxiClean, and when she passed out on the trampoline and I woke her by pelting her with moldy scones, and when she expressed her reticence to skinny-dip while silkworms dangled from the tree behind her like tiny larval paratroopers. She even painted a sign for my album-crowded house reading HOME IS WHERE THE STUFF IS.

Ah, those were the days; we seemed bound for glory: marriage, death, some freckly kids left to handle our CD estate. But when we started to suck, as complicated people often will, our reliance on MMJ became a problem. James's nonchalantly gorgeous songs, once so reinforcing, now conjured an affectionate atmosphere that we failed to emulate. The songs were mafia thugs, putting pressure on us to live up to their drama. Even "Lowdown" became a sore spot: on the surface a bouncy, flippant ditty brimming with impossible promises, but actually about wounded people vowing not to put each other through any more crap. Its refrains of "you never gotta fight with me" and "you only gotta dance with me" seemed like buoys we'd already drifted beyond. We'd go to parties and perform the combative vaudeville of an unspooling relationship. "Hi, yes, we're here together, but don't be bourgeois and presume we're in love." "Yes, in fact, we steadfastly refuse to love each other." And people would laugh at the meta-couple's antics, and wonder what was the secret of our salubrious, self-correcting rapport.

So we drove two hours south to see My Morning Jacket one last time. They were awesome. Awesome. But we didn't even stand together. And after the show, we reached out, separately, to the band, freighting strangers with our speeches about what they meant to us. When she and I found ourselves, rather incidentally, in proximity to each other again, she said, giddily, "He's my new boyfriend!" When I traced the beeline from her big brown eyes to discern the identity of the beau nouveau, I realized, to my horror, that she was looking at *all of them.* Not necessarily a damning infraction, but we were eager to implode. Suffice to say, later that night this wonderful woman found reason to strand me in Orlando. She drove off just after whipping out her digital camera and taking a picture of me in the street, shooting her a gallant bird, capturing perfectly the climax of a pattern of abuse and dismissal that manifested only in gestures. She spent the night at a notorious gay bar/hotel with comforters assuring her that I was a good man, and I spent the night at a Greyhound station with a drunk explaining to me that manhole covers were "nature's pancakes." Before she moved away, we cleaned her apartment without speaking, all hard feelings. I don't recommend playing My Morning Jacket albums, which consist of fifty percent heartbreakers, in an empty house where you used to have fun and comfort. She's a union organizer in the Motor City now, getting buckets of dirty water thrown on her by frustrated factory workers and taking orders from a puckish Albanian. If some horrible Detroitian circumstance befell her, surely that would be My Morning Jacket's fault, and not mine, right?

My Morning Jacket is an ideal divergenic fix. Music's transportative power must explain why those men to whom I am bloodbound love it so; music provides escape, and hoarding it equips their rooms—and lives—with multiple escape routes. The work of Jim James and his boys is admittedly better suited to accompany your slightly seedy, loafering, lost twenties than it is your thirties' reductive Sisyphean quests for money, or orgasm, or that gross attention called respect.

With My Morning Jacket on my headphones, a bike constitutional can be epic (though technically against the law). Their music delivers me past the house where the black woman who told me she used to call whites "ofays" sits in her bra and jean shorts on the porch and it takes me past the office of the ophthalmologist who calls blacks "equatorials." It helps me pedal around the mother whose son carries her oxygen tank, the hose between them a kind of umbilical leash.

On a fitness kick, I listened to MMJ while I jogged around the upper level of a gym where a depressing basketball camp was being conducted, the unremarkable gloryhounds colliding with their own teammates in oversized logo-billboard outfits and shoes that resembled tanks. MMJ soothed me and some friends on a road trip when sleep deprivation and caffeine mania had us groupthinking that the deer on the shoulder were teasing us with suicidal lunges. *At Dawn* shepherded me through that dolorous day that my cactus died and it didn't symbolize anything.

Once, tipsy at a beach hotel, I dove into the pool with my headphones still on. And I hope to never grow so foggy that I forget the spring afternoon I spent playing MMJ and watching a Carolina wren build a nest in a guitar amp I'd used to prop open a kitchen window. Am I blathering yet? Forgive me, I've been recruited by a music that accentuates the purgative, that makes me sick for how radio was ruined, that situates itself at all the best crossroads—it's gothic but transparent, smart and sentimental, slippery but firm, demotic and difficult, weapon and tourniquet....

Reverb is such an integral component of My Morning Jacket's galvanism that it could be regarded as the band's sixth member. The same way that black-and-white footage is used to communicate filmic pasts, reverb provides MMJ with an instantly fermented, nostalgic sound, that of an oldies station struck by magic lightning, harkening to the cavernous levels used to inflate the minimal arrangements of so many legendary Sun sessions and so many doo-wop and r&b classics. (For a band often labeled as modern hillbilly psychedelia, MMJ's soulfulness runs deep. Anyone doubting Jim James's worship of various incarnations of Marvin Gaye need only consult "War Begun," "The Bear," or "Come Closer." See also "They Ran," which functions as a nitrous-oxidized homage to Berry Gordy, and the band's cover of Nubian diva Erykah Badu's "Tyrone," which holds its own against Wilco's magnificent, Mayfield-lite "Jesus, Etc." as an artful slab of Caucasian soul.) The reverbiana of Joy Division and Galaxie 500—two rock touchstones for placing MMJ—was ascribed to those bands by their madmen producers Martin Hannett and Kramer, respectively, whereas My Morning Jacket inflicted reverb on themselves—possibly, initially, like so many do-it-yourselfers trying to maximize the scope of their four-track cranny, to make up for their low-budget recording apparatus (on Quaid's grandparents' farm). And then, possibly, because it suited them so well, like it did Roy Orbison, enshrining his bellows with a nebulous quality, an interiority—the resonance of the psyche's amphitheater.

Whether James is singing in his punk wail, soft "black," deep country, nimble swain, or spastic castrato mode, reverb is his substrate. *At Dawn*'s mixer is listed in the liner notes as Dave "Would you like a little music with your reverb?"

Trumfio, no doubt based on a comment he made regarding how this band lets reverb affect their music the way certain narcotics transmogrify thought, or the sex drive. I have watched Jim James rattle soundmen during concert setups. "More reverb," he'll ask. "But that's already way too much." "Uhnh-uhnh. More." Minor adjustment. "More." Adjustment. "More," James will say until the monitors are threatening to succumb to a feedback skree. MMJ's tunes reflect but also go beyond the exaggerated industrial-wasteland solitude of Joy Division and the plastic vastness of Galaxie 500; James can sound aquatic, or like he's broadcasting from some interplanetary outpost, a ranger station that the budgetary committee ceased to fund but forgot to shut down. (This cosmic tincture made MMJ's desolate cover of Elton John's "Rocket Man" a no-brainer.)

"Phone Went West," arguably the band's most instantly hummable, and thus crowd-pleasing, song is lacquered just to the point of amniotic stillness that the poet Joe Wenderoth conveyed when he called an empty fast-food restaurant "the false eternity of the womb." While the band delivers an otherworldly reggae-prom arrangement whose drums explode around the five-and-a half-minute mark, James yowls and re-yowls a passive prophecy, "There will be a knock on your back door!" The listener infers that the knock won't be acknowledged. The song's refrain, "Tell me there's nobody else in the world," works both as a slogan for a poisonously exclusive relationship, and as a plea for confirmation of the speaker's grandiose loneliness, like Beckett's Krapp, who guesses from his living room filled with sound equipment that the "earth might be uninhabited." It's as if a biblical rapture transpired, and the speaker is relieved to be left behind.

As an ardent dabbler in mix-CD alchemy who strives to produce a rewarding mood arc with each compilation, I must say that the Bible's orthodox DJs did a mean job of sequencing that thing, especially with that four-book stretch during which the praise songs of Psalms lead into the advice columns of Proverbs following the national doom-treatise of Ecclesiastes, ending with the erotica of Song of Solomon. My Morning Jacket wanders gracefully through the turf of Psalms, Proverbs, and Solomon, offering nuggets of appreciation for the gift of life, of can-do positivity, and of fleshly magnetism. James frequently cites his intuition that he is being guided by things beyond his understanding, by voices and spirits. Demos from *At Dawn* include "Lead Me Father," which could be sung at a Wesleyan picnic. The band is always thanking a "God," and like the Power Team, those weightlifting Christian motivational speakers, the band takes the stage with an athletic confidence, huddles, sometimes high-fives, and openly discusses what they see as their music's redemptive mission. I've never seen them drink. When James sings about stealing or cocaine, or kicking someone's head in, he does it with an innocence that takes me back to how pure even a toxic scrapyard seems after snowfall. MMJ's mysticism doesn't belie their capitalism, however; just like late-night televangelists, the band are mantrapreneurs, business-minded spiritualists who want their product to reach everyone. ("Old September Blues" is awkwardly beautiful; it's a cost-benefit-analysis as ballad, with James expressing his gratitude for someone who was "always . . . an asset" and "never . . . a drawback.") MMJ even participated in the commodification of the holy days by making an "Xmas" record.

For all that gusto, their discography bogs down considerably, as the Bible does, in the despairing acceptance of Ecclesiastes' existential morass. How can I not think of MMJ's reverb when I read, "Better is a handful of quietness than two hands full of toil and a striving after wind"? The author, pen-named Qoheleth, or the Teacher, is bummed, big-time, and thankfully my *New Oxford Annotated Bible* does me the favor that my bubbly, biased *New Student Bible* wouldn't; it admits that the book's God's-in-control, "it's all good" moments were tacked on by a cautious editor. James's line, "There will be bigotry and there will be open minds," from "I Will Be There When You Die," parallels the passages in Ecclesiastes that inspired the Byrds' "Turn! Turn! Turn!" (written by Pete Seeger) and T.S. Eliot's "The Love Song of J. Alfred Prufrock."

The book's refutation of novelty complements MMJ's retrofitted tones. "Take me out of this dead-end nightmare," the speaker of MMJ's "Nashville to Kentucky" cries, as worn down as Qoheleth, who doesn't sound very different from contemporary absurdists frustrated with their estrangement from purpose and authority. All is vain toil under the sun to Qoheleth, and we moderns have the rank benefit of knowing that even that sun's only got about five billion years left.

Though on some tracks James vaunts a chipper faith in hard work, he addresses the anhedonia brought on by torpor and the idea that "trying gets nothing done," on "Death Is the Easy Way," voicing concern for a person whom nothing "gets . . . high." Anyone who flinches when the weather forecaster says "tomorrow will be almost exactly like today" could commiserate with MMJ or Qoheleth. When James sings of not letting your "silly dreams/Fall in between/The crack of the bed and the wall," you know that to have focused on that dead space, the speaker is hurting, or lying awake nights. Qoheleth holds forth on the transience of youth, and James sings of a lost urgency, "I needed it most/When I was eighteen/But now that I'm older/I don't need many things." The song goes on to bemoan a relationship that even the "heavens" can't help. Things just are how they are, Qoheleth says, and they repeat, and we don't know why, and he adds, "Who can straighten what God has made crooked?" James prefers to let his own creations' crookedness speak for itself, reluctant to explain where his songs come from, or how one is supposed to regard the twenty-four-minute "Cobra," which shifts from a bizarre Prince-meets-the-Oak-Ridge-Boys groove into flophouse

Hendrix, into ambient drone, into banjo drone, finishing with a slurred "shout-out." I think James would like the short section called "Hurrah!" from "The Dog Among the Rills" by Winfield Townley Scott:

Madam, your little boy has
Bat ears;
And, Madam, some of my poems are
Cock-eyed;
But we had 'em—
Didn't we!

The band's two bleakest songs are the ones chosen to provide the last words on their respective releases, before chill-out instrumental codas. "I Think I'm Going to Hell" closed *The Tennessee Fire*, and it's, uh, self-explanatory. *At Dawn* wraps up with "Strangulation," perhaps an extension of "The Dark," on which James sang of "God's fingers choking me." "Strangulation" though, looks outward, as much of *At Dawn* does, at people who feel optionless and plundered. The character's nihilist wish is to not "feel a thing," and the song's final fourth is a two-minute caterwaul, with James screaming as if being forcibly escorted toward the vestibule beneath this world's blinking EXIT sign. Chapter 9, Verse 4: "But he who is joined with all the living has hope, for a living dog is better than a dead lion."

A church-faith, once indoctrinated, can be difficult to de-bug. Even Ecclesiastes' doubting author says my writing and book-love won't save me, that knowledge and sadness increase correlatively. Plus: "Of making many books there is no end, and much study is a weariness of the flesh." As for the obsessive music collecting, I can sometimes hear, mentally, slightly reverbed, a visiting preacher from one of the mountaintop camp meetings I attended as a lad telling me that my CD racks are altars I've built to false gods. Pity me for clinging to a child's literalism, but what would heaven even *be*? Everybody sporting J. Crew, gathering berries and corn? I can't buy the capitalist streets-of-gold thing, and that version of eternal paradise in which we are supposed to become spirit-blobs may free us of our troubling bodies and thoughts, but it underscores the sci-fi nonsensicality of "perfection" and "total fulfillment." Hell is simply more understandable, more navigable a concept. Even if you don't go for envisioning it as the Dantean torture-scape, or a Bruckheimer fireball, you could comprehend the tastefully simple all-darkness format. Then again, our nightmares seem more linear than our sweeter dreams. I pick on the religion I inherited, and quasi-shirked, but my faith in bands isn't any more rational. The rockist and the fundamentalist carry hot, hero-clogged heads. We don't outgrow our extremism because we're so invested in it, and, needing our lives to make sense to us, we construct self-fulfilling prophecies.

Jim James sings, "[I] try to walk this earth an honest man, but evil waves at me its ugly hand." He understands not only Ecclesiastes' moral that all is vanity, but also that, conversely, vanity is, sometimes, all. On the ponderous "Bermuda Highway," he makes the very anti-Christian confession, "I wonder why that meek guy got all the fame/Maybe I'm to blame/For his short, bitter, fucked-up life." And no matter how a life is spent, dying is losing to Jim James, as was evident from the first MMJ show I saw without the woman I'd squandered. The concert was August 16, in Washington, D.C., and James opened with a soul-charring solo cover of "Suspicious Minds," the King's chronicle of a smothering, paranoid relationship. James introduced the song with a warm smile, saying, "Twenty-five years ago tonight, Elvis Presley lost his way." Then came the reverb, and he began to sing: "We're caught in a trap...."

At my day job, I have regular encounters with a kid whose sadistic, Cromwellian, fundamentalist parents lock him in his room at night to keep him from becoming "worldly." He is one of the most tormented and traumatized people I've ever met. I try to help him view his parents' treatment of him as abuse, and to set up an intervention, but he declines, having adjusted to the hopelessness of his plight. He is eighteen, but they've got him terrified of even the most mundane daily maneuvers. One day I invited him to grab some take-out with me, and My Morning Jacket's *At Dawn* was cued up in my car stereo, sounding majestic despite having to poot out of my ruined speakers. Neither of us made conversation; I wanted to hear some MMJ, and I thought he was nervous about not having permission from his censors to join me for a drive. We ate in the car with the music on, sucked Cokes as we watched lovers in the park across the street compose their own concordances. On our way back, he pointed to my CD player and said, "I'm not allowed to listen to music." I thought, *Who are his parents, the Taliban?* He continued, "But if I could listen to music, I would want to listen to this."

Janis Joplin

LOOKING FOR HER IN PORT ARTHUR, TEXAS
by Cynthia Shearer

■■■

It's not deep in the heart of Texas—it's more like the service entrance. Driving around downtown Port Arthur, Texas, you pass the Golden Light Social Club, then something called Club Say What where an ominous-looking van—the kind used by villains in 1970s TV movies—is parked in front. Nearby, paint peels from pastel shotgun shacks, while banana trees stand beside them. A gaunt, tranced woman walks the pavement, wearing bedroom shoes at high noon, as if she is navigating by her own jones to find her next fix. No cars move on the street. You want to find the water, the people, the life you would expect in the town that birthed the voice of Janis Joplin.

The Port Arthur Port Authority (like that old joke about the Department of Redundancy Department) on Procter Street is closed for lunch. A sign reads PORT OF PORT ARTHUR EXPANSION, but the site is padlocked and deserted. Procter Street is a wide deserted boulevard straight out of an old Western ghost town, except the time period is 1960-ish.

A Zenith Radio storefront window has some kind of World War II exhibit—mannequins sporting military uniforms. A loudspeaker affixed to a corner building across from an old fortress-like bank plays Tejano radio music to the empty street. All that is missing is the tumbleweed.

There are two stores open: a Goodwill Store and Kizzy Konnection, an African-American import place. Kizzy Konnection, "your connection to African Imports," is as much a museum as anything. The main import here is nostalgia for the African continent—each bolt of fabric printed with zebras and giraffes curates a memory of loss.

"How long have you been here?" you ask the proprietress.

"I'm not African," she misreads the question. "I grew up here."

"So do you know where Janis Joplin lived?"

"No," she says. "But it was down that way somewhere. It's not there anymore. You need to go to the museum down the street. And go around the corner to the barbershop," she says. "They have pictures of all the old places on the wall you can look at. The whole town, all of it. The barber can tell you stories."

The Museum of the Gulf Coast is a large, white-stone building that faces Procter Street. As small, eclectic historical museums go, it has one of the best reputations in the country. A sign on the front entrance tells you to go around back.

The first thing you see is the largest indoor mural in Texas, depicting the old Hotel Sabine. The mural was rescued from an attic in San Antonio (pronounced "San AnTONyuh" here) and "restored" before hanging here in its quasi-primitive starkness. A wide, soft Texas sky in the background, flat green land in the foreground, little animals in the grasses.

One of that cheery, well-meaning race known as docents comes over, wearing a windsuit—vivid parachute cloth sewn into a kind of retirement uniform. "The animals were painted to cover the profanity," she says. "There used to be profanity on it."

"Vandalism?" you ask.

"No," she says. "It used to hang in a bar. The artist painted it to pay off a big bar debt."

You ask her what kind of profanity.

She shrugs. "Just whatever men'd want hanging up in a bar, I guess. I'll tell them to start the movie for you."

The movie is shown in a small theater with lush, expensive chairs. It begins with the kind of music you used to hear in old Social Studies class films. Freeze-dried history.

Land masses appear, disappear. The area was all underwater once. Then: volcanoes, ice sheets, grasslands, Indians, the Spaniards, Sam Houston, then the timber and cattle barons lead into: *boomtown*. Then bust.

No Janis.

Outside the little theater the aged docent is once again upon you. The museum holds the combined attics of the patriarchal *they*—thrown in with enough black, Mexican, and Chinese history to keep the place eligible for federal funding. "See that cannon?" she says. "It fought in the Spanish-American War. In Cuba. And on Armistice Day, they loaded it with ham sandwiches and shot it off, and it blew out all the windows on Procter Street."

You ask why ham sandwiches.

She says she doesn't know. Never thought about it before.

You must proceed very slowly in this place so you will know where Janis fit in the local cosmology. The people of Port Arthur want you to understand their shared story, so you read slowly the scripted panels that accompany the artifacts.

There were the trilobites. *Though this animal did not exist long on the earth, it was widespread.*

There were the Indians, including a lovely girl named Kisselpoo, whose tribe was known to engage in ritual cannibalism.

Then there were the Spaniards with their parchment rumors of cities of gold, and their quaint name for a nearby island: *Malhado*. Bad luck.

A lovely old map depicts oil claims. The names are proof that the patriarchy of yore had its own sense of poetry: *Lone Acre Oil Co., The Gladys, Saratoga Oil and Pipeline, Queen of Waco, Paragon, The Drummers, Alamo Oil Company, The Ground Floor.* Under the same roof with the trilobites these extinct companies also seem like short-lived beasts.

There is a photo of a beached whale, turn of the century. Triple-masted schooners anchored in Port Arthur in the 1920s, stately in their moorings next to Model-Ts on the docks. A Nero-esque bust of General Sam Houston.

You pore over the specimens of water hyacinths, sailfin mollies, mourning doves, barn owls, blue-winged teal, cormorants. These creatures have everything to do with Janis Joplin, if you hear what you are reading the way Pentecostals hear in tongues. *Indigo bunting: common . . . this vividly colored bird sings through a series of varied high-pitched phrases . . . common . . . loud burst of whistled notes, downslurred toward the end.*

A docent is right on your heels with a group of mostly black schoolchildren, assuring them that the oil companies are not responsible for dirtying the bay; why, even the explorer Cabeza da Vaca, upon arrival from the Old World, found balls of tar floating in it.

Upstairs, there is the Big Bopper, another widespread, short-lived phenomenon, along with a macabre display of the hairbrush, Bufferin, dice, and Zippo lighter salvaged from his Dopp kit at the site of the plane crash that ended his life—and Buddy Holly's and Richie Valens's—in 1959. There is his elegant black-inked manuscript music to "Little Red Ridin' Hood," later to be recorded by Sam the Sham and the Pharoahs.

Tex Ritter's aqua cowboy coat.

Grammar-school pictures of Johnny and Edgar Winter—startling white egrets even then.

George Jones album covers.

And then there she is, Janis. Inexplicable as a sailfin molly. The first thing you see is the photo from the *Pearl* album cover, in her frou-frou clothes. Her high-school annual is open to the page that reveals she had a B average, and was in the

Art Club, the Future Teachers of America, and the Slide Rule Club. Her slide rule holds the pages open.

Her slide rule.

There is a pair of pen and ink sketches she did, pumpkin-headed scarecrows, like what you would've gotten if Dürer had had a sense of humor. There are certificates of her achievement in English, journalism, and art from Woodrow Wilson Junior High.

Her Bible.

A note to her mother, written when she was a kid:

> Dear mrs. S.W. Joplin.
> In gratefulness for being such a wonderful mother for 14 years, I would like for you to have dinner with me at Luby's on Saturday the 16th.
> Janis Lyn Joplin

A newspaper clipping from the *Port Arthur News*: Kris Kristofferson came to town for her birthday, over twenty years after she died. He said, "She reminded me of a little girl wearing dress-up clothes. If she had lived, I think she would have had a lot of happiness. She would have found out what a strong influence she was on so many people, and it would have maintained her."

In the center of the Port Arthur music exhibit there is a console of video screens; you can choose from a menu of musicians birthed or claimed by Port Arthur—Clifton Chenier, Harry James, Tex Ritter, Gatemouth Brown, and more. Press a button and you get a couple of minutes of old film footage of Janis, maybe live at the Fillmore, just a piece of her voice: *Cry, cry, baby.*

There is a "close replica" of her psychedelic Porsche, and it spooks the hell out of everybody except the children, looking like some kind of antiquated death-mobile with its mushroom motif, and a big eye on the hood that sees nothing, admits nothing.

You think of Hendrix and Morrison and Cobain. Maybe fame is civilization's euphemism for ritual cannibalism.

Outside, the sky is like a school of gray mackerel, eastbound, blowing. There is no sign for the Uptown Barbershop, it's just there, like an afterthought in an alley. In the window you see a white-haired man getting his hair cut by a barber whose own appearance suggests that he, like the building, is as he was in the 1960s. They are the only human beings to be seen for several city blocks. The deserted high-rise Hotel Sabine towers over a vacant parking lot outside that window.

"The lady in the African store told me I should come see your walls if I want to know about Port Arthur," you say.

The proprietor nods, and you make your way over to the back wall, where a mass of yellowing newspaper clippings are taped and tacked to the walls.

KENNEDY ASSASSINATED, big headline, black mourning font.

A newsletter, *The Oil Can*, 1939, laminated like a truck-stop menu.

A local golf star, shot.

An obit for the legendary madam Marcella Chadwell lovingly rendered by a reporter from the Beaumont newspaper, full-page feature.

A centerfold bimbo—following some law of the pornographer's: the sneer must increase in proportion to the ludicrous size of the breasts.

The barber and the customer are discussing who is the most powerful man in Port Arthur.

"No, he's been downsized to number two," the customer insists.

Another headline in funereal black: GRIM VIGIL FOR 33 MISSING ON TEXACO SHIP CONTINUES. And another, the *Sulphur Queen*, which went down in 1963, with photos of all the missing crewmen. There are thirty-three small portraits of some very good-looking men, arranged like a Moose Lodge, except they belong to the loyal order of the dead.

"I used to cut some of their hair," the barber offers, and comes over. "They never found them, I guess."

You begin to understand. This is barbershop history. The oil men on the shore, the sea of money changing hands in the standing-room-only photo of the now-deserted bank building. This also is the history of the patriarchal *they*, told at a slant. The barber has been telling stories on his walls for decades. All human events are connected and admissible evidence in this history, proffered without comment in the way men don't cloud the air with small talk sometimes.

The barber points to the old poster. DREAMLAND COLORED.

"Do you know what that means?" he asks. "Colored. That was a colored theater. For colored folks. Can you believe we used to have six? Five white, one colored."

"Where is everybody?" the question slips out before you have time to think. "What *happened* here?"

"That man," the barber says, pointing to a yellowing photo. "His name was Tom James. He ran out the gambling and the prostitution."

"And urban renewal," his customer offers. "Tell 'bout the urban renewal."

Nothing has been renewed out there in the *Twilight Zone* streets.

They launch into a contrapuntal explanation, a mishmash of misinformation.

"Ya condemn the buildings the blacks had, see. Twenty-five-foot lots, mostly."

"Ya tell them they can come back when it's all clean."

"They buy houses outside downtown."

"Ya pass an ordinance: minimum fifty-foot lots. They not gon' come back. They don't want two mortgages."

All this time you're trying to take in the walls, the *walls,* the riot of clippings and photographs. A sepia photograph of the original Hotel Sabine, a lovely old white-frame.

A grouping of yellowing index cards, dealt out like a solitaire hand. *Department stores, gas stations, brothels.*

Brothels?

Then a list of ladies' names with Marcella Chadwell's at the top. The other names are charmingly ordinary. A boom-time telephone directory for the patriarchy of yore.

The white-haired customer says aloud one of the names of the women on the list. He is freshly shaven, smiling benevolently. "My wife went to high school with her. A more beautiful person to be associated with you would not find." His voice is so soft that you know he is commemorating something unspeakable and important that he would like for you to understand. "She was a true lady. She always tried to keep the kids out of it."

You continue to peruse the walls.

A full-color spread of a bleached blonde with breasts like big tankers, next to the immortalized napalmed Vietnamese girl running naked down the road.

Sirhan Sirhan.

A schooner.

A calendar: bygone bimbo breasts like big fog lights.

The whale that beached itself at the turn of the century, again.

A big beached blonde in a stream: Ann Margret.

A *Life* magazine clipping of a 1939 Klan nighttime rally in Georgia, the old Nashes and Buicks like docked ships around a central bonfire, the white-robed men like sinister insects answering some call only they can hear. Their women are looking on with horrific approval at their protectors.

A small clipping of the hanged bodies of Mussolini and his mistress.

"Where'd you find that Klan postcard?" you ask, and a little tremor of irritation passes over the barber's face.

"Over Vidor," he gestures in the direction of the next town. "That was supposed to be a big Klan place. That parking lot out there? Used to be another big hotel. I used to comb those old rooms and find all kinds of stuff. Pictures, magazines."

"They say we talk too much about the negatives," the barber's customer offers.

"But if it happened, it happened," the barber adds.

Then, as your eyes scan the walls, *boom.* There she is, Janis, with her family. A nicotine-stained newspaper photo from the time, when the measure of a woman was whether she was a good girl or a bad girl, clean or dirty. Sister and mother, each coiffed in a kind of carapace for the head, armor for the feminine hygiene wars. But Janis's hair is sagebrush-wild, and her grin is a free gift from a spendthrift: *You know you got it, if it makes you feel good.*

No porno sneer like the jug queens sneer for their money.

Something about Janis's clean, honest smile makes you want to grieve right there for what was lost from this earth when she died. But you have an instinct not to do it in front of these particular natives of Port Arthur.

"Did you know Janis Joplin?" you ask the barber.

"Used to sit right there," he points to an empty red leatherette and chrome chair. "When I would cut her brother's hair."

Maybe she looked at some of these same clippings on the walls of Ivory Joe Hunter, Big Bopper, Tex Ritter—and an assortment of less fortunate local singers who passed into obscurity—who are remembered here for their 1950s appearances at the local nightspots. And for a minute, it feels like you have found her, the little girl waiting in the barbershop, maybe looking up at those yellow index cards, squinting, reading BROTHELS.

"She was a weirdo," the barber says. "A sick little weirdo. I was in that book they did about her."

"Tell about all the men," the customer adds. "She just didn't care. She did not respect herself. Tell about the artwork. She was a sick young lady. She OD'd. Go down to the museum. They have some stuff."

In that barbershop, you can remember yourself what it was like to be a white girl in a button-down white man's town in the 1960s. You remember the summer you were fourteen, the first time you heard her voice, on the radio, singing "Summertime," and you knew that being a woman was going to be more fun than anyone had ever told you before.

That photo on the cover of her album *Pearl* suddenly makes sense. She was parodying a Port Arthur madam. Marcella, perhaps. Maybe she was playing a joke on Port Arthur, and that joke enabled her to get away from whatever agoraphobia of the soul grants some men permission to revere a madam who charged money for it, and to condemn Janis for giving it away for free.

You drive around in the dark, past the thousand gold lights of the refineries as they spout blue dragon flame. The highway seems a whole river of human beings who have no choice at that moment but to trust the movement to somewhere else. You flip the radio dial, looking for Tish Hinojosa's clear voice, but the Tejano station has by then begun to sound like stylized passion, styling mousse for the ears, a collective trance. There is an imitation Barry Manilow of Tejano, a Tom Jones, a Michael Jackson, a Salt 'n' Pepa. You make a mental note to come back here, sometime when there is more time. Flat as it is, Port Arthur is a big scenic overlook from which you can see America's entire musical dharma.

If you are far away from your loved ones, under that exquisite black velvet night that is otherwise going to waste, you need to believe that somebody will think to play a song of Janis's all the way through. You want some DJ to release her sand-papery, slide-rule purr once more into the general traffic of radio dust-motes. Because you need to believe some girl who doesn't yet know fear will lie down for the first time with a boy who doesn't yet know mistrust, and they will teach each other the best things about themselves—*You know you got it, chile, if it makes you feel good.*

And it won't matter if the boy and the girl can hear Janis's voice or not. It's out there, and it's irrevocable.

Chris Bell

THE LEGACY OF BIG STAR'S "OTHER GENIUS"
by John Jeremiah Sullivan

━━━━

One thing you do not find much of in *It Came From Memphis,* Robert Gordon's history of the deeply, richly twisted cultural scene that occupied that city from roughly 1950–75, is tragedy. (Within the scene itself, that is; outside of it, the whole period could look pretty tragic.) There's awfulness: people rushing headlong into bad ends, talent going unrecognized, that sort of thing. But overall, the sense Gordon gives of the time and place is one of antic, at times frustrated, exuberance. The freaks were out, day and night, and they found one another. One result was rock & roll. Another was professional wrestling.

The story of Christopher Bell, which Gordon includes, is an exception, a tragedy, though in other ways it remains quintessential: He was a rich white kid from an affluent Memphis neighborhood, whose well-greased path through conventional society got ambushed by rock in high school, he formed the requisite cover bands (the awesomely named Christmas Future was one), playing not roots music per se, but the "new" stuff: Hendrix, British Invasion. Eventually he angled his way into Ardent Studios, where he became an apprentice engineer, taking actual morning lessons (8:00 A.M. sharp, drunk or sober) from the studio's founder, John Fry. At Ardent he met, or was reintroduced to, Alex Chilton. They'd known each other in high school, but since then Chilton had become marginally successful as the lead singer of the Box Tops ("Give me a ticket for an aer-o-plane ...."). When Chilton grew tired of fame, he knocked around Greenwich Village as a desultory folkie, then came home, not really knowing what to do with himself. He and Bell reconnected. They tried out new tunes on each other. Chilton was impressed enough that he tried to drag Bell back to New York with him. The idea was to play as a duo, but Bell didn't want to leave Memphis. So Chilton stayed.

The result, with Andy Hummel on bass and Jody Stephens on drums, was Big Star. And the less said about Big Star here the better, since Chris Bell's near-anonymity has much to do with his status as the "other genius" in that much written-about, much emulated band. Suffice it to say that Big Star invented power pop, loosely defined as unapologetically pretty and sophisticated melodies, with prominent harmony, played loudly and, at times, with an edge that approaches punk. (Didn't the Beatles do this? you ask. Yes. But pop fans live by razor-thin and barely defensible categories, and this is one.) Big Star made three records, each of which has multiple all-but-perfect songs on it. The third album, most often called just *Third*, is the masterpiece. It's a huge, dark, haunted house of a record, every song a room, and stylistically no one song seems to have anything to do with any other. But Chris Bell had nothing to do with *Third*. It is an Alex Chilton project in all but name.

Bell's presence fades from Big Star neatly, album by album. On the first, *#1 Record,* he was the dominant songwriter, sang half the lead vocals, and co-engineered. On the second, *Radio City,* he contributed only to the songwriting. That's saying quite a lot, in this case, since we have it on Andy Hummel's authority that Bell was the principal writer on "Back of a Car," a song that Rob Gieringer, in Judith Beeman's excellent, short-lived Big Star 'zine (also called *Back of a Car*), describes simply and without exaggeration as "one of the best pop songs ever written." By the time the third album came to be recorded, Bell was no longer a member of the band, and seems even to have become estranged from the band's social circle.

What happened was, in its particulars, a rock & roll cliché. Bell couldn't understand why Big Star wasn't famous. They had made a first-rate record, he believed (correctly, as the last thirty years have shown). What could possibly be the problem? The critics liked it, sure, but Bell wanted the screaming crowds at the airport. He needed to feel reciprocation from the world. Chilton had seen all that already, some version of it, and knew what it was worth—or knew, at least, that it couldn't be counted on. But the career defeats and the audience indifference were more than Bell's fragile psyche could bear. Making things worse was the tendency of the media to focus on Chilton, when they chose to pay attention to Big Star at all. At the time this was natural, even good for the band, since people knew who Chilton was. But mercenary logic like that never speaks to the tormented artist.

It's possible that Chris Bell was headed for a breakdown regardless. Certainly he was prone to mental illness. Robert Gordon reports that even before *Radio City* came out, Bell "was actually seeing things." Heroin found him, as it routinely finds those who have least business messing with it.

Something rarely mentioned in writing about Bell, but that appears to have been widely recognized by those who knew him, is his homosexuality. Five years ago, in Memphis, there was a rumor moving through the music world that he had been in love with Chilton, and that Chilton's lack of response may have hastened the breakup of Big Star. It borders on sensationalistic to mention this stuff, and Gordon may purposefully have left it out of *It Came From Memphis* because he doubted its veracity. Most of the subsequent interviews with people involved in Big Star sooner or later come to a statement along the lines of, "Chris was having personal problems, and I won't say any more about that."

If he was gay, well, Memphis in the '70s may have been full of freaks, but it was still in West Tennessee. The performance artist Randall Lyon, a highly influential Memphis scenester and open homosexual who knew Bell, remarked to Gordon, "I was always out front about my shit, and their problem was they didn't know what to do with a hip queer. It says a lot about the whole period."

Whatever the specifics of Bell's affectionate leanings, it's a safe bet they were tortured; most things about him were. His voice, on the recordings, is too sensitive. That's meant not as an aesthetic judgment. It wasn't too sensitive for the material, in other words. It was too sensitive for life. Listen to him sing, closely, and if you don't know a thing about what happened to him, you know that the guy who possessed that voice is probably not going to last in this world.

This is true not so much of Bell's work with Big Star but of his later solo material, collected long after the fact on a Rykodisc release titled *I Am the Cosmos*. It's not really an album, just a bunch of tracks recorded from 1974–78 in Memphis and a boutique studio in provincial France. Bell's brother, David, took him to Europe to help him go clean and generally get himself together, and David Bell's liner notes to *I Am the Cosmos* are a loving, wrenching tribute to a brother whose demons his family could no more fathom than help fight.

We can't know how much of *I Am the Cosmos* Bell wanted released, and the quality of the fifteen tracks is wildly inconsistent. (For that matter, the first two Big Star albums are less consistent than most of their evangelists are willing to confess—rescuers from obscurity understandably feel that their job demands extreme enthusiasm.) Some of Bell's songs feel generic, others are knockoffs of songs that Big Star did better, one attempt at barrelhouse—"Fight at the Table"—is sort of embarrassing. But the four (by my count) stand-out songs are so good that you just shake your head: at the idea that, with the exception of a rare and now quite valuable 45, these songs went unheard for fourteen years; and at the fact that Bell never got to make a bona fide album of his own, never got to make his own *Third*.

I Am the Cosmos starts breezily, with one of the greatest, saddest early-'70s goodbyes to the dreams of the late-'60s counterculture. Joni Mitchell had already sung that we had to get ourselves back to the garden. Chris Bell knew that the garden had been mowed. If it was still there, it was no use: He had the spider inside of him. His falsetto is somehow both angelic and howling.

> Every night I tell myself
> I am the cosmos, I am the wind
> But that don't get you back again

It would be funny, that verse, if it weren't so sad. It's still a bit funny, I think intentionally, which is another sign of the maturity Bell was growing into, taking himself less seriously. The contemporary power-pop band the Posies, two of whose members round out the current Big Star reunion line-up, do a superb cover of "I Am the Cosmos," their note-for-note fidelity a tribute to how well constructed it is. Halfway through it there's one of the coolest *yeah, yeah, yeah*s in pop, a descending ethereal three-note thing that waterfalls down while the guitar rips back and forth between A and Em7. There's a crudity to the song's beauty.

The second track, "Better Save Yourself," opens jarringly.

> I know you're right
> He treats you nice
> It's suicide
> I know, I tried it twice

We have it from David Bell that his brother had at some point tried to kill himself. In the throes of whatever drove him to it, he found Jesus, further complicating the psychological picture of his post–Big Star years. In "Better Save Yourself," he goes on to sing "You shoulda gave your love to Jesus/Couldn't do you no harm." The past tense there is creepy. The righteous blues were about exhorting the listener (maybe the singer, too) to get right with God, but it's too late for whomever Bell's talking to. "Shoulda Saved Yourself" would have been a more accurate title.

"You and Your Sister" is the sweetest of Chris Bell's songs, three minutes and eleven seconds of flawless pop craftsmanship, the goofy half-cleverness of the verses ("Your sister says that I'm no good/I'd reassure her if I could") expertly balanced with the real beauty of Bell's falsetto on the chorus:

> All I want to do
> Is to spend some time with you
> So I can hold you, hold you

Chilton said to Robert Gordon, "Most of the Big Star stuff was searching for how to get through two verses without saying anything really stupid. . . ." Add "playing" to "saying," and you have as apt a description of the task involved in writing good pop songs as has ever been articulated. Good songwriters can learn as much from listening to bad music as they do from listening to what they love. They memorize pitfalls, dead-ends; the how, as opposed to the what, of poor taste and cliché. It's a strange, hair-splitting science, since, let's face it, when you're thinking in Shostakovich terms, the distance between a Brian Wilson objet d'art and a breakfast-cereal jingle is about three atoms wide. For a pop songwriter, each new composition presents countless temptations and traps, moments when the song wants to become "stupid," wants to go to the obvious chord or rhyme, wants to sound too close (as opposed to the just close enough) to what we've heard before. The game is to thread your way through these traps without sounding like you're trying to be unpredictable—melodically, lyrically, in whatever way. Success comes when you've taken all the crap the genre gives you to work with—limited instrumentation, limited melodic possibilities, limited time—and made beauty of it, then disguised the beauty as more of what we like to hear on the radio. Isn't that what makes those classics, like "Baby, It's You," so moving, so overwhelming, what makes you have to pull your car to the side of the road when they come on? The beauty in them is subversive. It doesn't belong. It's been smuggled in under the radar of suburban teenage taste and purchasing power. That's why pop music is *the* art for our time: It's an art of crap. And not in a self-conscious sense, not like a sculpture made of garbage and shown at the Whitney, which is only a way of saying that "low" materials can be made to serve the demands of "high" art. No, pop music really *is* crap. It's about transcending *through* crap. It's about standing there with your stupid guitar, and your stupid words, and your stupid band, and not being stupid.

An example of what this sounds like, when pulled off, is Bell's "Though I Know She Lies." It's primarily an acoustic song, not quite like anything else he did during or after Big Star. There's nothing revolutionary about it, except that it's gorgeous, and full of space, and that it's the hardest kind of song to write, insofar as in the wrong hands it would turn to purest treacle. The guitars on "Though I Know She Lies" are badly recorded—the electric cracks up at the high end—which has probably kept it off some compilations in the past. But the vocal performance is chilling and tender.

> When I look through your eyes
> I tend to get bitter
> Maybe I'm best advised
> To look to myself

It doesn't really even sound like Chris Bell; he'd never sung that well before, which makes it even harder to take, since it was the last, or one of the last things he did. *So* confident, and at the same time, somehow, so vulnerable, with bared nerves. The song needs to be heard on headphones, because it's clear that he means to be singing straight into your head. Most striking of all is that by the end of the song, he no longer sounds like the person who started out singing it. The song itself, the experience of performing this vocal, seems to have done something to him, worn him out. Three and a half minutes have gone by, but he sounds ten years older. The chorus is simple:

> I fall every time
> though I know she lies
> I can't stay away

But it's how he holds the words in his mouth, sings "staaay aaawaaay" from the back of his throat, like he's physically trying to hold himself down in the bed, knowing he shouldn't go over there, shouldn't call. There is only one line of harmony in the song. It comes out of nowhere, on the bridge, a quiet falsetto, maybe Bell's own. You can miss it so easily—you have to squeeze the headphones to the sides of your head. The line is "Keeping me in the dark."

That's all I know about Christopher Bell. The Chairs, a power-pop band from Sweden, wrote a song about him in the mid '90s. One leans again on Robert Gordon for the end of the story, which is that a couple of days after Christmas, in 1978, Bell crashed his car into a telephone pole on Poplar Avenue in Memphis, and was killed. As with most fatal single-car accidents involving chronically depressed people, suicide has always been suspected, never proved.

He was coming home from a rehearsal, which means music was still a part of his life. That's no consolation, but I like hearing it anyway.

Jim White

THE ORIGINAL HICK-HOPPER by Lee Durkee

Jim and I are in his dilapidated van, driving around Washington Square Park an hour before sound check at the Village Underground. We are, like so many others, looking for a parking spot, a place to rest and talk. Jim is at the wheel, swearing. Tall and lanky with long, black hair and sideburns, he looks like a gas-station attendant from some music video fantasy; his accent, more twang than drawl, is thick Pensacola, a city that claims more churches per capita than any other in the South (and therefore the universe). One of its churches is a small Pentecostal one where for a decade Jim was a less-than-fervent member not above faking the occasional bout of glossolalia. Ten years as a Pentecostal, ten as a New York cabbie. . . . Call it a wash.

When the obscenities subside, Jim's voice returns to a smooth, fast river of observation, non sequitur, and storytelling that you can just ride along on and watch its banks. For instance, you mention Pensacola, and you get: "It's a beautiful, quiet, cheap place to live, but it's very conservative, and it's got its hands around the neck of life, and it's just slowly choking you, and you don't really notice it when you first get there 'cause they're such pretty hands. . . . You're just thinking . . . what pretty hands . . . and you know what? *They're around-my-neck!*"

You mention Manhattan, and you get: "The great thing about New York is shit just flying at you from every direction. I was standing outside the Museum of Natural History today—my sweetie's here with our daughter, and we wanted to take her to see the dinosaurs—there it is, man, every cabdriver's nightmare: the woman throwing her door open into traffic—and this hip-hop kid came walking up to me and out of nowhere showed me a picture of Tyra Banks in a bathing suit and says, 'Man, what do you think about this?' He'd never seen me before. I said that I'd have to think twice before I even said a word, and he said, 'I can't even think about it not even once because it hurts too bad,' and he turned and walked away. New York's got this kind of thing where if you keep the windows open long enough, all kinds of interesting birds will fly in."

There are a few interesting birds flying around inside Jim's new CD, *No Such Place*, on Luaka Bop, David Byrne's West Village label. Although Jim has been forever cast as "alternative country," the fact remains that there is a strong urban wind of static, intercom, reverb, and police megaphone blowing through these thirteen songs that his own label calls "trip-folk" but which Jim likes to call "hick-hop." (Not to argue with the likes of Mr. Byrne, but this ain't folk.) Whatever it is, it's dark medicine, this music, dimly lit if at all, by its humor and desperate faith.

There are no parking spaces along Washington Square, which is an old haunt of Jim's, one of many here, not all of them kindly remembered. "It almost killed me," he says of New York. "I've been back a couple of times, three or four times since I moved and quit driving a cab, and I still got, like, this yellow mind I get in the city and start driving like a madman, cussing everybody." As he pauses, the various strange birds of the West Village flutter inside the van's open windows. Electronic whirls and twirls, a car alarm, some horn blowers, hollerers and hawkers, screamers and boomboxers. New York spring.

"Music is a real fragmented lifestyle," he suddenly picks up—I'm pretty sure not where we left off—then lays on the horn to assert us toward a fire hydrant. "There was a certain rhythm to driving a cab, at least. You pick up your fares, you drop off your fares, you pick up your fares. . . . You never know where you're going or anything like that, but there's a rhythm to it. But there's no rhythm to this at all, and it's funny because it's rhythm that's what you're doing, you're doing music, which is supposed to be rhythmic—*No, I'm not honking at that thing you're shaking there, boney, I'm honking at your bad pedestrian skills!*—Sorry. The New York cabdriver just comes flying out of me. People are so astonished when they're riding around with me and I seem like a fairly polite person, and then suddenly I start calling someone fuckhead," he sticks his head out of the window, "YO, FUCK-HEAD! GET OUT OF THE WAY!" He shrugs. "It's reflexes. Anyway, my sweetie made a real good living here so her memories of New York are Edenic. It's just this paradise. Meanwhile, I lived here for ten years hand-to-mouth, driving a cab and making movies on shoestring budgets, and I think of New York, and I taste dirt in my mouth because it was so hard on me here so many times I was sick to the point of death and guys with guns threatening to shoot me when I was driving a cab and taking shit from people all the time and having to ride my bike home across the Manhattan bridge. . . . I don't know if you've ever had to ride a bike home across the Manhattan Bridge at three o'clock in the morning, but *it-ain't-no-fun.*"

We park illegally, doing what Jim calls the alternate-side-of-the-street-Watusi near the giant cement arch flanked by two statues of George Washington: soldier and statesman. A tall hurricane fence surrounds the entire structure so that no one can pass underneath it, which I think is kind of the purpose of an arch, being passed underneath. The fence was built to discourage the local artists-at-large, who are having a hard time of it these days, especially since some scientist, probably Giuliani's sister, invented the Teflon subway car. My girlfriend was raised in Queens and remembers the good old days when every square inch of every subway car was art.

Eyeing that arch, Jim says, "Yeah, even though there's a big sign on that thing that says, LET US RAISE A STANDARD TO WHICH THE WISE AND HONEST CAN REPAIR, they still sell crack right under it. I used to laugh like hell about that."

He laughs nostalgically now while I watch a drug peddler searching the crowd for a hungry eye. We talk a little more about New York and how hard it can be on the artist soul. Jim was a student at the NYU film school and used to finance his films on cab tips, working fifty-hour weeks for months, then quitting and spending it all in one week of production. He's earned money in stranger ways, too: as a professional surfer in Florida, a professional model in Europe. But whatever hardships he has endured, he has at least put them to good use in *No Such Place*, his second album, two years overdue. (Jim looks to be in his late thirties, like me; anyway, we both call them albums.) *No Such Place* is a haunted collection of songs, its poetry filtered between realms, leaving Jim's voice with the lonesome and, at times, disembodied sound of a Patsy Cline record played over a PA system to an empty midway on the closing night of the state fair.

When I was a kid, a friend once told me that you could listen to dead peoples' voices on the shortwave radio. I believed him and used to sneak out of bed and into my dark closet late at night and slowly spin that dial listening to all the static-eaten ghosts. This notion that voices never die has stuck with me, and it's not too far removed from what you get listening to Jim White's broken ballads. This ghost-in-the-machine effect is strongest in the dusky remake of Roger Miller's "King of the Road." As Jim tells the story, he first performed the song while deathly ill, battling disease and depression in a Florida beach house. Some friends had come over to cheer him up, they claimed, and after a while they demanded he join in the reverie. Half delirious, Jim dragged himself out of bed and moments later found himself speaking in tongues for real.

"Somebody shouted, 'Sing something!'" he recalls now. "And like I was possessed, I suddenly started singing 'King of the Road' like David Byrne." Here Jim belts out a few lines in that shouting delivery that trademarked the Talking Heads. "I'd been playing guitar for twenty-five years, and I'd never learned one song by another person. I don't know how to do it. I just don't have the patience to sit and learn. It's a form of narcissism, like the only thing you're interested in is yourself. I learned half of 'Stairway to Heaven,' and I learned the first half of 'Fire and Rain.'

Anyway, the record company hated the song ['King of the Road']," he adds, smiling grandly. "It was like pouring vinegar in their eyes."

It wasn't the only battle won over Warner Brothers, the parent company of Luaka Bop. Four years earlier, during the production of Jim's first CD, *Wrong-Eyed Jesus*, Byrne got worried that Jim's music might be coming across a bit too hostile and remote instead of swampy and mystical, so he advised Jim that what that first album needed was a "handshake to the world."

"Yeah, David told me it was a strange, interesting album, but you need to think of a handshake for the world because if people know you, they're going to like you. And I thought about it—I went to film school here at NYU, right behind you—and I remember that during the first film I showed, there was a kid in the class who said, 'I feel stupid watching this film, and I don't like feeling stupid, so I don't like the film.' Now there were a couple of people in the class who knew me and the way my mind works and loved it and were dedicated to it, and I thought, Well how can I get people to know me? If they know me, maybe they'll understand all these surrealist hillbilly references, for lack of a better term. So I sat down and wrote 'Wrong-Eyed Jesus.'"

"The Mysterious Tale of How I Shouted Wrong-Eyed Jesus" is of all things an accomplished short story included with the liner notes inside that first CD, and it went on to receive rave reviews. Even the one mixed review I found conceded high praise for the story, which tells the saga of a teenager, hitchhiking home from a minor drug deal one night, who gets picked up by a dirt-farming pervert. The inclusion of the story does exactly what Byrne had hoped for: it helps ground the music, which at times tends toward the ethereal, into the very solid, Southern landscape of Jim's childhood.

"Anyway, I presented the story to the record label, and Yale, the guy who runs the label, said no. Warner Brothers was never going to pay to have a story in a first album. Then David read it and said, 'Let's see what we can do about this.' So we fought this big *inter'nesting* war where we were fighting against our own people. We were shooting each other at Warner Brothers because there were people ready to lose their jobs for the sake of keeping the story in the album, and there were people who were willing to lose their jobs—you know, *Over my dead body that thing's going in there*—and we got away with it in the end, and I'm glad we did."

In fact, Jim has always considered himself a writer first and a musician second. He is faithful to both William Faulkner and Cormac McCarthy, but above all to Flannery O'Connor: "I didn't have a clue about my quote-unquote literary voice until I read Flannery O'Connor, and once I read that, particularly a story called 'The River,' I felt like I knew—like you'd been lost for fifty years, like the Israelites in the desert, and suddenly you see Israel, and you say, *Okay, that's where I have to settle*. That's how I felt when I read Flannery O'Connor."

His favorite novel, however, is a bit more obscure, a little-known Mexican classic called *Pedro Páramo,* written by Juan Rulfo, the grandfather of magic realism. Jim shows me the copy stashed in his van. By coincidence, it's one of my favorites, too, a novel told through a series of ghost ruminations arising out of a Mexican graveyard. Of the book, Jim says, "Rulfo's wandering back and forth between the ghost world and the literal world, and I got to a point where I was doing that a lot. Lots of times people kind of romanticize this idea of ghosts, and I learned the hard way—I talk about it in 'Ghost-Town of My Brain'—you can't take comfort in ghosts. That's not the point of their presence. You can learn from them certainly, but don't snuggle up with them too much because the physics of it will lead to disaster."

"Ghost-Town of My Brain" gives you a pretty good glimpse into Jim White. Performed almost somnambulantly, it is a song that didn't quite make it into this world, the spectral lyrics played against a heavy mix of percussion and a subtle background of banjo and lap steel. The delivery is full of lull, more subliminal than real, and groaned in a dark Waitsian voice.

But in spite of its ghosts, the new CD is balanced—more so than Jim's first one—with humor and even some lively tunes that could be called half-pop. One troubadour number, "God Was Drunk When He Made Me," is even a bit reminiscent of Jimmy Buffett (that is, young Buffett, before he started recording white-rap rants against popcorn prices and then opened up a chain store celebrating himself). Further balancing the album is its tenacious optimism, what I would call optimism-in-the-face-of-considerable-evidence-to-the-contrary, as witnessed in the beginning lines of the opening track:

> I'm handcuffed to a fence in Mississippi.
> My girlfriend blows a boozy good-bye kiss.
> I see flying squirrels and nightmares of stigmata.
> Then awakening to find my Trans-Am gone.
> Still I'm feeling pretty good about the future.
> Yeah, everything is peaches but the cream.
> I'm handcuffed to a fence in Mississippi,
> Where things is always better than they seem.

"Handcuffed to a Fence in Mississippi" pretty much sets the tone for the CD. It's a song that refuses to wallow, its music pulsating, Jim's voice seedy and bluesy and, at times, crooning. In true John Prine manner, the song doesn't feel it has to explain itself too much. It's also one of the tracks where you can hear the lingering possession of David Byrne loud and clear when Jim starts chant-lamenting: "My Trans-Am is missing/I guess there's no more kissing the girl who loved my car." The song's optimism is reinforced by a shaa-naa-naaah backup, and the irony of this optimism is reinforced by a police PA system repeating the refrain: "Things is always better than they seem."

Morcheeba, a British trip-bop trio, produced the second track, "The Wound That Never Heals," a spooky, sad ballad about a woman serial killer. But it's not the production that carries this song, it's more the absence of too much production that allows the grim beauty of its lyrics and distant, almost-spoken vocals to create this touching and haunted portrait of the murderess. Jim wrote the song after reading an unauthorized biography of Aileen Wuornos, a prostitute who killed seven men in Florida. But it's not a song solely about Aileen Wuornos, he points out. "None of the actions in the song parallel her actions." The song, as Jim tells it, was also written with a few former girlfriends in mind, women who had been victims of sexual abuse. "The Wound That Never Heals" begins with the stunning lines:

> Long about an hour before sunrise she drags his body down to the edge
> of the swollen river,
> Wrapped in a red velvet curtain stolen from the movie theater where
> she works.
> Quiet as a whisper, under the stanchions of a washed-out bridge,
> She cuts him loose and watches as the flood waters spin him around
> once then carry him away. . . .

Jim's lyrics are filled with the strongest, darkest poetry I've come across in music since the likes of Tom Waits and Shane MacGowan.

The third and last Morcheeba track is the catchiest song on the album, the upbeat "10 Miles to Go on a 9 Mile Road," which contains the trademark, preacherly lines:

> From the splinter in the hand,
> to the thorn in the heart,
> to the shotgun to the head,
> you got no choice but to learn to glean
> solace from pain or you'll end up cynical or dead.

These vocals are gruffly sung over a line of static that sounds, at times, like a computer going online. It's a bent, warped, wonderful song, almost like two diametrically opposed songs somehow welded together.

There are more subtle moments, too. Among them is the beautiful Sohichiro Suzuki–produced "Christmas Day," where again the music takes a step back and lets the songwriting have the floor, deservedly so, in this soft, understated number, another detached tale of grief and woe that has a couple parting at a Greyhound station. Strange electronic chimes haunt this song whenever the vocal pauses, which it does frequently and to great effect, in this meandering anti-serenade:

> I remember quite clearly . . .
> a bad Muzak version . . .
> of James Taylor's big hit . . .
> called 'Fire and Rain' . . .
> was playing as you crouched down . . .
> and tearfully kissed me . . .
> and I thought, 'Damn, what good fiction I will mold from this terrible
>   pain.'

When I ask Jim about that line—and it's a line that doesn't need much explaining to any writer—he smiles and says, "Yeah, my sister told me not to put that in. She said it makes it sound like you're not present in an emotional sense, you're thinking about the future, and I said, 'That's the point of the song.' It's that there's this emotional maelstrom all around me, and I'm thinking, How can I turn this into a story?"

Before Jim leaves for sound check, I ask him if, when touring Oxford, Mississippi, last week, he had visited Faulkner's house. (I'd noticed the Faulkner quote on the new CD, "Between grief and nothing I will take grief.") But no, Jim didn't have the time or desire. He'd rather find the ghost in the books.

"The town seemed like it was frozen in a way. It was frozen in the intentionality of showcasing Faulkner. I don't know if it was, but it kind of felt that way. I don't want to slam Oxford, but I had this hope of coming to Oxford and seeing this new metropolis of subversive thought . . . like a new epicenter of confusion and charm blending together and creating—"

"In Oxford?" I interrupted.

"Yeah, and it didn't feel that way—the thrift stores there are real overpriced! —but what happened to me in Oxford, and please write about this because any eccentric in Oxford will identify with it. We were in that bookstore in Oxford, which is a really nice bookstore, and me and the keyboard player were in there, and sometimes those oak worms fall on you, and he had one just crawling across his shoulder. And when I was a little kid I read *Horton Hears a Who* by Dr. Seuss, and so I have an extended sense of the universe and think that all life forms have some kind of right to live, and there he was, this worm. He didn't do anything wrong. He just happened to fall on somebody's shoulder, and so I picked him up off Clint's shoulder, and I started talking to him," he extends index finger in front of nose. "You know, like, *You're going to be okay. I'm going to take you and find you a nice bush,* and I walked out the store, and I'm walking along the sidewalk—I guess I was dressed kind of scruffy—and I'm talking to the worm like this, and people are staring, and I don't care, go ahead and stare, and I get to a nice row of bushes off the Square, and I'm saying, *You want to get on this bush right here,* and it wouldn't go, and I'm saying, *C'mon just do it,* and it won't. So I get in this big, long negotiation, and finally the worm gets off, and I'm telling it, *See that wasn't so bad, and you thought I wasn't going to be your buddy, and here I am helping you out,* and I get done talking to it, and I look up, and there's a cop right there just staring at me. And all he saw was this guy talking to his finger, talking to a bush. That fucker circled me for hours, waiting for me to throw a brick through a window." Jim pauses for breath, for thought. "Yeah, when I was deathly ill, I read Faulkner, and that shit will get inside your soul if you're deathly sick."

After Jim leaves for the Village Underground, I wander around Washington Square. I have a few hours to kill before the show, and so, while watching the drug deals of dusk, I put my flask to use with a dollar can of Coke. The cement lawn is filled with the usual parade of riffraff, and I'm feeling kind of sad and nostalgic because the previous day I'd given notice on my Lower East Side tenement. I'd been borderline leaving New York for months—I simply couldn't afford it. And now I sip my Coke and start thinking about returning to ice-shackled Vermont and getting back my old job bartending. I had finished my first novel and moved to the city in a gust of romantic optimism. Well, now I'm moving back. Which isn't so terrible, except after over a decade of bartending, it hurts to even think about cutting off another drunk, and I mean physically hurts, like my heart's wincing at it.

I wander over to check the inscription on that big arch, to see if Jim got it right. Sure enough, above the statue of General George, who had so successfully slaughtered the Hessians on Christmas, it states: LET US BUILD A STANDARD TO WHICH THE WISE AND HONEST CAN REPAIR. And sure enough, as I'm standing there, a short black guy with long, beaded dreads introduces himself as Medusa and asks if I am in need of anything.

I'm a bit late for the show, and my girlfriend is waiting for me outside the Village Underground. She is looking especially beautiful but is wearing diabolical shoes and so isn't in the best of moods. "Your eyes look funny," she says. I haven't yet told her about breaking my lease—I'll tell her tomorrow or the next day. Maybe she'll go with me to Vermont, but I doubt it—it's real hard to imagine her existing outside of New York City—and leaving without her, that hurts my heart to think about, too. We descend into the club and are steered toward the reserved Luaka Bop seats. The tavern is filled with white people of all ages, thrift-shop art on the walls, the obligatory net of smoke, the musicians on stage tuning. We settle in, get some drinks, and I'm probably the only person in the club who doesn't notice when David Byrne sits down right next to me. My girlfriend elbows me, whispers at me, and a few seconds later, I glance over. Sure enough. No big suit or anything, but David is looking himself, fit and healthy. "David, by the way, is a sweet, wonderful person," Jim had told me earlier. "He's a nice guy. He's a very distant person, and he has an angular mind, and if you take those two things as givens, you will not meet a nicer person."

Being quiet and shy, I am not about to bother him, but then Byrne leans over and holds out his hand and says, "Hi, I'm David."

I raise my palm in high-five position and say, "Dude!—Burning down the house!"

No, not really. I was happy to shake his hand, though.

Jim onstage is a master of self-deprecation. "I am doomed as a performer," he announces at one point. His shyness offsets his good looks and tallness. He's lost his straw cowboy hat, but he's still wearing the gas-station-attendant shirt. His version of "Handcuffed" is much livelier and more infused with humor than the recorded version. This is pretty much true straight through the set. It's a great show that ends with a randy encore of "God Was Drunk When He Made Me," not Jim's best song, but it's a good one to march them home on. (The CD ends in a more thematic fashion, the last track on the album being a reprise of the imagistic "Corvair," a song about an old car being overgrown by nature and becoming something other than a car.) Jim is up there enjoying himself, belting out in drunk-reverend fashion:

> If it was God that saved the miracle child from the peril of the fiery flame
> Well then it musta been Him killed the two hundred others just to glo-
> rify His name.

People are clap-dancing and shouting for more, but it's the third encore already.

The house lights go on, and we escape upstairs to the street, the diabolical shoes causing us to opt for the F train on an otherwise beautiful night. We hold hands waiting for the F, which never comes quickly, but luckily on this night there is an old Japanese man playing the subterranean violin. He is wearing thick, taped glasses, and propped in front of him is a similarly duct-taped music stand. I don't know what he's playing, but it is very spring-sad and flight-filled, and whatever it is, the old Japanese guy appears utterly lost inside it, his eyes shut behind the thick lenses, a small smile playing on his lips. Two F trains roar in at once, converging at the station in an onslaught of noise so loud that parts of you disappear, but the old man keeps playing, even though not a soul can hear him now, except maybe the rats. We get in the F and leave him there, his eyes shut, his bow hand dropping down to turn a page of sheet music.

Jazz

Eartha Kitt

TIGRESS by Jack Hitt

———

In 1982, when I was twenty-four years old, I was ushered into an apartment in the West Village where Eartha Kitt suggested I sit beside her on a sofa. She was a famous woman in her fifties, promoting a new show, and still very much a striking figure. She had a Cary Grant jaw beneath a forehead high enough to rent a banner ad. Up top, she had a fluff of a 'do that would one day perhaps inspire Will Smith in his Fresh Prince phase. Across the marquee of her face was a severe Euclidean line, her mouth. She seemed to have a dozen extra teeth in it. When she opened it—which she did in that crazy, theatrical way—a gale of stage laughter followed, and it was then that a young man was invited to peer into an abyss that threatened to consume everything in the room.

At the time, I was trying out my interview style, which consisted of chatting the interviewee to death about how much we had in common until she realized she either had to put me out of my misery or never get a word in.

I was test-driving this novel technique on Kitt because I knew her story well, as do many by now. She grew up in the odd little place called North, South Carolina. Her father was white and her mother was black and Cherokee. People made fun of her mixed race. She was beaten as a child. And eventually her mother abandoned her. She was sent to New York and muscled her way into show business. I, on the other hand, grew up in Charleston, where I learned to sail at the Carolina Yacht Club and to dance the foxtrot at the Society Hall. My cascade of anecdotes meant to convince Ms. Kitt that our lives shared many similarities, because what's really the diff between being reared as a young dandy in the Lowcountry and ridiculed as a mongrel in the Piedmont? See, it all happened in the samè *state*. Oh, man, I may even have mentioned that I had once or twice dated a black woman. But well-intentioned white men from the South, when finding themselves seated on a sofa beside a comely black person, are sometimes possessed of an irresistible need to exhaust their store of I-know-black-people stories. (In 1991, the future editor of the *New York Times*, originally from Alabama, wrote a cover story in the magazine about how much he had liked his black maid. Swear to God.) Suddenly, Eartha Kitt interrupted me.

"I'm not black," the famous mouth explained. "I'm white." The abyss opened—a zephyr of laughter filled the room—and in I tumbled. I don't quite remember what happened after that. There were a few other questions, maybe. When I tried to revisit the subject of her youth, she simply repeated her angry epigram—"I'm white." Those words fell out of her mouth like two small, hot cinders. They were untouchable, unanswerable.

Was she just toying with a greenhorn reporter, or was she making some point about race? After all, couldn't she claim to be white with as much authority as I could assume that she was black? But as I rolled this failed interview around in my head—something I did for years and years—I never could shake that sense of anger, not just at the people who had rejected her but even at those who, however mawkishly, tried to embrace her. Kitt often tells interviewers, "I wasn't white enough to be white or black enough to be black." So the little yellow girl named Eartha Mae Kitt took her trilling pipes, hot body, and outrageous mouth to New York and Paris, and became a star.

Listen to her—pick any song, it doesn't matter—and it's hard not to hear that anger in every word and gesture. If you can find an old film of Kitt singing her signature song, "C'est Si Bon," you can see it. Your average chanteuse would take the staccato pop of those teeny French words and wail one of those '60's pep songs meant to leave you with an ain't-life-grand? cheerfulness.

Here's what Kitt did. The song goes back and forth between a chorus of straight-laced men hitting the title phrase twice, a kind of percussion to her lead. But then she comes in, moaning and purring those French words, "It's so good, it's so good." Back and forth she takes it with the men, back and forth, until you almost feel embarrassed, like you put your ear up to the wall of her bedroom. But then she suddenly sharpens her phrases into little daggers. On stage, she'd bulge her eyes, sometimes literally scratch at the audience, bare her teeth, and open the abyss.

In 1950 Orson Welles called Eartha Kitt "the most exciting woman in the world." Sigmund Freud long before coined his own phrase, *vagina dentata*.

Kitt could have been called the Catwoman long before she played the part on the *Batman* television series in the 1960s (where I first saw her—a kind of Ur-J. Lo, the first introduction to the Civil Rights–era suburbs of a female beauty best described later by Sir Mix-a-Lot). But Kitt's purr and her almond eyes and demeanor have always been misdescribed as catlike. Her stout muscular body and giant head and scarred psyche is very wounded animal—feline, sure, but much bigger. I wasn't surprised when I learned that at the foot of her bed she keeps the skin of an actual lioness, stuffed head intact.

Her songs are all about being profoundly alone and angry. Sometimes literally: "Spend hours by the phone—where is my baby?/Chew my fingers to the bone— where is my man?" But usually it's in the phrasing and that purr. On talk shows, she deploys her trademark sound, and it's all campy and silly and Catwoman on TV, usually calling it up from the back of her throat. But in her songs, it comes from the solar plexus and it's all present-tense melancholy and long-ago fury.

There's a desperate quality to Kitt, some remnant of that eagerness to get away from South Carolina. She conned her way into the Katherine Dunham Dance Co. And then, once in Paris, worked her way into the club circuit and followed the path carved a generation before by Josephine Baker. But Baker literally became a European, lived there, fought bravely in the French Resistance, and maintained her fame on Old World terms. Kitt, however, decided to come home and make it, American-style.

And so, every five years or so since her breakthrough moment in Paris in the 1950s, she's found a way to ramp up the purring legend for one more turn. In many ways, Catwoman on *Batman* was an attempt to make her name known to a generation that included, well, me. In the 1980s, she recorded a disco song. At a *Batman* reunion years ago, she delighted in making Julie Newmar admit that her purr was second-rate. She announced herself: "I am the real Catwoman," and then cattily looked at Newmar, whom Kitt had replaced on the show, and asked, "I don't know where you went or what happened to you. Did they take you off?" The actors who played Batman, Robin, and the Riddler were all there and all joshing about their status as washed-up has-beens. It's what you do to show your self-effacing humanity in such pop-culture situations. Of course, Kitt didn't exactly protest when asked to sing something, her way of separating herself from the claque of losers seated around her.

This act that Kitt pulled together in America—purring chanteuse who made it big in the "clubs"—both is and isn't true. As a career in Paris, you can actually pull off being a big-time singer in the clubs. But in America? It's largely a pose on talk shows or a plot twist in a movie. "I'm working on my act," says some singer in a hundred American movies, like Debbie Reynolds or Mickey Rooney or Doris Day or Judy Garland. But mostly it's fictional characters in America who get to make that claim, like Renée Zellweger's character in the recent *Chicago*, Liza Minnelli's lead in *Cabaret*, or Desi Arnaz on *I Love Lucy*. But, except for the back room of the Carlyle, America doesn't have the kind of cabaret culture that allows torch-song singers to make it big. Something like the Folies-Bergère? Doesn't really happen here in reality. So, the only alternative is to play one on TV.

Which is how Kitt jump-started the story of the abandoned yellow girl from South Carolina going to Paris and making it big. And it's where the purr comes in. No talk show is going to let her sing a whole song, so the purr is a kind of catchphrase suggesting sexy cabaret nightlife. She can let out one of her trademark *gggrrrrrrr*'s and the audience pounds out a roar of applause that makes them feel like they are sophisticates catching the show at old Havana's Tropicana or Paris's Moulin Rouge. But since the only cabaret clubs that succeed in the big time in America are the fictional ones, you play the role with occasional appearances on *The Mike Douglas Show, The Tonight Show,* or *The Merv Griffin Show.* Or for a different generation, on the sofa beside David Letterman, Conan O'Brien, or Craig Ferguson.

From Charo's "cuchi-cuchi" to Flavor Flav's "Boyeeee!," the life of the post-hit entertainer is marked by a long forced march through the talk-show outback, sounding out one's catchphrase to the same automatic applause. But with Kitt, you get one difference that makes her songs irresistible. You can hear it in every note she sings. Eartha Kitt's story—the anger, the melancholy, the desperation—is audible there, in every quivering, trilling purr. On one album, every song was charged with her primary emotions, especially that desperation of American celebrity: "Do or Die," "My Discarded Men," "All by Myself," and "Hit Them Where It Hurts." All of these songs on an album entitled: *I'm Still Here.* You sure are, Eartha Mae. And for the same reasons that make me stop to watch a house fire, I'm still listening.

Henry "Red" Allen

A NEW ORLEANS TRUMPETER AND THE MAN WHO
LOOMED OVER HIM by David Gates

━━━━━

I stumbled onto Henry "Red" Allen when I was maybe fifteen, in that haphazard, ahistorical, assbackwards way you discover music as a kid. Thanks to the Columbia Record Club, the Amazon.com of its day—this would've been 1962 or '63—I'd already become entranced by Louis Armstrong: his live *Ambassador Satch* album from the '50s and one volume of his studio-created Hot Fives from the '20s. I was mad to hear more jazz, and particularly more jazz trumpet, so I ordered a Dizzy Gillespie record—headspinning after Louis, but exhilarating—and then an anthology of sorts called *The Sound of Jazz,* recorded at the rehearsal for a 1957 TV show of the same name. Amazing people on it: Billie Holiday and Lester Young in elegantly wasted decline, Coleman Hawkins, Ben Webster, Count Basie, and Jimmy Rushing still at the top of their games, the whimsical and tortured Pee Wee Russell, the modernists' favorite old-timer, who was the Thelonious Monk of the clarinet. It was like the cast of the best movie you've ever seen. But the first thing you heard (well, no: the band hit one quick opening chord) was Red Allen's trumpet kicking off Armstrong's stop-time "Wild Man Blues," and even then I could hear that he was unique. He had a strong, straightforward attack like Armstrong's, but his tone was drier, on the one hand, than Armstrong's fat, brassy sound and, on the other, less astringent than Gillespie's. And—the important thing, though I never articulated it to myself then—a subtle melancholy somewhere in all that bright, bold agility. It spoke directly to a kid like me, for reasons I won't need to explain to anybody who was a kid like me.

But there was so much I didn't know. For one thing, I didn't know that "Wild

Man Blues" was an Armstrong piece; I'd never heard—or heard of—his 1927 version, with the Hot Seven. Nor, for some reason, did I discern Armstrong's influence in Allen's singing on the other song he did on the record, "Rosetta," though it's plain as day now. Nor was I aware that "Rosetta" had been one of Allen's signature recordings back in the '30s. Nor did I understand that *The Sound of Jazz* was a moderate-Republican representation of the true state of jazz in 1957, favoring what was then called the "mainstream" and omitting both New Orleans revivalists and post-Parker modernists (except for the mellow, almost folkie Jimmy Guiffre Trio with Jim Hall). I'm glad I didn't know these things then, because I would probably have suspected Allen was the show's second choice after they couldn't get Armstrong himself. (Probably not true: Smart producers would have known that Armstrong wasn't much of a team player, and that his showmanship would have disrupted the collegiality.) I would have divined that Allen's role was to do a sophisticated tip of the hat to jazz's New Orleans roots without getting all Dixieland about it. (I didn't even know Allen was from New Orleans.) And I would have been apt to dismiss these glimpses of Allen as nostalgic rehashes of revered originals, rather than out-of-context wonders. It took me a while to develop that sort of knowingness, and much longer to get over it.

So, in my innocence, I craved more Red Allen, and soon I found it: a 1959 recording called *Red Allen Meets Kid Ory*. Perfect, I thought: not just my man, but also the guy who'd been the trombonist for the Hot Five—still, amazingly, alive and playing. (Three decades seemed more amazing then than it does now.) The record turned out to be a disappointment. Allen sounded okay, but the band was rickety and corny compared with the sleekly powerful rhythm section and all-star soloists on *The Sound of Jazz*, and Ory seemed to have become an even cruder player than he was in the '20s, though maybe that was just because you now heard him in unforgiving hi-fi. (By this time, my idea of a trombonist was Jack Teagarden or Dickie Wells.) Ory's solos were downright painful, and he clunked up the ensembles; you could only wring enjoyment out of the thing by trying to pick the trumpet out of the muddle and waiting for Allen's solo choruses to come around. I did my best to like the record, since I'd chosen it and I've always hated to be proved wrong, but it dropped out of the rotation after a few plays, and I eventually gave it away to somebody, along with a bunch of other stuff I wish I had now, in a rash purge of my pre-bop records, except the Armstrongs (couldn't part with those). I kept *The Sound of Jazz*, too, but that was pretty much the end of it with me and Red Allen.

Then, forty years later, the damnedest thing happened. On some whim, I pulled out my old *Sound of Jazz* LP and listened to it from beginning to end for probably the first time since I'd been in high school, and a couple of days later—I don't expect you to believe this, but it happened—I got a call from an editor at *The*

Oxford American asking me if I might be interested in writing about Red Allen. Red Allen? Did he mean Red Allen the bluegrass singer (whom I don't much care for) or *my* Red Allen? And sure enough. I headed for the record store—record stores, actually—but all I could find in New York were copies of a British import called *Swing Out*, with material from 1929 to 1946. (And so sloppily assembled that it gets the track numbers wrong.) *Swing Out* gave a useful overview of Allen in the process of self-creation, with the original 1934 "Rosetta" (with an unaccompanied introduction that, like the similar introduction to the 1930 "Dancing Dave," seems intended to one-up Armstrong's intro to "West End Blues") and other Allen benchmarks, including the Ellingtonian "Feeling Drowsy" (1929) and the light-footed yet bluesy "Rug Cutter's Swing" (1934). Amazon.com had a wider selection, but some of it was unavailable, and some of it was those year-by-year, for-completists-only discs that you might play once on a long car trip. I passed up *World on a String,* a 1957 set with Hawkins that I've since learned is supposed to be Allen's masterpiece. (I still haven't heard it. I'm saving it as a treat for my old age. And—you want the truth?—because I didn't want to be disappointed.) *Red Allen Meets Kid Ory* wasn't on CD, but I found a disc with the two of them live in Denmark the same year, so I thought I'd test my memory. (Which proved accurate; I doubt I'll play this turkey a second time.) And I chose one more CD, *Henry "Red" Allen and His Quartet Live, 1965,* recorded at a Long Island restaurant two years before he died, to hear Allen doing a perfectly ordinary gig, with nothing to prove and only a pianist with whom to share solo space.

There was a Red Allen biography (who knew?), so I went to—ahem—*my local independent bookstore* and had them order that, too. The jacket of John Chilton's *Ride, Red, Ride* calls its author, a British writer and trumpet player, "a close friend" of Allen's, though it's apparent from the book that they were acquaintances who hung out some when Allen toured the U.K. Poor Chilton will never sell the movie rights to a life like Red Allen's: Allen seems to have been a nice guy, maybe a little distant, but not self-destructive, not a doper, not a drunk. In his early years, in fact, Allen was a teetotaler, the guy fellow band members could trust to handle the money. (By the time Chilton met him, he'd sip sherry or have a beer with you; while in the U.K., he'd come to like stout.) His sense of decorum once led him to berate the New Orleans singer Blue Lu Barker for hanging her laundry out the window after she'd moved to New York.

He was married, to the same woman, until he died. He did die pretty young—sixty-one—but from pancreatic cancer rather than an overdose, car wreck, or jealous husband. Chilton reports nary a fistfight, and seldom a squabble. About the only way you could get Allen riled was to talk too much with him about Louis Armstrong, or to make unfavorable comparisons; Chilton once saw him bellow at an obnoxious club patron who suggested Allen wasn't musician enough to play Armstrong's "Cornet Chop Suey." ("I think I could play it in every key, but I have my own repertoire and I won't be playing it for *you*.") On the other hand, you could also get Allen's goat by comparing him *favorably* with Armstrong. "Don't say that," he told an admirer at another U.K. gig who'd told him he was better than Louis, "don't ever say that! Louis is the king."

In fact, if Allen's life had any great drama or tension or pathos at all, it was in the way Armstrong loomed over it. Like Armstrong, half a dozen years older, he was born in New Orleans, though to relatively genteel parents. (Armstrong's mother was a prostitute.) His father, Henry Allen, Sr., a foreman longshoreman, ran one of the city's best brass bands; Armstrong played in it, as did Sidney Bechet and the legendary, never-recorded Buddy Bolden. Like Armstrong, Allen played in one of Fate Marable's riverboat bands. He joined King Oliver, then in St. Louis, in 1927. In 1922, Armstrong had also gotten his start with Oliver, in Chicago. Allen joined Luis Russell's band in New York in 1929; Armstrong was fronting it. In one publicity handout, Allen was billed as Armstrong's "understudy." Years later, when someone played Allen one of the Russell recordings on which he and Armstrong shared solos, Chilton reports that Allen said, "My, my, those two trumpets do sound alike, don't they?" Then he ended the discussion "by shaking his finger in an unfathomable gesture." In early 1930, Armstrong was in the studio when the Russell band cut "Saratoga Shout," with a romping thirty-two-bar solo by Allen, and, as Chilton tells it, Armstrong "offered genuine congratulations, much to the young man's delight. One suspects that Louis, even then, knew that Red would never overtake him."

Ouch. And this from Allen's own biographer. And, of course, it's true, as Allen himself clearly understood. Allen was a brilliant—and, after a while, a brilliantly original—jazz musician. Armstrong was something far beyond that—beyond jazz, really: an intuitive genius, and one of the twentieth century's transforming figures, popular music's equivalent of Einstein, Picasso, or Joyce. What must it have been like to sit next to him on the bandstand? True, Allen was arguably more of a musician. He got around his horn faster—he seldom relied, as Armstrong did, on belting out the same high note over and over when tempos got fast—and I doubt Armstrong could have transposed "Cornet Chop Suey" into every key. But mere musicianship ultimately wasn't the issue; if Armstrong taught Allen's generation how to play jazz, he also taught them humility. Allen's recorded solos are daring, inventive, sometimes surprising explorations, but Armstrong's best solos are like pieces of architecture; no one could hope to surpass his sense of form and his way of balancing phrase against phrase, sound against silence. On the earlier tracks on *Swing Out,* you hear Allen appropriating Armstrong's mannerisms, both on trumpet and in his singing: the gravelly voice (Allen's natural singing voice was smoother), the scatted nonsense syllables, the ironic semi-detachment from such second-rate pop songs as "My Galveston Gal" and "Roll Along, Prairie Moon." But even from the first, you can also hear the difference: Despite the Armstrong-like high notes (and one glissando right out of Armstrong's playbook) on "Feeling Drowsy," Armstrong would never have sounded this reflective and restrained—as if Allen were choosing not to be hammy. As he moves through the 1930s, he comes to sound more and more like Red Allen: more tricky, more elusive, more inclined to color his sound with growls and smears, more willing to incorporate passing dissonances—more like what we know as modern jazz.

Some critics have argued that Allen is the missing link between Armstrong and Roy Eldridge, who's considered the obvious link between Armstrong and Gillespie. (This obsession with who begat whom grows out of the old view of jazz history as a march to modernism—a tempting approach, but one in which individual figures tend to be valued as much for their evolutionary function as for their own achievements.) Chilton, though he has every reason to puff up his subject's importance, doesn't believe Allen had much influence on Eldridge; neither did Eldridge himself. "I like Red," Eldridge once told Nat Hentoff, "but oh God, no! When I first came to New York I used to wonder as people were saying he was playing wonderful chords. . . . He used to come and sit in with Teddy Hill, and I felt something was wrong. I didn't know exactly what it was until I went with Fletcher [Henderson] and from the experience there I knew he had often been playing wrong notes." (By the way, as knowledgeable a scholar as Gunther Schuller doesn't believe Eldridge's denial.) Eldridge, in effect, was calling Allen a primitive, who achieved his quasi-modernist effects not because of a sophisticated grasp of chord theory, but by accident. I'm not enough of a musician to decide this, but Eldridge was—and so is Chilton, who writes that Eldridge based his solos on "a consummate knowledge of harmony and chordal substitutions whereas Red's improvisations relied mainly on his ear and his remarkable musical instinct."

Yet post-bop trumpet-player Don Ellis took an apparently opposite view. In a 1965 *DownBeat* article, Ellis made the remarkable claim that Allen—then considered a nostalgia-mongering sellout for his crowd-pleasing performances at Manhattan's Dixieland-oriented Metropole Café—was in fact "the most creative and avant-garde trumpet player in New York." Every time he went to hear Allen, Ellis wrote, "I have said to myself, 'It can't be true. All those wild things he's doing must be lucky accidents. After all, he's been around almost as long as Louis, and it is simply impossible that he could be playing that modern.' . . . What other trumpet player plays such asymmetrical rhythms . . . ? Who else has the amazing variety of tonal colors, bends, smears, half-valve effects, rips, glissandos, flutter tonguing, all combined with iron chops and complete control?" This may say more about Ellis than about Allen: It's not unheard of for a rebel to fantasize that a revered forefather is secretly his comrade-in-arms. (There should be a term for the Oedipus complex in reverse.) Some of these effects, which Ellis considered avant-garde, were heard by others—including Chilton—as tasteless and grating. (Chilton calls one Allen mannerism, a high-register half-valve effect, "a squeezed-out squeal . . .

that rapidly loses its enthralling quality.") I suspect Chilton is right: Allen was simply a musical pragmatist, whose intuitions led him to an increasingly unusual and distinctive style. He played what sounded good to him, and didn't much care how he happened to be categorized. He did sound the way Ellis described him—which is a better job of describing than I could do—but he was entirely innocent of any avant-garde agenda. He had no sense of defiance, no urge to *épater le bourgeois*: Hell, the bourgeois kept him in paying gigs. "I don't go for putting people in different categories like Dixieland, Chicago, West Coast, and so on," he told one interviewer. "I listen to everybody, you know. Bop didn't bother me. This was just another style. It's all kinds of new chords, but all of them wind up with the same spark plug. I had no squawk when bop came in. I had no days off unless I wanted them."

So that was the real issue: whether you worked or not. Allen had come up at a time when jazz at least verged on becoming popular entertainment, and like many musicians of the pre-bop era, he never got his head around the idea that he was practicing an elite art form. Despite his shyness, he cultivated a good-time onstage persona, counting off every tune with his trademark "Wamp! Wamp!" and playing to the customers with such numbers as "Drink Hearty." The only thing for which he really faulted the boppers was their neglect of—in fact their contempt for—showmanship; the one thing for which his admirers faulted him was his overeagerness to please his public. The sympathetic critic Dan Morgenstern caught a show at the Metropole and reported that Allen would "start a solo and get a groove going, and then abruptly jerk the horn away from his chops to yell 'Hey, my good man!' to greet a fan who'd just walked in." J.C. Higginbotham, the master trombonist who for years was Allen's closest musical collaborator, once went so far as to invoke the T-word. "In front of [clarinetist] Buster Bailey and me," Higginbotham claimed, "he said, 'I'll admit I'm an Uncle Tom to make a dollar.'" Maybe he did, maybe he didn't. But this hot-button accusation was too much for Morgenstern. Allen, he wrote, "had real good old-fashioned manners . . . but, in spite of Higgy's claim, not in a Tomming way."

The true problem—which Allen would not have seen as a problem—was conceptual, not racial. Allen considered himself an entertainer, and artistry was part of the package. Chilton once saw him tame an audience of American servicemen, few of whom knew who he was, "not by firing the heavy artillery of his sing-along routines, but subtly, by playing pianissimo solo. . . . He got down off the bandstand and strolled from table to table whispering open-trumpet phrases to young ears that had never before been charmed by improvisation. He blew so softly and with such control that within minutes the entire audience became appreciatively silent, totally absorbed in Red's music." This was hardly the Miles/Mingus method of dealing with a philistine audience. The post-bop generation demanded respect; in this case, at least, Allen commanded it.

Still, listening to those 1965 recordings at the Blue Spruce Inn, in Roslyn, Long

Island, you wish Allen had been a little more artsy-fartsy. You can only feel vicariously humiliated by hearing him play the faux-Greek novelty "Never on Sunday," presumably by request—I'm unwilling to think he chose the tune. (Whoever put the disc together should have known nobody who'd buy a Red Allen record in the first place would sit still for it, however instructive it is in a grimly documentarian way.) And sure enough, he also seemed to feel obliged to serve up the Armstrong hits of the day, "Mack the Knife" and "Hello, Dolly," which he delivered at much faster tempos than Armstrong's sedate versions, perhaps to cut the old man down to size, perhaps to get through them sooner. He gets as close as he ever got to rock & roll on the obviously ad-hoc blues "Blue Spruce Boogie," egged on by Sammy Price's barrelhouse piano. And then there's his autobiographical New Orleans medley ("Sidney Bechet, Louis Armstrong, so many of the boys," he tells the crowd. "I was there with 'em. I couldn't miss—my father had the band"), ending with "When the Saints Go Marching In," a tune so notoriously overplayed that for years seriousminded traditionalists had taken to refusing requests for it. To Allen, though, "Didn't He Ramble" and "Just a Closer Walk With Thee" and "The Saints" had a genuine personal resonance that predated the jazz culture wars of his day. He delivers his mini-sermon and his repeated "Hallelujahs!" in all seriousness, apparently, and takes "The Saints" at a boppish tempo, and his minimalist-modernist trumpet solo makes no concession to any expectation of good-time Dixieland.

Allen is nothing short of masterly on Ory's "Muskrat Ramble"—if he was tired of playing this Hot Five warhorse, you'd never know it—and his own "Crazy Blues." His singing on "St. Louis Blues" has an intriguing touch of Joe Williams—in his vocals, as in his trumpet-playing, he'd almost entirely gotten over Armstrong. But the most absorbing pieces on the album are the furiously uptempo "Lover Come Back to Me" and "Caravan," and the mid-tempo "Satin Doll," on which his playing ventures far from his classic '30s sound, and from the refinements he'd made on it well into the '50s. Even at the zippiest pace, he sounds both headlong and ruminative; at points in "Caravan" and "Satin Doll," he veers almost perversely out of key—those "wrong notes" Eldridge complained about, except that by 1965 such excursions had become part of jazz's lingua franca. Critics at the time wondered if Allen had been listening to Miles Davis, as of course he had: By his own admission, he listened to everything. He told Hentoff that he liked Miles's work "very much," but denied any direct influence—if anything, it was the other way around. "The fact is that Miles used to come around to hear me during his first years in New York." And surely Miles would have denied any direct influence as well. Who really knows what "influence" consists of anyway? Is it a process of imitation, or of what Harold Bloom calls "strong misreading"—a fruitfully wacky take on an earlier master's achievement—or simply of hearing something that gets you thinking for a minute? Who knows what was really going on in Allen's head during these tunes: Was he searching for something new, or simply running a few random notes to please a segment of the crowd he thought might want a touch of modernity? Had he taken Don Ellis's article (published that same year) too seriously? Or what? We'll never know. Probably Allen didn't either.

What I hear in Red Allen is a musician coming along in Armstrong's wake, into a period of continuing revolution, part of which he might have helped foment. The four decades of his career spanned all of jazz's significant history: from New Orleans to swing to bop to free jazz to the beginning of jazz-rock. The year Allen began playing with King Oliver, Armstrong was still recording with Kid Ory and Johnnie Dodds. The year he died, Miles was recording with Wayne Shorter and Herbie Hancock. Allen once met Buddy Bolden; one of the mourners at Allen's funeral was Ornette Coleman. During his lifetime, Allen was generally considered either an old-timer or someone in the rear guard of the mainstream.

Today, we can hear him as a musician who reflected something of all the times through which he lived; if he had a particular attachment to, and identification with, the period in which he was the hot young horn, who can blame him? Allen wasn't a restless spirit like Miles, who evolved from a colleague of Charlie Parker to a rival (or so he hoped) of Sly Stone and James Brown. Allen was a musician with a solid sense of who he was, and that sense left him free to play within its confines.

It's been a hell of a four decades since I first heard him. Jazz history has pretty much come to an end: After about 1970, free jazz couldn't get much freer, jazz-rock couldn't get much rockier, and the mainstream—Joshua Redman, the Marsalises—hasn't evolved much beyond Coltrane's *Giant Steps* and Miles's Shorter-Hancock period. The war between the Ancients and the Moderns has become a non-issue, and it's now possible to hear independent-minded musicians like Allen in context, without worrying about which side they chose (or refused to choose) all those years ago. And I've become more forgiving as well, though I wish I'd never heard his "Never on Sunday." Red Allen, torn between imitation and innovation, between his need to please and his need to stretch himself, between his reverence for a dead past and his good wishes for a future in which he would never participate—he reminds me of me. For a little while there when I was kid, I took him to heart. And here we are again.

Folk/ Bluegrass

Doc Watson

SITTING ON TOP OF THE WORLD by William Gay

The week before MerleFest I went by to check on Grady, and he was putting a fuel pump on his RV. It was a huge RV so ancient it looked like something the Joads might have fled the Dust Bowl in, and something was always going wrong with it. Grady had skinned knuckles and a half-drunk beer and a home-rolled Prince Albert cigarette stuck to his lower lip that waggled when he talked.

He was not in the best of moods.

"I don't think I'm going to this one," he said. "It's got to where all this traveling around costs too much money. I believe I've about seen everything anyway."

I looked at the RV. It was emblazoned with hand-painted legends memorializing bluegrass festivals past. The Bean Blossom Festival, the Foggy Mountain Festival, MerleFest '96, '97, '98. Maybe he *had* seen everything. He told me about Dylan at the 1964 Newport Folk Festival, cracking a bullwhip and preening as the newly crowned King of Folk. Another time at Newport, his RV had been parked next to the one belonging to Mother Maybelle Carter. They had sat in lawn chairs and watched twilight come on, and she had shown him how to play the autoharp, placing his fingers just so to form the chords.

Grady told me a lot of things, but he had the goods to back it all up. The walls of the house he rented were papered with a surrealistic collage of photographs of the high and the mighty, the late and the great: Bill Monroe, the Stanley Brothers, Flatt and Scruggs, Don Reno and Red Smiley. Grady was in a lot of the pictures. Bill Monroe was embracing him like a long-lost brother in one, and there were pictures of Grady's own band, the Greenbriar Boys, skinny guys in Hank Williams suits standing before old-timey WSM microphones as if they were frozen back in the black-and-white '40s.

"If you go, go up and talk to Doc Watson," Grady said.

"I may. I always wanted to know where he got that arrangement for 'Sitting on Top of the World.'"

"He got it off that old record by the Mississippi Sheiks."

"I heard that record. That's not the arrangement."

"Well, hell. Just go up and ask him. Walk right up to him, he'll tell you. He's not stuck up like a lot of them are. He's a hell of a nice guy."

"Well, he's blind. Maybe that makes him a little more approachable."

"A blind man can be a prick the same as anybody else," he said. "He's just a hell of a nice guy."

Early in the morning of October 23, 1985, Arthel "Doc" Watson received the worst news a father can get: His son was dead. Eddy Merle Watson had been plowing on a steep hillside when the tractor he was driving overturned and rolled on him.

It was a blow that Doc almost did not recover from. It was a blow that resonated on a number of levels: Aside from the incalculable loss of a child, Doc had lost a friend and a fellow musician. For a time it seemed he might even lose the music as well, because Merle and Doc and the music were one.

In 1964, when he was fourteen, Merle had learned to play guitar while his father was away. He had learned to play it so well that when Doc went back on the road, Merle went with him. That fall they played the Berkeley Folk Festival, and he was all over the place on Doc's next album, *Southbound*. They toured and recorded together for the next twenty-one years, right up to that morning in 1985.

Merle became a proficient blues guitarist, and some of the albums subtly reflect his love for the genre. But he could pick flattop guitar with the best of them, and he could frail the banjo in the style of country performers like Uncle Dave Macon. When he died he was a few days away from winning *Frets* magazine's Bluegrass Picker of the Year award.

In what may be one of the few purely altruistic gestures in the music business, a handful of folks decided to do something. A friend of Doc's, Bill Young, together with "B" Townes and Ala Sue Wyke, approached Doc with a proposition. Townes is Dean of Resource Development at Wilkes Community College, in Wilkesboro, North Carolina, and the three of them convinced Doc to play a benefit concert on the campus. The funds raised would be used to create a memorial garden in Merle's honor.

Doc agreed, and a few of Merle's friends, including the banjoist Tim O'Brien, volunteered their time and ended up playing from the beds of two flatbed trucks.

That was the first MerleFest, in 1988. By contrast, the festival in 1999, while still held on the college campus, was a vast sprawl of tents and stages and concessions accommodating more than a hundred performers and over sixty-two thousand people in the audience.

There was not a flatbed truck in sight.

The first night of the festival was cold and rainy, but the performances went on inside tents, where hundreds of folding chairs were arranged in rows. When you came out of the tents, the wind would be blowing and the rain would sting your face, but nobody seemed to mind. Earlier there had been a little grumbling when the performer list had been released: Hootie and the Blowfish? Steve Earle? These were not the descendants of Bill Monroe. Earle had been touring with the bluegrass great Del McCoury, but there was a loose-cannon quality about him, and he was a lot more edgy and confrontational than, say, Ralph Stanley.

But never mind. This audience could take it in stride. They had come to have a good time, and by God they were going to have a good time.

There is a kind of bond between participant and observer; common heritage maybe, the unspoken reverence for certain values: family, home, and the tattered remains of the American Dream. Disparate elements of the audience mingled as easily as Freemasons meeting far from home and exchanging the password. Except here no password was needed. The fact that you were here seemed password enough.

The second day was sunny and as perfect as days in April get, and the shuttles were busy early ferrying folks down to the main gate. The parking lot is a mile or so from the festival, and buses carry festival-goers down a winding road to the entrance. Watching this potential audience disembark, you are struck by the fact that there seems to be no type, no average, and that many spectrums of America are represented: middle-aged hippies and their new-SUV-driving yuppie offspring; farmers and farmers' wives; factory-workers; the well-off in expensive outdoor gear from L.L. Bean; and longhaired young men in beards and fool's motley who seem determined to be ready should the '60s clock in again.

And just as you are about to decide that there is no common element among the spectators, you notice the percentage of people carrying instruments. Guitars and banjos in hardshells. Cased fiddles tucked under the arm and God knows how many harmonicas pocketed like concealed weapons.

You don't see this at a rock concert or at the Grand Ole Opry, folks coming equipped to make their own music should the need arise. But bluegrass is widely perceived as handmade music, as opposed to, say, the output of the song factories on Nashville's Music Row. The people who love bluegrass love it enough to learn to play it, and they are intensely loyal—to the music, to the performers, and to one another. That love of music is the common factor, the source of the brotherhood.

Wandering past tents and the open-air stages, you hear it segue from bluegrass to old-time rustic to a tent where a Cajun scrapes his fiddle at breakneck speed, and young girls jerk and sway with their partners on sawdust-strewn floors. MerleFest is a growth industry. Attendance has grown every year that the festival has been in existence, but not as fast as the number of vendors and service providers: You can buy the usual tapes and CDs of your favorites; T-shirts and sweatshirts and blankets and plaster busts of musicians and folk art and homemade jewelry; Italian food and Mexican food and downhome American food; anything you want to drink, unless you want it to contain alcohol—alcohol is forbidden on the grounds.

During the course of the four-day festival, you learn that a lot of these people know one another. They know one another well enough to remember the names of their respective children and what everybody does for a living. They will meet again before the year is out, whether they live in Alabama or Pennsylvania. They begin in the spring, at MerleFest, and through the careful allocation of vacation days or the advent of three-day weekends, their paths will cross at bluegrass festivals in the South, or in Midwestern states like Michigan or Indiana, where bluegrass is almost a religion. They will see the shows and late in the day will get together and grill out and catch up on old times. Likely they will make a little music themselves.

In a sense they are a family, loose and nomadic but keeping in touch, and at the very bottom of things family is what they believe bluegrass music is all about.

Family and Doc Watson.

Doc Watson, blinded by an eye infection during infancy, first learned to play the harmonica. From there he went to a banjo with a drum made from the skin of a house cat. But when he'd listen to records, the guitar was what he liked, and he began fooling around with one his brother had borrowed. His father heard Doc and told him that if he could learn a song by the end of the day, he would buy Doc one of his own. When his father came in from work that night, Doc played "When Roses Bloom in Dixieland," and the next day Doc owned a guitar.

Watson was playing on the radio at age nineteen, and in the years between learning that first song and becoming an icon, he played roadhouses and church socials and square dances. He played all kinds of music—country, rockabilly, swing, blues, folk songs, Appalachian ballads about young women wronged by their lovers.

It is amazing to listen to the Folkways records Doc made with Clarence "Tom" Ashley in the early days of the '60s. His style seems fully formed—the complex picking, the impeccable interaction between bass and treble strings, the breath-less, death-defying runs he interjects into spaces of time so small there seems scarcely room to accommodate them. You keep listening for him to miss a note, deaden a string, but he does not. There have been countless long and drunken arguments over how many guitars, one or two, were playing on a particular track.

It was one guitar, Doc's guitar.

In every great performer's life there are watershed concerts, events that forever alter the rest of the career from what has gone before. For Doc one of these came in 1963, when he was brought to the Newport Folk Festival by the folklorist Ralph Rinzler. Doc was forty-one years old. He sang about blackberry blossoms, shady groves, houses of the rising sun, and the sad fatalism of sitting on top of the world. When he began, he was an unknown guitarist with a pleasant baritone, on a long and winding road from Deep Gap, North Carolina. When he was helped from the chair and led from the stage, he was on his way to a contract with Vanguard Records, and he had reinvented forever the way folk musicians approached the guitar.

There are more than a hundred performers at MerleFest, and there are no slouches. These are the heavy hitters and brand-name pickers of bluegrass, everyone from hardshell traditionalists to the avant-garde, folks who through virtuoso playing and infusions from jazz are moving bluegrass into uncharted territory.

But no one questions what this thing is all about.

The Texas singer-songwriter Guy Clark usually performs his song "Dublin Blues" during his sets, a song that has the quatrain:

> I have seen the *David*
> I've seen the *Mona Lisa* too
> I have heard Doc Watson
> Play "Columbus Stockade Blues"

At the mention of Watson's name there is thunderous and spontaneous applause. It happens the same way before different audiences each time Clark performs the song.

When Doc is led up the wooden steps to the stage, he approaches from the rear, and the first thing you see is his silver hair. At the sight of it, the audience erupts. Doc is guided across the stage to where folding chairs have been positioned before the microphones. He is assisted into a chair, and he feels for the guitar in the open case beside his seat. He takes the guitar and sits cradling it, his face turned toward the crowd he can feel but not see.

A stocky young man with a black beard has seated himself in the chair beside Doc's. He has taken up a guitar as well. He touches Watson's arm, and Watson leans toward the microphone.

"This is my grandson Richard," he says, "and he's going to help me out a little here. This is Merle's boy."

The crowd erupts again. The torch has passed.

Doc's guitar kicks off a set of country blues, old Jimmie Rodgers songs, and the song Clark referenced. The third generation holds his own with ease, as if perhaps guitar-playing was simply a matter of genetics.

Between songs, Doc jokes with the audience, tells a couple of stories. They eat it up. They're eager to laugh at his stories, and maybe they've heard them before—their laughter anticipates the punchlines. They love him. He could sell them used cars with blown transmissions, refrigerators that keep things warm instead of cold. His voice is comforting and reassuring. He could be a neighbor sitting on the edge of your porch, or rocking right slow in the willow rocker.

Except for the playing. The picking is impeccable: the hands sure and quick, the notes clean and distinct, and the absolute right note to go where he picks it.

Those cannot be seventy-six-year-old hands, we are thinking.

Maybe they are not of a mortal at all, maybe with the guitar clasped to him and his fingers moving over the strings, he is a god, sitting on top of the world.

When the set ends, Doc begins to rise, his hand reaching for the hand that without seeing he knows is reaching for his own, and the hands touch, and an illusion shatters: The audience sees that he is not a god at all but a mortal with frailties like the rest of us.

"Chet Atkins is the best guitar player in the world," Doc said.

"I figured you'd say Merle Travis."

"Well, Merle was a great influence on me. I named Merle after him, and we finally met when we did that *Will the Circle Be Unbroken* record. But Chet's the best. He can play anything."

"That's what people say about you," I said.

"I'm slowing down a little. I'm getting older, and I can feel my hands stiffening up. I don't tour as much as I used to. I can feel myself slowing down, some of the runs are slower."

Close-up, Watson's face is pleasant, ruddy, the silver hair a little thin but waved neatly back, every strand in place. He does not wear dark glasses, as most blind performers do, and in fact, it is easy to forget that he is blind: The lids are lowered, the eyes just slits, and he looks almost as if he's just squinting into strong sunlight.

"Where'd you come up with the picking on 'Sitting on Top of the World'?"

Watson laughed. "I made that up," he said, "that's my arrangement. I heard it off that old Mississippi Sheiks record. You might not have heard of them. But I changed it. I just played it the way I wanted it."

"What do you think about the way MerleFest has grown? It's pretty big business now."

"Well, it's good for the music. It's good for Merle, to keep people thinking about him. And people have to make a living, have to sell records. It's good to know so many people love this kind of music enough to come way down here to hear it."

"Do you think it's changing? Music, I mean?"

"Music is always changing," Doc said. "But it's all music, just people getting together and playing. One thing I noticed, though, somebody told me there were some complaints about one of the performers using some pretty rough language over the mike during his show. I don't care for that. This has always been a family thing, women and kids, and that young fellow needs to remember where he is.'"

It was almost dark, and gospel music was rising from the tents when I walked down the road toward the parking lot. It was Sunday, the last day of the festival, and gospel was mostly what today had been about. There had been Lucinda Williams, but mostly it had been gospel, like Sundays on old-time radio when the Sabbath was a day of respite from the secular.

Off to the right were the campgrounds. You could see the RVs, but they were hazy and ambiguous through the failing light, and music was rising from there, too—the plinking of a banjo, a fiddle sawing its way through some old reel.

What you could see best were the campfires scattered across the bottom-land, and for an illusory moment, time slipped, and it could have been a hobo camp or a campground for Okies on their way to the Golden State. There was a gully beyond the camp area. It was shrouded with trees, and fog lay between the trees like smoke, and it was easy to imagine Tom Joad slipping through them like a wraith, fleeing the vigilante men on his way upstate to organize the orange pickers. Or Woody Guthrie himself might ease up out of the fog, his fascist-killing guitar strung about his neck, a sly grin on his face that said all the world was a joke and only he was in on it. He'd warm his hands over the fire, for the night had turned chill, and he'd drink a cup of chicory coffee before heading down one of those long, lonesome roads Woody was always heading down.

Then I was closer, and I saw that the fires were charcoal and gas grills, where ground beef sizzled in tinfoil, and hot dogs dripped sputtering grease, and I saw that these people were much too affluent to be Okies and that the guitars they played were Fenders and Gibsons and Martins. They were guitars that Woody would never have been able to afford.

After a while Grady wandered up. I knew he'd made it, since I'd seen him a couple of times in crowds and had seen him playing guitar in a tent with other players, guys with homemade basses and washboards and Jew's harps and whatever fell to hand. I hadn't talked to him yet, though.

"You learn what you wanted to know?"

"Doc heard it off that old Mississippi Sheiks record," I said.

"I told you that."

"He invented the arrangement, though. It's his song now."

"But he did talk to you. Was I right about him, or not?"

"I guess you were right," I said.

I thought about it. It seemed to me that Doc embodied the kind of values that are going out of style and don't mean as much as they used to: self-respect and a respect for others, the stoic forbearance that Walker Evans photographed and James Agee wrote poems about. Something inside that was as immutable and unchanging as stone, that after a lifetime in show business still endured, still believed in the sanctity of womanhood, family, property lines, the church in the wildwood, the ultimate redeemability of humankind itself.

Life sometimes seems choreographed from the stage of a talk show, where barbaric guests haul forth dirty linen and a barbaric audience applauds, where presidents disassemble themselves before a voyeuristic media, where folks sell their souls to the highest bidder and then welsh on the deal. It was nice that Doc was still just being Doc, just being a hell of a nice guy.

But Doc's getting old, and those values are getting old, too. Maybe they're dying out. Maybe in the end there will just be the music. For there will always be the music. It is what Doc loves above all things—from show tunes like "Summertime" to music leaked up through time from old, worn 78s by Mississippi string bands, from the hollow, ghostly banjo of Dock Boggs to the contemporary folk of writers like Tom Paxton and Bob Dylan.

All kinds of music that will endure and help us endure. The music will never let you down.

Fred Neil

WHO WAS FRED? FRED WAS FRED WAS FRED by Mike Powell

In 1969 Fred Neil had a hit song and what was probably a lot of money. Fred Neil did not, however, have a telephone. The hit was called "Everybody's Talkin'," which he'd recorded for his 1967 album, *Fred Neil*; it was covered by Harry Nilsson and used as the theme for *Midnight Cowboy* in 1969. And then, you know, in drifted the royalty checks, milk of Hollywood kindness, and Fred spent the remainder of his life singing to dolphins and dying slowly. "One morning, we were sitting and having breakfast in Coconut Grove," Vince Martin, Fred's only real collaborator, recalls. "Joe Bike—he ran the bike shop in town, he was the man—Joe Bike came running over and said 'Freddie, Harry Nilsson's on the phone!'"

Fred Neil looked up from his breakfast and said, "Fuck 'im." Fred Neil, like a lot of human beings, wanted to be left alone. He never smiled, backlit, in front of a pile of screaming fans. He wrote a famous song but most people couldn't pick his face from a crowd. Fred Neil probably drank too much, and like anyone who drinks too much, his mood was erratic and temperament incompatible. But he never made theater of his disintegration. His excesses, if you'd even use such a sensational term, were private. He kept hurt between family walls. He broke a guitar string and walked offstage. Sometimes, he didn't show up for gigs, but when he didn't, nobody knows where he went. Fred Neil, who, in photographs, looks by turns plaintive, stoned, disaffected, yearning, and lots of other nebulous synonyms for melancholy—serene, maybe, but never happy—was, at best, an antihero, and at worst the kind of story people don't bother to tell.

Supposedly, the original theme for *Midnight Cowboy* was going to be Dylan's

"Lay, Lady, Lay." This is hilarious for at least one reason, namely that *Midnight Cowboy* is an emotionally torturous movie about broken dreams and the frailty of human psychology, and "Lay, Lady, Lay" is about the sex act. Which, sure, figures into the movie: There's the part where Jon Voight has that horrific flashback of his girlfriend being gang-raped. Or there's that part where, desperate and poor, he lets a nerd give him oral in a crummy movie theater. Plenty of sex in *Midnight Cowboy*. Legend has it that one studio executive was keen on shearing some of the racier stuff and propping up Elvis, just entering his pants-splitting phase, for Voight's part.

"Everybody's Talkin'," though, was an even more pointed proposition. Now, it's ubiquitous. It's a staple of lite radio; it's been violated by bad keyboard presets for anonymous reproduction. Forget the cliché of hearing a song browsing cereal at the grocery store, I've heard "Everybody's Talkin'" buying tripe in a Polish butcher shop. The context of hearing it has become so mundane that the meaning has become invisible. Just how we don't think too much about people who plan public transportation or the important relationship between the dwindling bee population and the future of almonds, we probably don't think too much about "Everybody's Talkin'," which is, essentially, an easily hummed song about being totally alienated from humanity.

This took me a while to realize. I was in an open-air market in Mexico City. Table after table of plastic irrelevance. These scenarios come with a built-in sense of displacement and anonymity—it could've been in New York or Nairobi or Oslo, as long as it wasn't home. You walk around and feign interest in poorly made goods and let your mind unravel on new ground. You let your surroundings swallow you.

A gigantic speaker blared Nilsson's version of "Everybody's Talkin'" through the dust—"Everybody's talkin' at me, I don't hear a word they're saying, only the echoes of my mind"—and for the first time, I stopped to think about it: *This song is sort of, in some minor but definite way, about what I'm doing right now, except what they're doing is more like yelling, and I'm not really all that good at Spanish to begin with.* When Harry sang, "I won't let you leave my love behind," it exploded like a non sequitur: Why does he care who leaves his love behind? Isn't he the one running? Is he singing to himself? Fred Neil wanted to disappear. When he died, not even his children knew where he was.

"You know, I talked to him not long before he passed," Charlie Brown tells me. Charlie Brown owned the Gaslight South club in Coconut Grove, where Fred and Vince Martin regularly played as a duo. Charlie Brown explains to me that he's a Quaker originally from Memphis and therefore doesn't own a telephone or "indulge in modern conveeeeeeeniences." He was one of the last people to be close to Fred. "He knew he was dying. And myself and another buddy had called him one day and said we were going to come down to see him, and we wanted to see him. . . . And he said, 'No, don't bother,' and hung up."

"So when was that?" I ask.

"It was about four or five months before he died. I'd say around '85, something like that. '84."

"No, no, he died in '01."

We debate the date, which feels sick, desperate.

"I thought it was long before then, but I guess not," he mutters.

Fred Neil was alive for sixty-five years. For the last twenty, he didn't play concerts. For the last thirty, he didn't release an album. One of his best friends misremembered his death-date by fifteen years.

"Fred grew into someone nobody could really understand," Vince Martin tells me. Vince Martin is what I guess the world would call a bohemian, which I come to realize is sort of like a hippie, but hard-bitten and more prone to cursing. He played on the Greenwich Village coffeehouse circuit and collaborated with Fred on a 1964 album called *Tear Down the Walls*.

He tells me about shit that Einstein and David Crosby said. He tells me shit about pure cocaine and what you learn from sleeping in cars in the dead of winter. Lots of cosmic hoopla. He slings every word with a calcified Beat wisdom, the assertion that I know life so open your damn ears. So I do. But I would hesitate to call Vince Martin gentle. "I'm not reticent"—he grits his teeth and repositions himself in his chair—"but just ask me what you want to ask and I'll tell you what I feel like telling you." Fred and Vince initially met in New York in 1961 at the back of a coffeeshop. They played all night. "Fred hadn't heard a white guy play the blues like that. He asked me where I learned, and I told him, 'My father's basement.'" They ran into each other a year later. Vince mentioned he was living in Coconut Grove. Fred asked where that was. "Florida," Vince told him; Fred started coming down to visit. "We used to go sailing. And I just thought he was from New York, because he never really said otherwise. One day we were on the boat and Freddie just jumped off into the water." He puts his hands on his head and stretches out his mouth, mocking panic. "But Freddie just—*choooooooooooooo*—swam like a fuckin' dolphin." Vince stared in disbelief. "I'm from St. Pete," Fred said as he surfaced.

Listening to Fred Neil's music leaves a distinct impression of his nature: Fred Neil sounds like a gentle little doe. A leaf trembling in the world's cruel winds. Oh life, rife with conflict and disappointment, take care of Fred Neil for he knows not how to weather you! His voice was a deep, placid baritone, but fluttered through melodic turns with the volatility of birds. Blues vocalists are often praised for sounding like their tragedies are worn into their throats like notches in a tree; Neil sounds paradoxically much more alert and much more passive. His best vocal passages aren't dried tears, they're winks. Smirks, even.

Fred Neil didn't write about changing the world, he wrote about how the world changed him—no, wait, about how the world ruined him. Just a country boy shuffling through the city. A victim. A sodden lump. What happened to po'

Fred on his journey? Something? Nothing? In interviews, friends are deferential—they refer to a mystical source of trauma. They sound like parents explaining a child's bad behavior. He throws food at strangers because. He spits on his hand before shaking because.

But nobody knows what Fred's trauma was. Other memories are clearer: "Fred used to stand behind me when we were playing," Vince Martin says, "and say nasty stuff. Just nasty. He'd say 'Sell your ass, sell your ass.'" Vince tells me Fred used to curse at the crowd when they would heckle him. Sometimes, there were punches. Sometimes, there was just old-fashioned manipulation: "There was something about Fred that made people want to cuddle him. Especially women. Everyone knew it. And he'd sit there and be acting soft with some girl, and I'd come up to him and say, 'Freddie, come on,' and he'd say, 'Not now, I'm doing good.'"

Charlie Brown spoke of Fred's Florida years, drinking cases of St. Pauli Girl and playing Pac-Man all day. "He got real good." That doesn't surprise me. At all. I mean, if I had a steady supply of three-figure checks, no job, beer, and nearly no friends, I think I'd become quite good at Pac-Man. Fred used to tape nuts to the inside of his cottage window in Woodstock and watch squirrels paw at them. In 2002, Charlie Brown told Henry Llach, "The squirrel would try and try to get it and Fred would just laugh and laugh." Some great artists have an insatiable thirst to create, some prefer heated Pac-Man sessions and malevolent tricks on squirrels. But maybe Fred Neil was, in the words of producer Paul Rothchild, just "a brilliant songwriter and a total scumbag." Maybe Fred Neil was an inattentive father and an unreliable friend and should've died alone, a little too young, slightly overweight, his most momentous achievement, physical, metaphysical, or otherwise, that he wrote a hit song and ran off with bank. The dippy passivity of "Everybody's Talkin'"—well, maybe that was a double-edged sword. Maybe it was a beautiful excuse for the way he wasted his own time. On *Fred Neil*, he admits, "Everything I have—I done it wrong"; he wrote a song called "Everything Happens," which is either a statement of ultimate enlightenment or, well, what deadbeats say before smiling and slipping out the side door.

In the liner notes for Water's 2006 reissue of Fred's self-titled album, guitarist and collaborator Peter Childs mused, "You want to know about Fred Neil? Grab a copy of his self-titled record, turn on the hi-fi, put on a good set of headphones, lay back and just listen to the music." No. This is an asinine thing to say. It's asinine for at least two reasons. One, people say it all the time and nobody bothers to think about what it means. Try saying it. Nobody will argue with you because it sounds cool and mythical and right to think that the artist conveys his or her life in their work. Because artists—folksingers, especially—are free and expressive and earnest people. Two dovetails nicely with One. We find a lot more in Fred Neil's life than in his music alone. Theory shattered. If being biographically comprehensive is some sort of a measure for great art, "Everybody's Talkin'" would be a terrible song without at least one reference to punching an audience member in the face.

Charlie Brown remembers him as "one of the most ruthless son of a bitches in the world," but Vince Martin's characterization seems more accurate, more impenetrable: "Fred was Fred was Fred was Fred." He says it three times during our conversation; each time, he shakes his head. "We used to hang out at the Seaquarium, where they filmed *Flipper*, and just play guitar for the dolphins. They'd hear it and come right up," Vince says. Fred actually co-founded and dedicated a lot of his later life to the Dolphin Project, an organization focused on dolphin rights and preservation. The British magazine *Mojo* published an article on Fred in 2000; later that year, Fred, who hadn't been publicly heard from in decades, wrote a letter to *Mojo*. It was about dolphins. Fred Neil cursed at audience members, cursed at Harry Nilsson, but figured out how to be compassionate to dolphins. Dolphins, those non-human creatures with the long noses and eighty teeth they don't even use to chew—they just swallow fish whole!—and tiny impassive eyes and gorgeous, squeaky dolphin-talk. People are difficult and disappointing. They lie. People are complicated animals who subvert instinct for disgusting reasons. A dolphin will not screw you out of money. A dolphin will probably not screw you out of anything.

But the most alluring aspect of Fred Neil's life is that he gave up in the most artless, crude way possible. He could've pulled off a reasonably well-reported suicide in exchange for his temperament. He didn't. He could've sprung up like a marionette for cash-in concerts. He didn't. He sat in front of the television with the volume down and played guitar. He did his thing with the dolphins. Fred Neil made peace with his alienation, made some money, made his closest friends feel confused, unwanted, and irrelevant, and then died.

What we do know about Fred is that he was more than a talent, he was a *presence*. Bob Dylan, another magnetic crank, beamed, "You couldn't touch him. Everything revolved around him." Supposedly, David Crosby wanted to name Crosby, Stills & Nash the hilariously dumb "Sons of Neil." "Everybody's Talkin'" has been covered, in my estimate, one billion times. In the early '60s, Fred Neil was not just another laughable Anglo in a tight sweater writing sterile paeans to freedom. He was a deity hovering over Greenwich Village. He played a twelve-string guitar—unusual then—and had a voice weaned on gospel. Fred knew jazz chords and was okay letting them in.

The cover of his second album, 1967's *Fred Neil*, shows him cradling the head of a wide-eyed, blank-faced kid. Fred's head is cocked to the side and his eyes slant down and away. He looks resigned. The kid looks faintly annoyed. Is he a demon? I am not sure. Fred cradles demon-boy as a cloud gathers beyond our scope. It took me a while to realize that the image's tone is the consecrated melancholy of a Madonna and child. It's quiet, momentous. Charlie Brown remembers Fred's idea of a joke: "You know what alimony is Charlie? It's the fuckin' you get for the fuckin' you got."

But the album itself. The album. Dylan had gone electric a year and a half earlier; in comparison to *Fred Neil*, his *Bringing It All Back Home* sounds like a guy banging a rock in a damp clearing. There is big, psychedelic-sounding tremolo guitar on *Fred Neil*. And twinkly noises! Drums thump in waltz time. Everything sounds completely narcotized, almost subaqueous. Fred's voice booms about dolphins and cocaine. Fred sings "Everybody's Talkin'," and bassist James E. "Chops" Bond, Jr., lives up to his name by losing the groove so comprehensively it's astonishing any group of people with functioning tympanic membranes didn't notice, let alone musicians recording on a major label. To prove just how loose he was, to God and everybody, Fred decided to squander the last eight minutes of the record on a subpar raga. Fred Neil, pity of pities, gets hot orange juice, is arrested for whistling, and guesses, pretty reasonably at this point, he'll die in an atomic explosion as soon as he reaches port. He didn't even mention he was a sailor. And the rub: "I should start over but, you know, I'd rather not—same thing's gonna happen again, and that's the bag I'm in."

So you move to Coconut Grove to talk to dolphins, skip to a cottage in Woodstock to scam on some tree squirrels, and you don't play a show for twenty years leading up to your death in Summerland Key, and you fall out with almost everyone you know, and they say that when you died the cancer had put a hole clear through your cheek, but nobody really knows because they burned your body and a few people came down to throw your ashes in the Gulf Stream because you wouldn't want to be stuck among all those corpses anyhow. What else?

Iris DeMent

TANGLED IN MY LIFE by **Kevin Brockmeier**

———

*There are songs that have saved lives, and songs that have ended
them.*

—Joshua Poteat

It seems to me that those of us who aren't musicians usually take one of two imaginative stances toward the songs we listen to—either we imagine ourselves as the singers or we imagine ourselves as the sung to. I am one of the sung to. When I concentrate on a song, it is as if someone is speaking directly to me, unreservedly and in total privacy. The voice that comes through my speakers strikes me as faraway, inaccessible, and yet somehow strangely intimate. Perhaps it is this presumption of intimacy on my part—a false presumption, I know—that makes certain tones so likely to set my teeth on edge: vanity, pugilism, boastfulness.

"Then you don't like rock & roll," a friend once told me when I confessed as much to him.

And I thought, Maybe so.

It's certainly true that I am out of sympathy with the main currents of a lot of rock music. I am constitutionally averse to swagger, unless it's delivered with a wink and a shrug, as if to say, "You and I both know that I can't really pull this off, but let's pretend that I can." In other words, nerd-swagger. And I am generally unmoved by the aesthetic of transgression that has energized so many rock bands, from the Who and the Sex Pistols down through Nirvana and the White Stripes. It's not that I disrespect it; I just don't find it very interesting, although, for the sake of completeness, I should say that most of it strikes me as fairly reflexive—little more than transgression for transgression's sake—and I tend to respond with more engagement to what I hear, rightly or wrongly, as heartbroken, principled, or playful transgression (see, respectively, Arcade Fire, New Model Army, and They Might Be Giants).

Once the basic elements of form and melody are in place, what I look for in a piece of music are vulnerability, openness, and purity of tone, along with enough precision or passion of delivery to keep me from becoming embarrassed on behalf of the singer, a feeling to which I'm all too prone. Beyond that, I'm after the same sensation I'm always after, both in life and in art—the sensation that I'm being presented with something that has been cherished by someone. In an essay about William Maxwell's short, masterly novel *So Long, See You Tomorrow*, Charles Baxter observes, "[Y]ou feel that you have been given considerably more of what is precious to its author than is often the case in novels of many hundreds of pages. What Maxwell has loved, he gives away in that book."

And ultimately, that's what I want from a song: a feeling that I'm being given what is most precious to its singer. Offer me that, along with a voice capable of delivering the message, and you'll win me over every time.

Which brings me to Iris DeMent, and to *My Life*.

My Life is the second of three albums of sweetly flowing country-folk songs that Iris DeMent recorded in the mid-1990s, following the poignant, confessional *Infamous Angel* and preceding the slightly more outward-looking and studio-lustered *The Way I Should*. Since then, she has remained largely silent, though in 2004 she returned to the CD bins with an album of gospel standards—and one original—called *Lifeline*.

Each of these albums has its treasures to offer, and indeed many of Iris's fans have found the warmth and tenderness of *Infamous Angel*, her debut, to be unsurpassable. For me, though, *My Life* has proven the richest and most enduring of her recordings. An intimate suite of heartache and yearning, lightened only occasionally by the kind of airy happiness that presents itself as a necessary-but-never-more-than-temporary renunciation of its own grief, it is one of exactly two albums I own that I wouldn't hesitate to call perfect. (The other is Van Morrison's *Astral Weeks*, which strikes me as *My Life*'s reverse image in many ways: an album that celebrates without ever denying how much there is to mourn in the world, whereas *My Life* mourns without ever denying how much there is to celebrate.) When I say that I consider the album perfect, I mean that I can't imagine what change might be made to it that could improve it. Not a single moment seems anything less than moving, honest, and inspired: no lyric, no vocal flourish, no shift in rhythm—nothing. The effect could easily have been ruined in the studio, but the album's producer, Jim Rooney, who also collaborated with Iris on *Infamous*

Angel and *Lifeline,* appears to have understood the demands of the material so thoroughly that he was able to provide Iris the best possible natural cushion for her melodies, so that when you listen to the album, it very nearly sounds as if everything has arisen spontaneously out of her own mind. This is no small accomplishment, particularly on a work of such interior and often wistful sensibilities, exactly the kind of album frequently saddled with a wrongheaded production strategy—cluttered, bombastic, glossy, or simply unimaginative—that turns the whole thing to mud.

In my experience, the perfect song, like the perfect short story, isn't all that unusual: there are many of them, and they lie relatively common on the ground. But the perfect album, like the perfect novel, is like one of those strange translucent creatures from the bottom of the ocean that are rarely ever seen by the human eye. It is nothing short of a miracle when one of them manages to make it to the surface alive.

Ordinarily, I've noticed, when critics write an essay in praise of an album, you'll find them offering at least some hint of an adversarial relationship with it, designed to stand as a signal that they're volunteering their honest, sophisticated response to the material. I'm a fiction writer, though, not a critic, so I'm resisting the temptation to contrive such a hint. My honest response to *My Life*—sophisticated or not—is simple adoration, complicated by nothing except my initial slight resistance to Iris's singing voice. For although, as must be obvious, I have become something of a missionary for *My Life* over the years, it took me several listens to appreciate it, and even longer before it found its place as one of the landmarks in my personal musical pantheon.

In 1994, when the album was released, the big-box record stores had yet to make their way to Little Rock, where I live, and most of the independents had already shut their doors. The Internet was not the vast library of MP3 files it is today—or if it was I had never taken the time to investigate it. Thus, I had never heard so much as a note of Iris's music before I picked up a copy of *My Life*. This was something I did frequently when I was in high school and college, sifting through the racks at Been Around Records or Camelot Music and buying an album I was totally unfamiliar with based on little more than the cover art or the song titles, the record label or the name of the band. By this method I discovered a whole host of mostly forgotten mediocrities—though I'm sure there is somebody out there who loves the Bambi Slam, I don't—but also a number of performers I still listen to today, like the Jean-Paul Sartre Experience and Billy Bragg.

The first time I put *My Life* on the stereo, I responded with pleasure to the melodies, the lyrics, and the general character of the songs. There was a hitch, though: I wasn't sure what to make of Iris's voice. It is as clear and unpolluted as any voice you're ever likely to hear, washing through the instruments like a warm Southern stream, but its timbre is unusual. The way it lifts up so ardently from the bed of the music, swaying along with the fiddle or the accordion, and bowing out around the vowels—well, it takes some getting used to. Moreover, I don't imagine you could enjoy any of Iris's albums without also enjoying her voice. The same could be said of any number of performers whose music I happen to appreciate: Tom Waits, Bill Morrissey, Joanna Newsom, Jeff Mangum—all of them are polarizing vocalists. Iris is unique among them, however, in that both the people who adore her without qualification and the people who bristle at the very sound of her will point to her voice in explanation. Her voice is, quite simply, where the personality of her music lies, and unless it speaks to you, nothing else she does will register.

It took me a few listens to grow comfortable with the way she sings, but when I did, I quickly realized how expressive her voice can be. It is capable of carrying so much exultation on the one hand and so much sorrow on the other, with so little costumery or ornamentation, that it can seem as if she has lived an entire life inside every note she delivers. And yet her vocals are always crafted to lend attention to the song rather than herself. She happens to sing well, but beyond that, she sings with the unmistakable stamp of experience, hard-won and cherished, so that the overall effect of her music, no matter how sad it becomes, is cleansing, invigorating.

It has always seemed to me that the best singers are the most evocative ones, which is a separate consideration from how conventionally pretty their voices might be. What's more depressing, after all, than those technically proficient, million-selling singers from whose tongues every trace of honest emotion has been extinguished, until there is nothing left of their songs but grace notes, one after the other, lined up on all sides of the melody like birds pecking at a chunk of bread? The songs on *My Life* are exactly the opposite of that. They are powerful in their simplicity, and Iris's voice flows naturally, right down the center of their melodies, just as it should.

I recognized all of this within a few weeks of first listening to *My Life*. Right away, I began including selections from it on the mix-tapes I made for my friends, particularly the plaintive piano anthem of the title track and the expansive and sublimely elegiac "No Time to Cry," Iris's meditation on the loss of her father. It was several years, though, before I truly found my way inside the album.

Just as most romantic relationships are founded on one ideal evening that is preserved in the memory of everything that follows, most artistic relationships are founded on one ideal moment of appreciation, an ideal reading moment for a book, or viewing moment for a movie, or listening moment for an album. In the case of *My Life*, my ideal listening moment came some five years after the album was released—on Monday, July 5, 1999, one of the most uncomfortable mornings of my life.

My friend Lewis and I, both of us living in Little Rock again after a few years away at college, had driven up to Fayetteville for the weekend to visit an old high-school friend of ours who was slowly finishing up his degree at the university, taking a half-dozen nonchalant credit hours at a time. Our only design for the trip was to sit around and catch up with him, maybe firing off a few bottle rockets after the sun fell on the Fourth, but when we reached his house, we found that he had already made plans for us to float the Buffalo River with him, which is how we ended up clustered around a campfire on Saturday night with his fiancée and seven or eight of their buddies. It was the first time in several years that I had been with a collection of people who seemed to understand one another's rhythms and fixations so well, and I was struck by the ease with which they settled into a pattern of communication, trading one-liners, anecdotes, and inside stories, and every so often, to bridge the silence, asking questions about the condition of the river. Once in a while I have surprised myself by intuitively finding my place in such a group, but that night I felt like I usually do when I'm surrounded by people I don't know very well: like a mediocre swimmer dropped unexpectedly into the Pacific. Mostly I just listened, waiting for my chance to throw out the occasional remark and watching the embers vary their configuration in the fire.

There was a beautiful girl in the group, with a long rope of red hair falling down her back and a smile that was broad in the center but tight at both the corners, as if it had been fastened together there with two small buttons. At one point I took the chair next to hers, but that was as brave as I could be. I sat beside her uncomfortably for a while, unable to break the stillness, opening my mouth from time to time as if I were about to say something and then closing it again, and when someone reached around from behind her to pat her leg and ask if she wanted a beer, she let out a gasp, believing for a split second that I had suddenly touched her.

It was past midnight before we retired to our tents. The people in the adjoining campsite were listening to pieces of a Tina Turner *Greatest Hits* album, "Let's Stay Together," "Private Dancer," and "We Don't Need Another Hero" cycling through their speakers in an endless loop. Two of them were having noisy sex in the tent directly next to mine. I waited a long time for the sounds to die away before I fell asleep.

Just before I faded out, I heard someone complain, "Tina Turner sucks."

Tina Turner doesn't suck, but having to listen to "Let's Stay Together," "Private Dancer," and "We Don't Need Another Hero" over and over again does.

I woke just as the sky was coloring up, and crawled out of the tent to stir through the remains of the fire with a stick. The ground beneath my sleeping bag had been terraced slightly on one side, and though the difference between the levels had seemed inconsequential at first, now I felt as if I had spent the entire night trying to keep from tumbling off the edge of a precipice. I was listless. My muscles were sore. I would have been happy to stay in the campsite reading all day.

But after everyone else woke up and began heading down to the river, I became embarrassed remembering how oddly I had behaved when I was sitting next to the girl with the red hair the night before, the nervous gasp she had given when she thought I had touched her, and I imagined that maybe I could redeem myself if I tagged along. I borrowed someone's sunscreen lotion and grabbed the middle seat of one of the boats just as it was launching from the shingle.

It was a long day, eight hours of slanting and lurching through mile-long stretches of white water, then floating gradually past sandbars and silver bluffs, sinkholes and wooded hillsides. I was wearing shorts and a T-shirt in lieu of a swimsuit. Since I didn't want my shoes drenched with river water, I had decided to go barefoot, and whenever we stopped to rest, I would pick my way delicately over the burning rocks along the shore and the slippery moss that papered the shallows. As the sun moved inch-by-inch across the sky, my arms grew tired. My mouth dried out, and my head began to swim. The same disease of silence that had overtaken me by the campfire engulfed me once again. The reflection of the light off the water seemed to get into my eyes and bleach the color from everything, making the dirt on the shore a sallow gray, my skin a chalky white. A plain, yellow butterfly rode my arm for the last thirty minutes of the ride, its wings flexing slowly back and forth. I thought about the girl in Salman Rushdie's *The Satanic Verses* who has a cloud of butterflies orbiting her body wherever she goes. That was all I could remember about her—the butterflies. The small yellow one on my arm did not fly away until we hitched our boats up onto the gravel at Buffalo Point.

My friend and a couple of his buddies piled into the truck they had left in the parking lot and drove back to the campsite to retrieve the rest of our cars, while Lewis and I stayed behind with the others. Set back from the shore was an old wooden hutch with a concrete floor, and in ones and twos we drifted over there to clean ourselves off or change out of our clothes. I assumed that the hutch was divided into separate compartments, like the park's restrooms, one for the men and one for the women. But as I made my way to the door, the girl with the red hair came hurrying out, clutching her sandals in her hands.

Inside I found a single open space with streaks of sunlight slanting through the boards. The gaps were wide enough for me to see outside, but the shading made it difficult for anyone else to see in. I had left such a strange impression of myself that she might easily have thought I had been trying to catch her undressed. Would the idea have surprised her at all, I wondered? I wrung the water out of my clothes and toweled myself off, then went to sit with the others at the edge of the parking lot, waiting for the cars to return to Buffalo Point.

As it happens, Iris was born not terribly far from this point—in Paragould, Arkansas, about a two-hour drive to the east. The landscape of Paragould is different from that of the Buffalo, the oak forests and limestone bluffs of the Ozarks fading away to the flatlands of the Arkansas Delta, but the climate is similar, and the summers Iris knew as a very young child must have been soaked in the same buzzing heat as ours was that day. At the age of three, she moved with her family—her father, mother, and thirteen older siblings—to Buena Park, California, where several times a week they worshiped at a charismatic Pentecostal church. It was there that Iris first heard many of the old piano hymns she would later record on *Lifeline*—the same songs she performed on doorsteps and street corners with her sisters and brothers, tambourine in hand; the same songs her mother sang at the upright piano in her bedroom whenever "the hard times came in for a long visit." Iris left the faith shortly before she moved to the Midwest to begin college, but she continued to feel the influence of the gospel music she had grown up singing, and she still attends services today at a church near her home in Kansas City, speaking admiringly of the openness of the congregation and of the living that comes out in their voices when they sing.

She began composing her own songs at the age of twenty-five and released her first album six years later, at the age of thirty-one. One of the earliest tunes she wrote was "Our Town," the song for which she's still best known today, introduced to many listeners when it played over the closing minutes of the final episode of *Northern Exposure*. Her most recent album of originals was released in 1996. In the decade since, she has continued to tour and perform, and though she has written songs, she says, "I haven't written twelve songs that I want to make a record of." In November 2002, she married the prolific and formidably talented songwriter Greg Brown. (If you don't know his albums, I recommend that you track down either *Down in There* or *Dream Café*, which jockey for position as my favorites.) On March 21, 2003, the evening after the U.S. invaded Iraq, she cancelled a show in Madison, Wisconsin, out of respect for those who were suffering the violence of what she believed to be an unjust war. This decision quickly drew the ire of many conservatives, who subjected her to a campaign of hate mail so venomous she was later driven to describe it as "a spiritual assault." It seems clear that, despite the peerless intimacy of her music, which can make you feel as if you have known her all her life—known her so well, in fact, that you find yourself using her first name when you write about her— she has tried to preserve her privacy, so I will close the curtain on her biography here.

Back in Fayetteville, the day after the canoeing trip, I woke early, my head pulsing with fever. I knew even before I made it to the mirror that I had been badly sunburned. Like a suit of clothes that had been left out to harden into its own planes by the weather, my skin no longer seemed to fit me right. There were mottled patches of red on my forehead, arms, and shoulders, and a large, sharply outlined stain, its color a violent beet-red I had never expected to see on my own body, that stretched across my ankle and onto my left calf. No one else was awake yet. I took my headphones and one of the CDs I had packed—it happened to be *My Life*— and slipped onto the front porch.

It has always been amazing to me that you can recognize a beautiful day even when you aren't capable of appreciating it. The sky was a pale, capacious blue. The sun had just begun to wick the moisture off the grass. In my exhaustion, I was more receptive to Iris's songs than I had ever been before, and as I sat on the stool watching a few early-morning cars coast noiselessly down the street, my head filled with the enveloping hum of the instruments, and I felt my eyes begin to sting. I got lost in the music, people sometimes say, and they mean it as the highest form of praise, but my experience that morning was exactly the opposite: The music gave me definition, made me clear to myself, I encountered myself in it. I thought about how long it had been since I was surrounded by the people I loved best, how easily damaged I had turned out to be, and I was convinced that I was feeling what Iris had been feeling as she performed the songs on the album. I had left so many people behind—too many already, and I was only a few years out of college. I had built and then abandoned one version of myself after another, and I liked the selves I had abandoned better than the one it seemed I had replaced them with, and I was so tired of building. I sat there in the shade of the porch trying not to move against my skin, absorbing the album as if I were generating every note directly out of my own experience, from the gliding contentment of "Sweet Is the Melody" to the high-lonesome ache of "Calling for You," from the rawboned sorrow of "Easy's Gettin' Harder Every Day" to the simple poetry of the title track:

> My life, it don't count for nothing
> When I look at this world, I feel so small
> My life, it's only a season
> A passing September that no one will recall
>
> But I gave joy to my mother
> I made my lover smile
> And I can give comfort to my friends when they're hurting
> I can make it seem better for a while
>
> My life, it's half the way traveled
> And still I have not found my way out of this night
> My life, it's tangled in wishes
> And so many things that just never turned out right

The friend I was visiting came to the screen door and spotted me on his stool. He made a tiny hello gesture with his fingers. When my eyes slid away from his, he turned and went back inside. The heat was starting to rise in the air, making my sunburn tighten over my skin. Still, I couldn't imagine what it would take for me to get up and follow him into the house. I remained there on the porch, letting the music filter slowly into me, until the last note had dwindled away and I could hear the insects chirring in the yard again, the car tires hissing down the street. It seemed to me then, as it does now, that my discomfort and hypersensitivity had somehow fastened me to the music, making it plain to me for the first time, and that the music in turn had somehow fastened me to the circumstances of my life.

I sat in the shade with my headphones resting around my neck, waiting for Lewis to wake up so that we could make the drive back to Little Rock.

I used to be one of the singers.

Anyone who knew me growing up will tell you that from the day I learned to speak there was always a tune in my mouth. My mom hated to take me grocery shopping with her when I was little because of the way I made every trip down the aisles a medley of commercial jingles. "Hi-C/Hi-C/It tastes so wonderfully." "Coast!/The scent opens your eyes." "So kiss a little longer/Stay close a little longer/Pull tight a little longer/Longer with Big Red." At Arkansas Governor's School, a few of us developed a game in which someone would name a word—any word—and the rest of us would have to come up with a song that contained that word in its lyrics. I rarely missed. A college friend of mine once told me about a dream she had in which she walked into a concert hall to find me sitting at a cafeteria table as though it were a grand piano. A hush fell over the audience as I began drumming on the tabletop with my fingers. "Come on Eileen," I sang.

Back then, in the din of a crowded party, when I didn't know anybody and my friends hadn't arrived yet, I liked to sit by myself singing in a corner, just loudly enough so that my voice blended into the background rustle of the conversations and no one else was quite able to hear me. I sang when I was walking to class, and when I was driving in traffic, and once, with a friend on a Spring Break trip to New York, in an elevator surrounded by complete strangers. I sang because it made me feel more alive—happier when I was happy, angrier when I was angry, sadder when I was sad. I sang because it seemed to join me to some rhythm I could sense flowing just beneath the surface of the world. I sang out of a mental tic that summoned a lyric up out of every sentence I heard, a melody up out of every lyric. I sang out of habit and need and egoism, and I sang because I was in love with the singers of the world, and I sang to feel like I was speaking to someone. I went on this way until my mid-twenties, when I, as Harold Brodkey once put it, "began at last to be like other people."

I don't know why I changed. All I can say for certain is that after I earned my graduate degree and moved back home, and my sense of time became governed by which book I was working on rather than which grade I was in, my desire to sing grew more and more sporadic. It still flared up occasionally when I was in the car and an old favorite surprised me on the radio, but this happened less frequently with every year, and after a while I ceased to expect it. The way I listened to music began to twist on me, becoming less theatrical, more interior. My ear for certain albums changed in ways I had not anticipated. A time came when I needed to be spoken to more than I needed to speak. And that was when I found Iris DeMent.

Ever since then, I have returned to her songs again and again when I wanted the comfort of hearing someone who was capable of transforming her sorrow into art. For though Iris is a country singer, with a country singer's lilting inflections and a country singer's lack of disguise, she has made her home in that fertile place where country meets the blues. Her music is music for mourning. There are times when no one can take your mourning away from you, but the great singers, like Iris, have the ability to lift it up and cradle it in their voices, and in that way make it complete.

R&B/
Soul

Ray Charles

HE HIT IT ON THE NOSE by Roy Blount, Jr.

━━━

I've been trying to write up Ray Charles ever since I interviewed him in 1983. We were in his dressing room at Lincoln Center, where he was to appear in the Kool Jazz Festival. As we shook hands, he felt up my arm from wrist to elbow. "If you're a woman," somebody told me, "he'll keep going on up till you stop him."

It was his way—since he couldn't look you in the eye—of checking the cut of a person's jib. He didn't say anything about my arm. What would you want Ray Charles to say about your arm? I didn't expect anything like, "Yeah! The boy has *got* it"—as he says to Jamie Foxx in a bonus track on the DVD of the movie *Ray*, after they play on separate keyboards till Foxx gets the signature harmonics right. Anyway, he gave no sign that he found my arm lacking. We had a cordial chat, although he got distracted. What he was distracted by is one reason I've never managed to write him up. Another reason was the slush he'd lately been recording.

"Where's Ray Charles?" I had asked the woman in the record store. "I can't find Ray Charles."

"Ray Charles," she said, "is Easy Listening."

And there he was, tucked away with Tom Jones and Engelbert Humperdinck. Maybe that didn't bother him, but it did me. I could remember the first time I heard "What'd I Say." *Ohhhh. Uuunh.* From deep down in the pool whence cometh everything from gospel to boogie-woogie.

It was 1959, the year I graduated from high school. Rock & roll had not bowled me over. (I still say that after Bo Diddley, everything is commentary.) Elvis was somebody trying too hard to impress the girls. But my jib never started coming into its own until I heard "What'd I Say." Since time immemorial people had been singing about misery and about jelly roll, but this was getting down to the things themselves, together, redeeming the one with the other, *in church*. This was what Jesus, the Founding Fathers, and Big Mama Thornton had been getting at. Ray Charles hit it on the nose, and there was something profoundly *droll* about it. Wasn't tending toward the overwrought, like that Marvin Gaye song, "Sexual Healing." Ray was singing *well*. Well, well, well. And then I came to find out he could play jazz, he could sing *country*.

Easy listening? I didn't want to grumble about Ray Charles. So I didn't write anything.

Now he's dead, but the movie has restored him to his prime. "Oh, I see, now, *yes*," I have heard several people say, whose teens are ten or twenty years more recent than mine. Now maybe I can write a little something.

First of all, I'd like to know who came up with that title, "What'd I Say." *What'd?* What kind of arrhythmic, unpronounceable, clogged contraction is that? Slipped that in on a blind man. He's not singing-shouting "What *did* I say?" It's "What I'm *saying*," with a self-delighted touch of "What am I saying?" It's a piece he improvised (as depicted in the movie) with the original Raelettes, most notably the sublime Margie Hendricks. In *Brother Ray*, his excellent autobiography written with David Ritz, which Ray meticulously proofread in braille, it's always "What I Say," and Ritz states explicitly that Ray meant it to be that. So let's get that straight from now on.

Okay. About Margie. In the movie she is played with feeling by Regina King, who has said, however, that she had a hard time getting a sense of the character because so few images of her survive. When, in the movie, the news of Margie's overdose death comes to Ray over the phone, you know it's awful. But you don't know how awful until you hear and see the real Margie singing. You can do that now, on a recently released Rhino DVD: *Ô-GENIO: Ray Charles Live in Brazil*. It was recorded in 1963, the day before he turned thirty-three. In a liner note Ritz says of Margie:

> She's among the most underrated of all soul singers, yet Ray placed her in the highest category. "Aretha, Gladys, Etta James—these gals are all bad," Ray told me, "but on any given night, Margie will scare you to death." This is one of those nights. Both in rehearsal and onstage, her attitude is irresistibly feisty, uncompromisingly funky. If Ray intimidates other singers, he sure as hell doesn't intimidate Margie. Vocally, she stands toe-to-toe with the boss, never gives an inch, pushes him to the edge. Her facial expression says, "I'm sassy, I'm salty, I'm singing this song to death."

Yes. Or rather, "*Yas* indeed. *Yas* indeed." And it's too bad none of that got into *Brother Ray*, in which she receives way too little credit. She and Ray were lovers, and it's a blot on his life and career that he let her slip away. "What kind of *mannn* are you? What kind of *mannn* are you?" the Raelettes sing. Genius that he was, that question must have stumped him sometimes in the night after Margie was gone.

In Brazil in '63, Margie, like the other three Raelettes (she's second from the left), is wearing a perky taffeta party dress with a big flat bow at the waist. Demure, except for her mouth. She's not very big and not very pretty (she has Michael Jackson's original nose, in fact she looks a bit like him when he looked real), but you can't take your eyes off her, the confident, slightly lopsided curl of her lip as she goes *Wow'r*. She works her mouth around as if she's winding up, and pooches her lips with zest on the let-go. If you have a hard time picturing two people twenty feet apart turning "You Are My Sunshine" into carnal knowledge, then you owe it to yourself to check out this DVD. On "Don't Set Me Free," Margie lets out a "No-n'-no-no-*no!*" that will make your blood run several directions at once.

When he sings "Margie," about there being only one and "Margie, it's you," the Raelettes aren't onstage, so we don't know whether the other three are giving her jealous looks, or. . . . Oh, well, I'm going to let Margie go now. I feel partly like I'm her father and partly like I wish I could have gone out with her in high school. But here's a question: When Ray sings, whom is Ray singing to? A good deal of the time, I'd say it's his mother, his only parent, and it's about having to leave her when he was still a boy so he could learn to be self-reliant. However warmly he may have felt toward his wife when he was at home, he was too much a habitué of the road to be feeling profound separation from her when he sings with such longing, "Now if I call her on the telephone/And tell her that I'm all alone," on "Hallelujah I Love Her So."

I talked to David Ritz back in 1983, and he did grumble about Ray Charles: "He's an interesting American businessman. His entire life is music, touring, and pussy. That's it. He's only written five or six tunes—once he made a lot of money he let other people write for him. He should deal more autobiographically with his art." But that was back then, when the man was coasting. When he was cooking, he could turn anything—"My Bonnie," even—into a personal grievance over primal love lost, sunshine taken away. He recorded lots of songs about light, vision, and tears: "I Can See Clearly Now," "Don't Let the Sun Catch You Cryin'," "I'll Be Seeing You," "Drown in My Own Tears," "Ma, She's Making Eyes at Me," "By the Light of the Silvery Moon," "Show Me the Sunshine." Just a few of them. He didn't sing, "*Hear* the gal with the red dress on." On his rendering of "Till There Was You," Ritz says, in his notes to *Brother Ray*, "if you listen closely, you'll hear him cry." That's a song with lines like, "There were birds in the sky/But I never saw them winging."

Don't want to explain a man by his songs, of course, nor the songs by the man. Here's one he sings with great conviction: "You Don't Know Me." When I tried to sound him out about the kind of work he was doing in 1983, he said, "I ain't never been so sure of what I was doing. But I've always been one of those people who had the balls or, what they call it in sports, confidence. My mother's training. I've been out here performing thirty-eight years. If I'm going to die, I'll kill myself. You've got some people want to tell you what to do, who are accountants, lawyers, who can't tap their feet to hardly anything—I hope you don't make that sound nasty."

I was pretty sure I wasn't going to be able to make it sound like much of anything. I asked him how he felt when Elvis came along.

"I think in all fairness about that," he said, "at the time, white families were not about to let their young girls go out and swoon over a black guy. And Elvis was the cat that came along at the time. Doing everything that black people had been doing *all* the time. Get out on stage and wiggle his behind, the white version. You had a lot of white artists doing clean-up versions. Like . . . who was it? He covered a lot of Little Richard—it was like food with no seasoning in it. Can't think of his name. He had a daughter who sang, too."

I didn't know who he was trying to think of. He got a faraway look on his face, as I tried to press him on why he carried seventeen musicians around with him, when his earlier work with a small combo had been so fine. "When you got a big plate, you can put as much as you want on it. If you want just a little bit to eat, just put a little bit on, but if you want a lot, you can have that too." He said a number of things that he'd said in interviews before. When I asked him why he thought he hadn't self-destructed like so many great American musicians, he said, "I have never let *anything, anything*—I have never let *nothing* come between me and my music. I have never been so out of it that I couldn't get up on stage and sing 'I Can't Stop Loving You.' And the fact I'm blind, that's bad enough—I better keep my *senses* about me."

Meanwhile, I could tell he was doggedly trying to remember something. The name of that other white guy besides Elvis.

"The key to survival is know what you're doing. People may not like it, but some people don't like sex, far as that goes. When it's time to start singing, you just—*Pat Boone!*"

Nearly the whole time of my only conversation with Ray Charles, he had been trying to think of Pat Boone. I didn't much want to share that with the world.

But, hey. Tell the truth, I sort of liked "Love Letters in the Sand" back when that came out, which was before "What I Say." I met Pat Boone once, a nice fella. We were in a green room, waiting to go on TV. Pat's topic was how Christians could have better sex, and feel good about it. Pat Boone is part of America.

If it hadn't been for Ray Charles, though, there wouldn't have been any America. According to Flip Wilson on one of his comedy albums, this is what happened when Christopher Columbus asked Queen Isabella to finance his voyage:

> She asked him about this America project, and he said, "If I don't discover America, there's not going to be Benjamin Franklin or a

'Star-Spangled Banner,' or land of the free and home of the brave—and no Ray Charles!"

When the Queen heard "no Ray Charles," she panicked. Queen say, "Ray Charles? You gon' find Ray Charles? He in America?"

Queen running through the halls screaming, "Chris gon' find Ray Charles!"

Dusty Springfield

THE QUEEN OF BLOND SOUL by Jerry Wexler

It was 1965, and I heard a mesmerizing voice pouring out of my car radio. I was on my way to my office in Manhattan from my home in Great Neck, Long Island. The song was "Some of Your Lovin'." The singer was one Dusty Springfield, whose voice—tender and pristine—conveyed a vulnerability both sexual and soulful. Her intonation was incredibly accurate, hitting every note on the nose, sustaining her tones to perfection, with a minimal vibrato that never wavered or quavered.

I wasn't just intrigued; I was excited.

Dusty was born Mary Isabel Catherine Bernadette O'Brien in London, I was soon to learn, and educated in English convent schools.

Such soul emanating from an Englishwoman, fair and blond as Jean Harlow? Well, why not? I was already converted to the idea of a white Brit being able to sing with soul by the likes of Joe Cocker and Rod Stewart.

My original fascination fortified by every new release, I followed Dusty's career attentively. During the next three years, she more than ratified her status as the queen of blue-eyed soul with great renditions of "The Look of Love," "You Don't Have to Say You Love Me," "Some of Your Lovin'," and other world-class ballads from writers like Bacharach and David, and Goffin and King.

One day, early in 1968, I got a phone call from one of the music business heavies, a lawyer named Stevens Weiss, who happened to be a neighbor of mine in Great Neck. He said that it had been decided to bring Dusty into America to record. "Would you be interested," he asked casually, "in producing Dusty Springfield?"

Would I not! With Stevens and her agent, Harold Davison, she contracted to record for Atlantic—with the proviso that I be her producer. This stipulation was called a "key man" clause—meaning that should I not be available for whatever reason, the agreement would be voided.

And so it was arranged for Dusty to come to New York to begin preparing for the session. I began an intense hunt for songs I could believe in—and that I hoped would please her. With the help of my assistants, Jerry Greenberg and Mark Myerson, we spent several months amassing a cornucopia of lead sheets, lyric sheets, and acetate demos (cassettes had yet to appear). In my zeal to provide her with the widest possible choice of material, we wound up with seventy or eighty songs.

I thought it would be comfortable for her to come out to Great Neck, where we could work without the distractions of a frantic record office. Dusty showed up at my door, and we went into my living room. We soon found ourselves ass-deep in acetates—on tables, chairs, shelves, the floor. I played her song after song, hoping for a response—would she like this one? If not, how about this next one?

Most of the day, and well into the night, I became first fatigued, and then spastic, as I moved from floor to player, then back to the shelves, the chairs, and the tables, in what turned eventually into a ballet of despair.

After going through my entire inventory, the box score was Wexler 80, Springfield 0. Out of my meticulously assembled treasure trove, the fair lady liked exactly none.

First, I had to cancel the recording session scheduled for Muscle Shoals, where my favorite rhythm section was standing by. Then, it was back to Blighty for herself, to review, to mull, perhaps to cogitate.

It was agreed, glumly on both our parts, that we would regroup some months later. And so we did: back to my house to have another go—with my assurance that fresh fodder would be on hand. In retrospect, my assurance was bogus, maybe even intentionally so. Instead of a new group of songs, I culled twenty from the original agglomeration of eighty or so that she had heard.

But this time she loved them all—immoderately and joyously. We reduced the candidates to thirteen and, because of prior commitments in Muscle Shoals, rescheduled to a studio in Memphis called American, the bailiwick of a brilliant producer-songwriter-guitarist named Chips Moman. At the time, Memphis was the undisputed music capital of the world. There were Beale Street, W.C. Handy, Sam Phillips's Sun Records, Stax Records on McLemore—and American, with Chips at the helm of a dynamite rhythm section consisting of Reggie Young on guitar, Gene Chrisman on drums, Bobby Wood and Bobby Emmons on keyboards, the late Tommy Cogbill on bass, Mike Leech on percussion, and a backing group that I had named the Sweet Inspirations when they first worked behind Aretha Franklin.

By now, we had settled for eleven tunes: four by Goffin and King; two by an emerging Randy Newman; Barry Mann and Cynthia Weil's "Just a Little Lovin'"; a Bacharach and David song; "The Windmills of Your Mind," from the movie *The*

Thomas Crown Affair; and a sly piece of seduction called "Breakfast in Bed," written by two of my favorite Muscle Shoals musicians, Donnie Fritts and the late—and much-lamented—Eddie Hinton.

And so, with the collaboration of two worthy cohorts from Atlantic, Arif Mardin and Tom Dowd, we descended on a studio that turned out to be on the funky and primitive side—but with superb acoustics and engineering—and began to lay down tracks.

We learned not to wait for Dusty to show up before we started. Dusty was preoccupied for hours every morning in a makeup procedure that was virtually an exercise in lamination. Although she was ravishingly gorgeous, her doubts and insecurities about her appearance amounted to neurosis. She also thought that her legs were less than lovely, and so when she finally arrived she was swathed in yard goods to the floor.

Days went by. We laid down some smoking tracks, but whenever I called on her to sing, she refused. I never got a note out of her throughout the entire Memphis sessions. Not even a scratch vocal, which would have greatly facilitated our arranging process.

Her insecurity about her looks extended to her singing, marvelous artist though she was. Later on, she spoke on a BBC program about her fear:

> Jerry's gone in print saying I was the most insecure singer he's come across. He didn't realize how intimidated I was. Because they were telling stories and talking about Aretha, and I'm going, "What am I doing on this label? Why are they recording me?" And that showed in the time it took to get vocal performances out of me. Because if there's one thing that inhibits good singing it's fear, or allowing the natural critic in me to criticize a note before it left my throat. My intimidation probably came out as scowls and fears and grumblings.

If I may quote myself, I told Anthony DeCurtis when he was preparing the *Rolling Stone* obituary for Dusty (who died this past March) that:

> Dusty had an absolute commitment to perfectibility. Now, a lot of people have that—*but they just don't get there!* Dusty got there. She was timorous; almost neurotic about letting a vocal go for fear that it might not meet her empyrean standards. But the thing is: she always met them.

Change venue to New York, a recording studio on Fifty-seventh Street. It was the moment of truth . . . showtime. There were no sidemen present, just me, Arif, and Tom. The tracks were anchored by the Sweet Inspirations' backgrounds—and pure hell ensued. The psychic struggle between Dusty and me was Machiavellian.

Singers always call for more track in their headphones; my method has always been to give them less. This forces them to project harder, with raised volume and intensity. But Dusty insisted on calling for more and more track, and pretty soon the band track was a blasting roar. I put on the phones to see how the level was coming through, and two bars were enough—the volume was agonizing.

But she then began to do what she had come for. She sang! She kept saying, "Bring up the track, I can still hear myself!" This contravenes all traditional rules of recording: simply imagine Dusty producing vocals without hearing herself sing! But what vocals: perfect intonation, every note correct, gorgeous tone production, and her own trademark, idiosyncratic phrasing.

With Arif and Tom providing rich and melodious strings and horns, the cult favorite *Dusty in Memphis* was born, the recording that eventually became her defining work.

It was about the time of the Memphis sessions that the aforementioned Stevens Weiss offered us the rights to a group of ex-Yardbirds who were forming a new band. Negotiations were under way when Dusty, in a state of high excitement, said, "Jerry, you simply must sign them! I have worked with them, and they are England's best!" Her enthusiasm was infectious, and before they had recorded a single note we signed them to a long-term, worldwide contract. They were to call themselves Led Zeppelin.

When I went to see the movie *Pulp Fiction*, I was surprised and knocked out to hear "Son of a Preacher Man" on the soundtrack—and so must have been a few others; by all testimony it re-invigorated her career.

As a member of the nominating committee for the Rock and Roll Hall of Fame, I kept proposing her year after year, and was overjoyed when she was finally nominated.

Last summer, I got her phone number in England from my dear friend Vicki Wickham, her longtime friend and former manager. It had been decades since I last spoke to Dusty, and I had an overwhelming urge to talk with her and congratulate her for the award. By then, I'm afraid, she was terminally ill, and her caretaker said that Dusty couldn't come to the phone.

We never did get to speak again.

Joe Tex

HIDDEN MEANINGS (a short story) by Michael Parker

━━━━━

In the song "Ain't Gonna Bump No More No Big Fat Woman" by Joe Tex, the speaker or the narrator of this song, a man previously injured before the song's opening chords by a large, aggressive-type woman in a disco-type bar, refuses to bump with the "big fat woman" of the title. In doing so he is merely exercising his right to an injury-free existence thus insuring him the ability to work and provide for him and his family if he has one, I don't know it doesn't ever say. In this paper I will prove there is a hidden meaning that everybody doesn't get in this popular Song, Saying or Incident from Public Life. I will attempt to make it clear that we as people when we hear this song we automatically think "novelty" or we link it up together with other songs we perceive in our mind's eye to be just kind of one-hit wonders or comical lacking a serious point. It could put one in the mind of, to mention some songs from this same era, "Convoy" or "Disco Duck." What I will lay out for my audience is that taking this song in such a way as to focus only on it's comical side, which it is really funny nevertheless that is a serious error which ultimately will result in damage to the artist in this case Joe Tex also to the listener, that is you or whoever.

"Three nights ago/I was at a disco." (Tex, line 1.) Thus begins the song "Ain't Gonna Bump No More No Big Fat Woman" by the artist Joe Tex. The speaker has had some time, in particular three full days, to think about what has occurred to him in the incident in the disco-type establishment. One thing and this is my first big point is that time makes you wiser. Whenever Jeremy and I first broke up I was so ignorant of the situation that had led to us breaking up but then a whole lot of days past and little by little I got a handle on it. The Speaker in "Ain't Gonna Bump No More No Big Fat Woman" has had some time now to go over in his mind's eye the events that occurred roughly three days prior to the song being sung. Would you not agree that he sees his life more clear? A lot of the Tellers in the stories you have made us read this semester they wait a while then tell their story thus knowing it by heart and being able to tell it better though with an "I" narrator you are always talking about some kind of "discrepancy" or "pocket of awareness" where the "I" acts like they know themselves but what the reader is supposed to get is they really don't. Well, see I don't think you can basically say that about the narrator of "Ain't Gonna Bump No More ..." because when our story begins he comes across as very clear-headed and in possession of the "facts" of this "case" so to speak on account of time having passed thus allowing him wisdom. So the first thing I'd like to point out is Treatment of Time.

There is a hidden meaning that everybody doesn't get in this particular Song, Saying or Incident from Public Life. What everybody thinks whenever they hear this song is that this dude is being real ugly toward this woman because she is sort of a big woman. You are always talking about how the author or in this case the writer of the song is a construction of the culture. Say if he's of the white race or the male gender when he's writing he's putting in all these attitudes about say minority people or women without even knowing it, in particular ideals of femininity. Did I fully understand you to say that all white men authors basically want to sleep with the female characters they create? Well, that just might be one area where you and me actually agree because it has been my experience based upon my previous relationships especially my last one with Jeremy that men are mostly just wanting to sleep with any woman that will let them. In the song "Ain't Gonna Bump No More No Big Fat Woman," let's say if you were to bring it in and play it in class and we were to then discuss it I am willing to bet that the first question you would ask, based on my perfect attendance is, What Attitudes Toward Women are Implied or Explicitly Expressed by the Speaker or Narrator of this Song? I can see it right now up on the board. That Lindsay girl who sits up under you practically, the one who talks more than you almost would jump right in with, "He doesn't like this woman because she is not the slender submissive ideal woman" on and on. One thing and I'll say this again come Evaluation time is you ought to get better at cutting people like Lindsay off. Why we have to listen to her go off on every man in every story we read or rap song you bring in (which, okay, we know you're "down" with Lauryn Hill or whoever but it seems like sometimes I could just sit out in the parking lot and listen to 102 JAMZ and not have to climb three flights of stairs and get the same thing) is beyond me seeing as how I work two jobs to pay for this course and I didn't see her name up under the instructor line in the course offerings plus why should I listen to her on the subject of men when it's clear she hates every last one of them? All I'm saying is she acts like she's taking up for the oppressed people when she goes around oppressing right and left and you just stand up there letting her go on. I'm about sick of her mouth. Somebody left the toilet running, I say to the girl who sits behind me whenever Lindsay gets cranked up on the subject of how awful men are.

Okay at this point you're wondering why I'm taking up for the speaker or narrator of "Ain't Gonna Bump No More" instead of the big fat woman seeing as how I'm 5'1" and weigh 149. That is if you even know who I am which I have my doubts based on the look on your face when you call the roll and the fact that you get me, Melanie Sudduth and Amanda Wheeler mixed up probably because we're A: always here, which you don't really seem to respect all that much. I mean, it seems like you like somebody better if they show up late or half the time like that boy Sean, B: real quiet and C: kind of on the heavy side. To me that is what you call a supreme irony the fact that you and that Lindsay girl spend half the class talking about Ideals of Beauty and all and how shallow men are but then you tend to favor all the dudes and chicks in the class which could be considered "hot" or as they used to say in the seventies which is my favorite decade which is why I chose to analyze a song from that era, "so fine." So, supreme irony is employed.

As to why I'm going to go ahead and go on record taking up for the Speaker and not the Big Fat Woman. Well, to me see he was just minding his own business and this woman would not leave him be. You can tell in the lines, "She was rarin' to go, that chick was rarin' to go" (Tex, line 4) that he has got some respect for her and he admires her skill on the dance floor. It's just that she throws her weight around, literally! To me it is her that is in the wrong. The fact that she is overweight or as the speaker says "Fat" don't have anything to do with it. She keeps at him and he says, "I told her to go on and leave me alone/I ain't getting down/You done hurt my hip once." (Tex, lines 25–27.) She would not leave him alone. What she ought to of done whenever he said no was just go off with somebody else. I learned this the hard way after the Passage of Time following Jeremy and my's breakup. See I sort of chased after him calling him all the time and he was seeing somebody else and my calling him up and letting him come over to my apartment and cooking him supper and sometimes even letting him stay the night. Well, if I only knew then what I know now. Which is this was the worse thing I could of done. Big Fat Woman would not leave the Speaker in the song which might or might not be the Artist Joe Tex alone. Also who is to blame for her getting so big? Did somebody put a gun to her head and force her to eat milkshakes from CookOut? Jeremy whenever he left made a comment about the fact that I had definitely fell prey to the Freshman Fifteen or whatever. In high school whenever we started dating I was on the girl's softball team I weighed 110 pounds. We as people nowadays don't seem to want to take responsibility for our actions if you ask me which I guess you did by assigning this paper on the topic of Analyze a Hidden Meaning in a Song,

Saying or Incident from Public Life which that particular topic seems kind of broad to me. I didn't have any trouble deciding what to write on though because I am crazy about the song "Ain't Gonna Bump No More" and it is true as my paper has set out to prove that people take it the wrong way and don't get its real meaning also it employs Treatment of Time and Supreme Irony.

One thing I would like to say about the assignment though is okay, you say you want to hear what we think and for us to put ourselves in our papers but then on my last paper you wrote all over it and said in your Ending Comments that my paper lacked clarity and focus and was sprawling and not cohesive or well organized. Well, okay I had just worked a shift at the Coach House Restaurant and then right after that a shift at the Evergreen Nursing Home which this is my second job and I was up all night writing that paper on the "Tell-Tale Heart" which who's fault is that I can hear you saying right now. Your right. I ought to of gotten to it earlier but all that aside what I want to ask you is okay have you ever considered that clarity and focus is just like your way of seeing the world? Like to you A leads to B leads to C but I might like want to put F before B because I've had some Life Experiences different than yours one being having to work two jobs and go to school full time which maybe you yourself had to do but something tells me I doubt it. So all I'm saying is maybe you ought to reconsider when you start going off on clarity and logic and stuff that there are, let's call them issues, behind the way I write which on the one hand when we're analyzing say "Lady with the Tiny Dog" you are all over discussing the issues which led to the story being written in the way it is and on the other if it's me doing the writing you don't want to even acknowledge that stuff is influencing my Narrative Rhythm too. I mean, I don't see the difference really. So that is my point about Life Experiences and Narrative Rhythm, etc.

The speaker in the song "Ain't Gonna Bump No More No Big Fat Woman" says no to the Big Fat Woman in part because the one time he did get up and bump with her she "did a dip, almost broke my hip." (Tex, line 5.) Dancing with this particular woman on account of her size and her aggressive behavior would clearly be considered Risky or even Hazardous to the speaker or narrator's health. Should he have gone ahead and done what you and Lindsay wanted him to do and got up there and danced with her because she was beautiful on the inside and he was wanting to thwart the trajectory of typical male response or whatever he could have ended up missing work, not being able to provide for his family if he has one it never really says, falling behind on his car payment, etc. All I'm saying is what is more important for him to act right and get up and dance with the Big Fat Woman even though she has prior to that moment almost broke his hip? Or should he ought to stay seated and be able to get up the next morning and go to work?

I say the ladder one of these choices is the best one partially because my Daddy has worked at Rencoe Mills for twenty-two years and has not missed a single day which to me that is saying something. I myself have not missed class one time and I can tell even though you put all that in the syllabus about showing up you basically think I'm sort of sad I bet. For doing what's right! You'd rather Sean come in all late and sweaty and plop down in front of you and roll his shirt up so you can gawk at his barbed wire tat which his Daddy probably paid for and say back the same things you say only translated into his particular language which I don't hardly know what he's even talking about using those big words it's clear he don't even know what they mean. I mean, between him and Lindsay, my God. I loved it whenever he said, "It's like the ulcerous filament of her being is being masticated from the inside out," talking about that crazy lady in the "Yellow Wallpaper" (which if you ask me her problem was she needed a shift emptying bedpans at the nursing home same as that selfish bitch what's her name, that little boy's mother in the "Rocking Horse Winner.") You'd rather Sean or Lindsay disrespect all your so-called rules and hand their mess in late so long as everything they say is something you already sort of said.

What you want is for everybody to A: Look hot and B: agree with you. A good thing for you to think about is, let's say you were in a disco-type establishment and approached by a big fat man. Let's say this dude was "getting down, he was rarin' to go." Okay, you get up and dance with him once and he nearly breaks your hip, he bumps you on the floor. Would you get up there and dance with him again? My Daddy would get home from work and sit in this one chair with this reading lamp switched on and shining in his lap even though I never saw him read a word but "The Trader" which was all advertisements for used boats and trucks and camper tops and tools. He went to work at six, got off at three, ate supper at five thirty. The rest of the night he sat in that chair drinking coffee with that lamplight in his lap. He would slap me and my sister Connie whenever he thought we were lying about something. If we didn't say anything how could we be lying so we stopped talking. He hardly ever said a word to me my whole life except, "Y'all mind your mama." Whenever I first met Jeremy in high school he'd call me up at night, we used to talk for hours on the phone. I never knew really how to talk to anyone like that. Everything that happened to me, it was interesting to Jeremy or at least he acted like it was. He would say, "What's up, girl?" and I would say, "nothing" or sometimes "nothing much" and I would hate myself for saying nothing and being nothing. But then he'd say, "Well, what did you have for supper?" and I'd burst into tears because some boy asked me what did I have for supper. I would cry and cry. Then there'd be that awful thing you know when you're crying and the boy's like what is it what did I say and you don't know how to tell him he didn't do nothing wrong you just love his heart to bits and pieces just for calling you up on the telephone. Or you don't want to NOT let him know that nobody ever asked you such a silly thing as what did you eat for supper and neither can you come out and just straight tell him, I never got asked that before. Sometimes my life is like this song comes on the radio and I've forgot the words but then the chorus comes along and I only know the first like two words of every line. I'll come in midway, say around about "No More No Big Fat Woman." I only know half of what I know I guess. I went out in the sun and got burned bad and then the skin peeled off and can you blame me for not wanting to go outside anymore? She ought to go find her a big fat man. The only time my Daddy'd get out of his chair nights was when a storm blew up out of the woods which he liked to watch from the screen porch. The rain smelled rusty like the screen. He'd let us come out there if we'd be quiet and let him enjoy his storm blowing up but if we said anything he'd yell at us. I could hate Jeremy for saying I'm just not attracted to you anymore but hating him's not going to bring me any of what you call clarity. Even when the stuff I was telling him was so boring, like, then I went by the QuikMart and got seven dollars worth of premium and a Diet Cheerwine he'd make like it was important. Sometimes though he wouldn't say anything and I'd be going on and on like you or Lindsay and I'd get nervous and say, "Hello?" and he'd say, "I'm here I'm just listening." My Daddy would let us stay right through the thunder and even some lightning striking the trees in the woods back of the house. We couldn't speak or he'd make us go inside. I know, I know, maybe Jeremy got quiet because he was watching "South Park" or something. Still I never had anyone before or since say to me, I'm here I'm just listening.

I'm going to get another C minus over a D plus. You're going to write in your Ending Comments that this paper sprawls lacks cohesion or is not well organized. Well, that's alright because we both know that what you call clarity means a whole lot less than whether or not I think the speaker in the song "Ain't Gonna Bump No More No Big Fat Woman" ought to get up and dance with the woman who "done hurt my hip, she done knocked me down." (Tex, line 39.) I say, No he shouldn't. You say, Yes he should. In this Popular Song, Saying or Incident from Public Life there is a Hidden Meaning that everybody doesn't get. Well, I get it and all I'm saying is you don't and even though I've spent however many pages explaining it to you you're never going to get it. If you get to feel sorry for me because I come to class every time and write down all the stupid stuff that Sean says and also for being a little on the heavy side I guess I get to feel sorry for you for acting like you truly understand a song like "Ain't Gone Bump No More No Big Fat Woman" by the artist Joe Tex.

In my conclusion, Treatment of Time, Supreme Irony and Life Experiences are delved into in my paper. There is a hidden meaning in this Song, Saying or Incident from Public Life. Looking only at the comical side is a error which will result in damage to the artist and also to the listener which is you or whoever.

Ike Turner

STILL SMOKING by John Lewis

Ike Turner lives on a quiet suburban street about thirty miles north of San Diego. His gray ranch-style house with sky blue trim has a picket fence in front, a two-car garage, and a well-maintained lawn. A small black cross hangs from the fence gate. The front door is open, and before I can knock on the screen door, a petite blond woman appears. I introduce myself to Jeanette Turner. "You're late," she says. "Ike was expecting you an hour ago."

A bit apprehensively, I follow Jeanette into the dining room, where Ike has just finished his lunch. Sitting back in his chair, he's wearing black Tommy Hilfiger sweats, Reebok running shoes, and a taciturn expression. After Jeanette's introduction, I apologize for being late and study a once-angular face that has gotten rounder and softer over the years. He listens and nods gravely.

Suddenly, Ike stands and smiles. He leans over and pokes me in the ribs. "Shit, we're just glad you made it," he says. "While you're here, make yourself totally at home. You don't have to keep your shoes on. You can put your pajamas on and look at the TV if you want. Whatever you want to do. You're totally welcome. Baby, I want you to make yourself at home."

He leads me to a recording studio in the next room. Exposed beams run across the ceiling, and pictures of Ike at various stages in his career hang on the walls. A 1964 shot of the Ike and Tina Turner Revue, fourteen members strong, with the band in suits and Ikettes in long dresses, catches my eye. Ike takes a seat behind a Kurzweil keyboard and squints at the color screen of a nearby computer monitor. After a few points and clicks of the mouse, the rhythm track to "Rocket 88," a propulsive rocker from the early '50s, begins blasting through a pair of speakers. "This song is from the old days," he says. "Check this out, I'm workin' on a new version."

Sitting on the edge of his chair, both legs pumping to the beat, Ike layers a piano part over the rhythm track. As his left hand bounces across the keys, his right hand punctuates the groove with a flurry of notes. He scoots the chair closer to the keyboard, hunches his back, and percussively bangs the keys. A smile spreads across his face, and he lets out some grunts. For a few seconds, he stands up and plays.

When the song ends, he lets out a whoop and laughs. "That's gonna be on my next CD," he says. "I'm cuttin' a blues CD of songs from when I was just startin' up, stuff by folks like Elmore James, Muddy [Waters], and them. See, kids today know my name, but they don't really know who I am. I want to share what I do because, you know, I got my music and my own story to tell."

At this point in his career, he seems in danger of being written out of the history of rock & roll, the music he helped pioneer. His reputation as a domineering badass has overshadowed his musical legacy. As a musician, most people know him only as Tina's former foil, the rail-thin, sinister-looking guy who lurked in the shadows as she shook and shimmied in the spotlight. But Ike was much more than that.

"From the time I first heard him, I thought Ike was extremely talented," says Sun Records founder Sam Phillips. "He's an exceptional musician, and more than that, he is a creative musician. . . . As a piano player, he's not quite in a league with Jerry Lee Lewis, but he's about as talented as anybody I've worked with."

"People talk about me and Elvis Presley and all these other people, but the original rocker was Ike Turner," Little Richard writes in the introduction to Ike's soon-to-be-published autobiography. "That's who I copied from."

"I saw him as one of the masters of the tight rhythm-and-blues band," writes B.B. King, in his book *Blues All Around Me.* "He came up with hot grooves and snappy songs that were way ahead of their time. When they talk about rock & roll, I see Ike as one of the founding fathers."

"He helped turn boogie-woogie into rock & roll," says Memphis pianist-producer Jim Dickinson. "That's a pretty important thing."

Ike Turner was born sixty-seven years ago in Clarksdale, the heart of the Mississippi Delta. His mother, Beatrice, was a seamstress who grew her own cotton. "My mother used to rent a space to grow cotton across Highway 61," recalls Ike. "I used to walk out there with her, and she would be pickin' cotton, and I'd just be messin' around. I would see the cars come down the highway, and I'd say to myself, 'Goddawg, man. Suppose everybody that was in all those cars knew who I was. That would be great, wouldn't it?'"

Ike laughs. "I wasn't but five or six years old," he adds. "Why would I even care whether people knew me?"

It wasn't long before he discovered the piano. He and Ernest Lane, a childhood friend, were walking home from school one day and heard music coming from Lane's house. "Ernest's daddy had a piano in the livin' room," says Ike. "We looked in the window, and I saw Pinetop Perkins playin' that piano. I never saw nothin' like that in my life. You could hardly see his fingers, man. . . . I went home and told Mama, 'Mama, I want me a piano.'

"See, my mother raised me like this: If I wanted a bicycle, she would ask me, 'How much does it cost?' I say, 'It costs ten dollars,' and she'd say, 'Here's my five dollars. When you get your five, you go get it.' Then, I would go and pick up Coca-Cola bottles and sell them to the store. I would sell scrap iron. Another thing I would do was I would buy baby chickens—twelve baby chickens—and I would raise them up and sell them to the store. I was hustlin' like that from the time I was a kid."

This time, Ike's mother made him a different proposition. If he passed the second grade, he'd get a piano. So when Ike received his report card showing that he'd been promoted to the third grade, he sprinted all the way home. "She already had the piano in the house," he says. "Yeah, boy! I was set. Wow!"

His mother gave him a dollar a week for piano lessons. "[The teacher] was playin' de-de-de-de, all that a-b-c stuff," recalls Ike. "She would play me a song, and I'd sit down there and play it back to her. Anything I heard, I could play. The lessons were so borin' to me. I didn't want to do that. I wanted to do that Pinetop shit."

It wasn't long before he was skipping the lessons and spending his money at the pool hall. "I would go there and shoot that dollar up in pool," he says. "All the time, Pinetop was showin' me that boogie-woogie stuff. I'd get home, and Mama would ask me, 'Sonny, what you learn?' and I'd play her what Pinetop taught me. She'd say, 'Ooh, my baby learnin'. Yeah!'"

Ike roars with laughter. Then he quiets and turns serious at the recollection of a fire that destroyed his childhood home. "It was a Saturday, and we were at the movies," he says. "That's when our house burned down. My piano got burned down. Shit, man. All the hammers, the wires inside were popped loose. Wasn't nothing left but the soundboard in the back.

"That's when I learned how to make a piano. First, I got some sandpaper and a wirebrush, and I wirebrushed that thing down as good as I could. Then, I went and got me a felt hat, some cement glue, some shoestring, and car tires. I can make a piano with that. You know the part of a tire right around the rim? If you burn that little part around the rim there, that's the same wire in there that makes the sound inside a piano. I burned me four or five car tires, stretched that wire across the yard, and me and Lane sandpapered this wire down. Then, we rolled it up and rewired that piano.

"I took the hat, cut it up, and glued the felt on the hammers with cement glue. I tied shoestring to the hammers, so they'd pull back and forth. I didn't even know they made tunin' hammers, so I went and got a socket wrench from a garage. I put that little socket wrench on there and started tunin' that piano. That's when I learned how to tune a piano. I can make and tune a piano, man. After I did that, I started goin' around to churches fixin' pianos to make a little extra money."

Jeanette enters the studio, saying she's going to the market. Ike stands. "How much you gonna need?" he asks, pulling a roll of bills from his pocket.

She says, "A hundred ought to do it." And he peels bills off the roll and hands them to her.

"Why don't you take the Lincoln?" he says. "I got an errand to run, too."

A few minutes later, Ike and I are barreling up Highway 78—in a tan Mercedes sedan with IKEREVU plates—on our way to LensCrafters. As he speaks, he constantly cranes his neck, looking for openings in traffic. The speedometer often hits 100 miles per hour. At one point he has to brake abruptly for a motorcyclist. "That boy on the bike gonna get run over," he says. "He's takin' his life in his hands on a road like this. And I can't see too good, either. There'd be nothin' but a spot o' grease in the street."

I ask about his father, Izear Luster Turner. "He was a minister," he says. "He died when I was real young, man. He was goin' with this black chick that was goin' with this white guy. When they came to get him, when they kicked the door down, I remember the fall. I was in my mother's arms, and they knocked her down when they came in there. It was a couple of pickup-truck loads of whites in khaki pants and khaki shirts. Mama was tryin' to hold on to Daddy, and they pulled her loose. She was cryin' and hollerin' and screamin' and all.

"When they brought him back, they threw him in the front yard. He was all bloody. They had kicked holes in his stomach. Mama tried to take him to the hospital in Clarksdale, but they wouldn't accept Daddy because it was for whites only.... The health department put up a little tent outside of my house—because those wounds smelled so bad—and he stayed there for three years, and he died."

Ike also recalls being molested at the age of six by a neighborhood woman and getting beaten with barbed wire by his stepfather. He shakes his head. "Kids, man," he says. "You have to watch what you do because they remember stuff from way back."

After having his glasses adjusted at the mall, where the LensCrafters employees greet him like an old friend, we speed home to a dinner of fried catfish, cornbread, potatoes, greens, rice, and iced tea. He eyes the plate Jeanette sets in front of him and pats his slightly paunchy stomach. "People keep tellin' me that I've put on a few pounds," he says.

"One thing's for sure," says Jeanette, "you will eat good at the Turners'."

"There's nothing else to do here," Ike adds, with a chuckle. "Eat and play music, that's all I do."

Ike and Jeanette met in East St. Louis eleven years ago. At the time, she was singing with a local band, and he was battling a cocaine addiction and barely making a living. By his account, they fell in love and "slept on a lot of floors together." When Ike was busted and sent to prison in 1990, Jeanette kept in touch, and after his parole two years later, she moved in with him and started singing in his band, the Ike Turner Revue. They were married at a Las Vegas casino on July 4, 1995. It was Ike's thirteenth marriage and Jeanette's first.

When asked how this marriage is different from the twelve others, Ike pauses between bites of catfish. After claiming to be too shy to talk about it, he gets serious for a minute. "Before, I was just doin' it to be married," he says, "Didn't mean nothin'. This time, it's like I've got another part of me. It's another kind of life for me. I don't care if the sun don't shine, because it's just us. I ain't ever felt like that before."

The seriousness disappears. "Don't be askin' me stuff like that in front of her," he says, laughing. "Look, I ain't answerin' no more questions today."

"You just start gettin' a little sentimental, and he's gonna hide," says Jeanette. "He'll turn shy on you in a hurry."

Ike steers the conversation to his early days in the music business. As a teenager, he was a DJ at WROX radio in Clarksdale and played piano at local roadhouses and juke joints. His first band, the Tophatters, was a school band that eventually split into two camps—the Dukes of Swing, who could read music, and the Kings of Rhythm, who could not. Ike went with the latter group.

The Kings of Rhythm were a dynamic live band. They played the r&b tunes that were popular on the jukeboxes, including hits by Amos Milburn and Roy Milton. At a typical show, the audience would jitterbug, camel walk, and do the hammer as Ike pounded the piano, the horn section stepped in unison, and the guitarists performed backflips as they played. B.B. King was so impressed with the group that he recommended them to Sam Phillips. "B.B. made an appointment for us with Sam," says Ike. "He was the one who suggested we go to Sam's studio and make a record."

The record turned out to be "Rocket 88," which is considered by Phillips to be the first rock & roll song. With a driving beat, distorted guitar, and sheer attitude, the tune hit Number One on Billboard's r&b chart in 1951. But to Ike's eternal dismay, it was credited to vocalist-saxophonist Jackie Brenston rather than the Kings of Rhythm. Ike claims the song was written by the entire group on the way to the session.

After the success of "Rocket 88," Ike frequented Phillips's studio and one day happened upon a B.B. King session for Modern/RPM Records. The recording wasn't going well. "At the time, B.B. was playin' semi-jazz," Ike recalls, "because that's how Phineas Newborn, Jr., [King's piano player] played. When they took intermission to rest or eat a hamburger or somethin', I eased in and started messin' with the piano. Joe Bihari [co-owner of Modern/RPM] heard it and started hollerin', 'That's what I want, right there!'"

Impressed by the pianist's taste in music, especially his feel for the blues,

Bihari hired him as a talent scout to canvass the South for musicians to record. Bihari bought Ike a 1949 Buick Roadmaster, gave him a salary of one hundred dollars a week, and paid his travel expenses. "He was sendin' me his clothes, too," Ike says, "the clothes he didn't want. The coat would hang way down on me, but I was *clean*, man. I was livin'."

On arriving in a new town, he'd go to the pool hall and ask about singers in the area. He'd do the same thing at the local churches. Then he'd locate the singers, audition them, and take notes on their performances. A few months later, he'd return with Bihari and a trunkful of portable recording equipment. "We'd find a house with a piano in it and give [the owner] a bottle of whiskey to use it," says Ike. "We'd set up in the living room, and a lot of times we only had one microphone, that was it. We recorded a lot of people that way."

From late 1951 to 1954, the duo recorded Howlin' Wolf, Elmore James, B.B. King, Junior Parker, Sonny Boy Williamson, and many others under such makeshift conditions. They cut classics like Wolf's "Moanin' at Midnight" and James's "Dust My Broom," and Ike often accompanied the artists on piano. Nearly half a century later, the particulars of those now-historic sessions are fuzzy.

"I remember personalities more," Ike says. "The last time I saw Wolf, I was swingin' at him with a mop. He owed me money and said he didn't have it, but I knew he did. I told him I wasn't gonna play no more, and I started callin' him names and shit. He come up on me, and I swung at him with a mop handle. He was big, man!"

Elmore James, he says, "was big as Wolf. And he could holler, boy. You could hear him holler for miles around."

B.B. King was "friendly and down-to-earth, just like he is today. He's earthy as can be, ain't got no star shit in him."

When Ike finishes eating, Jeanette clears the dishes, and he returns to the studio to work on a gritty, gutbucket version of "Catfish Blues." By ten o'clock, he's exhausted and ready for bed, so I retire to a guest room decorated with frilly pillows and floral draperies. Fifteen minutes later, there's a knock at the door. It's Ike, wearing pajamas with smiley faces and puppy dogs printed on them. "I just wanted to say good night," he says. Then he shakes my hand, gives me a hug, and leaves.

At nine o'clock the next morning, the house is quiet. Jeanette has gone to a voice lesson. She's left a tall glass of carrot and parsley juice on the kitchen counter for me. I take it to the living room and sit on the sofa.

With skylights letting in the California sun, the room is bright. White nubbed carpeting covers the floor. A wrapped Duraflame log sits inside the fireplace. An entertainment center and a bookcase—with such titles as *Divided Soul: The Life of Marvin Gaye, 88 Songwriting Wrongs and How to Right Them*, and *The Encyclopedia of Common Diseases* on the shelves—dominate one wall. Three television remotes, a plastic nativity scene, two glass angels, and an open Bible turned to the Book of Psalms are on the coffee table.

Ike joins me, wearing gray sweats and looking a bit groggy. He turns on the television and pops a tape in the VCR. It features Ike's recent appearances on the *Roseanne* talk show, *Extreme Gong*, and *Mad TV*, a comedy show with an ensemble cast. In one of the *Mad TV* skits, a cast member dressed as Tina Turner orders a pizza, and the delivery man turns out to be Ike, or rather a cast member playing Ike. When Tina asks why he's delivering pizzas, he says it's the only job he can get since *What's Love Got to Do With It* destroyed his career.

The real Ike chuckles at this. "Tina's gettin' like two million a night now," he says. "It's unbelievable. Right now, I need a hit record on Ike. One hit record on me would put me in the superstar bracket, because I already have the notoriety."

Ike met Annie Mae Bullock, an audacious country girl with high cheekbones and a gritty voice, at a Kings of Rhythm gig in the mid-'50s. By that time, he had moved the band to East St. Louis and was playing as many as fourteen shows a week. After hearing her sing, he groomed her as a front-woman and suggested she change her name to Tina Turner. Around that time, he also switched from piano to guitar so he could lead the band more easily.

When Tina was ready for the spotlight, the Ike and Tina Turner Revue was born. Together, the couple toured relentlessly, counted the Rolling Stones and Phil Spector among their fans, and topped the charts with "Proud Mary," "A Fool in Love," and "It's Gonna Work Out Fine." Ike says the tours would last for eleven months, "from the last day of January until December. We'd drive our bus all over the United States, from Florida to Maine to Seattle."

Ike ran the show with browbeating tenacity. "Everything that came out of Tina's mouth came from me," he says matter-of-factly. "Every step the Ikettes did came from me. I choreographed their dance routines and told everybody the do's and don't's."

If crossed, Ike was liable to get violent. In Tina's autobiography, *I, Tina,* Ike seems to yell, slap, and punch more than he plays music. In the movie *What's Love Got to Do With It,* he is portrayed as a raging psychopath. Although he's quick to claim the film caricatures his shortcomings, he doesn't deny having wreaked havoc on the lives of those around him, especially Tina. "It wasn't easy back in those days," he explains. "It's hard to be with somebody twenty-four hours a day and not have arguments and fights. It's especially hard when you tell somebody, 'Hey, this is the dress you wear when you sing that,' and you hear 'Fuck you,' with the attitude and everything."

Is he sorry for the things he did? "Let me say it like this," he says. "I love me today because everything I've ever done made me what I am today. Because I love me today, I have no regrets about what I did. But there are some things I did that I don't like. . . . I just can't go around defendin' myself with people."

Jeanette returns from her voice lesson and begins cooking breakfast. As Ike talks about the post-Tina years, the smell of bacon, eggs, and pan-fried potatoes fills the house. "When me and Tina broke up, I was afraid of rejection," he says, "so instead of doin' music, I grabbed me some drugs. . . . When you doin' cocaine like I was, you do nothin' but wake up and get some more. Sometimes I would record songs in a hotel room with a little piano I had, but mostly I was just procrastinatin' and philosophizin'."

And getting busted. Ike was arrested about a dozen times between 1976 and 1990, the year a California judge sentenced him to four years in prison for cocaine possession. In jail, he was "too scared to mess with it," so he quit drugs and "never looked back."

The phone rings, and Jeanette hollers from the kitchen. "Ike, your blood work came back normal," she says.

"I ain't dyin'?" he asks.

"No."

"Well, why am I itchin'?"

"Everything's normal. You must have dry skin."

"I been scratchin' my butt off, man," he says. "And I been gettin' a feelin', hit me right in my heart. Bam! When it goes away, I can feel the aftereffects of it, so I went to the heart doctor. Albert King had a thing like that, and all he did was start takin' Tums. I ain't goin' out like that."

Otherwise, Ike says he's healthy and feels great. He doesn't smoke or drink. He takes brisk walks through the neighborhood each day with Jeanette. He laughs a lot. And he plays music.

With the bacon still sizzling, he returns to the studio and begins playing the theme to *Chariots of Fire*. As he plays, he talks about getting back into the music business. In fact, a recent flurry of activity points to a resurgence of interest in his career. In 1996 he released a self-produced solo effort, *Without Love . . . I Have Nothing*. More recently, he contributed boogie-woogie piano to John Lee Hooker's *Best of Friends* record and made a guest appearance on *Chef Aid: The South Park Album*. Guitar wiz Jonny Lang covered Ike's "Matchbox" on his major label debut, *Lie to Me*, and Los Lobos guitarist-singer Cesar Rosas recorded a version of "You've Got to Lose" for his solo disk, *Soul Disguise*.

Still, Ike says that "it's been hard to get a record deal" and speculates it's because of his tarnished reputation. "I'm not hard to get along with," he says, but abruptly changes his mind. "Well, maybe I am hard to get along with."

The *Chariots of Fire* theme has given way to a familiar-sounding melody. It's from the mid-'70s, but I can't instantly place it. Ike sings in a scratchy voice.

Man got a woman to take his seed

He's got the power but she's got the need

She spends her lifetime tryin' to please her man

Does all the little things only a woman can

But she cries and moans too often

He smokes and drinks and sometimes

He don't come home at all

And then the chorus:

Only women bleed

Only women bleed

Only women bleed.

After a second verse and chorus, he adds a spoken-word part:

It's always black eyes all the time

Clean up the lawn

Clean up the grass

Cook me somethin' to eat

Always somethin'.

The song ends with Ike's distinctive baritone, the same voice he used for the "rollin' on the river" part in "Proud Mary":

A woman supposed to bleed

She supposed to bleed

If you think like this

She supposed to bleed

If she don't give me what I need.

He finishes, and I ask if he's thinking about re-recording the song, which already appeared on his 1980 solo record, *The Edge*. "Probably," he says. "I like it."

I ask him if he has any reservations about how the song might be received, coming from him. "Coming from me?" he asks. "Alice Cooper had it out. Why would people take it different from me?"

He seems genuinely perplexed until I remind him of his reputation as a wife-beater. "Aw man, I don't care about that," he says. "They can associate it with what they want. That shit don't faze me anymore. I care less about what they think. I just do what I feel."

He turns away and leaves the studio. It must be time for breakfast.

Family

My Mother's Blues

WHY SHE WON'T LEAVE NEW ORLEANS by **Sheryl St. Germain**

━━━━

My mother's sitting in her ruined backyard, the one haunted by the memories of children and swing sets, sandboxes, plastic pools, and Slip 'n Slides. Almost everything that wasn't knocked down, split in two, or uprooted by Katrina was drowned or damaged by the water that covered the yard for no one knows how many days. Skeletons of shade-giving pecan and avocado trees, hibiscus, bay leaf, holly, and the snaky vines of wisteria remind her of how vibrant this yard used to be. Once, there was even an addition to the house back here, a small room with large, screened windows and a ceiling fan where she and my father played card games late at night with friends, a room where he drank scotch and she drank wine and where they talked about the future.

My mother is sitting on a porch swing that is set on a cracked and roofless cement floor, all that's left of that room she and my father added onto the house, and that was destroyed by another hurricane years ago. Her neighbor's house is empty, the tree that stabbed its heart still there, upside down, the treetop buried in the house, the roots reaching out to the sky. If she looks at it in just the right light, it almost looks like a living Medusa, with the roots curling around like woody dreadlocks.

My mother is drinking a glass of wine and listening to music, a mix of New Orleans jazz and blues. She's not listening to anything intellectual or edgy, no Coltrane or Charlie Parker, not anything like what her daughter who doesn't live here anymore might listen to. No, she's listening to music she's always listened to, music that reminds her of people she loved who are gone, and her youth, which is gone, and her city, which also feels gone, and she's listening to music that deepens the sadness she already feels, and somehow the music's sadness combined with her own grief makes her feel exquisitely present in what has become her life in this city, and that's somehow weirdly better than actually feeling better. The music resonates with something ancient and animal inside her body, and she feels like the vibrating string of that resonance.

The music is coming from the back window of the living room, which she's left open, and she's turned it up loud because the cars on Williams Blvd. make lots of noise, and now that the airport, just a couple miles away, is back in business, the sound of planes often seems to speak for the sky, and the sound of planes is not music, will never be music, and even after almost fifty years of living in this house, the sound of planes still makes her feel helpless.

I don't know exactly what she's listening to since she's alone and I'm not there, but if I had to guess, I'd say she's listening to something with piano in it, since she loves piano: She's the one who insisted all five of her kids take lessons, who negotiated those free lessons from a neighbor. She was the one who scraped and saved to pay for a piano over many years, though she never touched it except to dust or move it.

She might be listening to Professor Longhair or Dr. John or Fats Domino or James Booker. She loves the way those New Orleans guys punch the piano, how they mix up blues and boogie-woogie and the parade rhythms of carnival, all sloppy and sexy-like. The piano also reminds her of her mother, who played by ear. *New Awleans,* Dr. John croons, *city of a million dreams, you never know how nice it seems when you way down South in New Awleans.*

My mother sips her wine, thinks of her life as a child growing up in the Quarter, *Yes it's true I got those Basin Street blues.* She thinks of JazzFest and seeing James Booker there years ago; she and her friends will go again this year even though her legs hurt more and more as she gets older and it gets more and more painful for her to walk. She doesn't want to think about that much, but she knows she probably only has a few more years where she'll be able to walk unaided.

James Booker. Only *he* sounds like this—that heartbroken, raw piano. Only someone who spent time in Angola, she thinks, could play like that. *I went down to St. James Infirmary, I heard my baby cry,* he sings, *I was so brokenhearted, she was gone somewhere, in the bye and bye.*

My mother is alone in her backyard because her parents are dead and her husband is dead and her two sons are dead and her sister and two brothers are dead and her two daughters do not live in this city that she will not leave. Her daughters live in nice Northern cities that are safe, with less crime than New Orleans, cities far from hurricanes and floods, but they are not *interesting* cities, in my mother's opinion, and this is still the most damning thing she can say about another city, that it's just not *interesting.* And besides, people talk different in those cities, and those cities are not *this city*, this city where she was born, this city where she had sex for the first and last time, this city where she married, then birthed and raised five children, this city where her sons, her husband, her mother and father and grandmother and grandfather and great-grandmother and great-grandfather and great-great grandparents and great-great-great grandparents are buried. Two hundred years of ancestors are buried in this muddy soil. She will not leave them; she will not desert them as her daughters have deserted her. *Down the road, came junco partner, he was loaded as he could be . . . knocked out, and loaded, and he was wobblin' all over the street.* Only here, she thinks, would we sing songs celebrating drunks, and she drinks a drink to my father, tilting her glass to the Medusa tree in her neighbor's yard.

Those cities her daughters live in don't have food like they have here, either, she thinks, no thick-rouxed gumbos and jambalayas and Creole sauces and crawfish and crabs and oysters and shrimp and red beans and rice, and roast beef po-boys, and they don't have *interestingly* named streets like *Desire* or *Tchoupitoulas* or *Melpomene* or *Humanity*, she thinks, and what can you say, really, about the imagination of cities that give their streets names like *Main* or *First* or *Second,* and what about cities that don't have King Cakes, or voodoo dolls or beads or Mardi Gras or crawfish festivals or rice festivals or oyster festivals, and those people in those other cities don't have the Mississippi *and* Lake Pontchartrain and they don't smell like this city, spicy and rank and full of color, and she's certain they don't even have a sense of humor, or *interesting* politicians, and she thinks that maybe people in those other cities might not even know how to dance, really, and they don't have the Saints or Al Hirt or Pete Fountain and now that I think of it, maybe that's what she's listening to as she sits alone in her backyard. Maybe she's listening to Pete Fountain's clarinet all high and sweet like a gladiola, and maybe she's singing along *when the saints go marchin' in, oh lord, I want to be in that number,* and how could she leave New Orleans now, *now* when the Saints are doing so well? She remembers when all the fans wore paper bags on their heads and called themselves the *Aints* because they were so embarrassed at how bad the team was, but they went to games anyway, and she remembers when Archie Manning wasn't yet the father of Peyton, but the redheaded hero of the Saints, and now that they're so good, it would be wrong to leave, all that time wasted on them when they were bad, and she drinks to that, and maybe it's trumpet she's listening to, maybe loungey Al Hirt, maybe he's blowing "Do You Know What It Means to Miss New Orleans?" She and my father used to go to his club on Bourbon, and she still likes to go now and visit his statue in the Quarter, touch his trumpet, and remember all that is gone.

My mother is sitting alone in the swing my brother gave her on Mother's Day the year before he died, the year before Katrina, and even though it's already rusted she thinks she will never not use it, she will never give it away, she will never move away from this swing. There's just room enough for her to sit comfortably on it without someone else and now she's swinging to the *drip drop drip drop* of Fats Domino, *I'm walkin' to New Awlins,* and she's thinking about music and sorrow and music and forgetting and music and remembering, and she's thinking of how important music is to this city and how it's not important in this way to any other city, and even though one of her daughters lives in a big city in the Northeast where she says there's lots of jazz, my mother knows in her bones it's not like it is here, music here is the voice of the city, but in this other city, where her daughter lives, she's certain the music is just some extra thing, some little curlicue, something nice—she's sure it's very nice—but it's not *necessary* like it is here, and she's certain this city would die if it couldn't sing, and she drinks to that. *Jackomo fe nan e', Jackomo fe nan e', you don't like what the big chief say Jackomo fe nan e'.*

She pushes herself in the swing and all of a sudden she realizes almost all the songs she loves from this city are riffs and "improvisations"—a word her daughter likes to use—on loss—*brother, brother, brother John is gone. When the levee breaks, I'll have no place to stay.*

How could she go to another city where music and food were not the breath and heart of it? She's sure she'd feel like an alien, living somewhere else, somewhere not here, with all her records and cookbooks and history books and Mardi Gras beads and colorful old-lady clothes and costumes; people would just see her as an eccentric old woman. Here, she thinks as she swings, here I am someone, here the earth knows me, the water loves me. Here I'm a native. I've lived here so long, she thinks, the air smells like me, the trees and the bushes sometimes look like me, and when I die I'll just switch one shape for another.

My mother is sitting alone in her backyard because she's sad, and it seems better to be alone when she's sad. I'm old, she thinks, I am an old woman, and who wants to look at an old woman? She has girlfriends, and she knows they don't care about how old she is. They have an informal club and they sometimes all wear purple like in that poem "When I Am an Old Woman I Shall Wear Purple." She could call one of her friends to come sit with her now, but most of her friends are sad, too, and she doesn't want to make them even sadder. *My grandma and your grandma, sittin' by the fire, my grandma told your grandma, I'm gonna set your flag on fire, talking 'bout hey now, hey now Iko Iko an de'.*

It's getting dark now, the mosquitoes are out, and she slaps at her arms and thinks about going in. Later, maybe one of her friends will call her up and they'll go to a movie or out to listen to some music. They'll still be sad, though, because this city they love and will not abandon is so sick and broken and stinking. It's like a child, or a parent you love very much who is addicted or alcoholic or has been in a horrible accident and is now a quadriplegic, she thinks. Sometimes it seems to my mother that everyone who still lives in this city is depressed, although they are all trying not to be. They're sad because some of them are still living in trailers and some of them, like my mother, still have not had their houses repaired. The city is old, too, a gone pecan. *We're all gone pecans,* she says to herself, looking at the thousands of rotting pecans on the floor of the backyard. She's sad because it's hard for her to believe the city will ever be the same, and she wants it, she needs it, to be the same.

Maybe she's listening now to saxophone or clarinet, which she also loves. Maybe it's Lester Young's version of "Summertime," which she used to sing to me when I was a child, or "The Man I Love," a song that does not make her think of my father but rather of the boy she did not marry, the boy she didn't have a chance to fall out of love with. Or Sidney Bechet's "Black and Blue" or Louis Armstrong's. *What did I do to be so. . . .*

They call it stormy Monday, but Tuesday's just as bad. Lord and Wednesday's worse, Thursday's also sad. That's what it's like now, my mother thinks. Every day nothing's being done to help us and maybe soon I won't even remember what it used to be like, but she thinks if she keeps listening to the music, maybe it will help her remember.

My mother is sitting alone in her backyard feeling sorry for herself and not wanting to feel sorry for herself. She knows depression is a selfish thing, like a little cloud she carries around that keeps her from doing much for anyone, especially herself. She's sitting alone thinking of the last time she went out with one of her friends and they drove by the Lower Ninth and they saw again that the houses were still knifed into one another; and they went by the marina and Lake Pontchartrain where she loves to sit and dangle her feet in the water like she did when she was a kid and the boats were still all scrambled up. I'm seventy-five years old, she thinks, and maybe you just get more alone when you get older and maybe nothing will ever be fixed, and she thinks about how she's too old to fix anything, not even herself.

And as I write this I'm sitting here alone, like my mother, in my own bedroom in some Northeast city, listening to music, and it occurs to me all of a sudden that I'm not writing about my mother at all, that I'm writing about myself, my own loneliness and despair and love of the music she taught me to love, the music of our city, the city and music she won't leave, and I'm talking about *see that guy all dressed in green, Iko Iko an de'* and I'm talking about *Summertime and the livin' is easy* and I'm talking about *Brother John* and I'm talking about *I'm going back to Louisiana* and I'm talking about *Mama Roux!* and I'm talking about *way down yonder in New Orleans* and I'm talking about *I got my jambalya crawfish pie ya* and I'm talking about *when the levee breaks* and I'm talking about *I got nowhere to go* and I'm talking about I got *my saints marchin' in* and I'm talking about going down to *St. James Infirmary* and I'm talking about *I'm gonna be in that number* and I'm talking about *when junco partner comes down the road loaded* like my father, *knocked out, knocked out and loaded,* and I'm talking about my gone brother, I'm talking about *brother brother, brother Jay is gone* and I'm talking about *I know what it means to miss New Orleans.*

About a Girl

MY SISTER'S LOVE AFFAIR WITH COUNTRY MUSIC
by Wendy Brenner

A Partial List of Country Musicians My Sister Rachel Has Met Personally
(*"This doesn't mean I know them, just that I met them at least once,"
she clarifies, ever the soul of reason.*)

Vince Gill
Rodney Crowell
Rosanne Cash
Guy Clark
Gail Davies
Emmylou Harris
Sweethearts of the Rodeo
The Desert Rose Band
Kathy Mattea
Steve Earle
Roy Acuff
Minnie Pearl
Brenda Lee
Billy Walker
Jimmy Dean
(*"Jimmy Dean?" I ask. "The sausage guy?" Rachel: "Yes, the sausage guy.
He was a singer first. He sang 'Big Bad John' in the '60s."*)
John Hartford
Linda Davis

Jon Randall
Lorrie Morgan
Del McCoury
The Cox Family
Townes Van Zandt
Dwight Yoakam
The Marshall Tucker Band
Nikki Nelson (second lead singer of the group Highway 101)
Paul Overstreet
Hal Ketchum
J.C. Crowley
Louise Mandrell
Amy Grant
Peter Rowan
Barry and Holly Tashian
Robin and Linda Williams
A whole bunch of lesser-known, local-type performers and session musicians.

Disclaimer

While my sister is, inarguably, an "obsessive country-music fan," she is not a *crazed* fan. She doesn't stalk people, has never been arrested, doesn't do drugs, has never auditioned for a reality TV show. She has rented the same Nashville apartment and held the same job—bookkeeping for a property management company—for more than a decade, and she volunteers weekends in a therapeutic horseback-riding program for children with disabilities, and just because she once wrote a song about the ghost of Emmylou Harris's tour bus and waited after a show to present Emmylou with the typed-up lyrics, and just because she once got a thousand signatures on a petition to keep a Manhattan country-music station from switching to an all-talk format (including, somehow, the signatures of the Marshall Tucker Band—"They were around that week," she says vaguely, meaning "around" New York), and just because she moved by herself, a twenty-four-year-old nice Jewish girl from Chicago with no savings, connections, college degree, or job, to Nashville, Tennessee, a place she had never even visited, just so she could be close to the music—it's not like she's *crazy*.

To be fair, she met many of those listed before as both fan and employee, while she was working as a production secretary at Opryland Talent, one of her first jobs in Music City. Her position required her to behave professionally and appropriately—she couldn't, for example, get autographs, which was fine with her. "I don't do autographs," she says, with some disdain. She is a purist, that particular brand of music snob for whom it's all about the music. She actually still *listens* to her hundreds of vinyl LPs, and her cassettes, and even to her 45s, most of which have been in her possession for about thirty-five years.

The Opryland position was short-lived, and she was growing desperate, between jobs and short on cash, when she met the married duo Barry and Holly Tashian at a Unitarian church; they were selling their CDs, and my sister asked if they'd trade her one in exchange for a few hours of office work. They hired her on as a part-time Girl Friday, and for several happy years thereafter she got paid to immerse herself in their music, a mix of bluegrass, traditional country, and folk/Americana described by reviewers as "gentle," "soulful," and "unpretentious," adjectives that also describe my sister, but don't usually apply to the music business. The Tashians were neither naive nor novices, however. As a teenager, Barry had appeared on *The Ed Sullivan Show* (with his garage-pop band, the Remains) and toured with the Beatles; he later played on Gram Parsons's solo debut and recorded ten albums with Emmylou Harris. For my sister, it must have felt like she'd landed a job in heaven—and from what she has told me, the Tashians were most certainly her guardian angels, the kind you encounter when you're too young, or young at heart, to know you need watching over.

It was through Barry and Holly that my sister got a brief gig assisting a local college professor who was writing a book about country music; Rachel's duties were rote and clerical, securing reprint permissions on lyrics, calling ASCAP and other music licensers—yet again, she was happy. She didn't care about getting her own name into print, wasn't secretly angling for a recording contract. She wasn't All About Eve. She just loved country music, and in Nashville, it seemed, she could get paid for this.

Several years later, I met some colleagues of the professor for whom my sister had worked. I brought up the connection, and watched the shock of recognition, the rapid reinterpretation of me, or whoever they'd thought I was, the polite rearrangement of facial expressions. "Yes, that's right," one of them finally and carefully said. "She wasn't the usual type of person you see around our department." Another quickly added, "She was a breath of fresh air."

Flashback: Chicago, Illinois, Saturday Afternoon, Winter 1977

My sister and I slog through black slush and ice chunks in the gutters of Lincoln Avenue, a busy, sidewalkless four-lane that cuts through our suburb and into the city. We are thirteen and eleven, respectively, bundled in our fake down jackets, my sister in soggy sneakers, me in my new knee-high vinyl fashion boots from Fayva. We are hiking to Discount Records, a dark hole-in-the-wall shop my sister somehow knows about and frequents, even though she is too young to drive and the store is miles from our house, on a gritty block of pawnshops and take-out joints and taverns. She bikes there by herself when the streets aren't so icy, and bikes home with her album purchases under one arm, but I have no idea why she suddenly needs to go in the middle of winter, or why she invited me along—we're not close, don't usually hang out together. Usually she's in her bedroom with the door shut, listening to music or lying on the floor reading, and even if her door is open, trying to talk to her is infuriating. One time I started yelling at her, and nearly physically attacked her (which I did with some regularity throughout our childhood), because when I asked her what the book she was reading was about, she would only answer: "A girl."

She conned me into going to Discount Records by casually mentioning that she had recently seen Heart's original, unreleased *Magazine* LP there—only a few hundred copies were allegedly in circulation, she explained, because of the band's contractual dispute with the Mushroom label. This was news to me; I didn't read *Creem* and the other music magazines my sister subscribed to—they seemed slightly dangerous, like they were written in code. (What was up with Boy Howdy beer? I still don't understand.) But I got excited about the treasure-hunt aspect of the Heart story, the lottery angle. I didn't doubt for a moment, nor do I have any doubt today, that if anyone in America had seen a copy of the original *Magazine* at a record store, it was my thirteen-year-old sister, but the music itself was incidental to me. I spent my own allowance on unicorn posters and *Me!* perfume and Bonne Bell Lip Smackers. Yes, I loved singing along with "Magic Man," poring over photos of Ann and Nancy Wilson on *Little Queen* and *Dreamboat Annie,* wondering where they got their cute outfits, what size bras they wore, but I felt phony, like I was copying my sister when I said Heart was my favorite band, or claimed to even have a favorite band. No matter how strong my love for music, it would always be a weak imitation of my sister's.

We didn't see *Magazine* at Discount Records, and I don't recall whether we bought anything else. The day's highlight for me was getting fries and a hot apple pie at McDonald's. (Per our liberal upbringing, we were permitted to walk miles unchaperoned into the city to buy records, but corporate fast food was forbidden.) I still remember the glorious, illicit, yellow-plastic warmth and light of that restaurant, after walking so far in the damp and overcast cold. By the time we got home, after dark, my feet hurt so much I literally crawled up the stairs to my bedroom. My sister, of course, was in no pain whatsoever, and even then I felt this as a reproach—I was a lightweight.

"In My Room," original lyrics and score by Rachel Brenner, circa 1970*

I like to sit in my room.
In the corner there is a broom.

---

*Brian Wilson's song by the same title was released in 1963, coincidentally the year my sister was born.

The ceiling is red
And so is the bed.

My sister taught herself to read at age three, was labeled "gifted," "the sensitive one" (nobody said what that made me, the other one), was so smart her kinder-garten teachers skipped her ahead a grade in school. She wrote poems and was a talented artist and spontaneously composed music when she was seven or eight, perhaps inspired by our mandatory piano lessons, which inspired me only to fig-ure out and play endlessly the creepy, hypnotic four-note theme of Brian De Palma's 1973 horror film *Sisters*—starring Margot Kidder as good-and-evil Siamese twins—after I heard it one time on TV.

Somehow, though, by high school, she was no longer behaving like a gifted child. She had quit piano long ago (we both tended to abandon every kind of lesson—ballet, flute, guitar—the moment we were allowed to) and spent all her free time shut in her room. She wasn't doing drugs in there, hadn't "fallen in with a bad crowd"—she barely had a crowd, just the same few close friends. She moved anonymously through the halls of our giant public high school, amidst the anony-mous other 2,500 students, her grades plummeting, her teachers and doctors and guidance counselors offering no diagnoses and scant guidance. There was noth-ing wrong with her. Her standardized test scores were through the roof. The more my parents yelled at her, the more time she spent in her room. "Rachel's off in her own little dreamworld" became the family line, repeated over the years in tones of dismay, rage, worry, resignation. (The line on me was "Wendy's working her-self up into a tizzy again.")

What she was doing in her room, instead of homework, was typing up and compiling into binders the lyrics of every Fleetwood Mac song ever written, clip-ping and saving every magazine or newspaper article about Fleetwood Mac, track-ing down out-of-print LPs by the band's original members and by the members of all the bands they'd played in before or since, and ordering bootleg recordings of live performances and unreleased tracks and interviews from classified ads in the backs of magazines and catalogs from all over the world. Because I happened to live down the hall, I, too, came to know all the album titles and accompanying bizarre cover art by heart, burned in my memory even today, though I can't name all the students in a class I taught last year. *Kiln House, Bare Trees, Then Play On, Future Games, The Pious Bird of Good Omen*. She had the Buckingham–Nicks album and the solo album by Christine Perfect (Christine McVie's real maiden name) and tangential things by Chicken Shack and Walter Egan and John Mayall. I knew about how Jeremy Spencer got brainwashed by the Children of God, how Peter Green went crazy from too much LSD and on one tour refused to play anything but "Black Magic Woman" (of which he was the author), and about the brilliant but fragile Danny Kirwan, whom Bob Welch called "one of the strangest people

I've ever met." Now, of course, all of this—the trivia, the discographies, the bootlegs—can be found in five seconds on the Internet. In the '70s, my sister was the Internet.

At the time, I just wished she were *normal*. I was mortified by her weird hobby, her tentative, "sensitive" way of speaking, her uncombed and unfeathered hair, her failure to wear makeup to cover her acne. She was making me look bad by association. Did she not notice that nobody wore bell bottoms anymore? In our family, I was the only one who cared—panicked, actually—about what others thought of us. My nerdy parents were frantic about my sister's academic problems, but social uncoolness was like a badge of honor to them, a sign that one had *good values*. They practically bragged about how they themselves had never been in the "in crowd"; when kids teased or bullied us, they suggested we respond with clever puns.

Most teenagers would rather die than be seen with their families, I know, but I am ashamed now by how deeply ashamed of my sister I was then. Recently, I realized that seven of my iPod's "Top 25 Most Played" tracks are Fleetwood Mac songs from the 1970s—four of these in the top ten—and by way of penance or apology reported this to my sister, who seemed neither surprised nor especially interested. But then, I've always been slow to catch up with her. (The only thing keeping "Second Hand News" out of the number one spot is my obsessive playing of Santana's 1981 hit "Winning," which is somehow simultaneously plaintive and triumphant and thus seems like the perfect anthem for both the best and worst moments of my life, not that I ever noticed this in 1981.)

Despite the hand-wringing and dire warnings, my sister made it through high school and through four years at a Midwestern state university, from which she elected not to graduate. She had moved on from Fleetwood Mac by then and turned her attention to Broadway, and was writing letters to the actress Mary Gordon Murray—who coincidentally (or not) played a country singer on the soap *One Life to Live*—and Betty Buckley and other stars of the stage, many of whom responded with kindness and encouragement. When a couple of my sister's theater professors turned out to be less encouraging, she did an end run around them, skipped town during finals week with a few hundred dollars and two suitcases, and moved to New York City.

In between endless, hopeless cattle-call auditions and temp jobs, she hung out at a bar in the East Village that had a forgiving crowd of regulars and a country-heavy jukebox she liked to sing along to, maybe to let off steam, or maybe just to practice her singing, which wasn't getting her very far in auditions. "The jukebox was loud so I could kind of let it drown me out if I couldn't hit a note," she recalls. Sometimes other regulars joined in and sang harmony, or bought her drinks, or put in quarters for her. One guy who always sang along with her on Loretta Lynn's "You Ain't Woman Enough" later turned up on the front page of the *New York Daily News*, identified as one of the top drug dealers in Washington Square Park.

I remember silently wincing on the phone when Rachel told me, rather excitedly, about her new jukebox hobby. Why couldn't she just be *normal?* Yet as I write this, probably twenty or thirty of my graduate students, not to mention several fellow professors, are down at Martha's Karaoke Lounge in Wilmington, unironically and quite competitively belting out Patsy Cline and Hank Williams and Tammy Wynette, taking photos to post on their blogs. When was it ever cool to care so much what people think? I wonder. What the hell was my problem? Of course, now that karaoke's cool, my sister's not particularly interested in it. "I sing better than I used to, but not well enough to do it for anyone but myself," she says. "I sing because that's where I can express myself musically."

It was in New York, riding the LIRR back into Manhattan with a friend after an Emmylou Harris concert, that she wrote the song about the ghost of Emmylou's tour bus. "We were just being silly and trying to write something melodramatic," she says. "It was never supposed to be serious." She doesn't understand why I am suddenly so interested in this song, and despite my repeated entreaties, she insists no record of it survives, not even the title, which she claims not to remember, even though I'll bet money she can cite from memory every musician who played on each of Emmylou's albums. All she recalls about the tour-bus song, she says, is something about the "taillights disappearing into the night."

The Happiest Girl in the Whole U.S.A.

I have noticed on *The Bachelor* that you can always tell which girl the bachelor is going to pick by what he doesn't say, what he can't find words for. If he rhetorically lists positive traits—"She's warm, she's athletic, she's great with kids"—it's the death knell. About the girl he loves (forgive my loose usage of the term), he's like, "I don't know, whenever I see her, I just feel like—I don't know!"

The same goes for music, I've always thought. However well-schooled or personally impassioned, even the most genius critics aren't much better than Amazon.com's "personalized recommendations" at predicting what music you, or anyone, will love. What happens between you and the music in private, in your head, or soul, or wherever music is truly heard, is finally impossible to articulate.

When I ask my sister why country has outlasted her other musical obsessions, she mentions that it incorporates many different influences, that the industry is more accessible, the shows generally more intimate, than, say, mainstream rock—but then she adds, a little helplessly, "I don't know, maybe because it has more horses in it than any other kind of music?"

Certainly nothing in our heritage predisposed her toward the South. Our parents listened exclusively to classical, jazz, and the occasional Tom Lehrer album, and never so much as turned the radio dial to a pop station, let alone country. As kids, we owned a single country record, a K-Tel "Best of" LP that someone had given us as a gift, featuring Donna Fargo and Buck Owens and Roy Clark; we laughed at the cartoonish accents and melodramatic lyrics, made a game of hilariously acting out "I Fall to Pieces."

By way of explanation or testimonial, it is easier, and perhaps more accurate, for Rachel simply to cite her favorite country-music memories: sitting on the banks of the Ohio River in Owensboro, Kentucky, for sixteen hours straight, listening to bluegrass under the sun and stars; seeing John Hartford and Mike Compton perform on a midnight riverboat cruise; watching the Tashians from backstage the first time they performed on the Grand Ole Opry; seeing Emmylou perform with the Nashville Symphony at the Summer Lights Festival one day, and Guy Clark play at some smoky, low-lit little club the next. Love is always greater than the sum of experiences, but those experiences are all we can see or touch or hear, the only part of love anyone's ever been able to chart.

Sometimes I think my sister and I haven't changed at all over the years: I'm still the annoying, hyper one, she's still the dreamer. Living in the South has helped me to see her in a different light, the region having always accepted and celebrated its eccentrics—it's practically a requirement, a point of pride, to have one in the family. But I'm not so sure I would even call my sister eccentric anymore. Somehow, by internal radar or smarts or simply following her heart, she has always known how to find her way to the places that feel the most to her like home, places where being a music freak is considered anything but freakish, her own little dreamworlds on earth. We all should be so blessed.

Rockabilly

Jerry Lee Lewis

ONE NIGHT WITH THE KILLER by John Fergus Ryan

Twenty-five years ago, Esquire assigned me to write an article about Jerry Lee Lewis. I spent two days with him, then wrote the piece which my editor at Esquire rejected because, he said, I had made Jerry Lee into a nice guy when everyone in the country knew he was a brawling, hell-raising, wild man whose own friends called him "Killer."

What follows is the piece I wrote in 1970, an account of spending five hours with Jerry Lee in his dressing room as he waited to perform on the stage of the Mid-South Coliseum in Memphis.

I didn't see him again until several years later, while he was on probation for trying to crash the gates at Graceland with his Rolls-Royce. Jerry Lee had to report monthly to the office next door to mine at the Department of Corrections where I worked, so we saw each other often. But he never seemed to recognize me. And, for some reason, I never stopped him to ask if he recalled that memorable night in his dressing room in 1970.

1970

And there he was, Jerry Lee Lewis, host to a passel of in-laws and friends, sipping bourbon and Coke, joking, clowning, reflecting, while fifteen big diamonds and a bloodred ruby the size of a Wild Cherry Life Saver glistened upon his fingers.

It was eight o'clock on a Saturday night and Jerry Lee, once the Crown Prince of Rock & Roll, was making his first personal appearance in Memphis since *Cashbox* had named him and Buck Owens the most popular male country-music singers of the year.

Jerry Lee was waiting to go on.

Outside, a cold rain swept the streets and kept attendance down.

Show folks came and went.

Three young men, tall, rangy—an act in lime-green velveteen suits and white ruffle-front shirts—came offstage, past two pretty girls in red-and-white cowgirl costumes who were just going on.

Jerry Lee was in his element.

He was sitting in a folding chair, leaning against the fireproof brown tile wall of the dressing room in Memphis's Mid-South Coliseum, his feet braced against a closet door.

His black cowboy boots were worn and scuffed, and his gold-colored denim pants had scratch marks along the back of the right leg, where he struck matches to light his cigars.

He had arrived at the Coliseum in his 1970 Cadillac limousine and entered through the stage door, in the pouring rain, wearing no coat.

His manager, Cecil Harrelson, had followed, carrying Jerry Lee's costume in a paper sack and a two-quart bottle of Calvert Extra bourbon whiskey.

When they got to the dressing room, Jerry Lee's father-in-law; some other relatives; Rita Gillespie, a television director from London; and a country boy in a shiny blue suit, a clip-on necktie, and dusty, black vinyl, pointed-toe shoes, whom they called the Kid, were waiting with a six-pack of Cokes, paper cups, and a sack of crushed ice.

Jerry Lee poured a jigger of bourbon into a big, plastic iced tea mug, filled it with crushed ice and Coke, and then stirred it with his aluminum pocket comb.

"I always stir my drinks with my comb," he said, shaking it dry and putting it back in his hip pocket. "And I ain't had dandruff for years."

Rita Gillespie, who is trying to develop a network television show starring Jerry Lee Lewis, only drinks champagne and Jerry Lee had brought along a bottle for her. He had someone take it across the hall and open it there so no one in the crowded dressing room would be injured by the flying cork.

"Jerry is interested in doing a film," said Miss Gillespie, holding a waxed paper cup of champagne, "and we're looking for a property. It's difficult to find just the right one. He insists on playing the villain but he wants to escape punishment in the end."

She was wearing a red dress and red vinyl boots that came up to her knees and fit so close you wondered how she got them on, and was smoking a Turkish cigarette held in a long, gold holder.

"Jerry makes an excellent villain," she said. "Did you happen to see him in

Othello?" she asked, referring to a 1968 rock version of *Othello* staged in Los Angeles, in which Jerry Lee played Iago.

That Saturday night, as he sat in the dressing room at the Mid-South Coliseum, he had six albums in the country music Top Twenty. His new single, "Once More, With Feeling," out just a week, had sold over fifty thousand copies and was edging toward the top of the charts, a position it attained before the month was out.

The dressing room was filling up with people.

Three old musicians, who looked like what the young ones prancing by would look in twenty years, appeared at the door and waved to Jerry Lee.

"Just stopped by to pay our respects," said one, after Jerry Lee invited them in.

Jerry Lee looked at them. He knew them from somewhere. "I'm tryin' to remember where," he said.

"The Stompers," said one of them. "Eddie Bond's club. Eddie Bond and the Stompers."

"That's from where!" said Jerry Lee, shaking hands with them.

"We done a lotta pickin' together in them days, Jerry Lee," said one.

"Didn't we!" Jerry Lee agreed.

"We'll be out front, cheerin' for ya," said one of the men, and they left.

Jerry Lee took a sip of his bourbon and Coke.

"That's really bad weather, and I mean *bad* weather, outside," he said. "Rita, is your champagne all right?"

"Yes, Jerry. It's splendid. Thank you," said Rita Gillespie.

"Did you watch Sivad last night, Jerry Lee?" asked the Kid.

"Goooooooooood evening. I am Sivad, your Monster of Ceremonies," said Jerry Lee, doing an impression of Sivad, host of a late-evening Memphis television horror show who appears in full evening dress and wears two-inch fangs.

"Boris Karloff. Did you see it?" asked Jerry Lee. "Boris Karloff, *The Haunted Strangler.* Horror movies. That's all I ever watch. Well, that's not right, exactly. I go to every W.C. Fields picture I can find."

"He was on TV Sunday," said the Kid. "Did you ever read that book about him?"

"*Follies and Fortunes?* Sure I read it. You remember that part where he was doing his pool-table act and started getting laughs in the wrong places?"

"Yeah," interrupted the Kid. "They was a guy under the pool table doin' funny faces."

"Right," said Jerry Lee. "Under the table, who was it?"

"Ed Wynn," said someone in the room.

"Ed Wynn. Ed Wynn was under the table, cuttin' up, and Fields saw him and I mean bounced one a' them cue balls right off his head. And everybody thought it was part of the show.

"W.C. Fields was the greatest, I guess, they ever was," said Jerry Lee.

Fans and other musicians, somehow having made it past the four policemen and the steel-mesh door that protected the dressing-room area, continued to come in and out of the room to see, to touch, Jerry Lee Lewis.

One young man, whose mother was already in the dressing room, came in and introduced his fiancée to Jerry Lee.

"Hello, honey," said Jerry Lee, rising and taking her hand. "You're sure a mighty pretty little lady!"

Jerry Lee was pleased by all the people coming in.

"I never have hid myself from 'em. Let 'em all come, I say. I like it. When I go out to th' supermarket or picture show, I see they notice me. I see 'em lookin'."

The Kid said, "They're sayin' to theirselves, 'Look yonder. There's Johnny Cash!'" Everybody laughed.

"Now Elvis, he stays hid," said Jerry Lee. "You just can't get in his dressing room. Well, almost can't.

"When he did his first show in Las Vegas, I called him up long distance, to where he was stayin'. I been knowin' him, I guess fifteen years.

"Somebody answered, and I said, 'Let me speak to Elvis,' and they said he wasn't able to come to the phone just then, and I said I knew he was and that I wanted to speak to him. I said, 'Just tell him this is Jerry Lee Lewis talkin'.'

"He was there. You know where he was? In a steam bath! A steam bath!

"Anyway, he come to th' phone. I knew it was him, and the first thing he said was, 'Who is this?' and I played like I didn't know who he was and I said, 'Who is *this?*' and he said, 'This is *Gidget!* Who is *this?*'

"Well, I flew out there. He got me a table right at ringside, and I mean, he was great! Great! The audience went wild. Elvis got those old ladies with all that blue hair all stirred up, and I went over and finished 'em off."

Everybody laughed.

"Naw, I'm just kiddin'. But you talk about trouble gettin' into a dressing room! After the show there was a little party in Elvis's dressing room. Elvis, he's give up drinkin' sweet milk and Pepsi. He was drinkin' champagne.

"He told me that he'd come to Las Vegas because people had begun to figger he'd gone squirrely on 'em, hidin' away like he does. He wanted to show 'em it wadn't true. That's what he said.

"About that time ole Colonel Parker comes in and sees the party goin' on and says out loud to Elvis to get all of those people out of here. He meant it. People started getttin' out, but I just stood there at the bar. I told Elvis, I said, 'Elvis, if I was you I wouldn't let no loudmouth ole man tell me who I could have a drink with.'

"An' ole Parker jumped on me. I thought I was gonna hafta whup him. But then he put his arm around my shoulder and said he was just nervous and not to mind him.

"I don't know why Elvis stays away from the public like he does. I know he'd rather be out there with 'em. He loves to sing.

"There's just three from the '50s that have managed to make it into the '70s. Elvis Presley, Johnny Cash, an' me, Jerry Lee Lewis."

A short, very skinny man with a thin little mustache came in from nowhere and stood in front of Jerry Lee, with his arms folded, swaying a little.

The man stood there a full minute, swaying, looking Jerry Lee in the eye.

At last he spoke.

"You don't remember me, do you?"

He had a tooth missing in the front.

Jerry Lee looked at him a minute and then pointed a forefinger at him.

"I knew a fella once outta Beaumont, Texas, had a tooth missing," he said.

The little man shook his head and continued to stand there, his arms folded, swaying.

"You don't remember me, do you?" he repeated.

"I guess you're gonna hafta tell me," said Jerry Lee.

"I changed a tar on your Lincoln, outside a' Bunkie, Louisiana, about ten years ago."

"That's from where!" said Jerry Lee.

The little man beamed.

"You want a drink, Jerry Lee?" he asked.

"Have one a' mine," said Jerry Lee, pointing to the two-quart bottle of Calvert Extra, which was getting on toward empty.

"I got my own," said the man. "Look."

The little man was wearing pants so tight they must have been cut by a taxidermist. He started pulling up his right pants leg, and it fit so close it was taking all his strength just to get it up over his boot top.

At last he did, revealing a half-pint bottle of peach wine stuffed in his boot alongside his anklebone.

The little man's wife came in and took him out.

"That's the first real bootlegger I ever saw," said Jerry Lee, and there was much laughter.

Jerry Lee's barber, Sonny Bridges, of Southaven, Mississippi, came in with a lady and introduced her to Jerry Lee.

Bridges was a young, handsome man with long, red sideburns, easily better looking than any entertainer on the bill that night.

Bridges shook hands with everyone.

"Sonny is my only barber," said Jerry Lee. "Don't nobody else ever even touch my hair."

Another young man came in and introduced his fiancée. Jerry Lee rose, took her hand, and said, "Hello, honey. You're sure a mighty pretty little lady!"

The members of Jerry Lee's five-piece band were beginning to arrive, and they checked in with Cecil Harrelson.

Harrelson is the former husband of Jerry Lee's singing sister, Linda Gail, who now lives in Ferriday, Louisiana.

Another group of people came in and one young man among them introduced Jerry Lee to his fiancée. Jerry Lee rose, took her hand, and said, "Hello, honey. You're sure a mighty pretty little lady!"

Jerry Lee's drummer, Morris Tarrant, a slim, young Confederate with a drooping mustache, checked in.

Tarrant, who had just returned to Jerry Lee's band after making one tour with James Brown, had his wife and young daughter with him, and Jerry Lee rose and greeted them.

Four musicians in road costume—double-breasted coats, ruffle-front shirts—entered, and one of them, a big, young man with red hair, introduced his fiancée to Jerry Lee, the fourth man that evening to do so.

This time, Jerry Lee rose, took her hand, bent low, and kissed it, then said, "Hello, honey. You're sure a mighty pretty little lady!"

Jerry Lee and the red-haired young man were old friends and they talked a while, recalling past adventures.

"You remember those three girls that were waiting for us that time outside that Greek place in Amarillo?" asked the young man.

Jerry Lee scratched his head.

"You're not thinking of that time in Shreveport, are you?" he asked. "Are you stayin' for the show?"

"Can't do it," said the young man. "We got a show ourselves Monday night in Miami, and we're pulling out right now. We'll run into you again on the road, someplace."

"Yeah, sure. Someplace," said Jerry Lee, as he followed them to the dressing-room door and waved goodbye.

Jerry Lee's wife, Myra, and his six-year-old daughter, Phoebe, entered the dressing room.

Myra Lewis, twenty-seven, had been married to Jerry Lee for fourteen years and was a petite young lady who wore her hair long, in the Assembly of God fashion. She was dressed conservatively, without a trace of showbiz in her appearance.

Phoebe wore little white vinyl boots and jumped up in the lap of an older woman sitting in the room.

"I just came back to be sure what you're going to wear tonight," Myra said to Jerry Lee.

"Honey, I might go out there in just what I got on right now," he said.

"Now you wear your leather suit, Jerry Lee Lewis, and I mean it!"

Someone mentioned Jerry Lee's hair. In the early days, he wore it long enough to fall down past his chin. Now it is short and combed straight back all over.

"Jerry Lee's hair is just beautiful," said Myra, "and he doesn't put anything on it but QED."

"That's a pretty dress you got on, honey," said Jerry Lee.

Myra twirled around to show him the full skirt.

"I'm going out front and do some clapping," she said. "It makes me so mad! There are people sitting out there who don't ever clap. I don't think they ought to be out there if they're not going to clap!"

Myra Lewis went back out front.

By now, all the members of Jerry Lee's band had checked in with Cecil Harrelson and were waiting in the dressing room across the hall.

Harrelson, hair parted in the middle of his head with long, full sideburns, came in, poured a shot from the bottle of Calvert Extra, and put a little Coke in it.

"I don't care if it does make my ulcer hurt," he said.

The little man who had changed Jerry Lee's tire appeared in the room again, swaying a little more. He stood in front of Jerry Lee and looked at him awhile.

"They call me Pee Wee, and I don't care," he said. "I'm proud of it!"

"If it was me, I'd be, too," said Jerry Lee.

The little man swayed, almost falling, and Jerry Lee put out his arms to catch him.

"Be careful, Killer," said Jerry Lee.

"Jerry Lee, you sure you won't have a drink? Lemme tell you what I got." He leaned over and whispered in Jerry Lee's ear. "Peach wine."

Pee Wee's wife reappeared and led him back out the door.

On his way out, Pee Wee addressed the room: "I changed a tar on his Lincoln once. The one he set far to."

Dick West is Jerry Lee's bodyguard, driver, general assistant, and friend. A former professional wrestler, he selects and sees to the fitting of Jerry Lee's wardrobe.

He was in and out of the dressing room, taking infrequent nips from a drink he kept on a shelf in the closet.

West took me aside and showed me a .32 caliber revolver in a holster on his belt, hidden by the coat of his perfectly fitted suit.

"I have to carry a gun," he said. "We're always leaving these strange towns with big cash money on us. I just got this .32. I got a license to carry it. I did have a .45 automatic but it went off on me.

"We were in Oklahoma City, and I went outside to the car for something, bent over, and the .45 fell out of the holster, hit the pavement, and went off.

"The slug grazed right through my you-know-what. In one side, out the other. Clean as a whistle. Then it creased my belly and stopped in my thumb.

"There was so much blood, they all thought I was dead. They called Jerry Lee. He called my people. They called ever'body they knew and told them I was dead.

"But I came out of it. Healed up fine ever'where. Ever'where. I mean, it didn't even leave me any interesting scars I could start up a conversation about."

Dick West had to leave. Some of his wrestling fans were waiting to meet him at the steel-mesh gate.

It was getting near time for Jerry Lee to go on.

Ken Lovelace, who is married to Linda Gail, checked in. Lovelace plays guitar and fiddle in Jerry Lee's band and has a featured solo.

Charlie Rich stopped by the dressing room.

Charlie Rich, a big, gray-haired man of thirty-seven, has a sad, genius quality about him, and is much venerated by Jerry Lee and his associates.

He was appearing on the show that night, and, after he shook hands all around, he poured himself a healthy drink, and stood there drinking and swaying.

"Mr. Cholly," asked the Kid, "is this music all you do for a living?"

Charlie Rich stopped swaying and looked at the Kid.

"Do you mean . . . do I park cars?"

The Kid was silent a second or two, then he said, "I'm a gi'tar man."

"You really want to play the guitar?" asked Rich.

"You better believe it," said the Kid, grimly. Rich took a good pull on his cup of bourbon and Coke. "Try playing it holding it over your head," he said.

"You really mean it, Mr. Cholly?"

"How'd you do tonight, Charlie?" asked Jerry Lee.

Rich did not hear him.

"How'd it go out there?" repeated Jerry Lee.

"He ain't been on yet," said the Kid.

Jerry Lee's jaw dropped, and he looked around at everyone, rolling his eyes upward.

He went over to Rich and put his arm around his shoulder.

"You'd better slow down on that stuff, Killer. You got a show to do," he said.

Rich nodded. "Yeah. You're right. I think I better go wash my hair."

Charlie Rich left, and Jerry Lee poured his second drink, putting just about one jigger of bourbon in the big mug, and again stirring it with his comb.

"That Charlie Rich is great," he said. "He's got it. When I say 'it' I mean *talent*. He's not like these groups that come and go on one record they do with a lot of trick, electronic stuff.

"Man, if you can't entertain without a sound engineer, an' a man at a console mixin' for you, you're in trouble.

"That's the way it is with a lot of them makin' it in the music business these days. You put 'em on a stage by theirselves with just a guitar or piano, and they're lost.

"They'll all wind up back parkin' cars. That's where they belong, anyway. Pumpin' gas and parkin' cars."

Dusty Rhodes, brother of the late country entertainer Slim Rhodes, came in, said, "Hello and good luck," and left.

Jerry Lee's accountant came in and asked if it were true he was planning to buy an airplane.

"Got it picked out," said Jerry Lee. "Gonna cost $625,000."

"Let me just say one thing," said the accountant. "Make sure you get a good pilot and keep it maintained, regular. Promise?"

"I promise," said Jerry Lee.

A young lady came in and gave Jerry Lee some color photographs of himself that she had taken at the disc-jockey convention in Nashville. They showed him wearing a dark blue pinstripe suit, vest, striped tie, and he looked very respectable.

"You can keep them," she said, and left.

"Is that the one give you that ruby?" asked the Kid. Jerry Lee held his hands out in front of him.

He was wearing a gold identification bracelet with JERRY on it, three diamond cluster rings, and a ring with one big red stone.

"That's not her. I got this ring from a fan, a lady, up in Middle Tennessee. I didn't even think for a minute it was real. Then one time it fell off my hand, and the stone come out while I was on stage.

"Myra took it down to Gordon's Jewelers on Main Street to have it reset.

"They asked would she like to have it appraised, and she said she guessed so.

"Well it came back, and the man said he reckoned it would cost about the same as a diamond that size. Maybe more.

"It was *real!* And there I'd been stompin' it all over the stage!"

Cecil Harrelson and Morris Tarrant came back in, and Jerry Lee showed them the pictures the lady had left.

"Look here," he said. "Don't I look like a banker? That's the day they asked me to run for Governor of Tennessee.

"They were taken at the DJ convention in Nashville. Three days. I mean, for three days, I never went to bed. It was at the Andrew Jackson Hotel. Three whole days of me takin' nips and stayin' up.

"Second or third day, I don't remember which, I was in the lobby looking for the men's room an' I asked this fella standin' there which way it was.

"He said, 'It's down those steps, if you think you can make it.'

"I thanked him and started down. Then I caught on to what he meant by 'if I think I can make it.'

"I turned around and came up those steps after him. He went for me and I went for him. We grabbed one another and started in.

"I mean, we fought from one end of that hotel to the other, and finally we fell in through the door of the Capitol Records hospitality suite and started knocking over the displays.

"There was this guy in a bowtie standin' there, and I heard him draw himself up and say, 'This sort of thing would never happen in the Mercury Suite.'"

"What happened to th' one you was fightin', Jerry Lee?" asked the Kid. "Did you finally whup him?"

"I had to. He started pullin' my hair."

The show had been going on for over four hours, the rain was still coming down, and it was getting colder.

"This is flu weather," said Jerry Lee. "I've only had the flu once in my life. I caught it from Stonewall Jackson. I know that's where I got it. He had it an' was drinkin' outta my bottle."

Jerry Lee's band was going to accompany Charlie Rich, and they left to set up the stage.

"Don't forget to move the piano around so's they can all see Jerry Lee," called Cecil Harrelson as they left.

The half-gallon bottle of Calvert Extra was empty.

Jerry Lee, who had had about three good shots of it, was relaxed but bright-eyed, alive, eager.

It was time for him to put on his costume but his dressing room was too crowded with strangers for him to do it there.

He took off his shirt.

"That's a cashmere shirt," he said. "I don't wear nothin' but cashmere. Cashmere socks, pants, underwear. No, I'm just kiddin' about th' underwear.

"On the road, I buy a pair of Fruit of the Loom shorts in th' mornin' and throw 'em away at night."

He stepped out in the hall with no shirt on and did a little dance step, down to a big room where basketball teams dress out, and put on his garb there.

I went out to the side of the stage and waited.

Charlie Rich was on, sitting at a grand piano, which had had the lid removed, backed by Jerry Lee's five-piece band, and was singing one of his own songs:

"... after you're through with me, who will the next fool be?"

Charlie Rich finished his regular act, did two encores, and left the stage.

Jerry Lee Lewis was next.

It was now early Sunday morning, almost one o'clock, and there were still over six thousand people who had waited through it all to see him.

Dick West introduced him, and amid screams, cheers, and applause, Jerry

Lee Lewis walked onstage, wearing a mocha-colored leather suit, a yellow silk neckerchief, and yellow cowboy boots.

He sat down at the piano and started in.

Between songs, he threw in a little funny chatter, never much more than one sentence, but it was always just the right thing, done with perfect timing, perfect delivery, something he has developed performing before live audiences night after night for over twenty years.

Dick West appeared at my side in the darkness.

"How about that suit?" he asked. "All leather. Myra and me, we got it for him for Christmas. Picked it right off the rack at Izzy Rosen's and it fit perfect everywhere except the waist. We had to have it took up by a shoemaker."

Jerry Lee was doing all his famous songs, leering at the audience, exchanging a little blue banter with them, playing the piano with his foot.

He stood up, took off his coat, his neckerchief, wiped his brow, fanned the waistband of his leather pants to let a little cool air in, ran his comb through his hair, then picked up a huge guitar and accompanied his brother-in-law Ken Lovelace, who played an intricate solo on the electrically amplified fiddle.

Then Jerry Lee went back to the piano and sang a song that belongs to him, to Jerry Lee Lewis, like "Your Cheatin' Heart" belongs to Hank Williams, like "Louise" belongs to Chevalier, like "Falling in Love Again" belongs to Dietrich.

It was "One Has My Name, the Other Has My Heart," a song that can bring out the crying drunk in any man.

Jerry Lee finished that one, then took fire for the finale. Lewis doing his straight act was amazing enough. Lewis when he went into the big wind-up was unbelievable.

Jerry Lee suddenly stopped playing the piano, jumped up, knocked over the piano bench with the back of his legs, and stood there, his body quivering, in the throes of a cataleptic seizure.

The band got loud, louder, louder still, as Lewis struggled to break out of the spell. It reached a crescendo, and he burst free and screamed, went wild, attacked the piano, pounding, leaping, sensually thrusting and twisting his body.

He became Power, crazy raw Power.

He grabbed the hand mike and leapt up on the piano, stepping on the keyboard. Then, balancing himself on the thin wall of the sounding box, he sang, yelled, roared.

I watched, hypnotized, thrilled, delighted, but afraid, too, afraid something would go wrong and he would get loose among the audience.

The frenzy became unbearable and then, suddenly, too soon, it was over.

Jerry Lee picked up his coat, threw it over his shoulder, and left the stage.

He did not come back for an encore. He could not.

It is impossible to follow Jerry Lee Lewis, even for Jerry Lee Lewis.

The crowd started leaving.

Backstage, the fans, the faithful, were gone. The hall was empty.

Two old stagehands hurried toward the front.

"We'd better see what he done to that piano," said one.

Jerry Lee was in his dressing room and had changed back into his denims and black shirt.

Rita Gillespie was there, and the Kid, who was handing Jerry Lee pieces of paper to autograph.

"Make that one 'To Sarah Ann, with Love' and the others 'To Orma Jean, with Love' and 'To Momma and Daddy, with Love.'"

Jerry Lee was writing, in a daze.

He looked barely alive.

"Don't Jerry Lee get give out singing!" stated the Kid.

"You're the greatest entertainer I have ever seen," I said to Jerry Lee.

"Aw, I don't know about that," he said, shaking my hand.

Jerry Lee said goodbye to Rita and the Kid and hurried outside to the big limousine, where Cecil Harrelson and Dick West were waiting.

They had a long drive ahead of them.

It was Sunday morning, and they were due that night in Muskogee.

Southern Rock

The Allman Brothers

THE ONLY PLACE THEY REALLY FELT AT HOME WAS
MAMA LOUISE HUDSON'S SOUL-FOOD RESTAURANT
by John T. Edge

▬▬

In April 1969, a scraggly bunch of hippies made their way north from Jacksonville, Florida, to the Central Georgia town of Macon, a quiet citadel of red-brick churches, fading antebellum mansions, and row after row of mill houses. The hippies came at the behest of music promoter Phil Walden, who had made a name for himself—and for Macon—managing black soul artists like Otis Redding. Still reeling from the death of Redding a little more than a year before, Walden was in search of the next big thing. And he wanted this band in his town, under his watchful eye, far out of harm's way. "When they come to Macon," Walden told a reporter, "all they can do is eat fried chicken and make good music."

By the time the Allman Brothers Band hit town, the Summer of Love was already two years past. Martin Luther King, Jr., and Bobby Kennedy were dead. Watts was in ashes. Nixon was in the White House. The Chicago Seven were indicted. And yet Macon was still asleep.

"The revolution came late to Macon," says Newton Collier, who once played horns for Redding's band. "It took the Allman Brothers coming to town to shake things up." The interracial troupe of six was a sight to see on the streets of town: hair cascading down their backs or mushrooming skyward; faces obscured by bushy muttonchops and droopy mustaches; love beads and bear claws around their necks; bell-bottom jeans riding low on their hips.

"Nobody in Macon had long hair then," the Allman Brothers roadie Red Dog Campbell recalls. "When we moved into a house down on College Street, all of us would be sitting out on the porch, and traffic would line up both ways just so people could take a look at the hippies. People would be jerking their heads all around, breaking their necks just to look at us, yelling things at us. We had to look out after each other. Back then, if you saw one of us, you saw three or four. . . .

"One of the only places we really felt at home was down at Mama Louise's little restaurant. At the H&H, they didn't care if we were white or black or purple. Mama didn't say anything if we were trippin' our asses off. Now, she might tell me to come in the back door instead of the front when I was messed up, but really she just fed us fried chicken and loved us."

The late '60s was, of course, a heady time to be a rock & roller. Free love. Communal living. Cheap dope. A feeling of camaraderie that came with being part of the counterculture. But for all their swagger and bravado, for all the talk of drugs ingested and women seduced, the boys in the band were just that: boys, overgrown teenagers far from home, far from their mamas, set loose in a strange town. Of the original six, none were natives. Duane Allman and his younger brother, Gregg, were born in Tennessee; Dickey Betts and Butch Trucks in Florida; Jaimoe Johnson in Mississippi; and Berry Oakley in Illinois.

For the most part, the band stuck close to their self-styled "Hippie Crash Pad" that summer. Just a short walk down the street was Rose Hill Cemetery, a rambling antebellum graveyard of Italianate terraces dotted with marble statuary, carved into the bluffs of the Ocmulgee River. The cemetery proved to be a sanctuary for the band, a place to gather in the early morning hours and drink Ripple, smoke pot, maybe play a little acoustic guitar. Here, in the moonlit shadows of listing tombstones and spreading magnolias, the band composed the blues-rock songs that would make them famous. And before three years passed, Duane Allman and Berry Oakley would be interred here, side by side, each the victim of a motorcycle crash. In the years that followed, the time spent at Rose Hill would take on an eerie significance.

A few blocks in the opposite direction, in the midst of the black business district, was the headquarters of Phil Walden's Capricorn Records. One block west, on Forsyth Street, was the H&H. "It was the place to go for soul food in Macon," recalls Walden. "It was, how should I say this, economical. And when I brought the band to town, that was the place they were sent when they were hungry."

The H, as regulars called it, wasn't much to look at. "Back then it was in an old gas station," Campbell tells me. "The front room was something like a radiator shop. In the back Mama had set up a couple of tables and a counter with four or five stools. There was a big old floor fan to cool things off and a jukebox full of Clarence Carter and Wilson Pickett songs. That was about it, but man, it was a beautiful place to be, just beautiful."

Mama Louise did more than feed and nurture a ragtag group of musicians, says the keyboard player Chuck Leavell. "She felt the spirit of the time. Blacks and whites were working together, playing music together. It was almost like a religion. And Louise's cooking was a sort of soul-food sacrament."

Years before, while still living in Daytona Beach, Florida, Gregg Allman had made visits to a similar restaurant part of his pre-performance ritual.

"It was just what you'd expect, an aqua green, one-story building with red, white, and blue signs in the windows, with a screen door that wouldn't quite shut and a big fan on the ceiling," former bandmate Tommy Tucker told a reporter back in 1973. "We'd always order about six or eight barbecue sandwiches. Gregg thought that eating this soul food would give his voice an extra edge. It was sort of like a superstition with him. If he didn't eat soul food, he wouldn't have himself together that night."

This spring I went back to Macon in search of the ghosts of the Allman Brothers and the scents of Mama Louise's good home cooking. I was on familiar ground. I had attended grammar school a couple of blocks from the College Street flophouse that the band first called home. I remember standing on the playground, my fingers hooked in a chain-link fence, watching the parade of hippies that always seemed to be shuffling by. I remember the motorcycles that roared by late in the afternoon, trailing a plume of patchouli and petroleum.

In the company of my father, I ate my youthful fill of meatloaf and fried okra, ropy collard greens and candied yams at the newer H&H, the one on the ground floor of a squat bunker of a building, just across the street from the original location. The upstairs was home to the local bricklayers' union; next door was a beauty shop. In my mind's eye, I can see Mama Louise bustling about the orange and yellow dining room, her soft, brown face framed by a puff of coarse, black hair. I remember the sadness in her eyes, that devilish sidelong smile she flashed when you said something that tickled her. I remember the incessant boom of the jukebox, the rattle of the speakers as the first few chords of my favorite Allman Brothers song, "Statesboro Blues," filled the room. To this day, the bright taste of her sweet potato pie dances on the tip of my tongue.

I found her where I left her: at the stove, an oversized, misshapen serving spoon in one hand, a thick china platter in the other. "You want gravy on that rice, honey?" she asks a stoop-shouldered man perched at the counter.

"Yeah, Mama, gravy, a whole bunch of it," comes the reply. She drenches the rice, hands the plate over to a waitress, and turns to dish up the next order.

Mama Louise Hudson was nearly forty when she met Gregg and the rest of the band. Born in Youngstown, Ohio, she moved south with her parents to Warrenton, Georgia, when she was just six weeks old. Her father farmed on shares, picking cotton when the crop came in, doing odd jobs during lay-by time. By the age of ten, Mama Louise was cooking for the family, her bare feet planted on a wooden peach crate so that she could reach the fire, stirring pots of black-eyed peas and butter beans, baking skillets of coarse, white cornbread and tins of gooey pecan pie. Life was hard. Choices were few. She was married by the age of twenty and separated soon after.

In 1952, she set out for Macon with Lucy, the first of her four children. "My job was waiting tables and cooking down on Broadway for a man named McClinton," Mama Louise tells me, seated for a moment at one of the tables that dot the linoleum-floored room. "He had a place called Good Eats Café. It was a soul-food spot same as mine now." By 1959, she moved up the street to the B&L Snack Shop, where she further honed her skills.

In 1968, Mama Louise Hudson and her first cousin, Inez Hill, opened the café that still bears their initials. "Those were crazy times," she says. "That was back during the time when they were trying to integrate. There were all these long-haired boys hanging out down at Phil Walden's place. Some people wanted to make a fuss about it. I didn't pay much attention until one afternoon a whole bunch of them came in together. They acted like they were afraid or something. Two of them—it was Berry and Dickey—finally came up to the counter. Dickey told him, said, 'Ask the lady for something to eat.' Berry looked at him like he was crazy, and they went back outside. I was watching them, trying to see what they were up to. After a while they built up their nerve and came on back in. They asked me, 'Lady, you don't know us, but would you fix us two plates? When we get back off tour, we'll pay you.'"

At this point in the story, Mama Louise looks up at me, then drops her head low, almost to the tabletop. "Those boys were hungry," she says, shaking her head slowly. "Wasn't nothing bad about them. But all I did was come out with those two plates they were asking for. I felt like I was doing something wrong, but that's what I did. A couple of weeks later, they come back in, asking could they have something to eat. I told them yes, but it won't be no two plates and six forks this time. All y'all is eating."

The Allman Brothers struggled that first summer. "Money was real tight then," Gregg told me. "We had about three dollars a day for food, beer, everything. By the time we had some cold drinks, well, you could just about forget it. We were all skinny back then, real skinny. I guess if it hadn't been for Mama Louise, we might never have made it. Back then, a plate cost $1.25, and I'd dare you to finish it. She never asked us to pay when we didn't have the money, just put it on our tab, and kept putting it on our tab, and kept putting it on our tab. She called us her boys, and we called her Mama. I'll love her till the day I die."

In time, the band repaid its debt. By late 1971, their new album was ascending the charts, and their shows were selling out larger and larger halls. Mama Louise soon became a Sunday night fixture at the band's new quarters, a Tudor-style mansion north of downtown known as the Big House. Some nights she cooked; other nights it was Big Linda, Berry Oakley's wife. When Dickey Betts married Sandy Bluesky in a ceremony that included, among other rites, the sacrifice of a wild duck, Mama Louise was there, too.

And when the band headed to California on a leg of its summer 1972 tour, she boarded the plane with her boys. The initial plan was for her to cook at a Los Angeles press party, but she was having too much fun to think of work. "I just went around with the band," Mama Louise told a reporter back in August of that year. "We didn't do much sightseeing. We mostly just loafed around the hotel and went to the pool and the lounge. . . . I love the Allman Brothers' music and that sweet voice Gregg has behind it. Every album they make, they give it to me."

On the cover of their second album, *Idlewild South*, the band included her in the credits: "Vittles: Louise."

Today, Mama Louise Hudson's little restaurant is claimed as hallowed ground by the Allman faithful. The walls are covered with photos of the band: Duane on a lake bank, fishing pole in hand; Gregg and Duane, asleep on a tour bus; Dickey and Mama Louise, arm in arm. There's even a stained glass mushroom—a nod to the band's drug of choice—hanging in the front window. And though band member sightings are rarer these days, she still keeps in touch with her boys. "Now when they come by, they bring their families," says Hudson. "When they do, we just close down the restaurant and have a big party." In the pantheon of Allman Brothers Band belief, Mama Louise is now revered as a sort of saint, a kindhearted caretaker of wayward hippie souls.

On my way out of town, I stop off for one last meal: baked ham, creamed corn, rice and gravy, and snap beans. As I work to sop the last of the gravy from my plate, I fall into conversation with a man in an Allman Brothers T-shirt. He is quiet, almost reverential, a fellow traveler. When I ask him how he came to eat at the H&H, he begins reciting the very story Mama Louise told me just the day before. The only thing is, he embellishes the tale just a bit. The way he tells the story, Jesus fed the multitudes with a few loaves of barley bread and a string of fish. And Mama Louise fed the Allmans with a wing and a leg and a mess of greens.

Lynyrd Skynyrd

SONG OF THE SOUTH by Diane Roberts

After two notes, after one second, I know it. You'd know it, too—everybody would: It's everywhere every day on "classic rock" and oldies stations, it's a near-the-top selection on jukeboxes in bars called Ray's or the Cotton Patch, and it's played to ignite the soggy, waning hours of keg parties from the Blue Ridge Mountains to Lake Okeechobee. The chords chime, then somebody (Ronnie?) says, "Turn it up," and you do turn it up, unless you turn it off. You have one of two reactions: fight or flight. Whoop and dance like you ain't had no raisin', or retreat, embarrassed, hitting the scan button on the radio or scuttling to the ladies' room till it's all over.

"Sweet Home Alabama" has been following me around ("where the skies are so blue/and the governor's true"). Maybe it's because I'm not in Alabama this summer. Maybe it's some kind of karmic torture plotted by FM station managers all over the world. Or else it's a psychological projection, like the ghost in *Hamlet*, a memento mori ("Lord, I'm coming home to you"). I rarely hear the song on any of the Birmingham stations or in Tuscaloosa, except blasting out of the Kappa Alpha house after football games or played ironically at graduate-student parties, where the alert, young intellectuals, amazed that they are actually sleeping and eating in Alabama in the first place, dance to the flailing chords before deconstructing the words. And in Central Florida, a place that doesn't know if it's culturally part of the South or the North or, even worse, the Midwest, the song is ubiquitous, beating out for sheer volume the other revived rock-out fiestas of the '70s: "Walk This Way," "Stairway to Heaven," and even "Free Bird."

Of course, the perpetrators of "Sweet Home" came from Florida. Lynyrd Skynyrd was a garage band of psychedelic rednecks from the bad side of Jacksonville—not that Jacksonville, a nasty, race-riven port city, really *had* a good side. Ronnie Van Zant and his friends Gary Rossington, Allen Collins, Billy Powell, Leon Wilkeson, and Bob Burns all grew up in one of Jacksonville's working-class white barrios, playing music, courting trouble with the cops, and getting kicked out of school. The name of the band, said Van Zant, came from one Leonard Skinner, a high-school gym teacher who'd sent the boys to the principal's office for committing the crime of having long hair.

And Skynyrd had the kind of long hair that should have been against the law. Whereas the rock-boy hair of 1974 looked sexily androgynous on Mick Jagger, sexily intellectual on John Lennon, sexily rabbinical on Bob Dylan, or just plain sexy on Jim Morrison, Van Zant and the rest looked, well, trashy. The year 1974 was about the time that Southern white boys, having previously expended a lot of energy whupping on hippies, began to steal their 'dos. I'm not going on about Skynyrd's hair just to be cruel: The hair was an outer manifestation of their Rebel cap–cherishing, gun-fascinated inner selves, part of the "Sweet Home" aesthetic. Long hair on the likes of Lynyrd Skynyrd did not signify sympathy for the dead of Kent State or solidarity with the Chicago demonstrators or common cause with the freaky people of the Summer of Love. Lynyrd Skynyrd was anti-Establishment, but the Establishment they rebelled against were the liberal, earnest, righteous, Civil Rights–promoting, anti-war middle classes, the hippie aristocrats as personified by Neil Young.

As y'all know, "Sweet Home Alabama" was a response to Young's songs "Alabama" and the magisterial "Southern Man," in which Young wails against the "screamin' and bullwhip cracking" caused by Southern man.

Here was this art-rock poet, this bleeding-heart super-grouper, the author of the anti-Nixon "Ohio," the baroque "Cinnamon Girl," the mushy "Judy Blue Eyes," this outside agitator, this Canadian dissing the Motherland, insulting the Honor of the South. It was not to be borne. So Van Zant sneered:

Well, I hope Neil Young will remember
A Southern man don't need him around, anyhow

It was the Top 40 equivalent of a couple of guys, at least one of whom had had too much Jack Daniel's, shoving each other in a bar.

I was fourteen or fifteen when "Sweet Home Alabama" came out. I hated it immediately, and so did all my ninth-grade philosopher friends. Immured in an integrated (in terms of race, if not class) Tallahassee school, we would talk back to the song when it jangled out of our radios.

Lynyrd Skynyrd would go on to offend us with "Gimme Back My Bullets,"

"What's Your Name?," "Saturday Night Special," and the dreadful "Free Bird," that endless caterwaul of a tribute to Duane Allman (who had gotten himself killed in a motorcycle accident in 1971), but at the time nothing could be as bad as "Sweet Home." The fans who put it in the Top 10 had to be Confederate battle flag–waving high-school dropouts with SURRENDER, HELL! bumper stickers on their Chevy trucks, George Wallace supporters, philistines incapable of understanding the occult subtleties of "Jeepster" or "The End." The only antidote was repeated playing of Young's "Southern Man," with its evocation of lynchings, burning crosses, miscegenation, slavery: all the stuff we white Southerners knew we were guilty as sin of, all the stuff that made us wish we'd been old enough to march with King, or at least get beaten up in Chicago.

And yet—and yet. I've been in bars in New York and Tampa and once even London, and if "Sweet Home" starts playing, something strange happens. Certain people kind of look at one another and smile, moving their feet and shoulders just a little. You try to get a grip, recall that you hate this song, loathe its jingoism, its smugness, its willful white-boy ignorance—but those three guitars! Wanting, even subconsciously, to dance to "Sweet Home" is like feeling the urge to stand up when "Dixie" is played: recidivist, reactionary.

And yet—and yet. The people whose eyes you meet in the bar turn out to be from Macon or Mobile, Sunflower County or the Carolina Upcountry, and the song—the indefensible but nonetheless infectious, febrile anthem—drags us into a Southern solidarity that we are all thoroughly ashamed of but exhilarated by. And you just can't (go on, try), *can't* dance to "Southern Man."

Lynyrd Skynyrd

CAN YOU FIND SALVATION IN THE LATE-NIGHT MUSIC OF
A ROADHOUSE COVER BAND? (a short story) by Ron Rash

So it's somewhere between Saturday night and Sunday morning clock-wise, and I'm in a cinderblock roadhouse called The Last Chance, and I'm playing "Free Bird" for the fifth time tonight, but I'm thinking not of Ronnie Van Zant but of an artist dredged up from my former life, Willie Yeats, and his line "surely some revelation is at hand." The only rough beast slouching toward me, however, is my rhythm guitar player, Sammy Griffen, who is down on all fours, weaving through the maze of tables between bathroom and stage.

One of the sins of the 1960s was it introduced the redneck element of Southern society to drugs. If you were some Harvard professor like Timothy Leary, drugs might well expand your consciousness, but they worked just the opposite way for people like Sammy, shriveling the brain to a reptilian level of aggression and paranoia.

There is no telling what Sammy has snorted or swallowed in the bathroom, but his irises have expanded to the size of quarters. He passes a table and sees a bare leg, a female leg, and grabs hold. He pulls off an attached high heel and starts licking the foot. It takes about three seconds for a bigger foot, with a steel-capped toe, to swing into the back of Sammy's head like a football player kicking an extra point. Sammy curls up in a fetal position and passes out among the peanut shells and cigarette butts.

So now it's just Bobo the bass player, Hal Deaton the drummer, and me. I finish "Free Bird" so that means the next songs are my choice. "They got to have 'Free Bird' at least once an hour," Rodney said when he hired us, saying it like his clientele were diabetics needing insulin. "The rest of the time play what you want."

I turn to Bobo and Hal and play the opening chords of Gary Stewart's "Roarin'," and they fall in. Stewart's music was too intense and pure for Nashville, though they tried their best to pith his brain with cocaine, put a cowboy hat on his head, and make him into another talentless hack like Garth Brooks. Stewart ended his days hunkered down in Florida, for a while living in a trailer with the windows painted black, surviving on whatever songwriting residuals dribbled in from Nashville.

Such a lifestyle has its appeals, especially tonight as I look out at the human wreckage filling the tables of The Last Chance. One guy has his head on the table, eyes closed, vomit drooling from his mouth. Another has pulled out his false teeth. He reaches out and clamps them on the ear of the woman at an adjoining table. An immense female in a purple jumpsuit is crying while another female screams at her. And what I'm thinking is maybe it's time to halt all human reproduction. Let God or evolution or whatever put us here in the first place start again from scratch because this isn't working.

I too live in a trailer, but I have to leave it more often than I wish because I am not a genius, just a forty-year-old ex-high-school English teacher who has to make money in the present tense, and more money than I get from a twenty-hour-a-week day job proofing copy for the weekly newspaper. Which is why I'm here from seven to two, four nights a week, getting it done in the name of Lynyrd Skynyrd, alimony, and keeping the repo man away from my truck.

I will not bore you with the details of lost teaching jobs, lost wife and child. Let me just acknowledge that "mistakes were made," as the politicos say. The last principal I worked for made sure I can't get a teaching job anywhere north of the Amazon rain forest. My wife and kid are in California. All I am is a check that arrives the first of each month. Every time I call and try to speak to my kid, I get a message that says, "We'll return your call as soon as possible." "Soon as possible" evidently meaning never.

Beyond the tables of human wreckage, I see Hubert McClain sitting at the bar, beer in one hand and Louisville Slugger in the other. Hubert is our bouncer, two hundred and fifty pounds of atavistic Celtic violence coiled and ready to happen. On the front of the ballcap covering his survivalist buzz cut, a leering skeleton waves a sickle in one hand and a Confederate flag in the other. The symbolism is unclear, except that anyone wearing such a cap, especially while gripping a forty-six-ounce ball bat, is not someone you want to displease.

Sitting beside Hubert is Joe Don Byers, formerly Yusef Byers before he had his first name legally changed. While it seems every white male between fourteen and twenty-five is trying to look and act black, Joe Don is going the opposite way, a twenty-three-year-old black man trying to be not just white, but tobacco-spewing, country-music-listening white. But like the white kids with their ballcaps turned sideways and pants hanging halfway down their asses, Joe Don can't quite pull it off. The hubcap-sized belt buckle and snakeskin boots pass muster, but he wears his cowboy hat low over his right eye, the brim's rakish tilt making him look more like a cross-dressing pimp than John Wayne. His truck is another giveaway, a petty blue Toyota two-wheel-drive with four mud grips and a DALE EARNHARDT sticker on the back window—he's unaware that any true Earnhardt fan would rather pull a George Jones and ride a lawnmower than drive anything other than a Chevy.

Nevertheless, Joe Don is liked. Movies and other media have made it very clear to the clientele of The Last Chance that the most wretched human being in Rwanda or Bosnia would not want to be them. How can they not be grateful to Joe Don that at least one person out of five billion thinks they're worth emulating?

On the opposite side of the bar, the money side, Rodney is taking whatever people hand him—crumpled bills, handfuls of nickels and dimes, payroll checks, wedding rings, wristwatches. One time a guy offered a gold filling he'd dug out of his mouth with a pocketknife. Rodney took it and didn't even blink.

Watching him operate behind the bar, it's easy to believe Rodney is simply an updated version of Flem Snopes, the kind of guy whose first successful business venture was showing Polaroids of his naked sister to his junior-high peers. But that's not the case at all. Rodney graduated from the University of South Carolina with a degree in social work. He wanted to make the world better, but according to Rodney, the world wasn't interested.

Rodney's career as a social worker ended the same week it began. He had borrowed a local church bus to take some of Columbia's disadvantaged teenagers to a Braves game. Halfway to Atlanta the teenagers mutinied. They beat him with a tire iron, took his money and clothes, and left him naked and bleeding in a ditch. A week later, the same day Rodney got out of the hospital, the bus was found half-submerged in the Okefenokee Swamp. It took another month to round up the youths, several of whom had procured entry-level positions in a Miami drug cartel.

Rodney says that running The Last Chance is a philosophical statement. Above the cash register he's plastered one of those Darwinian bumper stickers with the fish outline and four evolving legs. Rodney's drawn a speech bubble in front of the fish's mouth. "Exterminate the brutes," the fish says. Advice Rodney seems to have taken to heart: The only mixed drink at The Last Chance, what Rodney calls "The Terminator," combines six ounces of Jack Daniel's, six ounces of Surry County moonshine, and six ounces of Sam's Choice tomato juice. Some customers claim a dash of lighter fluid is added for good measure. Not even Hubert has drunk more than three of these and remained standing. It usually takes only two to put the drinkers onto the floor, tomato juice dribbling down the chin like they've been shot in the mouth.

When we finish "Roarin'," only three or four people clap. None of them know the song or, for that matter, who Gary Stewart is. Radio and music television have anesthetized them to the degree that they can't recognize the real thing even when it comes out of their own gene pool.

And speaking of gene pools, I suddenly see Everette Evans, the man that, to my immense regret, is twenty-five percent of the genetic makeup of my son. He's standing in the doorway, a camcorder covering the right side of his face. The machine's making a sweep across the room like a Geiger counter. Everette lingers on Hubert a few seconds, then the various casualties of the evening before homing in on me.

I lay down the guitar and make my way toward the entrance, Everette still filming until I'm almost right on him. He jerks the camera down to waist level and points it at me like it's an Uzi.

"What are you up to, Everette?" I ask.

He grins at me, though it's one of those grins that's two parts malice and one part nervous, like a politician being asked to explain a hundred thousand dollars in small bills he's recently deposited in the bank.

"Donna got that letter from your lawyer, and we're just here getting some additional evidence as to your parental fitness."

"I don't see no 'we,'" I say. "Just one old meddling fool who, if he still had an ass, should have it kicked."

"Don't you be threatening me, Devon," Everette says. "I might just start this camcorder up again and get us some more incriminating evidence."

"And I just might take that camcorder and perform a colonoscopy on you with it. Donna doesn't seem to have a problem spending the money I make here."

"What's the problem, Devon?" Hubert asks, walking over from the bar.

"This man's filming The Last Chance so he can keep me from seeing my own son."

"We don't allow no filming of our shows," Hubert says, taking the camcorder out of Everette's hands. He jerks out the tape and douses it with the half-drunk Terminator he's been sipping. Hubert strikes a match and drops the tape on the floor. In five seconds the tape looks like black Jell-O.

Everette starts to crawfish back out the door.

"You ain't heard the last of this," he says. "You'll be collecting Social Security before you see that young'n of yours."

Rodney lifts a bullhorn from under the bar and announces it's 1:45 and anybody who wants a last drink had better get it now. There are few takers, most customers now lacking money or consciousness. The more responsible are trying to sober up before driving away.

I'm thinking to finish up with Steve Earle's "The Graveyard Shift" and Dwight Yoakam's "A Thousand Miles From Nowhere," but the drunk who's been using a pool of vomit for a pillow the last hour lifts his head. He fumbles a lighter out of his pocket and flicks it on.

"'Free Bird,'" he grunts, and lays his head back in the vomit.

And I'm thinking, why not? Ronnie Van Zant didn't have the talent of Gary Stewart or Steve Earle or Dwight Yoakam, but he did what he could with what he had. Skynyrd never pruned their Southern musical roots to give them "national appeal," and that gave their music, whatever else its failings, an honesty and an edge.

So I take out my slide from my jean pocket and start that long wailing solo for probably the millionth time in my life. I'm on automatic pilot, letting my fingers take care of business while my mind roams elsewhere.

Heads rise from tables and stare my way. Conversations stop. Couples arguing or groping each other stop. And this is the way it always is, as though Van Zant somehow found a conduit into the collective unconsciousness of his race. Whatever it is, they become serious and reflective, somehow more human. Maybe it's just the music's slow, surging build toward a rush that hits their synapses like a jolt of electricity, the same kind of thing that makes a dead frog twitch its legs. Or maybe something more—a yearning for the kind of freedom Van Zant's lyrics deal with, a need to lay their burdens down.

I see Rodney lowering the metal screen at the front of the bar. Rodney claims we live in a time when the traditional family structure has evolved into a "more subjective" way of being. He claims we are all family now.

As I finish "Free Bird," Rodney cuts on every light in the building, including some high-beam John Deere tractor lights he's rigged on the ceiling. It's like the last scene in a vampire movie. People start screaming and cursing. They cover their eyes, crawl under tables, and ultimately—and this is the goal—scurry toward the door and out into the dark, dragging the unconscious with them.

I'm off the clock now, but I don't unplug the amp. Instead, I play the opening chords to Elvis Costello's "Waiting for the End of the World." Lately, Costello has tried to be the second coming of Perry Como, but his first two albums were a kick-ass fusion of rage, cynicism, and longing. Those first nights after Donna left, I'd listened to Costello, and it had almost helped.

Hal is draped over his drumkit, passed out, and Bobo is headed to the door with the big woman in the purple jumpsuit. Sammy's still on the floor, so I'm flying solo.

I can't remember all the lyrics, so except for the refrain most of the lyrics make no sense, like I'm speaking in tongues or something, but it's 2 A.M. in Pickens, South Carolina, and not much of anything makes sense. All you can do is pick up your guitar and play. Which is what I'm doing. I'm laying down some mean guitar licks, I'm not much of a singer, but I'm giving all I got, and although The Last Chance is almost completely empty now, that's okay as well, because I'm merging the primal and existential, and I've cranked up the volume so loud that empty beer bottles are vibrating off tables, and the tractor beams are swaying like strobe lights, and whatever rough beast is asleep out there in the dark is getting its wake-up call to come lurching towards me, because I'm ready and waiting for whatever it's got.

Southern Heavy Metal

Southern Heavy Metal

AN ODE by Bret Anthony Johnston

━━━━━

If you grew up in Texas in the '80s and didn't wear a black Pantera concert jersey, you likely got your ass kicked by someone who did. (Or, like me, you wore the shirt and still got your ass kicked, but whatever.) In Louisiana, the requisite jersey was from the band Crowbar. North Carolina? Corrosion of Conformity.

These bands constitute the holy trinity of Southern Heavy Metal, but maybe you've never heard of them. Or maybe you've heard of them, but haven't *heard* them because you prefer blues jams to mosh pits and those black jerseys kind of terrify you, and generally lead you to believe the songs are about the devil and drugs and murder and other existential mayhem, and you've decided not to waste your time listening. Which decision should possibly be reconsidered, because after all, what was Robert Johnson singing about?

Here's the thing: Southern Heavy Metal *is* the blues. These musicians are our new bluesmen, and their patently subversive songs, with their essential themes of religion, sex, violence, and (headbangers, forgive me) hope, are the contemporary gutbucket blues. If blues music originally evolved from call-and-response field hollers, then Southern Heavy Metal is simply a louder call, a more deliberate and authoritative response, a holler that's impossible to ignore.

No surprise, then, that some of the hardest, most important metal hails from the South. Unlike the West Coast's overproduced fashion rock and the punky, vampire-obsessed theatrics that come from the East—both schools seem calibrated more for music videos than music—Southern metal has consistently offered a barrage of harshly distorted, raw musical fury. Poison was pretty; Twisted Sister pantomimed menace with rouge and lipstick; Pantera was ugly and plain-old pissed. Go to a Crowbar or C.O.C. show (only posers call them Corrosion of Conformity) and you'll find no dry-ice smoke, no drum kits rigged to pink strobe lights, no singers with teased, shellacked bangs, no guitarists in Jackson-Pollocked spandex. You'll find men who look like they've just been released from (or are being delivered to) Angola. In addition to sleeves of tattoos, Phil Anselmo, Pantera's vocalist, has the word "unscarred" inked in gothic letters across his abdomen. Whether this is meant to be ironic remains unclear. Either way, it's gnarly.

Which gnarliness returns us to why many have never heard of or heard these bands: This isn't your soccer mom's metal. Albums like Pantera's *Vulgar Display of Power,* Crowbar's *Obedience Thru Suffering,* and C.O.C.'s *Animosity* are not, thematically or musically, what one would call listener-friendly. The vocals are often abrasive and/or indecipherable, and the music so fast and complex and *loud* that the listener (black jersey notwithstanding) feels assaulted. But this is precisely the point. Whereas more marketable bands so conspicuously court your fanship (read: money) with sanitized pyrotechnics and saccharine power ballads and catchy, hummable melodies, the gods of Southern Heavy Metal *dare* you to listen, if you can take it; they urge you, as Anselmo says in "Walk," to "walk on home, boy." This is music of initiation, and most listeners don't have the stones for it. There's a reason more people drink wine coolers than Kentucky moonshine.

Once you've tasted the hard stuff, however, the bubbly goes down a little too smoothly and that vapid sweetness turns your stomach. For all of their bravado and overt aggression, there's a refreshing ballast to these bands, an unvarnished formidability that strikes the ear as distinctly Southern. This is hard to explain, but easy to recognize. It comes down to an anomalous and wholly unexpected intimacy that is forged between musicians and listeners, a deep and surprising kinship born from a sort of collective struggle. Try listening to songs like Pantera's "I'm Broken," C.O.C.'s "Albatross," even Crowbar's cover of Zeppelin's "No Quarter" *without* identifying with them, *without* recalling your own shortcomings and trespasses. Try listening to the brutally prescient "Stone the Crow" by Down (the group amounts to a Southern Heavy Metal dream team, a side project born from the aforementioned bands), and not relating it to post-Katrina New Orleans. Although the song was recorded a decade before the levees failed, the lyrics and music are as mournful and livid and inspiring as anything written since then:

> Flip through endless stories
> A life of a hand-written pain
> No one to share this hurt that is mine, mine, mine
> I never died before
> Can't be what happened yesterday. . . .
> Same old city, same old tale.

Such substance and timelessness is absent in most heavy metal, and in most music, so when you hear it, the sound is as unmistakable as a friend calling your name across a field—or screaming it. You want to dance and sing and throw your-self into a tempest of people who feel the same, who carry the same flag. Look, not to sound like a hippie—or a Yankee—but there's an oft-overlooked soulfulness to this kind of music, and a rare and undeniable and empathetic urgency, a sense that what you're hearing has come from years of regret and labor and pain and doubt and pride and loss. And what, in the past or present, is more deserving of song—or more Southern—than loss?

Blues:

Dept. of R.L.

Burnside

Authenticity Be Damned!

A DIRTY BLUES ALCHEMY THAT IS CORRUPT AND ALIVE
by Will Blythe

▬▬▬

Isn't one of the horrible secrets of the blues how boring they can sometimes be? Consider the great Eric Clapton, who can cop a Freddie King lick better than anyone, but whose blues tribute albums feel too precise and mannerly and ultimately vitiated—like repertory, for God's sake. They make you wish he'd left the key to the highway back under the mat at home. They lack the anguished soul of his magisterial *Layla and Other Assorted Love Songs*. And Clapton loves the blues like no other, yessir. But maybe you can love something so much that you kill it with reverence. Maybe then it stops loving you back.

There's no question, though, that the blues still loves R.L. Burnside, the seventy-six-year-old Mississippian, and that's probably because the records he makes these days don't kiss its hoary ass. Through some miracle of dirty alchemy, his blues jukes right past issues of authenticity and purity that bedevil the devil's music, or at least its fans. Anxious to maintain their special connection to the music, many blues buffs want it to stay the same forever, like lovers in the first onslaught of romance want their beloveds to never change.

Born on November 23, 1926, R.L. Burnside grew up on a plantation near Oxford, Mississippi, where his family members were sharecroppers. He first tried to play harmonica, but as he says, "I never could get that to work." As is frequently the case with his generation of Mississippi musicians, Burnside serendipitously enjoyed the most casual of connections to the blues gods—as if Mount Olympus stood just outside his screen door. In his late teens, he learned guitar from the magnificent Fred McDowell, who lived no more than a mile or two from Burnside's family. Often, after taking cotton to the gin, Burnside would stop by McDowell's to hear him make that slide guitar whine.

When Burnside moved from Mississippi to Chicago in the '40s to try and make a little more money—that classic migration—he learned that his first cousin, Anna Mae, was married to none other than Muddy Waters. The two men worked at the same Chicago foundry, and after their shifts, Burnside routinely ended up at the Zanzibar Club and Waters's home, where the master showed Burnside plenty of licks on the slide guitar.

Chicago, however, turned out to be a horror. Within a single year, five members of Burnside's family, including his father, were murdered there. In two songs on *Wish I Was in Heaven Sitting Down* (Fat Possum), "Hard Time Killing Floor" and "R.L.'s Story," Burnside matter-of-factly recites the details of the killings while electronica swirls around his narration like ghosts of the dead.

> Two brothers and my father was killed in Chicago
> That's why I don't like living there . . .
> Hard times, yea, everywhere I go
> It's rough, rough, rougher than ever before.

The details take the songs out of the realm of myth, in which it is possible to see death as mere folklore, and into the vicinity of Burnside's own history, where it still hurts.

He went back to Mississippi, working again as a sharecropper (he picked cotton on a plantation as late as 1984). Around 1960, he killed a local man whom he had accused of being a bully. In a *New Yorker* profile of Matthew Johnson, the founder of Fat Possum Records, Jay McInerney notes the badass exchange Burnside had with the judge after the singer was charged with homicide. "The judge asked [Burnside] if he had intended to kill the man. 'It was between him and the Lord, him dyin',' Burnside says. 'I just shot him in the head.'" He was sent up to the Parchman prison farm, where he served only six months before being released.

R.L. Burnside was the kind of bluesman—or "magic Negro," to borrow Spike Lee's phrase—who I went in search of as a young man. When I was growing up in North Carolina, I participated in a not uncommon white Southern tradition of revering black people (a custom probably closely related to the other white Southern tradition of abusing black people). In college, this reverence took the form of driving over to Durham every other week or so of my senior spring to imbibe the wisdom of Richard Trice, who had been a bluesman back in the '30s and '40s and a confederate of the more notorious Blind Boy Fuller. In an act of Christian repentance, Trice had given up playing the blues. To rid himself of the evidence, he sold me his electric guitar—which didn't work—and case for sixty dollars. We would sit in his little wood house, his wife watching TV in the other room, and he would tell me about his life. I hung on every word as if he were a drawling, hard-living Greek philosopher. My accent and expressions tended to ape his own. I have tapes of our talks and they are embarrassing in that respect. To hear the tapes, you would have thought you were listening to two grizzled black survivors of the '30s. Of course, one of us actually was.

I saw Richard—and other blues singers—as repositories of secret wisdom, alternative strategies for life. Real poverty was so foreign to my experience that it looked picturesque. Shotgun houses, flapping tin roofs, newspaper insulation, turnip patches—these were the beautiful visuals in a theme park of rough history. Richard's wisdom seemed to come from chthonic depths—something out of a tree, out of the dirt—that had nothing to do with hard living. Hard living struck me as quaint, not hard.

So, at twenty-one, I was far more of an Etch A Sketch than I should have been. It's true that naïveté has some charm—I was open, solicitous, interested. But stupid. I was searching for authentic exemplars of Southern culture, men whose lives seemed pulpier, more extravagant than my own. Not so overdetermined. In my own way, I must have felt like an outsider. I was trying to find something more real than I was—a quest as old as Plato, I've come to learn, but in my case, rather than ideal forms, I was looking for the anti-ideal forms—and old blues singers represented the bawdy end point of my quest. They were heroes of weak impulse control. They said terrible things to people, they shot them, stole women, made fools of themselves, drank things that weren't originally meant for drinking. A lot of times, they didn't show up places. They didn't seem to have jobs, wore the same clothes for days on end, had more children than they knew what to do with.

This was real life! Amazingly authentic!

At the same time I was doing all of this fieldwork, searching for the divine secrets of real negritude, something else really interesting was happening right under my big nose. One of my roommates was a black guy from Asheville, North Carolina. Curt struck me as such an odd duck that I didn't realize he represented the future (or, as was actually the case, the present as well). He told me he was a Buddhist. He meditated on top of his bed. He smoked a lot of dope (we all did) and dropped a lot of acid (which he kept chilled in our little dorm fridge). He was mixing up psychedelics and blackness (just like Parliament-Funkadelic, one of his favorite groups) in a way that was producing a new cultural blend. He loved all sorts of music that I didn't think of as black—Santana, Hot Tuna, Jimi Hendrix, the jazz guitarist Larry Coryell. Could he have been the only black guy I ever met who loved the Grateful Dead? Yes, I think so. There were other guys like Curt around (minus the affection for Jerry Garcia). I remember one such fellow being described as "not a real black guy."

Curt liked what he liked. Notions of authenticity didn't seem to trouble him. He was into scrambling things (which hallucinogens can certainly facilitate). He had no idea what a black guy like himself was supposed to be. He had no idea that he was supposed to be more real than the rest of us.

It appears that R.L. Burnside has been similarly fortunate in escaping the strictures of the blues cult of authenticity, though this seems primarily a phenomenon of his later years. Listen to him, for instance, on *My Black Name A-Ringin'*, a recording made in 1969 and re-released four years ago on the Adelphi/Genes label. At forty-two, his voice is quieter, more introspective, hemmed-in a bit by tradition. He seems to be performing folk songs correctly, and hasn't put his own steel-toed stamp on the material. The howling, swaggering R.L. of his old age has yet to appear. Burnside here is a brooder. The guitar style, too, is softer, acoustic, and only occasionally do the driving rhythms that fire up his Fat Possum records make cameo appearances. It's still a good record, but as good as it is, it's exactly the sort of album that pleases the so-called purists. The liner notes betray that obsession with authenticity that too often tries to set limits on a form, that erects categories rather than merges them, and that results in a collector's mentality rather than a dancer's. "These delightful people were real," exclaims the writer of Burnside and kin. Ah yes, we know about real.

Thirty years later, Burnside turns into a King Lear of the cotton fields, smirking, raging, howling, joking, and raising up such a ribald racket that even an unfeeling God would have to take notice. Burnside has thrown the archives up in the air and lit a fire in the library. His voice is deeper, rougher, more commanding. Let's take as prime examples of the new Burnside the brilliant Fat Possum releases *Come On In* (1998) and *Wish I Was in Heaven Sitting Down* (2000). The reviews suggested that these aren't records for the purists, as if some blues essence was being besmirched by the scratching and looping, the very hip-hoppedness of it all.

They are indeed a producer's records—Tom Rothrock on *Come On In* and an assortment of producers on *Wish I Was in Heaven Sitting Down*. Burnside handed in the raw tapes; the producers turned them into sonic theater. Like Jamaican dub, like lots of hip-hop. They chopped and looped and layered in that great American garage tradition of souping up the family ride. The music is constructed, not played. Burnside on these CDs is often only—only!—a trademark of himself, his voice floating over the beats like something Moby or Fatboy Slim, those omnivorous and unapologetic borrowers, those librarians of soul riffs, would have cooked up. The records function as a kind of electronic Mississippi, the sound effects rising like mist over the Delta. In some ways, they're advertisements, soundtracks, more than songs. And yes, that does sound a little bit corrupt. Or, at least playful.

What I love about them, however, is that for all of their corruption, they turn the blues from history back into music, from archives into beats, from something to catalog to something to dance to. The generations mingle in these records. With frenetic scratching underneath its hammering Delta propulsion, "Miss Maybelle" is a vat of old-fashioned blues cooking over a nuclear stove. Naturally, it boils over. For all of the technology employed here, for all of the studio engineering, this is a punk record. As they say, play it loud.

If the blues dies from anything, it will be from trying too hard to remain the blues. So goodbye, Authenticity. So long, too, to your stuck-up cousin Cool. Piss off, little Miss Purity. Don't let the screen door hit you on the way out, Real. Long live the Impure, the Corrupt, the Mixed-up, and the Mongrel. Forever and Ever. Amen.

P.S. Long live R.L. Burnside, too.

Why I Wear My Mojo Hand

CHAOS THEORY, APPLIED by Robert Palmer

▬▬▬

Blues and trouble, that's the cliché. The reality is: blues and chaos. Blues is supposed to be—what?—*nurtured* by trouble? So is most art that reaches deep inside and demands unflinching honesty. Is blues *about* trouble? No more than it is about good-time Saturday nights and murder most foul, sharecroppers' servitude, and sweet home Chicago. Is blues a *cause* of trouble? Not directly. But what sort of thing almost inevitably causes trouble in our oppressively regimented world? You guessed it: chaos.

The blues-and-chaos equation first presented itself to me back in the mid-'60s, when a bunch of us in Memphis—mostly musicians, artists, and a smattering of smugglers and dealers—organized and presented the first Memphis Blues Festivals in the Overton Park Shell. For years I believed the remarkable levels of chaos in everything remotely connected with those festivals resulted from a bunch of hippies trying to turn elderly blues singers into anarchist father-figures. Now I'm not so sure. In any case, that was some years before I met R.L. Burnside.

R.L. was an outstanding disciple of one of the greatest of all bluesmen, Mississippi Fred McDowell, who had been a Memphis Blues Festival regular. By the early 1970s, R.L. had really come into his own. The juke joints he ran, in Coldwater and elsewhere around the North Mississippi hill country, were as famous for their level of violence as for R.L.'s outstanding music, which rolled out of his jacked-up guitar amp in dark, turbulent waves—sometimes punctuated by gunshots, especially on Saturday nights. In fact, R.L. himself has been reported waving a (presumably loaded) pistol in at least one crowded joint. If that strikes you as akin to yelling "Fire!" in a crowded theater, well, that's R.L. The man is a connoisseur of chaos; he attracts it, admires it, and then absorbs it, like a black hole sucking reality itself into the chaos of Nothing.

Back in 1993, when I found myself producing a Burnside session for the album that became *Too Bad Jim*, a succession of chaotic eruptions seemed to threaten the entire project. A wooden string bass fell to pieces in the studio. Then the drum kit collapsed into kindling after being given a single light tap. Then a heavy glass door fell out of its mounting and gave me a skull-rattling knock upside the head. Out of the corner of my eye, I glanced over at R.L.—he was enjoying himself like a kid at a Disney movie. The performances he recorded that day were highlights of the album.

I decided, out of near-desperation, to fight fire with fire. Using objects and materials you can find in any good botanica (a shop that sells candles, herbs, and various Santeria/Voodoo supplies and accessories), and dedicating them with a simple, made-up ritual I thought appropriate, I made myself a chaos-buster, a post-Heisenberg-Uncertainty-Principle Mojo hand. And the next time I went in the studio with R.L., I made sure the mojo was secreted on my person. The session went well. Toward the end we were taking a break, standing around in the studio, when it happened again: A tall screen, or "baffle," began to tip over, as usual for no apparent reason. It fell, and on the way down it hit stalwart engineer Robbie Norris on his head. This time, I was all smiles. "It works!" I crowed, giving my mojo charm a surreptitious rub. Robbie was gingerly rubbing the top of his head. "Yeah," he said, "it works *for you*."

But of course, that's just what you expect from magic: If it affects the practitioner's reality, and in the way desired, it *works*. Chaos theory is one way of explaining the mechanics involved. Another, more poetic, and perhaps wiser way of explaining it is called "the blues." Rarely have chaos and uncertainty been so *listenable*; and I'll almost certainly be listening for the rest of my life. If I choose to pack my mojo, well, once again the blues says it best: "Ain't Nobody's Business If I Do."

Walking After Midnight

I BEGAN TO SEE THAT THE BLUES IS REALLY NEWS
FROM AN OLDER PLACE by Sven Birkerts

▄▄▄▄

I am not a man bent on gathering souvenirs of my passage through this world, but I seem to have made certain exceptions, including one for Oxford, Mississippi, where I spent two balmy spring days a few years back. I went there to participate in the annual Oxford Conference for the Book. Usually I come back from places with nothing at all to show. From Oxford, I have a coffee cup bearing the wonderfully conventional inscription YOU'LL ALWAYS COME BACK!, a Xeroxed recipe for "shrimp and grits" from a restaurant called the City Grocery, and a cassette of R.L. Burnside's *Too Bad Jim*. I had conceived this as a little reflection about the Burnside, why, apart from its smashing immediacy, I listen to it as often as I do, but it will have to be about everything, for whenever I listen to Burnside—and now that I drive ninety miles each way to a weekly teaching job, I listen often—a whole densely specific set of memories collects around me.

I'm not sure exactly what special combination of factors singled this weekend out in my life. In part, I'm sure, it was the abrupt transition from an ice-locked Boston winter to a place where the warmth and early ripeness of the season were coming like an exhalation from the soil. That, combined with my outsider's fascination with the South, and the knowledge that Faulkner had taken in and alchemized some of these very same vistas; and the fact that Barry Hannah, whom I knew from a Vermont summer writing program, made Oxford his home. I had heard enough stories from Barry to give the whole surrounding area an aura of faint familiarity.

But even these ties and associations do not get it—Oxford matters to me because it was the site and occasion for a peculiar immersion experience, one that has no obvious connection to the blues of R.L. Burnside but one that I think about every time I play the tape. Indeed, I play the tape to think about the experience.

It was, I think, April, and I was driven down from the Memphis airport by a student assistant, who dropped me at my motel. He had taken me for a loop around the town square—past the famous courthouse, past Square Books—and then, just as I was about to get out of the van, he gave me his last tour-guide tip. With a long leftward inclination of his head, he told me: "Faulkner is buried in a cemetery just down that way—it's a nice walk."

A strange weekend altogether. I was not then (and am only slightly more so now) a veteran of writers' conferences—of their intensities and camaraderies and vinous confessionals. From this one I have stirred together all sorts of nonsequential impressions—spotting an utterly befuddled Andrei Codrescu standing on a street corner; gawking at author photos on the stairway at Square Books, then later—another day—sitting at a signing table upstairs on the store's veranda, next to John Berendt, who did not seem to mind that his line stretched for blocks while I was absolutely free to watch him affix his signature to endless hardcover copies of his book; getting the "behind the scenes" tour of Faulkner's house from the curator Cynthia Shearer, and thinking how terribly confining spaces could seem when there were almost no appliances, when the aspect of the world was almost entirely limited to the panorama that pressed up to the window-glass; eating shrimp and grits at the City Grocery with Barry and his wife, Susan, and noting a stir in the room when an old gentleman with a chest full of medals walked in the door. "That's the real Santini," someone whispered—never mind that his son Pat Conroy, technically more famous, was sitting right there by the wall. Of course there was much, much more, but only one part of my visit stands out with a fully contoured clarity.

On my second night, keyed up from bar talk with writers, from drink, I found I was having a very hard time getting to sleep. When I did, at last, sink down, it was short-lived. A car radio, a tailpipe backfiring—something had me up again—and when I consulted the clock (which I should not have done), I saw that it was nearly five A.M. There was no point in trying. As my eyes were too tired for reading, and as it was too early to think about finding breakfast, I decided to take a long walk. It was warm enough, I remember, to go without a jacket, and having come in from New England rigors, I exulted in the feeling of air on my skin. Then, standing in front of the motel, surprised by the absolute silence of the moment, I remembered what my student driver had told me on parting. Faulkner's grave—I would find it.

That stroll, in the very first brightening moments of the day, along whatever side street I had chosen, put me under a spell. I was exhausted, of course, on top of being overstimulated, and maybe still slightly under the influence of the wine I'd been sampling earlier. The streets were profoundly silent—no passing cars, no barking dogs, no birds yet—and, block after block, here were only my footsteps, the intimate tide of my own breathing. I felt something unusual, a sharpened sensitivity to impressions—or so it seemed—but also an accompanying feeling of connection, of pressing depth. The world seemed very present, charged. I have known only a handful of these moments in my life.

I idled along the sidewalk, right up close to the sleeping houses. Doors sealed against the night, objects—children's bikes, tools, discarded bottles—in their inanimate repose, the upstairs windows now picking up the first strokes of light. At some point I started playing with the idea that I had taken a turn back in time; that this earthly silence, and this aspect of slumbering houses, was just what someone, my doppelgänger, might have encountered walking here thirty or forty years ago.

I tried on the notion as I walked, tried guiding myself backward in increments, and then, suddenly, the line of houses and trees broke and there, across the way, was the cemetery. And I could see that the sun would very soon be coming up over the horizon. But the mood—that feeling I had of being enfolded in another time—held up as I went in through the gates. Now I was among the stones, the names, the dates. Graveyards always provoke contemplation; this one was feeding directly into my preoccupation. I moved along in that same enormous silence, only stopping every few feet, not just to read the names and dates—and what resonant old names some of them were—but to go through that inevitable sequence of projective fancies: This person was once alive, walked these streets, stood at the sweet center of his—of her—life, thought strange thoughts, and knew the world. Perform this maneuver of the imagination—once, twice, more—and the hold on the present begins to loosen, which is clearly what happened, because all at once I had the most peculiar sensation: I felt time to be a medium, almost substantial, and I somehow grasped that the farther back into the past we look, the more people could be seen to live in that medium, in its midst. And I saw that now, in the present, we have all but lost that sense of immersion, that we move over the surface like water striders. Characterizing the feeling this way sounds all wrong—untrue to the event—but I don't know how else to come at it. The point was simply that people once inhabited their time and place in ways most of us would find almost impossible to imagine. I believed, at that moment, that I could feel the difference, feel how much more condensed and bound, and perhaps poignant, living may have felt. These streets, these houses, the background recollection of Faulkner's books, the still transparency of the morning hour—it seemed to me that, if I only willed it, I could be in the skin, behind the eyes, of a person living before the inner form of things was utterly shattered. I could feel the distance as would a person who mainly walked from place to place, whose life was deeply circumscribed by locale; feel time as it was felt when seasons and hours of the day were all determining, when one stood, waited, and had occasion, always, to observe the look and movement of things. It seemed unimaginable to me as I stood there that we had moved so quickly away, that the world inhabited, until quite recently, not just by our immediate ancestors (maybe even our parents), but also by the painters, writers, and composers we revere, no longer really existed. That there was a huge range of common human experiences, many of the humblest sort, that we could no longer fully claim. Standing on a road and watching a figure slowly approaching from afar, or hearing a train whistle and feeling the sweet sorrow of distance, or pining long days for a letter and having it finally arrive. . . .

There, that morning, I finally felt—fully and deeply—what I had been supposing for a long time: I thought I understood the nature and the terms of the change. We have freed ourselves significantly from the confinements of slow time and fixed place—though I would add that they very likely did not start to seem quite so confining until the possibilities of escape were made available. We are surrounded as those others, our ancestors, never could be, with diversions of every description for the mind and senses; against boredom we have assembled an arsenal. I thought back to those low-ceilinged, cluttered, yet somehow barren, rooms in Faulkner's house—the antiquated look and feel of everything—and I wondered for an instant how they all coped with time back then. But I was looking with the eyes of the present. Those now-vacated spaces were once, of course, teeming—with talk, innuendo, expectation, history, with all the human elements that render a space intimate. I had an impression not just of the open-window insect buzz of a summer afternoon but also of the lamplit intensities that became available when the whole of the larger world was swallowed by night.

Then it was time to go. The immersion sensation was running out—I felt it wearing off like a drug. I hadn't found Faulkner's grave, but I decided I would look for it another time. I thought that if I got back to the motel soon I could still lie down for a bit before the day's events. And without lingering or looking back, I left the cemetery and headed back.

There remains only to close the circle, and this I can do. For as it happened, I had to leave the conference a half-day early. I would miss the last party—much talked-up because R.L. Burnside was going to play—which I was, in fact, very sorry about. Not just because I love good blues, but because my entire Oxford experience had been vivid, so full, so right, and it seemed a violation of the charmed rhythm of things to step away before it was all over. It would be like a piece of music—a blues—cut off before resolving back into its dominant chord. But so it went—a round of hasty good-byes, small talk with my driver as the town rapidly shrank away in the side-view mirror. End of event.

Except that one afternoon not long after, the mail brought me a small package, a gift cassette of Burnside's *Too Bad Jim* sent along by Cynthia Shearer. And with that tape came completion. I put on the tape and through some strange sorcery the music at once closed off the weekend, resolved it—and, over time, over many listenings, it has come to contain it. This is peculiar, I know, how the raw slashing redundancy of "Goin' Down South" can hold—and trigger—memories of graveyard reverie, but the logic of association is peculiar, too. It was a long time before I got an inkling of how this connection really worked.

I was off track, I now see, in thinking that my musings about time were one kind of thing, and the syncopations of Mississippi blues another. On the surface, yes, there could be no less likely pairing, never mind that the blues are right at home among tombstones. But one day not so long ago, driving home from a less-than-brilliant day of teaching, and blasting Burnside at thought-cancelling volume, it snapped into clarity for me. This music could hold those wispy daydreams because there was, in fact, something kindred between the two. Because the music, not just Burnside but the whole deep tradition of that blues, came straight up out of that prior world, that utterly unmediated life. Listening from one angle, from outside, you hear the rough jangle, identify maybe the traces of Robert Johnson and Lightnin' Hopkins, but when that angle collapses, when insistence suddenly plants you *there,* so that you feel the music around you on every side, an environment of sorrow and release, then you get how this really is news from an older place. This is life lived up to the limit of the skin and no further—the life of the heart, of wanting, getting, and mainly losing—and it is very much, for me, about back then. Odd that a small cassette can call up so many different kinds of memories and that it can so reliably stand for something. After all, it's just one rough-voiced man hammering his version of the age-old blues.

Homage to a Juke Joint

WHEN THE MUSIC INSIDE MEETS THE MUSIC OUTSIDE
by Beth Ann Fennelly

I was visiting Oxford, Mississippi, in 1999, when I got invited to Junior Kimbrough's juke joint in the tiny community of Chulahoma, near Holly Springs. I didn't jump at the chance—I was with my husband on his book tour and was tuckered out. We'd married a few months prior, and we were young enough when the tour began that staying in a different hotel every night and eating out three meals a day seemed glamorous. By the time we'd reached Oxford, however, we'd partied with every Birkenstocked bookstore employee in the South, and we were jaded. All the clothes in my duffel were dirty. And tight. Our car smelled like Road Trip. But R.L. Burnside, a living legend, was supposed to be playing. Junior Kimbrough himself had died the previous year, rumored to have left behind thirty-six children, some of whom kept Junior's Place running.

A blues music producer, Amos Harvey, drove my husband and me and some local bookstore folks past the graceful Greek Revivals of Oxford and out into the country. We crossed the Tallahatchie Bridge, eventually turning from a gravel road onto hilly Highway 4. We passed trailers sitting back from the road, leeching their power from light poles wearing boas of kudzu, sometimes a group of men standing around a fire in a can, though the temperature neared the century mark. Roadkill studded the gravel shoulder, stars above big as asteroids, one orange moon trailing us like a balloon lashed to our bumper. Although there was no road sign, Amos knew when to turn and pulled over where a long line of cars was parked.

Getting out of the car and seeing just black folks, I felt mighty white. About the whitest, in fact, I'd ever felt. But there didn't seem to be any menace in the air.

We slowly approached the juke, a rambling gray wooden structure with a tin roof. Someone said the building had been built 130 years ago and had first been used as a general store, then a horse stable, then a church. Large plywood boards had been added to make porches, and groups of people stood about, talking and passing a plastic milk container, which they then passed to us, too. I swallowed, scorching my throat. White lightning. We each bought our own. It came in reused Veryfine juice jars.

Inside was a pool table so close to the door that the players had to wait to shoot until we'd entered. Little alcoves branched off to the sides and were lined with the kind of couches that, once you sat in them, didn't easily let you go. At the back was a jukebox, and to the right, under a few clip-on shop lights hanging from the ceiling, an area for the band. Elsewhere the lights were dim and the clothing bright—women accessorized with high heels and matching handbags, cleavage, spirals of gold chains. The men weren't dressed in shorts or jeans like the guys I'd come with. They wore pressed trousers, leather shoes, and belts—a few in full suits, though it was so humid everyone was sweating, and the dancing hadn't even started yet. The walls were bright, too, with murals—I guess you'd call it folk art, though the term has come to smack of a studied preciousness. These were genuinely expressive, but unsigned by the artists. There was a black Southern belle looking like Bo Peep with a pink ruffled hoopskirt and shepherd's crook. There was a Diana Ross, glazed with glitter paint, taken from the pages of *Ebony*. There was a wonderful Oprah Winfrey, whom I remember as being dressed like the Virgin Mary. There was a Busch beer mural from the "Come to the mountains, come to the sea" era, and behind the instruments—two guitars and a drum kit, cabinet-sized speakers—was a giant seascape full of volcanic rock and crashing waves wearing mustaches of foam.

In the back left corner was the bar, a wooden board separating the clientele from the two large and sexy barmaids who'd fetch from the avocado-colored fridge a Bud or a Busch. Each beer cost a buck-fifty, which they'd slip into the purple Crown Royal drawstring bags they wore around their wrists.

That night the kitchen served two items: the chicken drumstick and the chicken sandwich. The drumstick was handed to you with a napkin wrapped around the bony end. The sandwich, which came on a paper plate, featured a piece of white bread topped with two drumsticks nestling inversely, like new shoes, topped with another piece of white bread.

The two young men who had been up plugging in the amps picked up the guitars and played a few bars of a droning, propulsive funk blues. This is the heavily rhythm-oriented, hypnotic hill-country blues the area is known for, pioneered by folks like Fred McDowell and made famous by Junior Kimbrough, among others. The Burnside family played here regularly, as well as others who'd found an expanded audience through the recordings they'd made for Fat Possum Records in Oxford.

Finally, R.L. came out. "Well, well, well," he baritoned into the microphone, picked up his guitar, and sat down. He drank from a glass of whiskey that sat beside his chair. "This glass has a hole in it," he said. "A big hole, right here on the top." In the next moment the wallboards were thumping and the bass was so loud I could feel it throbbing in my breastbone. He was playing "Poor Black Mattie." ("Need no heater fireplace by my bed," Burnside sang, using his slide to drive the repeating guitar riffs, "Woman I got keeps me cherry red.") The dance floor pulsed with couples—no stilted, single-sex clusters reminiscent of high-school mixers— and the dancing was provocative, talented, unself-conscious. Leaning against my post, I wanted to join but thought better of it, though my telltale foot was tapping.

Behind me, a long, low voice crooned in my ear, "How 'bout you and me join in?" I turned around to find a tall, thin man wearing the most lovely suit, dove gray pinstriped with plum. His shoes, belt, and tie were plum-colored. So was his jaunty fedora, which he removed and rested on a duct-taped chair. He nodded toward the dance floor, and he offered me his hook.

Yes, his hook. Should I dance with a man with a hook for a hand? Headlines ran through my head. I heard, states away, my mother gasp. "You can pretend I'm a pirate if it helps," he said. He grinned and his gold tooth winked. What the hell: My husband didn't dance unless Styx was playing. So I followed him onto the floor, where he laid that hook on my hip and spun me expertly. He spun me out and reeled me in. He dipped me down and shimmied me back up. He made the music inside me meet the music outside me: Everything harmonized raucously for a few blazing moments.

Then the music stopped, after just three songs. R.L.'s wife of close to fifty years was taking him home. "Awh, Mama," he was protesting, but laughing. Someone said she'd objected to a song he'd played, or didn't play. So his grandson Cedric climbed behind the drum kit and with Kenny Brown on guitar they picked up that emphatic, roiling rhythm full of one-chord riffs, and everyone danced again and drank moonshine until the moon wasn't shining anymore.

Three years later I'd move to Mississippi, but I never returned to Junior's. I couldn't—it burned down in 2000. I've heard someone torched it, wrongfully thinking there was insurance money to be had, but I don't know about that.

Every now and then, someone talks about rebuilding Junior's. But some things can't be replicated. They exist on this earth for a while, and then they're gone. You can rebuild an Applebee's or a Hilton Hotel bar. You can't rebuild a Junior's. You can't rebuild that soul. I'm proud I can claim it: Children, I went there once. I danced a dance of great power and joy. This was years ago, before the flames came to embroider the blue gown of the Oprah Virgin Mary, before her brown hands blistered, before she cried her soot tears, her eyes cast downward to the clearing where R.L. Burnside used to play and where, once, a shop light glinted off a hook that gently, gently, gently brushed a lock of sweaty hair from off my forehead.

Rock &
Roll II

Captain Beefheart

WE COULD REALLY USE SOME MYSTERY IN OUR MUSIC
THESE DAYS by Mark Richard

▬▬▬

Come back, Captain Beefheart, come back! I was a mere prat of a child when my friend Bob dropped a needle into *Clear Spot*. I was just twelve, maybe thirteen, the youngest disc jockey in the country, or so said the man who swore he could get me on *Johnny Carson* but never did. My friend Bob used to come to the little 1,000-watt AM station where I worked in the afternoons after school, and he would drop off albums for mc to play. Bob told me you were a child prodigy, Captain Beefheart, and people were buying your sculptures when you were four, is that true? That you met Frank Zappa when you were twelve, maybe thirteen, is that right? I know you played on Zappa's *Hot Rats* and *Bongo Fury*. How old were you then? When Bob came into the little radio station that afternoon, I think I was playing Savoy Brown. Bob just came into the studio and stopped the turntable and dropped the needle into *Clear Spot*, and we turned up the studio monitors so loud the ladies next door at Town and Country Beauty Parlor complained. But the station manager didn't call. He had quit calling after the times he called up to say Clapton's solo on the extended play "Layla" sounded like someone killing a cat; that Grand Funk Railroad made him want to drive his car into a telephone pole; that he had seen the album wrapper for Mott the Hoople and they were obviously all queer as three-dollar bills. Why couldn't I just play the old rock & roll like Pat Boone and Simon and Garfunkel?

You see, Captain Beefheart, ours was a small Southern town and this was the late '60s, early '70s, before album rock made it to our FM stations. My voice plummeted overnight. I hear that's more common in Africa among boys who've grown up chanting. I would have said to you that my voice, in its depth and inflection from that day to this, is a cross between Barry White and Richard Burton, the ebonics honestly homegrown in our black-majority though Nat Turner–killing Tidewater Virginia county; the anglophonic faux Brit Os merely leftover cradle rot from the spawnings of nearby colonial Williamsburg. Richard Burton? My wife laughed in my face when I told her. More like Barry White and *Foghorn Leghorn*, she snorted.

I got the job at the radio station because my father thought working for two dollars an hour would keep me out of trouble with the police in whose jail I had already sat, age twelve. Tiny, tiny, small was our radio station, with its antenna speared on the edge of our cemetery so that when we were driving past the tombstones on the way to school, the signal broadcast itself through the car radio even if it was turned off. Some people said they could hear our radio station playing in some of the graves, having something to do with the metal vaults and the fillings in the heads of some of our deceased moldering down there. Your music, you could faintly hear it, Captain, rattling the molars, tweetering, woofing in the skulls of old dowagers way down in the ground, songs like "Click Clack" that I played over and over. That song, that train ride, a masterpiece. A masterpiece. Do you see how your songs became a secret language in a small Southern town among me and Bob and our friends who used to come by the station on Saturdays with armloads of albums for me to play so they would have something to listen to when they took their hippie girlfriends out to the sand pits to smoke reefer and drink beer and all go skinny-dipping? My other friend Steve and I used to scrawl your song and album titles across girls' lockers at school. *Lick My Decals Off, Baby.* They used to love that one. And how easy to put off our mothers or teachers, or somebody, with a shrug and answer, "There ain't no Santa Claus on the evenin' stage." Steve and I were in our gothic, pre-driver's-license days, him already over six feet, and both of us shrouded in our Army-surplus trenchcoats, ghoulish and processional through neighbors' yards at dusk just as they were sitting down to their chicken-fried, bacon-seasoned dinners, both of us chanting through their open windows, "Bring out your dead!" There was nothing to be done with us, no reason to call the station when we played "I'm Gonna Booglarize You Baby" instead of the National Anthem on Saturday night sign-offs. Your music, Captain, was a passport to a place from which I never returned.

They say your first album that you made with the Magic Band, *Safe As Milk*, was John Lennon's favorite album, is that for real? Your album *The Spotlight Kid* I think is my favorite. When I went to college I wrote a collection of short stories I presumptuously titled *The Adventures of the Spotlight Kid*. Some of the stories were about going to the sand pits to smoke reefer and drink beer and skinny-dip with hippie girls. I wrote a novel called *Fishboy* based on your song "Grow Fins" ("If ya don't leave me alone, I'm gonna take up with a mermaid, an' leave you landlubbin' women alone"). Come back, Captain Beefheart, come back. Maybe my favorite album after all is *Shiny Beast (Bat Chain Puller)*. I always go back to *Clear Spot,* though, for songs like "Sun Zoom Spark" and "Long Neck Bottles," which any Memphis player would have loved to have cut for himself. The song "Clear Spot" is Faulkner's *The Wild Palms.* I read once that you wrote the twenty-eight songs on *Trout Mask Replica* in eight-and-a-half hours. Zappa produced it and let you do whatever you wanted to do. And that you wrote all the music for everyone in the Magic Band—you wrote all the music and then showed them how to play it on their instruments, because you could. And all that cover art you drew and painted. Big books of it now selling for hundreds, thousands of dollars. I hear that's what you do now, that you're holed up in Northern California in Denis Johnson country and painting. Is that right? No more music? We could really use some mystery in our music these days. I could really use it. I "get" most songs on the radio on the first take, so it's hard to listen to them again like I listen to you.

My friend Bob says he met you once right in our small Southern town. On the main drag all that was open after dinner was Galloway's Gulf Gas Station, where a bunch of our friends worked over the years, Bobo, Hatch, Al. Bob says he and Hatch were making the nightly perimeter check around town in Hatch's little TR6 with the top down, and they circled back to Galloway's and found two professional wrestlers, Brute Bernard and Skull Murphy, pumping their own gas at the pump in the days before self-serve. Bob said, Aren't you Brute Bernard and Skull Murphy? and Bob says Brute Bernard and Skull Murphy weren't happy about being recognized out of the ring. Bob says he and Hatch took off again, making another perimeter check of the town in Hatch's little TR6, and when they came back to Galloway's, there was a Chrysler New Yorker at the pump pulling a U-Haul. Inside the station were a bunch of guys dressed up in zoot suits and big hats, wearing all sorts of things. Bob says he went into the station where the guys were paying for the gas and buying cheese crackers and Cokes and said, Who are you? and one of the guys said, Jethro Tull is playing in Norfolk tomorrow night, and Bob said, Yeah, but you're not Jethro Tull, and the guy said, That's right, we're Captain Beefheart's Magic Band, we're opening for Jethro Tull, and Bob said, Where's the Captain? And the guy pointed out to you sitting in the dim recesses of the backseat of the Chrysler New Yorker. Bob says he went out and introduced himself to you and talked to you for about three minutes, and Bob says that you were completely uninterested in talking to him but he says that was all right, and the next night he and Hatch went to see you open for Jethro Tull in Norfolk. He says the drummer came out wearing panties on his head, his hair sticking out the leg holes in two big shocks. Bob says that after you finished playing he and Hatch were among about twelve people who actually clapped but that Bob had stood up and clapped until his hands were sore even though he says he didn't get what it was all about. He says he looked around at the rest of the Jethro Tull audience. They definitely didn't get it, Bob says. And Bob says when he looked up at you onstage, he wondered if you got what it was all about, either.

Did you, Captain Beefheart? Did you get it?

Come back, we need you. Give us mystery again. I dread our cemetery, and I fear the music that might now fill my skull and teeth with eternal yearning.

The Sex Pistols

IN ENEMY TERRITORY: THEIR SOUTHERN TOUR OF '78
by Mark Binelli

―――――

We've heard a lot about these boys and if they behave themselves, we'll give them a right friendly welcome. Memphis is a clean city. We aim to keep it that way. We will not tolerate any real or simulated sex onstage. No, sir. They can be nude if they like. They can spit. They can even vomit. No law against that, but there must be no lewd or indecent behavior.

—Vice Squad Lt. Ronald Howell, before the
Sex Pistols' January 6, 1978, concert in Memphis,
from *Punk Diary: 1970–1979* by George Gimarc

They probably chose not to play in New York because it would have been the obvious thing to do. . . . It would have been a pushover.

—Warner Bros. spokesperson Marion Perkins,
Atlanta Constitution, January 5, 1978

Twenty years ago, the most notorious British punk-rock band made its stateside debut at a strip mall in Atlanta. Fans of the Sex Pistols began lining up at four P.M. for the group's sold-out (actually, oversold) show at the Great Southeast Music Hall, a five-hundred-capacity club that shared a parking lot with a Kmart. As the sun set, the preachers arrived, eager to save the spike-haired and the safety-pinned. There were also reporters on hand to bear witness for the *New York Times*, the *Village Voice, Time, Newsweek*, Reuters, and all three networks.

"After the show, we walked outside, and I remember Charles Kuralt was there doing a taped piece," says Atlanta photographer Rick Diamond. "I don't know what the relevance was, but somebody had brought a pig's ear—a real pig's ear—and it kept getting thrown onstage and then back into the crowd and onstage again. So Charles Kuralt was trying to do this interview and this pig's ear comes flying into the frame. They had to cut and start over."

It's difficult to pinpoint when Sex Pistols–brand, U.K.-minted-and-testmarketed Anarchy™ truly collided head-on with the American South, but one could make a strong case for the sight of the venerable *On the Road* correspondent nearly getting pelted with sub-scrapple. The moment arguably sums up the essence of the band's legendary, ill-fated U.S. tour, a glorious, entropic conflagration of media hype and willful subversion.

That most of the above took place well below the Mason-Dixon line is thanks largely to the machinations of Malcolm McLaren, the group's manager and would-be Colonel Parker. An art-school washout and the owner of a London bondage boutique called Sex, McLaren brought the Pistols together in the mid-'70s as a snarling, nihilistic assault on corporate rock & roll and society at large. The group's final lineup featured singer Johnny Rotten, guitarist Steve Jones, bassist Sid Vicious, and drummer Paul Cook. Rotten and Vicious were old friends and quickly became punk icons—the former as the movement's caustic voice, the latter as its mindless id.

As one might expect, the Pistols didn't hurt for exposure. They dressed outrageously, cursed on television, beat up journalists, got beaten up by punk-haters, were banned by BBC radio, and sold millions of records. After their debut album, *Never Mind the Bollocks, Here's the Sex Pistols*, a tour of the United States was the inevitable next step. According to tour manager Noel Monk's book *12 Days on the Road*, McLaren initially insisted on playing only three North American dates: New York, Tijuana, and Tupelo, Mississippi. After that plan was quickly vetoed by Warner Bros., the band's American record label, McLaren pressed for an all-Southern tour, hoping to stir up controversy by performing to potentially hostile crowds far from any punk strongholds. The label agreed, but only if the band first played some Northern dates, including an appearance on *Saturday Night Live*. McLaren, however, had waited too long to apply for visas for the bandmembers, all of whom had arrest records. By the time the Pistols made it through customs, they'd missed the initial tour dates and had to start off exactly where McLaren planned—in Atlanta. Of the abbreviated tour's seven dates, five would be in the South.

When the Sex Pistols landed in Atlanta on January 4, 1978, there wasn't much in the way of a punk scene waiting to greet them. "There were probably four or five punk bands playing around at the time," recalls longtime Atlanta musician

Rex Patton. "There was one group, the Knobs, from North Carolina, I think. The highlight of their set was the lead singer would take a chainsaw onstage and saw off his wooden foot."

By the time the Pistols arrived, the group had already become, to borrow an album title from the Flatlanders, more a legend than a band. Reports of the boys' unruly behavior had been exaggerated to an absurd degree. Authorities in the South had heard rumors of onstage rapes and of band members urinating on the audience; consequently, vice-squad officers from Memphis, Baton Rouge, San Antonio, and Tulsa all flew into Atlanta to find out what to expect at the upcoming shows in their respective cities.

Of course, it was in the interest of McLaren and the band to feed this sort of hype. "We wanted them to cause a stir and do what they do," acknowledges Warner Bros. director of publicity Bob Merlis. "That's what attracted us to signing them. It wasn't just their youthful good looks." At a sound check the day before their performance, Patton says the band members were warming up just like "normal" musicians—until they spotted some reporters. "Then they started spitting, drooling down the mike. It was an act, very mercenary. They knew all along what they were doing, but people just ate it up."

Still, not all of the Pistols' excesses can be written off as public-relations stunts—particularly in the case of Vicious, a violent, masochistic heroin addict who had no trouble living up to his reputation. On the first day of the tour, according to 12 Days on the Road, he attacked one of his own bodyguards in the restroom of an Atlanta restaurant. The bodyguard, a burly ex-biker, repeatedly slammed the bassist's head against a sink. Vicious then slumped to the floor and mumbled, "Now we can be friends."

By all accounts, the Great Southeast Music Hall was a media circus the night of the concert. The frenzied crowd had its share of true believers and hostile elements, but most were simply gawkers who'd heard the freak show was in town. Lech Kowalski's 1981 documentary film of the early punk-rock scene, D.O.A., features concert footage from much of the tour, including Atlanta. In shots of the audience, the mustache contingent far outnumbers the dyed-mohawk contingent.

Inexplicably, Rex Patton's '60s cover band, Cruis-o-matic, was hired to open for the Pistols. "The punks all hated our guts," says Patton. "We decided that the norm for that night would be safety pins and torn shirts, so if anyone was going to be a rebel, they'd dress opposite that. So for the one time in our careers, we wore Izod shirts and khaki pants. The *Village Voice* said we were 'a good-time party band whom we will hereby refer to as the Shitheads.' It zoomed right over everyone's heads. The crowd was rabid. We were only supposed to play for forty minutes, but we ended up having to play for an hour and ten minutes. By that time, even our girlfriends were booing us."

The Pistols went over considerably better. In *D.O.A.*, Rotten can be seen prowling the stage during "Anarchy in the U.K.," so gnarled and bent over he could be auditioning for an eccentric production of *Richard III*. The sound is muddy, sloppy—and utterly electrifying. At the end of the song, when Rotten finally stands up straight to howl, "I wanna be anarchy!" his fist raised in what would've been a Black Power salute ten years earlier, the potentially hackneyed pose comes off like a plausible call to arms. "Aren't we the worst thing you've ever seen?" Rotten later asks the crowd. "We're ugly and we know it." One gum-smacking female convert tells the camera, "When I saw Johnny Rotten's face, I thought I'd vomit, he's so beautiful." Another woman, a peroxide blonde in a denim jacket, adds: "I wanna be a Sex Pistols holster." The local press wasn't so quickly won over. "The Sex Pistols are going through a sophomoric anti-establishment phase," sniffed music writer Scott Gain in a front-page story in the next day's *Atlanta Journal*. "No one takes their philosophy seriously for a moment." In a *really* low blow, he described the scene as "almost like an innocent Halloween party."

After the concert, while the rest of the band went club-hopping—their stops included a nearby transvestite bar—Vicious eluded his babysitters and disappeared for the rest of the evening. The next day, the band and crew had to head off to the next date, in Memphis, without him. (Amazingly, the bandmembers managed to visit Graceland without offending pilgrims in town for a weekend-long celebration of Elvis's birthday.) A few hours later, Vicious finally turned up at Piedmont Hospital in Atlanta. After scoring some heroin, he'd gotten bored and carved the words GIMME A FIX into his chest.

In Memphis, the rest of the band was furious with Vicious. There was more trouble at that evening's venue, the now-defunct Taliesyn Ballroom. Fire marshals insisted on installing seats in the hall, cutting its capacity to seven hundred. Unfortunately, nine hundred tickets had already been sold, and angry ticketholders not allowed inside the club nearly rioted, breaking several windows before being dispersed by a SWAT team.

Jim Dickinson, a Memphis musician and record producer who played, most recently, on Bob Dylan's *Time Out of Mind*, made it inside. "I'll never forget it. It's in my top ten all-time concerts, for sure," says the fifty-six-year-old Dickinson. "The Sex Pistols walked in *through* the audience, literally pushing their way up to the stage. Sid was the show. As far as I'm concerned, they were just playing along with him. He certainly was primitive, making a horrible noise. Nonetheless, he was the lead instrument. When they walked in, he had what I guess you could call a suit on: a tie, a jacket, a white dress shirt. When they stood onstage, all the lights went off, and then when they came back up, he'd ripped off all of his clothes except for his pants and his tie, and you could see I NEED A FIX or something like that, looking like he'd gashed it into his chest with a needle. He was absolutely brilliant, what he was doing to the instrument. He may not have known it—he certainly didn't—but he was brilliant.

"It was offensive and frontal and aggressive in a way that I thought was gone from rock & roll. Part of the idea of rock & roll in the '50s—it was purely one-generational music; and through the commercialization of rock & roll over the years, all of that was gone before the punks, and I was glad to see it back. There was something so hostile. It wasn't just in your face, it was up your nose."

But this negative energy was rapidly tearing the band apart. That so many rock careers peak and perish in spectacular, almost cinematic flameouts comes as no surprise—we're talking about extreme personalities who are worshiped like gods and constantly rewarded for acting up. With the Sex Pistols, though, everything was accelerated. Along with the normal pressures of any tour, the bandmembers were starting to hate one another, Vicious was becoming increasingly unstable, the crowds seemed to be getting more violent and confrontational, *and they were in enemy territory.* "There was this sort of unspecified thought that, because we were in the Deep South, some harm might be visited upon them," says Bob Merlis. "It was twenty years ago. I don't know if the *band* knew exactly where they were. They had more of a Wild West image, I think. Steve Jones had a sheriff's badge on, and he kept saying, 'Look, I'm a *cher-iff.*'"

Death threats awaited the Pistols in San Antonio. They performed at a converted bowling alley called Randy's Rodeo, where the crowd began hurling glass bottles at the band after Rotten posited that all cowboys were homosexuals (but in much ruder terms). Vicious eventually removed his bass mid-song and repeatedly smashed it over the head of a bearded redneck who'd been taunting him from the foot of the stage. "He knew I meant physical harm," complains Vicious's target in *D.O.A.* "I would've been glad to take him on or his buddy Johnny. I came here to openly cause dissent in the Sex Pistols because I believe negatively in what they're doing, and, as far as I'm concerned, they're not worth killing."

In Baton Rouge, the Sex Pistols played at the Kingfish, a converted grocery store named for Huey Long. During the concert, a female fan jumped onstage and began to perform a sexual act on Vicious. Bodyguards eventually pulled her away. The following evening at the legendary Longhorn Ballroom in Dallas—the club was founded by Bob Wills, once managed by Jack Ruby, and decorated with portraits of patron saints like Hank Williams and Tex Ritter—another woman made it past security to present Vicious with a unique term of endearment: She brutally head-butted him in the face, giving him a bloody nose. Earlier in the concert, Vicious had slashed his own chest with a broken beer bottle, so that in much of the existing footage, he looks like he just crawled away from a car wreck.

Only two more dates remained on the tour, Tulsa and San Francisco. The shows became increasingly sloppy and erratic, and by San Francisco, the group had clearly stopped caring.

The day after the show, at the height of their fame and notoriety, the Sex Pistols broke up. Eventually, Rotten reverted to his given name, John Lydon, and started a new band, Public Image Ltd., which would achieve middling success over the next decade or so. Jones and Cook worked as sidemen in various projects. Vicious sank deeper into junkiedom, finally overdosing about a year later—while out on bail for allegedly stabbing his girlfriend to death.

It's hard to say what might've happened if the Sex Pistols had toured the United States as originally planned. Certainly, the band would have met with more receptive crowds in the North. Perhaps the lower tension levels would have reduced the potential for volatile behavior. The Pistols might have stayed together, and the group could have released a few more increasingly mediocre records before finally fizzling out as tired self-parodies. Instead, thanks largely to the pressures of the tour, they went out in a blaze. Sid Vicious's eventual demise was senseless and pathetic, but the Pistols, as a band, exited with rare style. They left the fans wanting more, they left a good-looking corpse, and they left their own near-mythical status intact. In the end, the South's major contribution to punk rock—excluding, of course, the fabulous Knobs—may have been, perversely, its role in destroying the most prominent punk group of the day, in forcing the Sex Pistols finally to live up to their own cry of "No Future." And, really, how much more punk can you get?

R&B:

Dept. of

Al Green

Raw and Born Again

THE SOUND THAT PROMISES TO TAKE US HOME
by Jeff Sharlet

━━━

Let's look at the facts about Al Green. Or rather, *the* fact, the biographical detail he does not discuss, the moment around which the whole story turns: at 4 A.M., October 18, 1974, when the last, great, sweet falsetto soul singer of the South eased into a bath after a long night of recording and got a pan of boiling-hot grits poured on him by a spurned lover. The woman who chose grits as her revenge was twenty-nine-year-old Mary Woodson, just another notch in a long line of ladies, and not even the one who occupied the greater portion of Al Green's erotic imagination (that would have been Juanita, a whore he'd proudly pimped to white business-men), nor the one who troubled him most at the time (that would have been Linda Wells, a former "secretary," who had charged him that summer with assaulting her with a bottle). In 1974, Al Green had behind him twenty million records sold and five consecutive hits. For two years, he'd been crooning and moaning the soundtrack of American romance, with a voice later described as the "lovingest" ever to turn to the tradition of Southern soul. So? Mary Woodson snuck into his Memphis split-level home and found some grits boiling—or boiled them herself while he washed—and she snuck up on him just as he was getting out of the tub and dumped the whole pan on his skinny bones, that slinky S of biceps and pecs and stomach later pictured on the *Greatest Hits* album beneath his strange, ugly-beautiful mug, the hangdog eyes and the missing chin and the teenage boy's beard and the earnest, love-me smile so at odds with the seduction of his bare-chested glory. She scalded it all. Shoulders, back, belly. Burning grits probably dripped down into the crack of his ass. He must have bellowed, raw and deep, no falsetto when your skin is sizzling off of you. Mary Woodson had done what she'd come to Memphis to do, and so she went into the bedroom and retrieved Al Green's .38 and tried to shoot herself. She missed twice, but got lucky the third time. The police found in her purse a note declaring her intentions and her reasons. "The more I trust you," she'd written, "the more you let me down."

Pretty much anyone who's ever heard "Love and Happiness" in a bar or in some cheesy movie or in an elevator knows some basic outline of this story. They know, too, about how Al Green understood the grits and the burns all over his body and the suicide of one of his conquests not so much as a sign that he had sinned, grievously, against a whole lot of females, but rather that God wanted him to raise up a church, which he did, the Full Gospel Tabernacle, in Memphis, which he then filled with sacred music instead of sex music.

Not such a stretch as it might have seemed; Al Green grew up on gospel, started singing it at age nine in the tiny town of Jacknash, Arkansas, toured with his brothers until as a teenager he discovered Jackie Wilson, and his father discovered that he'd discovered Jackie Wilson, and kicked him out of the combo for listening to music that betrayed the Lord. A man inclined to read worldly events as divine portents might look at that expulsion from Godly music, into what became a spectacularly successful career of singing about getting it on and loving and staying together and making it simmer a long time, as fated.

Al Green did not. Even as success thickened around him he lived a life of the blues and sang soul and somewhere deep in his heart, or in the back of his mind, or maybe down there in his crotch, he saved some piece of himself for his return to gospel.

In greater or lesser detail, every Al Green fan knows this legend. They probably know, too, that Al Green is what is called, on therapeutic television, a "survivor." Consider his peers: Sam Cooke, shot to death by a motel clerk in 1964 after he'd barged into her office, half naked, searching for the girl he may or may not have raped minutes before; Marvin Gaye, shot to death at age forty-four by his own father on April Fool's Day, 1984; Otis Redding and his band gone down in a plane; the long, awful dwindling of Curtis Mayfield. Michael Jackson, who bears mentioning in the company of Al Green for the sake of his falsetto, has his own problems.

But the Reverend Al Green, he survived. Everything, in fact, has worked out rather well. He lives modestly, in both the spiritual and sexual sense, in a house behind his church, which stands at 787 Reverend Al Green Road, just off Elvis Presley Boulevard. He still dances. "He wears out Bibles like he does shoes," one of his flock told a Memphis stringer for the A.P., on the occasion of his silver anniversary in the pulpit. After eight years in the gospel desert, his back turned on his hits, God has given him permission to sing his early, sexy songs again. He's lived to see himself ossified in Cleveland's Rock and Roll Hall of Fame, to cameo on *Ally McBeal,* to duet with Lyle Lovett. Starbucks canonization cannot be long in coming.

This is all as it should be, the artist as a comfortable older man. Maybe the best thing that ever happened to Al Green's career was that panful of boiling grits that burned him. The story has become a folktale. The grits are Al Green's crossroads. He did not gain knowledge of the world and its weaknesses; he abandoned it, left it behind when he checked out of the hospital, raw-skinned and born-again.

There's a style of country singing known as "high lonesome," innocent and broken and sad, like that of a wounded child. It's contrived, of course. The high-lonesome singer, in fact, must be a mature artist in full control. He must fully possess his song before he exposes the apparent pain that afflicts him.

Al Green has recorded a few country tunes, but he was never a high-lonesome man. And yet his voice worked the same vulnerability, that stance of innocence, of a singer powerless before the intense emotion of his song. We might name it "high tenderness."

High tenderness is just as sweetly desolate as high lonesome. A falsetto, after all, is artificial, not from the heart but from the throat. It belongs naturally to neither man nor woman; it's a homeless sound, and yet it promises to take us back home, to some place that is real, to a feeling so intense it can't be expressed with an ordinary tenor or a soprano. Falsettos are true and false at the same time.

For instance: The man who in 1972 sang "Let's Stay Together" could not. The man who was "Tired of Being Alone" never had been. He sang not from experience but from ambition. The "artifice" of falsetto, writes scholar Anne-Lise François, "is inseparable from a presumption to heights, a reaching beyond one's natural limits—call it transcendence."

Here's a high-tender story. A few years ago, I shared a house with a man I'll call Bruce, a tightly wound North Carolinian with the body of a jockey and the face of a leprechaun, cloudy blue eyes above high cheekbones and lips like someone had tied a bow of red ribbon. He was a beautiful man, indifferent to the effect he had on women. We lived together in a house full of men; Bruce said he simply preferred their company. "Guys," he'd say, "are just more *competent.*" There was this little joke Bruce liked to play. When a man who was showering closed his eyes, Bruce would strip down in a flash and pad quietly up to him and stand as close as he could without touching. Then, when the victim opened his eyes and jumped, Bruce would stand perfectly still, his voice soft and reasonable. "Sorry, brother," he'd say. "Just wanted to freak you out."

Bruce wasn't gay. He wasn't, technically, anything. He was twenty-five, but he was a virgin; it was a religious thing. He asked me once what sex with a woman was like "emotionally," but before I could even think of how to answer, he silenced me. Sex for him was like a falsetto, pure and nonexistent in the natural order of things. It was like that story of Robert Johnson at the crossroads, or Al Green burned and born-again. A myth, elusive and sweet. Bruce didn't need to sully it with details for it to be true.

One day we got to discussing Al Green, and I mentioned that I'd seen Al Green perform, up in Massachusetts. This bothered Bruce. He was a Southerner, and I was not, and he did not like this news of Yankee privilege. Also, he was certain I considered him racist, because that's what he believed all New Yorkers thought about all North Carolinians.

As it happened, I did think that. About Bruce, anyway, ever since he'd gently made the case for the Stars and Bars as a symbol of his heritage. Still, Bruce wanted me to know that as a Southern white man, he was blacker than me. There was, he said, an "Alabama blacksnake" in his pants. He was not just black, he was a black *man*, and I was nothing but a white boy. "Agreed," I said, hoping to calm him. I told him Casper the Friendly Ghost was blacker than me. But Bruce could not be deterred. He left the room and returned with a box and put in a CD and cranked up "Here I Am (Come and Take Me)," and he started not so much to dance as to groove. His hands balled into fists, his sapphire eyes crinkled. He began singing, a honey falsetto just like the Reverend's, "Here I a-a-m. . . ." He heard me laughing, applauding, but he didn't stop. I don't think he could've. He grabbed his crotch and shook his head like a rag, going deeper and deeper into Green. Then he froze, dropped back to his ordinary voice as if he was narrating. "I used to work in this pizza parlor," he said. "We had a poster of Al Green. He was, he was—man! Shirtless, leather pants. *Low* leather pants." Bruce grabbed his crotch. "Hips cocked," Bruce said, and shook his head and howled, slid across the floor, and grabbed my waist and held me so tight I could feel his pulse beating. Then he moonwalked away and buckled just a little with his feet spread wide, hands in the air, testifying, baring his torso. It wasn't real, of course, and it was thick with the blues of a misplaced exoticism, and a lust so lost and confused that it had got stuck on a soul song three decades old, worn as some kind of identity, black and white, maybe man and woman, used and spurned and virgin, the high-tender gospel of one Southern white boy, true and false, innocent, broken, and sad.

Only His Voice Made Us Feel This Way

IT IS LIKE CHURCH by **Susan Straight**

—————

The young girls look at us like we're ghosts when Al Green comes on the boom box in the driveway, just as the sun is going down and we're done putting up the rest of the ribs in foil-covered pans, when all of us, the women who are their mothers and aunts, are sitting in folding chairs with our feet out in front of us because we've been on them all day cooking and putting up with Usher and Ciara blasting from the speakers of someone's truck parked in front of the yard.

It doesn't matter which gathering it is—whose birthday or which holiday—we always sit in a driveway or a living room, and one of our ex-husbands or one of us puts on music from the 1970s. Chaka Khan. Sly and the Family Stone. But when the men want us to get forgiving and misty-eyed, right after we clean up all that food, someone puts on Al Green.

We hear not the electrified drums that shake our ribs, but the sparkly snare drum and organ riff that tap companionably at our sternums—the long bones that cover our hearts. We hear Al Green say, "I'm so glad you're mine."

Even though we're not theirs now, the men on the other side of the yard, we might as well be, because we're all still here, looking at one another and remembering all those cars speeding down dirt roads out past the orange groves, remembering all those nights on the phone, all those house parties where the DJ played Al Green when it got to eleven or so and it was time to pair up and move more slowly, to have a hand planted on your backbone just where your spine ended.

My three daughters, and all their cousins, who are between twelve and twenty-five, study our faces as Al Green sings about the only thing he sings about—that which transformed us when we were young like they are, when our feet didn't hurt and we were in the darkened living rooms with the ancient record players spinning "Call Me" and "Let's Stay Together"—as he testifies about the only thing we cared about then. Love. Love and Happiness. Let's Get Married. Here I Am—Come and Take Me.

Our faces get softer. Our eyes narrow to slits as we study the men gathered at the huge smoker and the old trucks, drinking their Hennessys, slamming down dominoes, and hollering. They hear Al Green, too, and they smile, because Al used to work for them.

"Girl," Sandra says to me, leaning back and folding her hands across her stomach. "Girl, this song used to *kill* me. Every time. It was this one summer. You know."

The five beats—stark and sweet, we all know them, every one of us women in the driveway, my sisters-in-law and neighbors and relatives by marriage—and then the guitar plaintive and the organ comes rolling in to make it sacramental.

Love will make you do right. Love will make you do wrong.

We think we did right. We think the men did wrong.

But here we all are, the dishes of macaroni and greens and rice behind us on the tables, our kids playing basketball in the street or bent over car hoods looking at something, the girls walking in the other yards with their tight jeans and little tees.

They think we look old. The women gathered around me, all in our forties and early fifties. Like we're in Lutcher, Louisiana, or Grenada, Mississippi. Helena, Arkansas. Galveston, Texas.

Al Green was born in 1946 in Forrest City, Arkansas, the son of a sharecropper, like some of the parents in our neighborhood, too. Al Green started singing gospel at nine, but he must have already spent his childhood observing the storms of adult love, because by the time he moved to Grand Rapids, Michigan, with his family, he abandoned gospel for secular love, and some sin, but always kept his desire for redemption.

The story goes that when his father kicked him out of the family gospel group for listening to Jackie Wilson at sixteen, Al and a few friends formed their own r&b group and their own independent record company, Hotline. In 1969, while on tour in Texas, Green met Willie Mitchell, bandleader and vice president of Hi Records, and in Memphis, assembled with the horns and strings and organ and tightly wound beat, Mitchell helped Green find his style and sound. "Silky on top, rough on the bottom," Mitchell is said to have told Green, and that's what we grew up hearing all over America during the '70s, and here in Southern California, in a largely black neighborhood where much of life was transplanted from the South.

Sitting here in my father-in-law's driveway with all my women relatives and friends, I know nearly every one of us was born in Southern California. But aside from my parents, who were born in Switzerland and Canada, the parents of all the women around me were born in the South, and between the smells of smoked meat and the sound of Al Green moaning and his voice catching in his throat when he says, "Baby, I'm so—so thankful for your loving—glad you're mine," it feels like church and testifying and that kind of love and loss that the young girls are afraid of, that seems to come from a place with too many trees and not enough cars, of women sitting not in a club or an Escalade but in a driveway, on folding chairs, with faces so soft they look like they might cry.

It is like church, for us. Al Green's voice slides and purrs in his lovely throat. Take me to the river. Wash me down. Tell me all your troubles. Lay all your burdens down.

He wanted to love us and take care of us and take us to church in our own houses, in our living rooms, on our couches, which were not the couches we wanted. We wanted better couches, and less hard work, and for the men to stay home and stay married to us, and we loved our children once they were the ones sitting near us on the couch, but when Al Green came on the radio or someone played "I'm Still in Love With You" at the fortieth birthday party of the man who'd been one of the most handsome in our youth, we all melted.

I was twelve when he had his huge hit, "I'm Still in Love With You," and I heard it on my tiny yellow transistor radio that summer before we all went to junior high and understood slow dancing. At fourteen, I met my future husband, and my friends and I learned about the crucible of love at house parties and in cars packed with people and in backyards where Al Green's voice wafted through the pepper trees.

That was the year, 1974, when Al Green's former girlfriend broke into his house in Memphis and poured boiling grits on him while he was bathing, inflicting second-degree burns over his body before she killed herself in an adjacent bedroom with his gun.

We heard the older guys use his name as part of the lexicon of love and rejection and obsession: "You bet not mess with that woman, fool—she look like she can cook some grits. She do a Al Green on you, brother, you let her go."

But they've all let us go, and almost every one of us, the women sitting in the driveway tonight, are single mothers now. When we hear him sing "For the Good Times," we don't care. We had our times, and we would never trade them.

Our daughters stalk toward us and then away. One of them says, "You all look like—"

They don't know how we look, because they've never looked like that. I wonder if they ever will, with how they live and love—they don't have house parties and driveways and dances in the gym and in the park. They have cars rolling past, boys studying them, yes, but the voices are blaring gymnastic fantasies and X-rated instructions from huge car-stereo speakers, rappers that sound to our ancient ears like slightly bored field generals.

Yes, back in our day, there was going to be a bed, or a couch, or a place to practice love. Yes, there was going to be possible disappointment. But there seemed a holiness to it. We revered the love we knew would come, and even the hurt. Because being hurt was inevitable, we knew from watching our own parents.

But that deep, soul-scouring love, with Al Green testifying to how powerful it was—that's what we knew we would have.

Lay all my troubles down. Take me by the hand. Take me to the river—wash me down. We'll walk away with victory.

Only Al Green made Sandra feel this way, as she closes her eyes next to me and moves her shoulders, dances just a little in the folding chair. Revia, Doris, Tina, Shirley—we are a long line of women along the cement edge of the driveway.

The roll and trill of the organ like wavelets leaving ghostly foam arcs on the sand. The horns. And then he moans, "I wanna soothe you, baby, and wipe all your tears away...."

Tenderness and dancing close together in the dark of someone's living room, sloe gin or homebrew in a paper cup, knees bumping in time with the insistent drums that even our kids can hear now, watching us in the driveway.

They can't have this. There's almost a pity we feel for them, watching us. We love them, but we feel sorry that they won't know how deep these strings pull inside, the way love is all tangled up with this voice that means time gone past, but the memory of how we were once sanctified.

Dept.
of Elvis

Bill Haney

THE FIRST AND MOST INFLUENTIAL ELVIS IMPERSONATOR EVER
by Tom Graves

━━━

Bill Haney never liked being called an Elvis impersonator. "I'm a lousy imitator," he says. "If you asked me to sound like anybody, I couldn't. I don't know how to change my voice. People automatically started comparing my voice to his. I never once tried to sound like Elvis. I tried to sound like Bill Haney."

It has been more than a decade since Bill Haney, the world's first full-time Elvis impersonator, the man who little by little created what has become a permanent cultural iconography, hung up his jumpsuit and turned his back on the money, the crowds, the adulation, not to mention the competing fan clubs that stretched from Memphis to West Berlin. By the time he quit in 1982, there were an estimated two thousand people doing the same thing Bill Haney did for a living.

"There are too many bad Elvis acts out there stinking things up for the rest of us," he told a reporter at the time. There was a young Elvis, a fat Elvis, a black Elvis, a girl Elvis, a Mexican Elvis, even a midget Elvis. The image of Elvis Presley on those stages was becoming increasingly sick and twisted and ugly, and the camp aspect of it—those people who thought the whole thing was some great white-trash joke—well, it all got to be too much for the boy from Blytheville, Arkansas, the one who started it all when he fell in love with Jerry Lee Lewis's red-hot piano.

Bill Haney is now fifty-five years old—"thirteen years older than *he* was when he died," he says—and still carries himself with the athletic grace of his performing years. The lines around his eyes and the few telling signs of gray in his black hair are all that belie his youthful appearance. When he grins, which is often, Haney is still strikingly handsome, and one can guess what the effect of that smile must have been like in the early '70s when he was creating a new form of pop culture.

He is sitting in the break room of the Four Seasons Realty Company in West Memphis, Arkansas, a highly successful real-estate enterprise he and his wife of thirty-five years, Gail, own. The office is decorated in nouveau West Memphis with tall cathedral windows, designer awnings, and peach-colored, floral-pattern furniture. The teal carpet is thick and cushiony, the matching walls bright and filled with sunshine. Bill is wearing a short-sleeved shirt with a bright red tropical print, khaki pants, and canvas deck shoes. He looks as if he has made afternoon plans to go sailing.

On first meeting him one is startled to discover that he doesn't look a thing like Elvis and, to the practiced ear, Haney's flat Arkansas drawl is nothing like Elvis's mumbling Memphis brogue. Yet the longer Bill Haney talks, the weirder it gets. Maybe it's the crooked grin, the careful coiffure, or the deadpan Southern wit. Or maybe it's some more mysterious osmosis taking place. Whatever the source, Haney is off the scale on the Elvis meter. At times, one finds it impossible not to simply sit and stare.

Bill was four years old when music moved center stage into his life. He heard his next-door neighbor in Blytheville pounding out a boogie-woogie on the piano and told his mother, "I want to do that." She saw to it that Bill got piano lessons and everyone was surprised at how quickly the boy became fluent, but before reaching his teens he had quit all formal musical training and was rocking on his own. Although eager for any opportunity to perform, Bill was too shy to sing, even though he had a strong, distinctive tenor voice. As long as he was behind his keyboard, though, everything was fine.

Shortly after Bill turned fifteen, his father announced to the family that they would be moving to Southern California. His father had been a policeman in Blytheville for over twenty-five years, but was willing to risk his family's future on the promise of a better job with a better salary. But Bill didn't take to California.

"As soon as school was out for the summer, I'd head back this a-way," he says. "I never liked California and was homesick. I've wondered a lot of times if things would've changed if I'd stayed back here to begin with and hadn't had anything to do with California. But parents have to change jobs sometimes . . . back then everyone was goin' out there for the *gold*, the California gold. A lot more pay than you could make back here. I was there, but I hated it."

He was in high school when a swivel-hipped boy from back in Memphis took the music world by storm. "I wore my hair like Elvis. I always had. But at that time I thought Elvis was just a pretty boy for girls—you know, with 'Love Me Tender' and 'Teddy Bear' and all that, and those girls screamin'."

Bill was more interested in Chuck Berry and Little Richard and smooth piano players like Fats Domino. Then came the craziest, poundingest piano player the world had ever seen, a blond-haired demon who literally set his piano on fire: Jerry Lee Lewis, the Killer. Bill listened to all those singles on the Sun record label—"Great Balls of Fire," "Whole Lotta Shakin' Goin' On," "Breathless"—and was transformed into a flailing keyboard wild man. "Man, you oughta seen me," Bill says. "I wiped them pianos *out*. I was killin' pianos."

By the time he graduated from high school in Torrance, California, in 1958, Bill had won several amateur talent contests with his piano act, including one on a television show, *Town Hall Party* in Los Angeles, that featured many of the nation's best country and western artists. He was invited back on the show to compete with other finalists and won the quarterfinals. He was invited again for the annual finals and won that one, too.

RCA Records came knocking.

"RCA got in contact with me after my win on *Town Hall Party* and wanted to groom me as an instrumentalist like Dave 'Baby' Cortez, who had a popular organ act going at the time. I wasn't singing at all then, but I didn't want to be just an instrumentalist. I wanted to have a band, so RCA told me to go ahead and get one.

"Well, I found a group of boys from Arkansas out there and we got up a band called the Flares and cut some singles for RCA. RCA got behind the records and sent us on a promotional tour to push the singles and we went across the country and were supposed to end the tour on *American Bandstand*. We started the tour and this old boy who was our singer, well, his daddy got sick and he had to leave the band. That left me as the only one in the band that knew the words to the songs. We were doing covers of Chuck Berry, Carl Perkins, Little Richard, and everyone else, and when I took over on vocals everybody was sayin', 'Hey man, you sound a lot like Elvis. Do you know any of his stuff?' Well, I hadn't learned any Elvis material, except for a few things that old boy, our singer, had done. So I started pickin' it up.

"At that time, if you were going to get a club to hire you, you had to play what the people were asking for so you could get up a crowd. Every time I'd go to play, people'd say, 'Do you know this song? Do you know that song by Elvis?' As they'd start naming them off, I'd go and learn them. And so people started to associate my voice with his. Even the songs that wasn't his came out *Elvisy*. It was easy for me; I didn't have to learn how to train my voice to be similar to his. I think it was because the colloquialisms we had, being from the South, were the same as far as the way we pronounced things and all. But then whenever I'd hear him sing something, it was just [he snaps his fingers] . . . the song was just *natural* to me."

Although the singles the Flares cut for RCA didn't burn up the charts, Haney had tasted the musician's life and liked it.

"After winning those contests out in California, I decided what I wanted to do was either play baseball or play music. Man, I was heavy into baseball, but I decided to stick to music. Music just consumed me. You know, man, you see those pretty little girls and all and I says to myself, 'Forget baseball.'"

Still homesick for his native Arkansas, Haney moved back to Blytheville, recruited another band, and married a pretty hometown girl, Gail Slaughter. Throughout the late '50s and early '60s, he covered the Arkansas–Missouri Bootheel circuit, playing many of the roadhouse honky-tonks that Elvis had played when he was still called the Hillbilly Cat and recorded for Sam Phillips's Sun record label. The tough clubs and joints that Jerry Lee Lewis and Carl Perkins toured became Haney's stomping grounds—clubs like the Rebel Inn in Osceola, the B&B Club in Gobler, the Zanza Club in Haiti, Top Hat in Kennett, Twin Gables in Blytheville.

People kept requesting Elvis songs and Haney began to develop a core of fans who came just to hear him do Elvis. Even though he sat behind a piano, didn't particularly look like Elvis, and sang in a much lower key, people told him over and over again how much he reminded them of Elvis.

Unlike many musicians, Bill Haney was a savvy businessman. With a wife and two young daughters to support, he knew his success depended on his ability to deliver onstage and knew if he could pull in a packed house, his bookings would multiply, and he could demand more money. And Elvis had never let him down.

Although Haney had played throughout the South, he had purposely avoided Memphis. "I didn't move into the Memphis market because I was hesitant about going where that Elvis monster was. I didn't know how I'd be accepted over there based on the kind of stuff I was doin'. Well, I wound up playing on *Dance Party* a couple of times, which was a local music show on WHBQ television station in Memphis that was hosted by Wink Martindale. Anita Wood, who was Elvis's girlfriend at the time, was on the show that day, and I didn't know who she was. She walks up to me and says, 'You know, when you're on TV, you remind me a lot of a good friend of mine.' I says, 'Oh really?' I thought she was just some gal who was goin' to Memphis State University and just happened to be on there as an extra that day. She said, 'Yeah, and I'd like to introduce you to him, but he's out of the country right now." I says, 'Well, who is it?,' 'cause I was still in the dark. She says, 'Elvis Presley,' and I says, 'Oh yeah, man. I'd love to meet him.' But they busted up and that was that."

Around this time, Haney began to have doubts about his career as an entertainer. He'd had more fun than any man was entitled to and had left his mark in the small towns that dotted Memphis' tri-state expanse, but he wanted to be a devoted father and husband. Shortly after the Beatles had nudged Elvis off the charts, Haney decided to leave the business. He obtained a real-estate license and began to concentrate on selling homes and lots around Hardy, Arkansas. It was something he liked, was good at, and it provided a solid, steady income. But there was still that call of the wild.

"I played for all the parties the real-estate company I worked for would put on. And I played and practiced at home, keeping up with all the new stuff. When we had sold off most of the residential lots in Hardy, I told my wife I was going back into music. I missed it. I wanted to move the family back to Blytheville, and one day when I was visiting there I went out to the Ramada Inn and they had someone in the bar playing your ordinary, basic piano music. There were a few people there who knew me, and they asked if I'd get up and play something. I let 'em talk me into it, and so I got up and played and sang a few songs.

"The people just... God... they was goin' wild. They was coming in from the lobby and all over the hotel to watch me. Even the help was comin' out from everywhere. I knew I was onto something."

Bill Haney was by no means the first person to imitate Elvis Presley. Undoubtedly, there were Elvis imitators performing in living rooms all over Memphis the same night disc jockey Dewey Phillips premiered "That's All Right" on his radio show. Even before Elvis's historic appearances on *The Ed Sullivan Show*, several comedians had incorporated an Elvis bit into their routines, along with impersonations of Dean Martin, John Wayne, Kirk Douglas, and whoever else would get a laugh.

As early as the mid-'50s a British singer, Terry Dene, had a short-lived Elvis-inspired act that toured England. According to Elvis intimate George Klein, there were one or two other performers who did an Elvis song or two as part of their routine. But these artists performed much more comically and tongue-in-cheek than with the studied seriousness we associate with modern-day Elvis impersonators.

Ral Donner was one of the first successful Elvis soundalikes on record and was followed by Terry Stafford, who had a huge hit with "Suspicion" and was never heard from again.

Hollywood, in its own way, got in on the act with bland Elvis clones like Fabian, Tommy Sands, Frankie Avalon, and Ed "Kookie" Byrnes.

The great leap of faith had not yet happened; no one had been asked to *believe*, to pretend for an hour or two that the person on stage was not some talented mimic from Blytheville, Arkansas, but the real deal—the King himself in the flesh. This leap is what separated mere imitators from impersonators.

By 1968 Elvis Presley's career was in a serious decline. After his stint in the Army, the hits began to dry up. When Elvis gave up live performing for Hollywood B-movies and lackluster soundtrack albums, the Beatles and all the other Brits rendered him passé. Between 1962 and 1969, Elvis Presley, the King of Rock & Roll, didn't have a single Number One hit. He hadn't appeared on TV since he'd teamed with Frank Sinatra in 1960 after being discharged from the Army, and hadn't performed before a live audience in nearly decade. The movies were getting worse *practically frame by frame*; even the die-hard fans were beginning to wonder what had happened to Elvis.

Finally, in 1968, Elvis stood up to Colonel Tom Parker, his smothering manager. There would be no more dumb movies, and he would start performing again. He was also determined to make some more decent records. Elvis must have been stung when he met the Beatles in 1965 and they asked, "Why don't you go back to your old style of record?" He wanted to prove to the world he was still the King and filmed a television special, now known as the '68 *Comeback Special*, that fully restored him to his throne. Clad in skintight black leather, Elvis was all raw animal power. The world watched and the world responded. Elvis was back.

In 1971, an Elvis fan and singer named Dave Carlson from Oak Forest, Illinois, discovered the same thing Bill Haney had a few years earlier: Elvis fans, the true-blue fans who would be called Elvi in years to come, were starved for their idol. Carlson, like Haney, had started in bands singing a few Elvis songs. The Elvis fans wanted more and told him he sounded just like Elvis. Carlson soon found he could draw a consistently bigger crowd by playing to the Elvis contingent.

"You've got to remember," Carlson says today, "that for years in the '60s Elvis was unavailable. It was like he was in hiding, a recluse. Until 1969, he didn't perform live and nobody had seen him. Even when he started touring again, if you were lucky, he came to your city once. And in those big auditoriums and arenas who could feel close to him? He was underexposed to the public and had been for years.

"You've got to understand one thing about the real Elvis fans: they're like drug addicts. They can't get over Elvis or ever get enough of Elvis. These people were having severe withdrawal symptoms, and guys like me and Bill Haney, and one or two others who were out there before Elvis died—Johnny Harra and Elvis Wade—were filling that void, that emptiness. If you're a heroin addict and you can't get any heroin, morphine is a good substitute. Well, we were like that—the second-best thing. Sometimes the second-best thing can satisfy for a moment."

Bill Haney moved back to Blytheville and began performing regularly at the Ramada Inn there. Rather than performing Elvis oldies, he began to concentrate on the newer material, "Suspicious Minds," "C.C. Rider," "An American Trilogy," and "Polk Salad Annie," and tried to keep the song list as current as possible. The response was overwhelming. The people, especially the women, went crazy.

"I played at that Ramada Inn for about a year, and business was better than they had ever had. The manager got sent down to manage the Levee Lounge in Memphis at the Ramada Inn on Lamar Avenue. It was new at the time, and they were bringing in some big outfits, some big-name bands. He wanted me to come down there and play, but I was intimidated by it. . . . I was playing with a little ol' four-piece group and still singing from behind the piano. I went down there nervous as hell, you know. I never had worked Memphis. But the response was good, real good, so he fixed me up for another couple of weeks.

"We started off and people was acceptin' it and I got a little more comfortable. I decided to add a few things to the group. So I added a lightman, upgraded the equipment, hired me another keyboard player who played the strings stuff and the Hammond B-3 organ—I was still playing the piano—then we go along and I started wearing different stuff. Stuff that more closely resembled what *he* was wearing. I thought, 'Well, if I'm going to do this Elvis thing, I may as well give the flavor of it. What the hell, I'm not going to copy him.' Then I started having stuff made up for me, you know, jumpsuit-style and all. I started wearing it and people really liked it, it got a response. And I thought, 'Well, I can make it even better than that.' And I did some more and the response was even better.

"I seen that my Elvis act was really going over good even in his hometown, and I said to myself, 'Hey man, it's showtime.' But it wasn't until 1974 that I was doing a stand-up Elvis routine. I felt lost without that piano. Piano was a part of me and still is. But promoters and everybody kept telling me that I could make a lot more money if I could get out from behind the piano and do a stand-up.

"I said, 'Man, I can't do that.' I was thinkin', 'What am I gonna do with myself out there?'

"Charlie Hodge, who was one of Elvis's Memphis Mafia boys, used to come to the show a lot. He walked up and says, 'Man, you get your butt up off that piano and give those people something to see.' I said, 'Man, there *ain't* nothin' to see.' Hell, I'm proud of the piano work that I do and I didn't want to leave that. Charlie finally says, 'You either stand up out there or I'm goin' to embarrass the hell out of you.' So I got up and I was nervous, man . . . that's probably the second hardest thing I've ever done in my life. The first was ever singin' in front of people in the first place.

"Well, I got up there and as I went along I decided I'd see if I had enough balls to keep on with it. It's hard to do for someone like me who's a little bit reserved. Now even when I went stand-up, I never studied Elvis, so even now I don't know exactly what all he did. I'd seen some of his shows, of course, and I knew *basically* what he did. But I sure didn't want to *copy* nothin'. I'da felt like a idiot doin' that. So whatever I did, it was something that felt comfortable to me. If it was somethin' that would turn on the gals some way or other, if it was somethin' that would get their attention, I'd say, 'Hey, I think I'll do that again.' So you learn as you go along. I was learnin' more about this and that, and then I started getting braver and not letting it bother me. Like doing karate moves and all when I'd never took karate. I just punched with the beat. The thing is, it seemed to work because what I did was *me* and it was *natural* and wasn't like saying, 'Okay, he used two fingers to do this and he put his foot down here, and he. . . .' You know, I didn't want to get into that at all. I would've been too embarrassed to do that. I have to do it *my way.*"

When Bill Haney got away from the piano and stood by himself in the spotlight, the effect was complete. The jumpsuits, the belts, the spangles, the shades, the red scarves, and the note-perfect song arrangements made Bill Haney's act much more than a clever illusion—they made it *reality*.

The crowds had always been good, but they soon became unbelievable: standing room only every night, reservations weeks in advance, long queues. Haney was pulling down thousands of dollars a week and word got out that seeing Bill Haney perform was as good as seeing Elvis himself, maybe even better. Haney, after all, would nod toward your table and dedicate a special request, save a scarf just for you, speak to you sweetly during a break, maybe even give you a hug and a kiss and thank you from the bottom of his heart for coming out to see him.

Elvis fans weren't the only ones curious about this guy who looked and sang just like Elvis. Bill Burk, a columnist and music writer for the *Memphis Press-Scimitar* who had covered the Elvis beat for a number of years and is now the editor and publisher of *Elvis World* magazine, heard about Haney's unusual act and went to the Levee Lounge to check out the rumors. Like so many others, Burk was astounded by what he witnessed: "The crowd response to Haney was unreal. The girls would scream and crowd the stage and grab for the scarves.

"Bill's timing could not have been better for what he was doing. Elvis had been away from the public spotlight for a long time and when he made his comeback in 1968—it ignited the whole Elvis thing all over again. Plus, Haney was good. I've seen literally hundreds of Elvis impersonators over the years and only a handful have been worth a durn. Haney was about the best I ever heard."

Tourists who came to Memphis to see Graceland and maybe catch a glimpse of Elvis found out about Bill Haney and went home telling their friends about this amazing guy who imitated Elvis. Fan clubs began to form including a hard-core group of locals who dubbed themselves Haney's Honeys and wore special T-shirts to all his performances. A rival group called Haney's Heinies banded together and they engaged in a friendly, but earnest, competition with the Honeys.

The Elvis Presley fan clubs also heard about the Elvis wannabe and were none too pleased about some copycat who thought he wanted to be the King. Before one of his shows at the Levee Lounge, Haney was approached by a middle-aged woman who informed him she was the president of one of Elvis's largest fan clubs.

"I just want to know who the hell you think you are?"

"Just Bill Haney, ma'am," he answered.

"I want you to know one thing," she went on. "There is only one Elvis and there ain't never going to be another. Who are *you*? You don't look like him, there ain't nobody who sounds like him—"

"I hope you're not offended, lady," Haney politely interrupted. "I'm just doing a show based off his. That's all."

After the show, the club president approached him again, this time with tears in her eyes. "I want you to know something. I really enjoyed that. You are for real and I'm a Bill Haney fan now. *Believe me.*"

The hubbub over Bill Haney didn't escape the attention of the Memphis morning DJ Rick Dees, who is now one of the nation's best-known radio personalities. Dees has been poking good-natured fun at Elvis for a number of years with a series of hilarious imitations, including one about Elvis eating too many jelly doughnuts. Dees called Haney on the air to rib him about taking over Elvis's job and concocted an imaginary rivalry between the two, claiming Haney wanted to change the name of Elvis Presley Boulevard to Bill Haney Avenue. Dees staged a sing-out on the show between Haney and Elvis, and did both voices himself. The publicity brought even bigger crowds willing to pay more money to get in, including several of the secretaries who worked at Graceland, and practically all of Elvis's Memphis Mafia.

The commotion didn't go unnoticed at Graceland. Every time one of Elvis's songs would come on the radio out at Graceland, one of the Memphis Mafia would quip, "Hey man, there's that cat who sounds just like Bill Haney." And they would all laugh.

One weeknight after Haney's show, the Levee Lounge manager came up to him and asked, "Do you know who was here just a while ago?"

Haney shook his head no.

"Elvis."

"I looked at that manager and says, 'Man, you're kidding me.'

"He says, 'Naw, man.'

"And I says, '*Holy shit.*'

"And the manager says, 'Charlie Hodge is still here and he wants to talk to you. Elvis was sittin' right back there in that booth. I went back and let them in through the kitchen 'cause they called before they came and told me what they wanted. They didn't want any attention, they wanted lights out, and they wanted back in a dark corner somewhere.'

"And that's what they did. They turned the lights out back in the booth—several booths, actually—and he came in with a cowboy hat on, sat in the back with the lights all out. Nobody even knew he was there and there was people all around him. It's probably a good thing I didn't know about him being there. I probably would've got all tongue-tied on the stage.

"Well, the manager brings Charlie Hodge around and Charlie says, 'Hey man, where you want me to pick you up?'

"I says, 'What you mean?'

"And he says, 'You do want to meet Elvis, don't you?'

"I says, '*Oh, hell yeah.*'

"And Charlie says, 'Elvis told me to stay and bring you out to the house for awhile.'

"So we started over there to Graceland and I thought that was great, but the impact didn't hit me until those gates opened up and we started up the drive and I thought, '*Holy shit! I'm really gonna meet this guy!*' You know, hundreds and hundreds, *millions*, of people would like to meet him, and here *I* am going in to meet him.

"I went in the house, and Elvis was upstairs and me and Charlie just messed around in the Jungle Room, Charlie joking around and stuff. Finally, Charlie says, 'Hey man, c'mere, c'mere, Elvis is coming down the stairs.'

"Well, Charlie introduced me to him and Elvis stuck out his left hand and said, 'Excuse my right hand, man, I've got a burn.' I couldn't help but notice that his left hand was just full of diamonds. Both his hands were *unusually puffy*. Soft, puffy. When I seen him come down the stairs it was like there was some damn aura around the guy. I mean he was *different*. More different than anybody I've ever met. I've never met anybody who projected that type of electricity. It was . . . *different*. I've met a lot of stars in my lifetime . . . Jerry Lee Lewis, Roy Orbison, Johnny Cash, Ricky Nelson . . . and I never met anything like Presley. And never will.

"When I was out there with him he says to me, 'Hey man, come on outside. I wanta show you my motherfucking cars.' We went outside and there was a brand new Lincoln Mark IV; he had just given away five brand new Marks to people. He looks at me and says, 'Ain't this one a motherfucker man?' And I said, 'Yeah man, that is *nice*.' He made me feel pretty easy. We sat around in the house for a long time just talkin', jokin', and playin' with the dogs. Charlie was cuttin' up and asks him, 'Elvis, what do you think about ol' Haney?' Elvis looks at me and laughs and says, 'I like his *style*.'

"I went out to Graceland many more times after that, not to see him, but to visit all his people who I had become good friends with. That was the only time I went out there just to see Elvis. After that, my schedule of concerts and his schedule of concerts often was in conflict with each other, and I didn't get to see too much of him. Plus, he really wasn't in that good of health after that. We waved and said hi to each other and that was about it. You could really see he was changing. You could tell he was getting way, way overweight and didn't seem to be like he was. He stayed in his room nearly all the time; you just didn't see Elvis that much."

After meeting Elvis, Haney would frequently get calls from Graceland. "We've got a bunch of stuff Elvis doesn't want and we're going to bring it out to you," they would tell him. Haney was given teddy bears and other stuffed animals, sweaters, and even one of Elvis's custom-made jumpsuits that wasn't the color he had ordered. "It was brown," Haney says, "and he didn't like to wear browns. So they re-did Elvis another one in black with silver trimming."

On August 16, 1977, Haney was booked to play Hot Springs, Arkansas, and was relaxing in his motel room when one of his band members came into the room with a pained look on his face. "Did you hear about Elvis?"

When he was told that Elvis had died, Haney slumped in his bed and held his head in his hands. He felt as if he had lost a member of his family, perhaps even some part of himself. He wanted to cancel that night's show, but was under a tight contract; the show had to go on. He went onstage, but the crowd was unusually quiet and reserved. There was no screaming, no fainting, none of the usual frenzy. Instead, many of the women cried softly. "When I did some of his songs that really hit home," Haney says, "well, all I can say is it was real emotional. For me, too."

Elvis's death had both a positive and negative effect on Haney's career. He was soon out of the clubs and lounges and playing large arenas and coliseums. Only days after Elvis was laid to rest, Haney nearly sold out the Pine Bluff Coliseum in Arkansas, and the crowd reacted as if he were the King resurrected from the grave. "We took in over thirty-two thousand dollars that night on the gate. Conway Twitty and Loretta Lynn only did twenty-eight thousand, so that gives you some idea of what kind of impact his death had."

From there, Haney got an exclusive contract to play the Silver Bird in Las Vegas. The management there gave him a suite, a hairdresser, a makeup artist, and a wardrobe assistant. He played the Cow Palace in San Francisco and the Los Angeles Sports Arena. He was featured numerous times on television news programs. The money was better than Bill Haney had ever imagined. The road, however, was beginning to take its toll. He was tired, burnt out, and lonely for his family. His wife had begged him for years to get off the road and join her in the real-estate business again.

Before Elvis had died, there were only a handful of impersonators, all of whom, it would seem, had followed in Haney's footsteps. Now there were hundreds and they were turning the whole thing into a sour joke.

"I knew when he died others would be coming out of the woodwork," Haney says. "I always said I wouldn't became part of some circus. There were so many cheap acts—I mean, *cheap*—some guy wearin' a few dollars worth of bad clothes, didn't look like him, didn't sound like him except in the shower, got some musicians together and decided he wanted to do a show. That hurt the business, I couldn't watch those guys. They made me want to throw up."

The fans had changed also. After Elvis died the hard-core fans seemed to become more aggressive, almost militant. "They were people who idolized Elvis, and then Elvis was gone. Their second choice was me. They were great fans because they supported me everywhere I went. Without them, I never would have gone anywhere. They made things more exciting, they screamed and carried on and gave me a little taste of what Elvis would have felt like. But I've said many times that I never understood the people who would go crazy. I've seen women bite each other, get in fistfights, knock cops all around. At times, we would just be mobbed by fans and they would grab at you, pulling and tearing at your clothes. I would think, 'Man, these are some expensive friggin' suits to be tearin' up.' But they would go for anything, necklaces, belts, anything. There were quite a few who would climb up on stage and grab ahold of you and not turn loose. We would have to pry them off.

"I was hit one night by three girls all at the same time. These girls, I swear to God, looked like Green Bay Packers. They all hit me at the same time and knocked me about ten yards back, flat on my ass. I just laid back on my ass and sang the rest of the song looking up at the ceiling."

When asked how the fan worship affected his wife and their relationship, he sighs and answers, "Trouble, man. Lots of dark clouds. Lots of things to overcome, lots of growing up to do, lots of questions to answer, all kinds of shit. Many times I've asked myself if it was all worth it. All the late-night phone calls. I couldn't afford to have an unlisted number because I was doing my own bookings most of the time. I finally got to where I couldn't handle the calls anymore, though. Fans might call at any and all hours of the night; they might find out where you live and come by to sit around for awhile. I understand that part of it, I really do. They just didn't realize how inconvenient it could be. Imagine you've got a gal callin' you up at all hours, sayin' how much she loves you and all, and you've got a wife who's mad as hell layin' in bed right next to you. And you're trying to talk and be polite to some fan. It was a lot to go through.

"The girls coming up on stage, all the kissing, the worship aspect of it . . . it was pretty heavy, man, plus the fact there was some awful pretty girls around sometimes. To sum it up for you, if my wife didn't go along to the shows, we got along a lot better."

Elvis impersonator Dave Carlson, who continues to perform after twenty-five years of doing Elvis, is even more blunt about the problems associated with fan worship:

"At times it becomes a big monkey on your back. Some of those fans literally want a piece of you. Imagine what it's like to be idolized by overweight, ugly, blue-haired old ladies who want to fantasize about you as Elvis. I feel sorry for those people—that's all they have. But they get jealous of one another and they all think they're your number-one fan. If you forget to dedicate a song to them or speak to them at their table, they can turn on you and it can get very ugly. Some of the worse-off ones will claim to be having your baby and everything else. Imagine how that kind of thing goes over with your family.

"I've had kids who've grown up and come up to me and tell me their lives were ruined and they got into drugs and trouble because their mothers were in love with me and spent all their time at my concerts or in some lounge watching me. That's so sad.

"Now I only play private gigs, conventions, and so on. I make good money and don't have to deal with girls getting their arms broken stampeding the stage, or choking each other with the scarves I've given them. I'm a novelty act to the crowds I play now, and some of them enjoy it as a joke, or for laughs. But at least I don't have to put up with that frenzied kind of adulation anymore."

In 1982, Bill Haney quit the road and put the jumpsuits in the attic. He has played on rare occasions, including a gig at the National Homebuilders Convention where he shared the stage with Frankie Valli and the Commodores. He has toned down the Elvis and gotten back behind the piano. When he performs now, he plays a lot of songs Elvis never recorded. He also has gone back to wearing ordinary stage clothes. People still come out to see Elvis, but aren't that disappointed when all they get is Bill Haney. He can still do a mean Jerry Lee Lewis.

"I'm recording a gospel album right now," Haney says. "I'm trying to develop something that nobody can identify Elvis-wise. I don't want to sound like Elvis. If it sounds anything like Elvis, I won't do it. Seeing as how my voice was always connected to Elvis, I've started singing a little bit different . . . softer, easier. I've always been in a lower key-range than Elvis. *Always.* How someone could identify me singing a song in C that he would sing in E or F in a high voice, I don't know. But they did. It's weird."

Rock & Roll/ Pop III

R.E.M.

IT'S NOT LIKE YEARS AGO by Elizabeth Wurtzel

———

When I was in college in Massachusetts in the late '80s, what I remember most about the early spring-fever days was the way the dorm-room windows would be flung open to reveal that the student body seemed to be listening to one band and one band only: R.E.M. Indeed, you could walk across the budding grass on the campus green and hear one R.E.M. album blasting out of a building on the right side—say, the opening chords of "Radio Free Europe" from *Murmur* and hear a different R.E.M. song—maybe the exuberant "Exhuming McCarthy" off *Document* coming from somewhere off the left.

Now, mind you, I attended one of those Northeastern schools-with-attitude where the political consciousness and intellectual pretentiousness of R.E.M. would seem to fit in well with the mood of the times—this was back when people were building shanties in the middle of the main quad to protest South African apartheid —so the band's popularity was hardly surprising. But, amazingly, R.E.M. had sizable followings at all sorts of schools, even at Southern campuses where Reagan Youth drove BMWs, where sorority girls and homecoming queens ruled the social scene, and business-majors with country-club backgrounds would be prone, if they didn't know these guys were rock stars, to spit on the members of R.E.M. for looking like hippie trash. By some time in the middle '80s, R.E.M. found themselves occupying that strange rock & roll realm where they were idolized by people who, in real life, would never have invited them to rush their fraternities. The sad rule for most of us is that our reach almost always exceeds our grasp, but R.E.M. was grasping and holding onto an awful lot more than they were reaching for.

The point is, for most people R.E.M. had their breakthrough success two years ago when *Out of Time,* their seventh album (not counting the collected b-sides on *Dead Letter Office* or the anthology called *Eponymous*), made it to Number One on the Billboard charts. But to me, the band was successful beyond the point of no return when the girl who lived next door to me my freshman year, someone called Libby, who hailed from Greenwich, Connecticut, declared R.E.M. to be her favorite band on earth and played her collection nonstop. With just a wall to separate us I got it all—a steady diet of *Murmur* before breakfast, *Reckoning* at dinnertime, and *Fables of the Reconstruction* late into the night. Since that could make even the meekest among us long for some Black Sabbath, there hardly seemed to be any reason to get into the band myself. Long before any R.E.M. albums went gold or platinum, the band's omnipresence on the college scene made them as much an oppressive force in bookworm circles as the "mainstream" music they were supposed to be an "alternative" from was to the rest of the world.

Listening to R.E.M. also seemed to be a first step toward declaring yourself a member of some strange special-interest group, or becoming a category in some marketing expert's demographic study that would report that you, say, bought clothes at the Gap, drove a solar-powered car, lived in Seattle or Santa Fe, ate Terra Chips, drank Rolling Rock, subscribed to *Utne Reader,* and would be likely to purchase reusable diapers once you started having babies. Or something like that. All this is to say that R.E.M.'s music became popular about the same time that a standardized, commercial notion of an alternative lifestyle was developed, so that all the bric-a-brac and bohemian touches that college students invented for themselves, and thought were just theirs, actually became something that could be bought at a shopping mall anywhere in America. For me, it was a sorry enough thing that without even trying I had paisley-patterned tapestries on my ceilings and walls, took courses in poststructuralist literary theory, spent afternoons attending Eric Rohmer double features at the nearby revival house, tended to date men with long hair who wanted to be filmmakers—all of this was stereotypical enough without adding the R.E.M. imperative into the picture. Better to listen to Bruce Springsteen and be thought of as a mall-rat from New Jersey (then again, that amounts to slumming, a whole other cliché) than fall any deeper into earthy-crunchy collegiate reverie.

And just as an alternative lifestyle began to pick up steam as a statement that could be exploited commercially (hence, you were suddenly able to buy jeans with holes already punctured in the knees, or to purchase fishnet stockings with runs already snagged up the sides), you can map out the development of college radio from a minor and mostly ignored student endeavor to an actual growth industry. Because R.E.M. became rock stars via the support of college stations, record companies suddenly realized that promoting at the university level was a marketing technique worth trying. Student disc jockeys tend to be passionate about music, they're willing to talk up new bands that they're hot for, and they're an excellent tool for creating a band's buzz. Their audience may be small, but if you get all the college-radio listeners together, you've got a groundswell—enough people to get an album on the charts. R.E.M. had built itself up to multi-platinum status through gradual and incremental growth, and had maintained a base of deeply loyal fans throughout, mainly because their following began at the grass roots. Using R.E.M. as a model, record labels realized the importance of artist development and slow growth. They realized that the big hype might sell a million albums once but it won't build a band for a long-term career.

It seems reasonable to say, then, that R.E.M.'s success taught some record labels a few honorable lessons. But it also skewed the term "alternative" to define a new branch of commercial music with its own set of standards and indicators that defied the norm to create a norm of its own—usually, anything that might be described as "quirky" or "abrasive," or both, could qualify. While alternative music had always happened by accident—a band would discover somewhere along the way that they just didn't fit into any pre-existing categories—suddenly "alternative" itself became an anti-category category: Record labels set up alternative departments, and even bands that have become utterly mainstream—like R.E.M. and U2—can still be found on the alternative charts. Because of R.E.M., the odd-ball music that used to just barely subsist on the margins of pop-music culture is now marketed as aggressively, and expected to sell just as well, as Michael Bolton.

All of this would be fine, except that what works for R.E.M. is not likely to work for most other "alternative" bands. Despite some strange notion developed somewhere out there that R.E.M. is offbeat and different, in truth the band has always created a jingle-jangle, guitar-based prettiness that is simultaneously sweet and edgy, mixing the lush Rickenbacker folk-rock of the Byrds with the dark, dour alienation of the Velvet Underground to produce music that is really quite catchy. Playing off a guitar arpeggio and staccato drum beats that make a song sad and boppy at once is a really great idea—but it's not one that is difficult for an audience to grasp. In fact, one of the most enjoyable aspects of R.E.M. is that the music combines so many pre-existing elements of the musical vocabulary that it's always instantly familiar and easily digestible.

It was R.E.M.'s ability to sound like a pop band and still address an audience of hipsters that set them up for the kind of success they are now enjoying (just last year, Nirvana used the same formula: highly likeable pop songs combined with a grungy bad attitude). If R.E.M. became the ultimate college-radio band—and along with U2, they most certainly were the underground airwaves' strongest crossover success story—what it mainly served to prove was that college students are basically conservative and conventional in their musical proclivities, and that after years of a steady diet of punk rock—or of cacophonous, screechy noise music of one underground movement or another—they were probably quite pleased to find that something as melodious and pleasant as R.E.M. could now be passed off as alternative.

By this account, if sound alone were all that counted, R.E.M. could have won me and millions of other people over years ago. Even though I never much cared for the band, I could always admit that certain R.E.M. songs were astonishingly beautiful—the gorgeously layered guitars on "Fall on Me" and the willful, fitful steadfastness of their cover of a minor '60s hit called "I Am Superman," both of them on *Life's Rich Pageant*, were undeniably catchy. And "Stand," "Pop Song '89" and "Orange Crush," all off of the major-label debut *Green*, were great, dance-happy fun. But I just couldn't stand Michael Stipe's lyrics. I don't even mind that he slurs his words so much that they're impossible to understand (*Murmur* has been jokingly referred to as *Mumble*); I just hate that Stipe is too deliberately obscure and too fixated on ecology and other politically correct stances to bother writing songs that the less right-minded among us could actually fall in love with. In a recent article in the magazine *Pulse!*, Stipe's bandmates Mike Mills and Peter Buck were so stumped by questions about the songs' meaning that the writer Ira Robbins concluded that deciphering the lyrics is a task for which membership in R.E.M. apparently isn't much help.

Now, of course, for some people, not knowing what Stipe's talking about is the whole point. I'm sure there are listeners who like the way many of his songs are deliberately non-sensical, and I know there are many others who consider Stipe to be something of a hero because he doesn't write sappy, silly love songs that pander to the lowest common denominator. But I always thought that R.E.M.'s maverick musicality could be combined with a simple, pretty set of thoughtful romantic lyrics to concoct sappy, silly love songs that were, somehow, not so sappy and not so silly. I always thought that if Michael Stipe would just play the game a little bit, R.E.M. could create a masterpiece of a pop album.

That's precisely what happened with *Out of Time*, which was an R.E.M. album for the rest of us, for all the people who just didn't get it. Although *Out of Time* opens with "Radio Song '91," a bit of social commentary that includes a quick rap from Boogie Down Productions' KRS-One, the ills the song addresses—the stupidity of pop radio—are a bit more, shall we say, run-of-the-mill than the usual. But after that, with the exception of the irritating, nitrous-oxide giddy "Shiny Happy People," *Out of Time* is an album of love songs. From the groping uncertainty of "Losing My Religion" to the loneliness of "Half a World Away" to the desperation of "Low" to the ecstasy of "Me in Honey," for the first time ever R.E.M. was creating penetrable, human songs. This was real-people music dealing with real-people problems.

There are plenty who felt that Stipe's new concern with relationships, and his move away from the abstractions and wishy-washiness that had marked previous material, was a form of selling out—but I'm pretty sure that it was just a way of growing up. R.E.M. must have known it was time to make an adult record. Simple logic would seem to dictate that it is adolescent to be hung up on love and infatuation, and that it is much more grown-up to be concerned with the World, but R.E.M. proved that the reverse is often more true in the land of rock & roll—this is a band that has best expressed its maturity of thought not through astute social commentary, but in an ability to write about love and relationships with an emotional depth that requires some semblance of adulthood. And not long after *Out of Time* was released, U2's album *Achtung Baby!* came out, marking the first time that band produced an album that had nothing to do with apartheid or civil war in Ireland or world peace or political strife or much of anything other than Bono's girl troubles. It cannot be a coincidence that two bands whose careers have followed a similar trajectory would come to the same creative point at about the same time. And it also cannot be a coincidence that these were both bands' best albums to date.

So where do they go from here? It will probably be a few years before there are new signs of life from the U2 camp—it might take Bono that much time to recover from how foolish he looked in that leather lamé suit on the Zoo TV tour—but R.E.M. didn't go on the road after *Out of Time*, and the follow-up appeared just a year later. *Automatic for the People*, despite the Marxist, agitprop ring of its title—it's actually named for a Georgia restaurant—is a sober, somber affair that almost completely lacks the verve and energy of its predecessor. It seems to be the decompression after the tremendous inflation of *Out of Time*. In simple terms, *Out of Time* was a great, big, sweeping album, clearly R.E.M.'s bid for a magnum opus, and *Automatic* has a much narrower, softer focus, as if it were a zonked-out afterthought, or an attempt to say goodbye to all that. I don't mean this in thematic terms—*Automatic* marks Stipe's return to his usual global ponderings, alongside many more intimate songs—but musically this is definitely an album that was recorded sparingly and in a minor key. It is moody and introspective. Even though John Paul Jones, best known as the only member of Led Zeppelin not to make a pact with Satan, was brought in to do string arrangements—which would seem to imply all sorts of grandiose orchestration—any use of violins and cellos and whatnot is extremely simple and organic. Without reading the credits, you might not notice the strings at all. (I mean that as an extreme compliment to Jones—the world does not need another rock album with turgid, orchestral aspirations.)

Automatic opens ominously with the strumming acoustic guitar of "Drive," the album's first single, which many have noted bears an eerie resemblance to David Essex's glam-rock classic "Rock On"—although I think David Bowie's "Space Oddity," which is about being alienated in the most literal sense, is a more accurate reference point. Beginning with the monotone chants, "Smack/Crack/Bushwhacked," it's clear that this is meant to be a downbeat battle cry for our times. The song by itself is a powerful, forceful, statement that makes the most of

Stipe's deadpan delivery, but taken with the accompanying video it is absolutely startling. The clip is very raw—shot in grainy black and white, it shows Stipe in a flesh pit being passed around over the heads and hands of a huge throng of kids. Many of the frames are all arms and flashing light—with Stipe's striped boxers occasionally peeking out of his shorts. Every so often, the camera cuts to a shot of another member of the band, lost in the crowd, which is getting watered down and broken up by fire hoses. Most people in R.E.M.'s audience will not remember the scenes of police officers hosing down the Civil Rights protesters in the early '60s, and they may only know cinematic re-enactments of anti-war marchers being teargassed by the National Guard a decade later, but this new R.E.M. video creates the perfect image of a white riot, '90s-style: Here kids are gathered in a crowd, a crowd that seems to go on and on, a crowd protesting nothing at all, a crowd that's just causing a disturbance for its own sake. As Stipe is passed around, he looks gaunt and sickly, and with his arms spread out, he seems to be playing with the image of Jesus on the cross. But giving this video that kind of meaning would be extremely over-determined: The point is that this is a meaningless mass. "What if I ride/What if you walk/What if you rock around the clock/Tick tock," Stipe sings, and for once his non sequiturs seem to have a purpose; life is reduced to its central and repetitive futility. You want teenage Armageddon? the video seems to ask. Well you can have it! In the meantime, Stipe's voice acts as an inciter. "Hey/Kids/Shake a leg/Maybe you're crazy in the head." Hey kids, this is your wake-up call! But everyone is too busy passing Stipe around, living in the daydream nation, to even think of waking up. As the clip spirals to a close, images of a creepy, passive violence flash and linger.

Every time I've seen the "Drive" video, I have found it embarrassingly mes-merizing, but it is quite clever, and will probably remain so—although once MTV got it rolling on the heavy-rotation juggernaut, it began to deteriorate into par-ody. Just the same, it serves as a fine reminder of the stunning visual charisma that allowed Stipe's strange, white-boy arm-flinging dance in 1991's "Losing My Religion" video to stick out in so many people's minds. It's unfortunate, given this quality, that the band once again won't be touring, although the subdued nature of this album probably would not work well live. Other than "Drive," *Automatic*'s primary masterpiece is the low-key "Everybody Hurts," a ballad about caring and empathy which pushes Stipe's voice almost into a falsetto range that makes the song sound an awful lot like "Bridge Over Troubled Water." In fact, "Everybody Hurts" is an anthem in precisely that vein, and it's so sweet and sad and sorrow-ful and heartfelt that it would be kind of hokey if it weren't so beautiful. To keep the song in balance, R.E.M. used an old metronome-like drum machine instead of real drums, giving the beat a wooden, mechanical quality, in juxtaposition to Mike Mills's languid keyboards and Stipe's earnest singing. The idea, Mills explained in an interview, was for the sound to be "human and non-human at the same time." And "Everybody Hurts" is unique for R.E.M.'s body of work in that it offers one of the rare moments when Stipe seems to lose control, seems to be stretching his voice to allow emotion (as opposed to rumination) to get the best of him. Normally, R.E.M.'s touches of vulnerability have been provided by Mills's background singing—and his vocal trade-offs with Stipe give the song real tenderness—but on "Everybody Hurts," the elements are reduced to so little instrumentation that it is up to Stipe to provide all human depth, and he performs the task admirably.

On the other hand, "Try Not to Breathe," which has a winding, waltz-like pace, is the picture of Stipe in complete control. He seems to be contemplating suicide, perhaps Dr. Kevorkian–style, and claiming he can take control of the most difficult task of all—the ability to stop breathing ("I will try not to worry you/I have seen things that you will never see/Leave it to memory/And dare me to breathe"). The song itself has the rolling, lilting quality that's R.E.M.'s signature sound, which is why it seems calm and contented, despite the subject matter. Of course, mortality is a big topic on this album—sometimes dealt with in a humorous light, as Andy Kaufman and Elvis Presley, along with the "horrible asp" that troubled Egypt, are imagined in the afterlife in "Man on the Moon" ("Let's play Twister/Let's play Risk/I'll see you in heaven if you make the list"), but more often in the mournful tone of the dolorous, heavy "Sweetness Follows."

The nonsense quotient on this album is up to Stipe's usual levels—on "Monty Got a Raw Deal," Stipe even confesses that "nonsense has a welcome ring"—although perhaps, after all this time, it's gotten so that I actually appreciate the seemingly random references to black-eyed peas, Nescafé and ice, fallen stars, and *The Cat in the Hat* that Stipe makes in the whacked-out "Sidewinder Sleeps Tonight," which seems, in the final analysis, to be a song about a diner payphone (don't ask). I think that after the practice of actually writing linear, straightforward songs for *Out of Time*, Stipe's gibberish has gotten better. But I'll be damned if anyone can figure out what's going on with all the sampled voices in "Star Me Kitten," which is really supposed to be called "Fuck Me Kitten" (as in "**** Me Kitten"). At any rate, when Stipe finally asks, "Have we lost our minds?" it seems he's at long last on to something.

Perhaps Stipe's loveliest lyrics—which are almost old-fashioned and quaint in their way—are contained in the narrative of "Nightswimming," an elegiac reminiscence of youthful skinny-dipping—of youthful everything—with images so strong you can feel the longing in Stipe's voice:

> Nightswimming deserves a quiet night
> I'm not sure all these people understand
> It's not like years ago
> The fear of getting caught

The recklessness of water
They cannot see me naked
These things they go away
Replaced by everyday

Sadly, from a musical vantage point, "Nightswimming" is one of the less interesting songs on the album, pretty but plain, all strings and piano, but the nature of nostalgia is often more pleasant than exciting. And the ability to look back and evaluate the past in a thoughtful, unsentimental fashion was the one missing element in the emotional growth R.E.M. tried for on *Out of Time*. That was an album so firmly grounded in the present tense that it never surprised me to find out that there were people—my stepmother, for instance, or kids under the age of consent—who actually thought *Out of Time* was R.E.M.'s first album. It had all the forward-thinking energy of a debut—and all the spit and polish you'd expect from an experienced group of players. There's no doubt that *Out of Time* will always mark a climactic moment in the band's career, and it will probably be a touchstone for everything that follows—that's just the way it always is: Everyone's still waiting for Joni Mitchell to make another *Blue*, for Bob Dylan to come up with another *Blood on the Tracks*, for the Violent Femmes to match the fucked-up genius of their debut, and for AC/DC to do another *Back in Black*. It's admirable that, rather than balk under the pressure or try to duplicate the success, R.E.M. decided to make a good, solid album that suits the place and creative space they've arrived at now. *Automatic for the People* sounds like an album by a band with a strong, illustrious history—and, one hopes, many good years ahead.

Bobbie Gentry

AN ATTEMPT TO SOLVE ONE OF AMERICA'S
GREATEST MYSTERIES by Ron Carlson

We're so sure we know what it was and why they dropped it. A baby, they dropped a baby off the bridge. I'm here to reopen this troubling file. It's been more than thirty years, and we need finally to face the music. The multiple ambiguities in Bobbie Gentry's song "Ode to Billie Joe" require close scrutiny.

Okay, we all know it was *something*. They dropped *something* off the bridge, although there was, and is, more than one Tallahatchie Bridge, and we know there were two people on the bridge for a moment: Billie Joe McAllister and a girl who looked a lot like the narrator of our ballad. We have no hard proof that it was the narrator; it could have been anyone. Her own mother, a well-grounded country person, doesn't ask, as she well might have, "What the heck were you dropping off that bridge with Billie Joe?"

She simply makes a statement based on what the young preacher, Brother Taylor, reported. And how well did this Preacher Taylor character know our girl? He hasn't even been around for dinner yet. And he's young. He sees two people from some distance, it sounds like, and of course he thinks the girl looks like the narrator. It's his job as a preacher not to notice girls; girls *have* to look alike to this guy. As soon as a girl stands out, he's asking for trouble. Some witness. He can't even tell what they were dropping.

It's good he didn't catch it, because that would have hurt the song's staying power. He saw *something*—that's all we know.

Boy, did we take that and run. We, in our suspicious minds, are so willing to leap to conclusions about *something* we didn't even see what was dropped from a bridge. We don't even know which bridge. It takes so little to get us speculating the worst. What have we got? Three little things: (1) the preacher's hearsay evidence, (2) our wicked imaginations, and (3) some reported "recollections" by the narrator's brother about an event that occurred some time ago when Billie Joe and Tom and Brother—this was at the Carroll County picture show—tried to put a frog down the narrator's shirt. Come on, a frog! This is an innocent prank; kids do it all the time. It's barely flirting. Who hasn't tried to put an amphibian in a girl's clothing? And if there was any meaning to the little moment, maybe it had to do with Tom—who's he, anyway? We know he likes movies.

It's too bad about Billie Joe. We all agree. He allegedly has jumped from the Tallahatchie Bridge, one of them, and perished in the event. It's too bad. It's been pointed out that he didn't have a lick of sense, but as Momma notes, "It's a shame about Billie Joe, anyhow." Anyhow! This *anyhow* points so clearly to the fact that his alleged jumping from the bridge has nothing to do with any of the other events of this tough week on Choctaw Ridge. He might simply have been wiped out from his work at the sawmill and slipped. Things and people fall accidentally from bridges all the time. Look in the paper. It isn't proven that, suffering from shame and remorse, Billie Joe McAllister purposely ended his life. Is there a note? An eyewitness? I don't see any.

All we've got is that *something*, the most effective *something* in all of American pop lyrics, a *something* that holds the song to our imaginations like a rivet in an old metal bridge. Sure, we've thought the worst. It was their illegitimate child. Again, I don't think so. Listen to the evidence once more, please.

This ballad is a remarkable story, full of real inventory and with an honest time frame. It's four minutes and eleven seconds long, and a full two minutes and forty seconds are given to the family dinner conversation, an extended scene in which we get everyone's position regarding the morning's bad news about Billie Joe. Momma, pragmatic and matter-of-fact, "by the way"; Poppa, all business, no nonsense, "pass the biscuits"; Brother, incredulous, "another piece of apple pie"; and the narrator, who keeps her mouth shut. Just because she's silent doesn't necessarily mean anything. She's reporting the story and staying out of the way. Is there any hint in anything anybody says that she's recently been pregnant? Does Brother make any snide allusions to her sudden weight loss? Does Momma, who would know about such matters, suggest anywhere that she'll help her daughter take in some of the drapey muumuus she's been wearing for the past few months? No.

I'm here to say this *something* was not a baby, though such a thing in such a world could have triggered such a tragedy. In the current world, we read weekly about newborns left here and there, and the abandonments have a common theme—the mother acts alone. There is no "meet me on the bridge so we can do this bad deed together." Billie Joe and a girl who looked a lot like our girl dropped *something* off the Tallahatchie Bridge. Is this an effective way of disposing of a secret, or is it a way of announcing the end of *something*? I submit that it is much more the latter than the former. If you want to dispose of *something*, you go to any of the isolated spots on Choctaw Ridge, and you bury it out of the world's eye. If, on the other hand, you want to tell the community that *something* huge has changed forever, you meet and march to the center of a bridge tall enough that if you jumped from it later in the week it would kill you, and together you wait until a young man associated with the church, which is the central social organ in your world, walks by, as he does by custom every day, and when he can see what you are doing and who you are, you drop *something* from the bridge. It's done in daylight, and it's done on purpose.

"Ode to Billie Joe," a wonderful short story, rose to Number One on the charts in August of 1967, a tricky year by any measure, and stayed there four weeks. The little tale was odd and prescient. The war in Vietnam was approaching its fiercest and most confusing horror. In a year Robert Kennedy and Martin Luther King, Jr., would be dead, and so would Poppa. Momma would have lapsed into depression, and Brother would have sold out and bought a store in Tupelo. There is no evidence that he doesn't now work for Bell South.

Billie Joe McAllister and the narrator walked out on that old bridge, and what they ceremoniously dropped into the muddy water below was our innocence. It was a neat little package, but we were too young and too busy to notice. It still glows in the song as one of the most powerful *something*s in all of American music.

Randy Newman

(NOT) THROUGH ROSE-COLORED GLASSES
by Anthony Walton

▬▬▬

Nineteen seventy-four was the midpoint of an era when songwriters had *ambition*: Joni Mitchell's masterwork, *Court and Spark*; Paul Simon's plangent *Still Crazy After All These Years*; Carole King's epochal *Tapestry*; Marvin Gaye's weighing in with *What's Going On* and *Let's Get It On*; Stevie Wonder's unmatched four-year stretch of musical fecundity from *Music of My Mind* through *Songs in the Key of Life*; Jackson Browne's *Running on Empty* (not to mention *The Pretender*); Bruce Springsteen's *Born to Run*; even the Eagles' shedding of their frat-boy, good-time image with *Hotel California*. There were other, almost-forgotten masters in this era as well, like Alex Chilton, Janis Ian, Phoebe Snow, Nick Drake, and Gram Parsons. Alongside and above them all was, and is, Randy Newman.

In 1974, Randy Newman was a thirty-one-year-old Los Angeles–based singer and songwriter of near-unanimous critical praise but negligible commercial success. In a pattern that has continued through the present day, Newman is known as a "staff" songwriter, a craftsman who has turned out such small pop master-pieces as "I Think It's Going to Rain Today," "Love Story (You and Me)," "Living Without You," and "Mama Told Me Not to Come" for other artists to sing, including Judy Collins, Three Dog Night, Harry Nilsson, and Peggy Lee. These tunes are well-balanced little jewel boxes pieced together with the delicate craft of Cole Porter and the traditional American harmonies of Stephen Foster, blended with the modernist extensions of Aaron Copland and traces of Charles Ives. They are often ballads in minor keys, with lyrics expressing a painfully self-conscious awareness of the lonely heart in the modern era and, as with the finest blues, with quotidian details that show loss gaining a shadowed, spooky resonance. Consider these lines from "Living Without You":

> The milk truck hauls the sun up
> And the paper hits the door
> The subway shakes my floor
> And I think about you.

Newman's career as a corporate songwriter has continued to this day with "That'll Do," the Oscar-nominated theme song from *Babe: Pig in the City*; the wistful love ditty "I Love to See You Smile" from *Parenthood*; and another Oscar-nominated song, "You've Got a Friend in Me," from *Toy Story*. (He has also composed and conducted a slew of film scores.)

Through it all, though, Newman has pursued his true vocation as a writer *and* performer. In this arena, he has recorded such treasures as "Davy the Fat Boy," "Let's Burn Down the Cornfield," "Cowboy," "Underneath the Harlem Moon," "Sail Away," "Political Science," and "You Can Leave Your Hat On." But no one, not even Newman's small, discerning fan base, could have anticipated the album that quietly appeared in the stores (all of Newman's albums appear quietly) in 1974: *Good Old Boys*.

On this record Newman's sad, sardonic, and ruthless exploration of the margins of the American scene and spirit segued into something else altogether, a satire so accurate, so vicious, that it became compassionate: a series of tales of American (in this case, Southern) love, loss, and desolation, narrated by a collection of lonely and lovelorn freaks, misfits, dreamers, drifters, and psychotic Romeos. Taken together, these characters' pain and ignorance constitute a worldview, a vision in which irony cannot be separated from tragedy: Call it Stephen Foster on acid, Flannery O'Connor in song; at their best, these songs become *lieder*—art songs—of the American experience.

Imagine William Faulkner, around the time he wrote "A Rose for Emily," getting on the piano to tap out, with a bitter recalcitrance soaked in bourbon and cynicism, some existential rhythm and blues. That is the ambience in which *Good Old Boys* catalogs and narrates the psychic and spiritual toll the tragedy of race has had on the South. Newman says what he sees and thinks, and he pulls no punches, something very few white artists working in any genre are able or willing to do on this particular subject. He does this from the inside, with tough-minded compassion for the racist—realizing, as Martin Luther King, Jr., often communicated, that *both* sides suffered terribly from the death grip on America's collective soul that the Jim Crow system imposed.

Newman's ability in *Good Old Boys* to inhabit the interior lives of poor whites, broken and deranged by their marginal status in society, is uncanny, as this playful riff in "Birmingham" shows:

> Got a big black dog
> And his name is Dan
> Who lives in my backyard in Birmingham
> He is the meanest dog in Alabam'
> Get 'em Dan

This sort of thing can, on casual listening, seem snarky or smart-alecky, but "Birmingham" is immediately followed by a love song, "Marie," which contains these lines:

> You looked like a princess the night we met
> With your hair piled up high
> I will never forget
> I'm drunk right now baby
> But I've got to be
> Or I never could tell you
> What you mean to me

"Marie" is the third song on the album, the third card Newman plays during his sly poker game. The song is masterful because it gives the speaker—Newman's Ur-white Southerner—an inner life:

> I loved you the first time I saw you
> And I always will love you Marie

In "Birmingham" we learned that the narrator's wife was named "Mary/But she's called Marie"; it is the same man, speaking so full of bluff and bravado a moment ago.

This man is also depicted in "Rednecks," with its legendary and still controversial chorus:

> We're rednecks, we're rednecks
> And we don't know our ass
> From a hole in the ground
> We're rednecks, we're rednecks
> And we're keeping them niggers down
> We are keeping the niggers down.

Good Old Boys is a prism that reveals a different aspect of the South at every turn, conveying in one moment the rage and humiliation of defeated "crackers" and their avatar Huey Long—"Every Man a King," "Mr. President (Have Pity on the Working Man)," "Kingfish"—and, in the next, in allegory and with immense skill and beauty, the helplessness of the South as change is forced upon it, as in "Louisiana 1927":

> What has happened down here is the winds have changed
> Clouds roll in from the North and it starts to rain

The song relates the events of the historic 1927 Mississippi River floods, which devastated the South from Arkansas to the Louisiana delta; at the same time, the listener cannot escape Newman's double meaning, the transitions of the Civil Rights era:

> Louisiana, Louisiana
> They're trying to wash us away
> They're trying to wash us away.

With the song, which I nominate as the most beautiful ever written by an American, Newman reaches a level that few, if any, songwriters have attained. The quotations in the strings from the songwriters' tradition, taken with the stunning use of woodwinds, the gospel chords played on the piano, and the lyrics, achieve something that might have been thought impossible: the humanization of that flag-waving, know-nothing Rebel.

Good Old Boys must be listened to like a musical, or better, a symphony where the variations on a theme add up in the end to one unified and conceptual whole. What to make of the lonely heart who sings "Wedding in Cherokee County," another r&b song pulled inside out by a compositional sleight of hand?

> Man, don't you think I know she hates me
> Man, don't you think I know she's no good
> If she knew how she'd be unfaithful to me
> I think she'd kill me if she could
> Maybe she's crazy, I don't know
> Maybe that's why I love her so.

The speaker is another of them good old boys "hustlin' 'round Atlanta," but revealed, contextualized, and made majestic, even mythic, by Newman's compassion and skill.

One more thing: Newman has been criticized for nearly thirty years for his use of the "n-word" on this album—as if one could tell a true story of the South without it. As if one could tell a true story of the United States without it.

Now your Northern nigger's a negro
You see he's got his dignity
Down here we're too ignorant to realize
That the North has set the nigger free
Yes, he's free to be put in a cage
In Harlem in New York City
And he's free to be put in a cage
on the South Side of Chicago
And the West Side . . .
Gatherin' 'em up from miles around
Keepin' the niggers down.

If Ezra Pound is right and literature is news that stays news, then Randy Newman, with *Good Old Boys* and much of his other work, is trafficking in literature. I give him my vote for the Nobel Prize.

1967

(a poem) by Billy Collins

When I left the house for the backyard,
No hair was sprouting from the wallpaper,
Nor was blood dripping from the electrical outlets.
But the rules of perspective were being
Bent, especially by the living room,
And inanimate objects were beginning to get restless.
A drum solo was playing on the stereo—
Ginger Baker maybe, or that guy from Blue Cheer—
Which may have been the reason I left the house,
Because it was so loud and lacking
The comfort of a melody, the reassurance of a lyric,
Just heavy rumbling and the flare of cymbals.
I don't know how long I was out there
Smoking and looking up at the freezing stars,
But when I finally came back in,
The house was still engulfed in drumming,

And that's when it occurred to me,
As I stood there under a ceiling light

Coming to terms with the indoors,
That the drum solo I was listening to
Might not be the same drum solo
That was playing when I went outside.
Perhaps it was a different drum solo,
Or the same drum solo
Only now playing at a later time?

So many drum solos sound the same to me.
Plus, I really had no idea how long
I had been out there on the back steps
Smoking and studying the cold starry patterns,
And it seemed there was no way to find out,
Unless, of course, I asked someone for assistance.
But you were immersed in a big chair
Reading your own palm or just looking at it,
And Tom was dancing by the windows
With the headphones over his ears,
Eyeing his reflection in the dark glass.

And even if one of you were better prepared
For inquiry, I could not think of how
To phrase the question without snipping
The threads that held us all together.

I stood on the worn-out oriental rug
Thinking about the impossibility of the situation
And soon other situations began to take on
This feeling of desperate futility,
So many scenes tumbling in on me
That I gradually began to be unsure
If what I was hearing at that moment
Was the same drum solo that had been playing
When I came back into the house
After that immeasurable amount of time

Outside with the cold stars,
Or was it a different cut from the same record,
Or a piece from another record,
Or again, the same solo only now playing
For a second, third, or fourth time?

Other things happened that night.
Tom took everything down from the walls
Except a framed pencil sketch of a duck
Which he, and later we, found hilarious.
You and I had sex in a bed and behaved there
Like people somewhat other than ourselves.
But the confusion regarding the drum solo
And the time I spent under the icy stars
Was, for me, a definite highlight.

I will never figure this, or anything out,
I whispered to myself under the fierce drumming.
Then, from the world's largest refrigerator
I took an extremely cold bottle of beer
Which tasted just like soap,
And went outside and sat on the steps again
Under the cold stars of 1967
And peeled the wet label from the green glass
As I waited for this endless drum solo to end,

All the while contemplating
The history of human consciousness—
The many incredible angles it made
As it caromed silently
Across the yard and bounced down the halls of time.

Drivin' N' Cryin'

MISCHIEVOUS TAXIDERMY by Chris Bachelder

When people ask me about Southern rock I always go into this definition thing to break it down because America likes to reduce everything to a simplified version of what Southern rock is.

—Kevn Kinney

Music critics are hard-line evolutionists, determined to discover lineage, advantageous mutation, vectors of influence and descent. Family, genus, species. The Tree of Rock, as it were.

Though their categories and genealogies are occasionally oversimplified, commercially motivated, or just erroneous, the rage for order is not the problem. Identifying likeness and difference is helpful and necessary. After all, how can we appraise a thing if we don't understand what it is, where it came from?

George Shaw, who in 1798 was the first English naturalist to study the platypus, thought he sniffed a hoax when British colonists brought the creature back from Australia. Duck-billed and furry! He even took scissors to the pelt, looking for the stitches. He knew that clever Chinese taxidermists had for years fooled sailors with their wild creations (monkey + fish = mermaid). "It is impossible," Shaw wrote about the platypus in *The Naturalist's Miscellany* (1799), "not to entertain some doubts as to the genuine nature of the animal."

Like the intractable platypus, Atlanta stalwart Drivin' N' Cryin' appears to be the work of a mischievous taxidermist. Consider the taxonomic challenges: Here we have a thoroughly Southern band whose lead singer and songwriter, Kevn Kinney, is a Milwaukeean who once worked for a socialist newspaper; a band that always looked in publicity photos like the rougher, less reputable sister of Whitesnake; who made lovely use of fiddle, Hammond organ, banjo, and Peter Buck's dulcimer; who once recorded an earnest, raucous version of John Denver's "Leaving on a Jet Plane"; who seemed just as comfortable in an arena as a sticky-floored dive; who toured, at one time or another, with Bad Company, Bob Dylan, Cheap Trick, Soul Asylum, R.E.M., and Lynyrd Skynyrd; who was socially conscious not only in song but in deed, establishing an annual benefit concert for Atlanta's homeless; whose lyrics were inspired one minute by Woody ("dawn-maker give me dawns/that rise with me and show my wrongs"), the next minute by Angus ("Can you feel the lava runnin' through my veins?"); who was catalogued on such websites as Metal Chamber, Metal Mayhem, and Mother Metal right between Dokken and Dungeon; and whose T-shirt, finally, I am wearing in a fuzzy, pre-digital photograph (c. 1990) that seems to suggest, particularly to my wife, that I have a *mullet* (even though I have repeatedly asked her to consider, in the spirit of matrimony, that the alleged matter on the back of my neck might be a shadow, or perhaps a mouse).

No, it's not easy to ascertain the genuine nature of this animal. The problem for critics and fans was not that Drivin' N' Cryin' seemed to have arrived sui generis, from nowhere. The problem was that the band seemed to have arrived from *every*where, from all paths and points. Michael Stipe sang, "You can't get there from here," but Drivin' N' Cryin' got here from there. And there, there, and *there*.

Just to be clear, this is a celebration. I come to praise, not to bury. DNC was no hoax, no mythical beast, and no joke. This is *not* Spinal Tap. This band was a wondrous, unrepeatable freak of nature, the egg-laying mammal of Southern rock.

The name is bad, I concede. It's a high-school talent-show name, all adolescent drama and mini-mart punctuation. Listen up, you youngsters: Three apostrophes are more than enough for your musical outfit. The name Drivin' N' Cryin' (variously cased and punctuated throughout its career) is a statement of the band's musical range, but it's a vast understatement. Plenty of bands play drivers and criers, but Drivin' N' Cryin's drivers and criers clearly subdivide into other discrete categories. Listen closely to most any DNC disc—or, hell, listen not closely at all—and you'll hear, at some point, the punk of the Ramones and the Replacements; the rambling protest folk of Guthrie or early Dylan; the heavy metal of Zeppelin, Sabbath, and AC/DC; the old-time country of Hank; the Southern jamrawk of Skynyrd, Molly Hatchet, and the Allman Brothers; the post-Skynyrd clay-bake of the Georgia Satellites, .38 Special, and Jason and the Scorchers; and even—there's just no denying it—the spandex head-bangery of, say, Def Leppard and Mötley Crüe.

This all makes for a bracing auditory experience, but it also creates a problem that you can no doubt either guess or remember. While a Drivin' N' Cryin' CD likely appeals to divergent tastes, it is not likely to be *very* appealing to a *single* taste. As evidence for the band's scattershot appeal, consider the results of a recent Amazon.com search: Customers who bought DNC's bipolar masterpiece *Mystery Road* (1989) also bought CDs by: Cracker, Judas Priest, Kansas, the Black Crowes, Led Zeppelin, Ryan Adams, the Cars, and Bruce Springsteen.

If you need one, this seems as good a reason as any why the band never quite broke through nationally, though they hardly toiled in obscurity. They were regional superstars and mix-tape icons of the late '80s and early '90s, they toured cavernous venues with national breakout R.E.M. on the *Green* tour, and their 1991 release *Fly Me Courageous* went gold. Guadalcanal Diary would have appreciated such bad luck. Or Pylon. Or Let's Active. Or the Connells.

Please recall that for nearly a century after Shaw studied and named the platypus, British scientists hotly debated the animal's essence and classification. Those in the mammal camp insisted there were no eggs; those in the bird camp insisted there were no mammary glands. Each side saw what it wanted to see, just as Western scientists long regarded the zebra as a white horse with black stripes, while African scientists saw it as a black horse with white stripes (the Africans, it turned out, were correct).

Similarly, DNC listeners have no doubt always perceived altogether different critters. The best thing I know to do is acknowledge what I always heard (or what I most desperately *wanted* to hear, which is probably the same thing): a literate folk-rock band with an unfortunate and vaguely lycanthropic tendency to shout at the Devil. Drivin' N' Cryin' is the inverse of the typical metal band, which gets much, much worse—just really terrible—when it slows tempo and turns down the amps and takes a crack at vulnerability and sensitivity. Drivin' N' Cryin', though, was better and smarter at mid-tempo, mid-volume: Their melodies had more texture, Kinney's lyrics were more observant and interesting, and his singing was better. Kinney's high smoker's voice can be soulful, but when the band goes metal, he sounds as if someone has stepped on his tail. He spends much of *Mystery Road* singing about peace, poverty, and change, and then all of a sudden—full moon, hairy palms, fangs—he's howling about his boss—she's a woman and oh my God is she a bitch—on a song called "Malfunction Junction."

I know that the meticulous librarians at Mother Metal see another animal entirely. Their favorite DNC disc is no doubt 1993's *Smoke*, a real hair-slinger, and they can grudgingly certify *Fly Me Courageous* as genuine metal (even though "Let's Go Dancing" and "For You" are totally homo). *Whisper Tames the Lion* (1988) is decent, *Mystery Road* has, like, three or four rockers, tops ("Malfunction Junction" is a killer), and please don't even get them started on 1995's *Wrapped in Sky*, with its folk instrumentation and Latin melodies, total mall-radio pansy fare.

And then there are the punks, may God bless them, who probably liked the first two songs—"Scarred but Smarter" and "Keys to Me"—on the very first DNC disc, *Scarred but Smarter* (1986). Those two songs have speed and power and glory, and they sound as if they were recorded in the sewage-treatment plant where Kinney once worked. After that, though, with maybe a couple of exceptions, DNC sold out.

The Peter, Paul, and Mary fans? The John Denver faithful? They got their eyebrows singed by "Malfunction Junction" and they never, ever came back.

Since this would not be a proper music essay if I did not try to pass off some personal, ineffable, nostalgic impression as a stone-hard and verifiable truth, I proclaim now that *Mystery Road* is Drivin' N' Cryin's best recording (*Fly Me Courageous* is a respectable second), and that, furthermore, *Mystery Road* is a minor classic of Southern Rock.

This CD is the most obvious and interesting demonstration of the band's musical range, whether you call it catholic or confused. It's also their most observant, melodious, and quirky recording. *Mystery Road* begins with a mountain fiddle and a bluegrass beat in "Ain't It Strange" and ends with a one-minute, twenty-eight-second punk stomp, "Syllables," dedicated to the Ramones. In between, the band weaves—like either an Olympic slalom skier or a DUI suspect —through folk, rock, pop, country, and metal. The road is mysterious indeed; based on the musical clues, I would place *Mystery Road* at the confluence of Highway 61, Highway to Hell, Road to Ruin, and Abbey Road. No, it's not a through road. Watch for fallen rock.

It's true that the band indulges its metal yen on *Mystery Road*. Four songs— "Toy Never Played With," "Wild Dog Moon," "You Don't Know Me," and the aforementioned "Malfunction Junction"—feature the kind of clean, heavy riffs that would make David Lee Roth or Vince Neil screech in Pavlovian response. It is not in the least bit difficult to feel the lava in Kevn's veins.

It's also true that Kinney's lyrical muse occasionally goes AWOL, just flat *vanishes,* as in the following multi-metaphor pileup in the perfectly lovely "Honeysuckle Blue":

> Runnin' through these caverns of gold
> Runs a river of death indeed
> An old hotel serves as a shelter
> For children of the street
> Abandoned by the promised land
> Set sail on your own
> How much longer will the well
> Be dry for those who roam

Not to be a schoolmarm about this, but we do seem to pass through several ecological zones in a single verse. Also, sorry, but the aridity of the final lines comes as something of a surprise given all that river-running and sail-setting.

But enough with the red pencil. The fact is, Kinney can be an excellent songwriter. He's a humane and empathetic watcher—"Ain't It Strange" and "Honeysuckle Blue" are tender songs of observation—and he writes convincingly and poignantly from points of view not his own (an old man facing eviction in "House for Sale" and a neglected adolescent in "Straight to Hell"). The guy from Warrant or Poison couldn't do that.

"Peacemaker" and the percussionless "With the People" are pure folk: passion and principle without scorn, irony, or cynicism. The former is a prayer for courage and political imagination, the latter a sort of catchy primer on citizenship in a democracy. "Wild Dog Moon" is—well, I have no idea what "Wild Dog Moon" is, not a clue, but it's the single song that best represents both *Mystery Road* and the band's career. For three minutes and forty-five seconds, it's a werewolf rave-up, with Kinney free-associatin' about Bonnie and Clyde, whiskey, and a woman built, yes, like a red-brick house. (I did worry, as I played the disc repeatedly, that "Wild Dog Moon" might in some way *harm* my infant daughter.) But if you can manage to stay in the room, you'll then hear the song segue—you *can* get there from here—into its mournful folk epilogue. It's difficult to imagine the person who would be pleased by both segments of the song, a fact that is sort of pleasing in itself.

And then there's "Straight to Hell," *Mystery Road*'s penultimate song and perhaps DNC's most popular. If, in the early '90s, you attended a Southern land-grant university (red brick, crepe myrtle, clock tower), you probably recall smashed Greeks raising their red plastic beer cups and screaming the chorus in sloppy glee. When you're twenty, perhaps you think every song is about you, but now that we're all older, it's important to note that Kinney's young narrator is not going to hell because he failed his chemistry lab, dented Dad's Jeep, took nine upside-down keg hits, and dry-grinded his friend's date on a pile of coats. "Straight to Hell" is a plaintive, three-chord country heartbreaker about a boy more sinned against than sinning, a boy doomed to repeat the mistakes of his parents.

The father is long gone, and the mother is, well, indiscriminate with her affections. When the boy leaves the house to make way for a suitor—"the seventh one in seven days"—and then stays out all night, his mother berates him. The rhyme scheme has gone straight to hell when she tells him, "You're no good because you're running without love." At the end, running away from home, the boy turns back and shouts, "Help me, mother," clinging to the one who most let him down. This is a beautifully sad song, one of Kinney's best, and his high whine is perfect for the voice of this lost boy. It's a tragedy that "Straight to Hell" got hijacked by undergraduate substance abusers. Like "This Land Is Your Land" and "Born in the USA," the song is probably beyond rescue at this point.

My appreciation of *Mystery Road* is no doubt infused with nostalgia. I was eighteen when the disc was released, certainly more likely to respond to energy and passion than to consistency. I'm now nearly twice as old. I own more than one corduroy blazer; I know how to operate a Diaper Genie; I really love my Subaru Forester. My life has narrowed, taken shape and direction. I wouldn't want it any other way, but it's nice to listen again to such a youthful and exuberant work by a band that refuses—without petulance or self-righteousness—to settle down and be something. *Mystery Road* is hopeful, completely unself-conscious, radical in lyrics and spirit. Kinney sings about change and the band performs it, song to song to song. It's a daring, surprising, thrillingly uneven work by a band that believes anything is possible, musically and politically. The band's best work is a wonderful mess, a testament to the richness of Southern music.

For those about to rock—and also for those about to attend an annual fiddler's convention—Drivin' N' Cryin' salutes you.

Eighty-five years after Shaw skeptically catalogued the platypus, its mystery was solved, sort of. In 1884, W.H. Caldwell, an English biologist in Australia, sent a terse telegram, in Latin, to his colleagues in Montreal, indicating that he had hard evidence that the platypus is a mammal that lays eggs. The debate was over, but the mystery of the platypus only deepened. The animal flaunts our neat categories, and scientists have just had to deal with that. As Harry Burrell wrote in his definitive *The Platypus* (1927), "Every writer upon the platypus begins with an expression of wonder. Never was there such a disconcerting animal!"

I've referred to Drivin' N' Cryin' in the past tense, but the band still exists. In fact, DNC will board a Carnival luxury liner in early January for the Gimme Three Days Cruise, featuring Lynyrd Skynyrd. That's right, deal with it, a floating country/rock festival on a round-trip to the Bahamas.

Let me share my vision of the Gimme Three Days Cruise. DNC is rockin' the open seas, amps stacked atop shuffleboard courts, the first mate crowd-surfing across the deck. While rowdy Carnival passengers—sunburned, seasick, and rum-blasted—scream out for "Straight to Hell," their Bics aloft in the salty Caribbean air, Kinney and Nielsen veer from the set list and launch the band into "You Don't Know Me." It's the platypus anthem.

Jazz II

King Pleasure

CLARENCE BEEKS, AN ASTRONAUT OF JAZZ, EXPLORED
THE SPACE INSIDE THE SOUND by Michael Perry

━━━━

At times we are given to know that we are outside our territory: a Wisconsin boy, for instance, afoot in Oakdale, Tennessee, surprised by dogwoods blooming in April. I am standing on Piney Road, overlooking the river Sherwood Anderson called the Babahatchie. The spring sun is working the asphalt, loosening the scent of petroleum. It is a thick scent, molasses-brown and dumpy, the perfect base against which to draw in the fragrance of the dogwoods, like meringue over mud pie. Among the pines and kudzu trash, insects kite through the sunbeams like vigorous dust motes. The pitch of the land, imparted in this case by the nearby Cumberlands, feels exotic to a northwoods flatlander. I imagine things coming down from the hills.

I am trying to get a feel for this place, but I am also trying to get a feel for another time. A time when the valley below was choc-a-block with buildings. When young boys walked the streets in sandwich boards advertising shows at J.C. Alley's Opra House, when the beer at the Hole-in-the-Wall Saloon was chilled with ice cut from the river, when the vacant ridge along Piney Road was studded with houses. Oakdale was riding a boom in the early 1900s, stoked by the rails running the curve of the Babahatchie. The switching yards were filled with cars gathered for the twenty-two-mile run up to Pilot Mountain. Built trackside, the YMCA hosted around eight hundred passengers per day and served 209,000 meals per year. A new train rolled through every three minutes. The railroad was its own sort of river.

In 1922, somewhere back up in the hills where the old-timers say the black folks lived, out of sight of the trains but within earshot of their rumble and whine, a boy was born to Mr. and Mrs. Butler Beeks. They named him Clarence.

Butler Beeks worked on the railroad, as did most Oakdale residents—black or white. He owned forty-seven acres back in the ridges, and he kept a garden. Sometimes, coming down the footpath, he carried produce for the market. The locals recall little Clarence tagging behind. They also recall that Butler unfailingly doffed his hat upon meeting a lady.

Given directions by a local schoolteacher, I went back up Reynolds Road, where they say Clarence lived. I stood in the woods. There was no sign of a house. The sun cut through the trees all around. I was trying to think of this place at night, with maybe a whippoorwill calling, and young Clarence, six years old, waking upright (as he would tell it later) with a revelation that he was "the real savior of humanity."

Within the year, a great flood swept Oakdale. The theater was ruined. The bridge went down. Boxcars floated off the siding, the roundhouse was torn up, homes disappeared. When the water receded, it took the boom with it. The railroad never did come all the way back. During the boom, Oakdale reported some thirty-five hundred citizens. Today there are about three hundred. You can trace the decline back to the Great Flood of 1929. And shortly thereafter—no one is clear on the details—the real savior of humanity departed the region.

Afoot in the world of jazz, or bebop, or jive, I am outside my territory. I have an appreciation, not an understanding. I am underqualified to rank the who's who. I know from various sources that in November of 1951, Clarence Beeks came to the stage of the Apollo Theater in Harlem armed with lyrics written for James Moody's recording of the heretofore instrumental "I'm in the Mood for Love." To speak in the idiom, he broke the place up. Swinging his voice like a saxophone, he blew words like James Moody blew notes, and when it was over, Clarence was declared winner of Amateur Night at the Apollo. In early 1952, Clarence recorded the tune—renaming it "Moody's Mood for Love"—and it hit Number Five on the r&b charts. Also that year, *DownBeat* magazine named "Moody's Mood for Love" its Readers Poll Record of the Year. Clarence—having taken to calling himself "King Pleasure"—set off on tour, performing from the seat of a swiveling purple throne with a microphone incorporated into the armrest.

It should end there, on the upbeat.

The thing Clarence Beeks was doing, the singing like a saxophone, was known as *vocalese*. An evolution of the scat singing pioneered by Louis Armstrong in 1926, vocalese replaced the improvised, meaningless syllables of scat with fully realized lyrics written to mimic jazz solos note for note. The success of "Moody's Mood for Love" was definitive, and established Beeks as a pioneer in the genre. It seems clear, however, that he was following in the steps of Eddie Jefferson, a former tap dancer from Pittsburgh. According to an entry in Bill Milkowski's *Swing It! An Annotated History of Jive*, Jefferson was practicing vocalese as early as 1938, and replacing instrumental solos with lyrics in live sessions dated to 1949. According to several other sources, it was Jefferson who put the lyrics to "I'm in the Mood for Love." In *Swing It!* Milkowski writes that Beeks saw Jefferson perform the song at the Cotton Club in Cincinnati just prior to Beeks's performance at the Apollo. In later years, Jefferson would say that Beeks "copped" the lyrics. According to liner notes written by Ira Gitler in 1991, Beeks gave credit to Jefferson for creating vocalese (Beeks favored the term *blowing*—as in, blowing through an instrument), but claimed the lyrics as his own. Beeks had another Top Five hit in 1953 with "Red Top," and he kept recording into the early 1960s, but his acclaim was on the fade. When HiFi Jazz released his 1960 album *Golden Days,* Clarence wrote his own liner notes. He told the story of his being woke upright in Oakdale. As a result of the revelations of that time, he explained, he had formulated a philosophy of "Planetism." He called it the "ultimate 'ism,'" and while he felt the philosophy was incomplete, he deemed the "What I have found" important to humanity and worthy of enumeration, as follows:

1. That this is a charged-neutral material existence. . . .
2. People are in ideal and physical metamorphosis (evolution) to a planet-satellite (moon)—the second Earth satellite. . . .
3. People do not have to die. Life and death are matters of general adjustment (union) and maladjustment (separation). . . . All things come from "nothing" (space). . . . ALL things exist, live and react in relation [to] space.

By the mid-1960s, Clarence was living in California, and—again according to liner notes by Gitler—was sometimes "hostile" in phone conversations with friends. There were reports of him performing in Cincinnati as late as 1968, but when he died on March 21, 1981, he was living in Los Angeles. Quincy Jones reportedly paid for the funeral.

"As far as I know, I am the only child of my mother and father," says Constance Brewster, daughter of Clarence Beeks. We're speaking by phone—me in Wisconsin, she in Cincinnati. Constance says her mother and father separated before she was five. "He was very seldom around my supper table," she says. But she remembers him visiting. "He always brought me something I might like," she says. "Typewriters, bicycles, puppies." She giggles at the memory. Mostly though, she sounds cautious and weary. She feels her father and the family have been shorted. "We can listen to him on the radio now, singing the songs, knowing that the lyrics came from his brain, but yet everybody else takes credit for it. Even rap groups have sampled his stuff, or have used some of his lyrics. You have to work to make what you get, and you're supposed to be able to support your family and help them, and I'm sure that was his intention, but somehow it didn't fall that way. We're sittin' here broke and everyone else is livin' large."

Shortly before his death, Clarence Beeks asked Constance to bring him a copy of *Give Me the Night,* the George Benson album produced by Quincy Jones. "He liked this one particular song that he wanted to write lyrics to," says Constance. When Clarence discovered the album included a version of "Moody's Mood," he became upset. "He didn't know there was one of his songs on the album," she says. Eddie Jefferson is listed in the credits, but Constance objects. "There's no question about who wrote the lyrics—that came straight out of my dad's head. Out of his brain. Eddie Jefferson may have copied the style, lyrics, what have you, but that's about it. My dad wrote the lyrics. You can't take that away. He thought those up himself."

Eddie Jefferson won't be heard from. He died in 1979, shot down outside a Detroit music club. On *Golden Days,* the album through which Clarence proclaimed the ultimate "ism," Clarence obliquely offers: "I made this interpretation and developed Eddie's baby and delivered it to the public."

I ask Constance what she knows of Planetism.

"I don't know what he was talking about with that," she says.

There are questions, as likely grown out of disappointment as deception. The purple throne is lost to history. Dogwoods bloom and fall. Having stood where he was born, it is tempting to riff on the otherworldly little boy, to extrapolate from his professed vision. But listening to Constance, I am reminded that sometimes he was simply Daddy. When I listen to *Moody's Mood for Love,* the eighteen-song Blue Note retrospective released in 1992, I hear a musician in complete cool-headed command of his instrument. Steady in the steady parts, smooth in the smooth parts, and groovy when it counts. If he was troubled, or concerned with charged-neutral existence, it isn't evident in the bounce of "Jazz Jump" or the ha-ha-ha's of "Don't Get Scared." "Old Black Magic (Diaper Pin)" unfurls in a way that brings to mind a rippling satin ribbon. And perhaps I presume too much, but when he scats and yelps out the spider lines in "It Might as Well Be Spring," I recall the insects kiting through the sunlight up on the Piney Road ridge, and when I hear the opening lines of "Swan Blues," I think, That man was born hearing trains.

There are two versions of "Moody's Mood" included in the collection. Both are listed without credits, and in what appears to be yet another copyright-related move, under the original title "I'm in the Mood for Love." Pleasure utterly inhabits each version. There are a few rat-a-tat runs, a judicious smidge of vibrato here, a hip slur note there, a few skittery runs up and down the scale, but most of all, the feel that dominates is assuredness: He was at ease in the song.

All things exist, live, and react in relation to space. At times we are given to know that we are outside our territory. Clarence Beeks as King Pleasure—inside the song, living and reacting in relation to that musical space he understood so intuitively—was at home.

Back in Oakdale, there are flat spots carved into the hills where the boom-town houses once stood, and where, if you step to the edge, you can imagine how it might feel to be a boy looking down at the Babahatchie, ready to sing for the planet and all its satellites.

Bob Dorough

A ONE-MAN MOVEMENT by Paul Reyes

I stuck with a predictable clique of jazz music for a while, when I was younger—John Coltrane, Miles Davis, Thelonious Monk—then sought out less obvious talent. I backed up toward Ellington and Armstrong and Charlie Parker, but always remained fixed to the idea that transcendence in jazz ultimately depended on some degree of moody seriousness. An easy mistake, and lately I've taken small, important steps to correct it. I've shifted depths; my range of appreciation has improved. For this, Bob Dorough is largely responsible.

His byzantine career is exhausting to dig through. Finding his records takes work. But after considerable searching, and playing his songs, and cross-referencing, and patience, and ultimately cracking open the frigid attitude by which I considered his music an "acquired taste"—the flimsy compliment he's been accorded by critics to describe the strange wit of his songs—and simply after listening, without prejudice, to his music, I've eased into a fold wherein lies a delightful problem: Cursed with obscurity, Bob Dorough might nonetheless be a genius.

Obscurity precedes him as a jazzman; as Americana, as pop culture, he's more familiar to us, since he's the musical wizard behind the Saturday-morning jams known as *Schoolhouse Rock!*, a gig that proved rewarding and lucrative, but which also meant that his fan club, if he'd had one officially, would have mostly consisted of milk-spilling, pretzel-legged children splayed out on floors not five feet from the television, inadvertently mesmerized by his lysergic boogies on multiplication and the parts of speech. Who didn't really collect jazz records. But who would, many of them, a generation later, recognize his voice while waiting on tables in a club where he'd be working through his repertoire, and would ask him . . . and affectionately request . . . until eventually the *Schoolhouse Rock!* stuff got mixed in with the jazz stuff, and Dorough would end up using rock as a "proselytization of jazz," which to some degree has been working, since that is exactly how he piqued my interest and eventually led me to a kind of jazz enlightenment.

All of this, of course, relies on a kind of cultural accident, just because an ad executive wants his kid to learn the multiplication tables by putting them to music, and he happens to meet a jazzman who can do it, so that in 1973 television history gets tweaked a little bit, and the jazzman's career gets tweaked a lot.

He started out with bebop ambitions, in 1949, traveling by bus from Texas to New York with books and records as his only possessions. He waded through New York's jazz culture by way of small gigs on Manhattan's West Side, or in Brooklyn, or Queens, wherever they needed a piano player who could sing. He led a double life of sorts, obliging the East Side crowds with jazz standards—pleasant numbers like "Basie Blues" and Hoagy Carmichael's "Up a Lazy River" (songs he loved)—then jamming fanatically with other beboppers after hours.

He scurried among the clubs on 52nd Street—the Three Deuces, the Downbeat, the Onyx—seeking out Charlie Parker. He'd find him regularly at Birdland, or follow him to ballrooms. He showed up at a high-school prom just to see him.

In the liner notes to a reissue of his first album, *Devil May Care,* Dorough writes lovingly and with hepcat enthusiasm about the thunderbolt Parker was to him:

> Oh, it was *crazy* how we dug Bird. We'd give up pork chops for beans to have cab fare and admission to Birdland (cheep). We'd follow him whenever we could, session-gig-or-concert. . . . We loved every note he played. We loved the squeaks of his reed. We dug other people too, especially the giants and the survivors, Diz, Miles, Thelonious . . . but we really dug Bird . . . it was like idolatry . . . it was crazy . . . we were Bird-happy, Bird-struck and Bird-bent . . . and mostly, tryin' to learn to blow a little.

Occasionally, Parker would grace jam sessions at a basement apartment in the William Henry Hotel. There would always be one bass, one piano, one drum kit, and about fifty musicians sweating and smitten and pressing for a chance to play. Who knows how they lured Parker into it; promised him junk, no doubt. As for Dorough, he rarely ever got there early enough to sit in; usually he'd listen at the edge of the room. But on one night, when Dorough heard that Parker would be there, he rushed down in time for a good slot, and squeezed in among the piano players packed like gamblers around a hot hand at a craps table, listening to Parker flit through about twelve choruses of "(Back Home Again in) Indiana." When it was over, the standing players with tense politesse requested turns, and Dorough leaned into the piano player's ear and said: "Okay, man, you played a tune, now let me have one."

Lips on the reed, eyes to the side, Parker unfolded the melody for the next song, and the new sidemen fell in, Dorough among them. He would recount this night for friends who couldn't make it, share it proudly with his wife. The moment put a fire to his jazzman ambitions.

Months later, as luck would have it, he and Parker shared a stage. Buddy Jones, a mutual friend who often shuttled Parker around the city, showed up at Dorough's East Side coldwater flat one evening to see if he was booked.

No, nothing.

Then get your hat and coat, Jones told him. Bird needed a rhythm section and had asked Jones to put one together. Bob would be the piano man, that simple. ("My spine went icy cold," he says.) The gig was in Queens somewhere, a nondescript bar, but word got around and the place filled up. Dorough remembers Bird arriving in a cast up to his thigh. They sat him down and propped his leg up on a chair. The piano was an upright; Dorough faced the wall. Parker sat to his left. There wasn't much small talk. The songs were standards, no pressure. When Bird played the first few notes of "Besame Mucho," the drummer knew it was a rhumba. Dorough got there by the second chord, and the bass player followed. But why the cast? Dorough never asked him. "How could you?" he says, still awestruck. "How would you?"

Charlie Parker's death in 1955 was especially painful to jazz musicians in New York, where the music was such an intimate art, its players separated by just a few degrees. Hearing and walking among and—if you were lucky—playing with flesh-and-blood giants like Parker created a musical zeitgeist that was badly weakened by Parker's death.

Dorough had recently returned from Paris when it happened. By then, he had developed a singing style that drew from vocalese impresarios like Annie Ross, Eddie Jefferson, and King Pleasure, and was able to layer his various admirations —for the American songbook, for bebop and its offshoots—into one persona. As a tribute, he worked out a vocalese rendition of Parker's "Yardbird Suite," tacking lyrics to the horn's part. "I'd stand, waiting for a train or bus," he wrote, "vacant-eyed, staring, trying to make the lyrics fit the brilliant solo he'd recorded on Dial Records and which I'd first memorized. I didn't think he'd care if I had to stretch it here and there."

The song thrust his hyperactive, hyper-inflected, acrobatic Southern lilt at beboppers, traditionalists, and everyone else in the way. By giving his consonants unusual elbow room and letting syllables fall like a tall house of cards after Parker's lead—"When*he*had the*miserablewoes*/He seemed to pull-out-his-horn/And make each person lis-ten/And*feelthat*he'd *never*-known what bein' low down could be"—Dorough flashed a personality in place of whatever groomed savvy a crooner might have projected.

"Yardbird Suite" was a highlight of *Devil May Care* (1956), a strange, romantic, infectious record guided by a gamboling voice. His singing style on that record—and throughout his career—projects an unguarded joy, even on his melancholy rendition of Hoagy Carmichael's "Baltimore Oriole," as smooth and gray a version as Carmichael himself could have whispered.

The jazz press was only lukewarm to it, and the record flopped. (Over the years, it's been said that he sounds like "Nat King Cole impersonating Louis Armstrong" or "a high-pitched King Pleasure.") But *Devil* earned Dorough a cult status among fellow boppers and hardcore listeners. Mort Fega, the legendary host of WEVD's *Jazz Unlimited,* out of New York, was immediately hooked. "I became enamored of his style," he told NPR's *Jazz Profiles* in 1998, "and played the record generously. I created a lot of interest in it—as much interest that could be generated with the kind of performer Bob is. He doesn't have a broad appeal. Actually, he's too hip to have a broad appeal. His following to this day is very much a selective minority appeal."

Fega would often play Dorough during the "Best Kept Secrets" portion of his radio show, and eventually would sign him to the short-lived Focus label, which released Bob's second album, *Just About Everything,* in 1966. That record features a gnarlier voice, unafraid to swing lower than it did on *Devil,* slightly harder than the wispy thin-legged one his fans already knew. (He'd taken voice lessons while acting in a St. Louis production of *A Walk on the Wild Side,* and had learned how to project.) His style was bolder—and it would grow bolder still across a dozen albums—nasal, hyper-articulate, clutching a line longer than comfortable, hogging the ball, but always romantic in tone. *Just About Everything* includes some sneaking through other genres, too, including a ragtime uptempo cover of Bob Dylan's "Don't Think Twice, It's All Right," which, by its wily style and stubbornness, makes Dorough cousin to Dylan, or at least a kindred spirit.

By the time Dorough recorded for Focus, he'd been in the music business long enough that, according to Fega, "he had a wealth of experience as a record producer. There was no nervousness about what he did in the studio. He was like in his mother's arms. Very comfortable. It went down like milk and honey. It was easy."

Just About Everything turned out to be one of Fega's favorite projects, but failed to sell. In fact, none of Dorough's albums, published mostly on small if not his own household labels, would do much better than *Devil May Care.* But his cult status would hold steady, and in the meantime he'd gig relentlessly, meandering like a Zelig through music: writing commercial jingles, producing a pair of albums for Spanky & Our Gang (which included the chart hits "Sunday Mornin'" and "Like to

Get to Know You"), and working with the oddball counterculture noisemakers the Fugs (which led Allen Ginsberg to hire him to play piano and organ for a musical interpretation of William Blake's *Songs of Innocence and Experience*). He'd write songs popularized by others—"Comin' Home Baby" (written with his longtime bassist Ben Tucker), which became a Mel Tormé standard; "Devil May Care," "Nothing Like You," and "Love Came on Stealthy Fingers" by several artists—and songs others would ruin ("I've Got Just About Everything" by Tony Bennett). He would make a record of Lawrence Ferlinghetti poems set to jazz (*Jazz Canto, Vol. 1*) and share a billing with Lord Buckley, the beatnik performance artist who recited hipster renditions of Shakespeare monologues. Lenny Bruce would hire him to play accompaniment for *A Sick Evening With Lenny Bruce*. ("When the intermission's almost over," he'd instruct Dorough, "go in and play a few of your shticks. Get 'em back in.") Then *Schoolhouse Rock!* would make his voice famous.

The tight but loyal following would grow, slowly. He signed with Blue Note in 1997, his first major-label contract, and that resulted in three releases—*Right on My Way Home* (1997), *Too Much Coffee Man* (2000), and the live album *Who's on First* (2000) with Dave Frishberg, the dry doppelgänger to Bob's nerdy showmanship, with whom he wrote the popular "I'm Hip," a tune saturated with a wry self-awareness: "Well I'm dig/I'm in step/When it was hip to be hep/I was hep"; "I even call my girlfriend 'man'"; "Bobby Dylan—he knows my friend!"

My favorite album of that trio, and a nice bookend to *Devil May Care*, is *Too Much Coffee Man* (sans comma because it's a moniker). By the time it was released, Dorough had collected mostly guarded compliments from critics; but by snooping through blogs, talking with people who've heard him, and reading the feedback of customers who bought *Too Much Coffee Man* on Amazon.com (as I did), I got a clear sense of what the critics had missed, what's so uncanny about this jazzman's audience: With Dorough fans, appreciation gets slapped aside by passion. The hyperbole of those who bought that record proves it: "He has no equal," wrote one buyer. "He is jazz, he is piano, he is mood, he is a poet in disguise"; "This is an example of the reason American music is great: startling creativity"; "Thanks for the great gift of yourself, Bob"; "Get this . . . and listen to it 10 times. You'll be hooked. . . . Whatever you do, thank your personal god that this man is alive and well and still making important American music."

Unfortunately, such passion wasn't enough to sustain his run with Blue Note. Since 2000, he's recorded three albums, but on much smaller labels, including his own DeesBees Records. "If corporate strictures weren't what they were now," says Tom Evered, the man who brought Dorough to Blue Note, and who is himself a devoted fan, "I would gladly make another one with him. But it's hard to get airplay. It's hard to get exposure. It's difficult to get a record like that out to the public."

Any of the contemporaries Dorough's been compared with—Mose Allison,

King Pleasure, Randy Newman, Dave Frishberg—might be better singers technically, or better musicians technically, but none seems to trigger the same fever in ordinary people. And understand that Dorough's humor has a bottom under it: Though he may not win accolades for a dazzling technique, his music is unquestionably sophisticated, with a gifted touch for arrangement. So how does a jazzman inspire such admiration from his peers, and such rock-star devotion from his fans, and still hunker at the respectable but dimmer status of cabaret singers? The safe answer, of course, is that he's an acquired taste.

Born in Cherry Hill, Arkansas, Dorough was eight when his father took in a pair of vaudevillians passing through town. While staying with them, the duo prepared a routine for local schools, for which young Bob was recruited to sing such songs as "When Polly Was a Little Girl" and "My Blue Heaven."

Music was a family talent. Dorough's father played hymns on whatever organ he could find; his uncle favored cowboy songs on the guitar. Bob took a total of six piano lessons, then noodled around on his own, learning to play by ear. Later, violin lessons were a trial: "Just twenty kids playing 'My Country 'Tis of Thee'—all the same notes."

When the Doroughs moved to Plainview, Texas, Bob joined the high-school band and became a protégé of the band director, who taught him the principles of harmony, how to play the clarinet, and how to conduct. He found his groove in the dynamics of the ensemble. "Just sitting there and hearing the other kids playing different instruments," he says. "How it all fit together, and realizing that the part I played was important to the whole texture."

The Army drafted him in 1943, interrupting his studies in composition at Texas Tech University. He drifted through a few stateside bases with different Army bands, playing saxophone, more clarinet, and piano. He learned Nat King Cole, Louis Armstrong, Jack Teagarden, Hoagy Carmichael. He wound up in Hot Springs, Arkansas, while it served as an ersatz rehabilitation village, where he played afternoon "tea dances" for veterans returning from overseas. He met his first wife, who moved with him to Amarillo at the end of his service, the duration of which—two years, nine months, and twenty-seven days—he's quick to rattle off.

In Amarillo, he began showing up at the Aviatrix, a club where several military musicians would reunite to play the big-band crowd pleasers that filled the nightly billing. Dorough met a pair of Air Force horn blowers who invited him over to listen to Dizzy Gillespie's "Hot House" and "Groovin' High," as well as Charlie Parker's "Ornithology." At first, the songs befuddled him. So they explained it—how "Hot House" was just a variation of "What Is This Thing Called Love?"; how "Groovin' High" came from "Whispering"; how "Ornithology" mirrored "How High the Moon." They played these songs over and over, distilling and decoding the phrasing. "They gave me the keys to the kingdom," he says, "in one simple session."

What clicked? Reflecting on it, he recognizes a genealogy: "As a student of composition, and of music in general," he says, "I had to know everything there was to know, if I could learn it. And, you know, bebop was highly affected by European music, the harmonies of French guys like Debussy and Ravel, and the rhythms of some of the wild guys like Stravinksy. The music was borrowing these rich harmonies for jazz, so it was easy to admire this cross-pollination. So I dug in. And, sure, I was enamored of bebop partly because it was bizarre."

He ordered dozens of records from *DownBeat* and wore them out on the turntable, all the while collecting letters from a friend who had moved to New York and gushed over what he'd been hearing in Harlem's clubs. Being outside that hot circle was too much: He headed North.

By 1952, Dorough was deep into what he calls his "lean period." For three dollars an hour, he worked as a session pianist at Henry LeTang's tap dance studio in Times Square. One afternoon, LeTang mentioned a five-dollar job in the main studio down the hall. Sugar Ray Robinson, retired from boxing, was putting together a variety show and needed a piano player. Henry introduced them, and said, "Play 'Green Eyes' for Sugar." Dorough played it, and when he was done, Sugar Ray said curtly, "You're going on the road with us." And that's all there was to it.

It was the beginning of a two-year gig as the show's musical director. Robinson hated to fly, so the cast and crew traveled by train—hitting Montreal, Chicago, Vancouver, and Los Angeles. The retinue swelled along the way: hairdresser, manager, chauffeur, valet, the wife and child (sometimes), more hangers-on.

The show included a retired vaudevillian named Joe Scott, who played the funny man to Sugar Ray's straight man, and a girl who sang in French, another who performed ballet, and several more who danced a can-can. It included a juggler and a handsome triple-threat ventriloquist, magician, and "pick-pocket extraordinary."

The job put Dorough with heroic company. He played opposite Earl Hines in Providence, opposite Louis Armstrong in Chicago ("I watched every set he played. It was always the same repertoire, four times a day, but beautiful"). He wrote and arranged charts, some of which were played by the Count Basie Orchestra as the opening act, after which Dorough would take over Basie's hot seat and lead the band.

Sugar Ray took the show to Paris, traveling first-class across the Atlantic on the *Île de France,* bringing along his pink Cadillac convertible for good measure. Opening night, at the Olympia theater, the show bombed. It wouldn't run long after that, but long enough, at least, to give Dorough the chance to snoop through the city's jazz clubs, to hear what was happening and pick up extra gigs. He found one at the Mars Club, a popular cabaret on the Right Bank, where the owner, an expatriate named Ben Benjamin, suggested that if Dorough ever quit Sugar Ray, he could play the Mars on a regular basis and, more importantly, play whatever he liked. The names of its alumni were written on the door: Bobby Short, Annie Ross, Billie Holiday, Eartha Kitt, Kenny Clarke, others.

When Sugar Ray announced, without ceremony, that the show had been cancelled and that they'd be returning stateside within a week, Dorough took Benjamin up on his offer. He began a five-month stretch playing seven nights a week at the Mars, developing a confidence in his style that had eluded him in New York, flexing the idiosyncrasies that felt so natural to him. "Something crystallized in Paris," he says. "I didn't reach some kind of level until that gig, where I could experiment and write my own songs, where I was the boss and no one could gainsay. It was the first time I got to do what I wanted to do."

He worked with Blossom Dearie, of the glass-menagerie voice (and who would later sing *Schoolhouse Rock!*'s "Figure Eight"), and recorded with her French vocal group, the Blue Stars of France. He befriended the journeymen piano players Aaron Bridgers ("an elegant expatriate") and Art Simmons. He backed up fellow Arkansan Maya Angelou, on tour as a chorus member with *Porgy and Bess*, for her repertoire of calypso numbers.

Homesick, he sailed back on the *Île de France* second-class (which was still rather nice) and returned to New York in 1955, "thinking I was hot stuff." He booked more nights in East Side rooms and was finally discovered by an agent, who signed him with Bethlehem Records. *Devil May Care* was released the next year, beginning its slow commercial burn.

Even if *Devil May Care* had sold well, it would have been difficult for Dorough to play regularly enough to build a following. He'd been arrested in 1953 for marijuana possession, at a gig in New Jersey, and had had his cabaret license revoked, part of a campaign to clean up jazz clubs that damaged many musicians' ability to play. Gigging thereafter was difficult at best, with his playing limited to one or two nights in small clubs just to avoid the attention of the Liquor Board. It was an exhausting way to nurture a record, never mind a following.

Meanwhile, Bethlehem Records was in trouble. Red Clyde, an A&R man who'd left Bethlehem to start Mode Records in Los Angeles, offered to record Dorough if he could make it out West. With Bethlehem spiraling and New York being so difficult to work in, there wasn't much to mull over. By way of a gig in Tucson, Arizona, Dorough reached Los Angeles in 1958.

Bethlehem soon folded, and Mode never got off the ground. Dorough was stranded, with no label whatsoever, but free to play as much as he wanted. He began buying his own records wholesale from Bethlehem's distributor (a buck a piece) and using them as calling cards for gigs. Whatever was left over he sold on the side.

He quickly plugged into L.A.'s jazz circuit, playing the Renaissance, the

Twelfth Knight, George's Caprice, and frequenting the Hillcrest. "It was incredible, what was happening there," he says. He crossed paths with the wild talent of Paul Bley, Dave Pike, and Eric Dolphy. He turned around one night to find Ornette Coleman on stage with him. ("I heard this strange alto sound come in suddenly, cranked my neck around, and he was blowin' this plastic horn. The sound was startling. It was blood curdling.")

Miles Davis came to L.A. with his sextet in 1959, settling in for an extended gig. While in town, Miles visited with Terry Morel, a friend he and Dorough had in common. One afternoon Davis noticed a copy of *Devil May Care* propped on Morel's shelf and asked to hear it. The next day he asked to hear it again. Excited by his apparent interest, Dorough asked Morel to bring him to one of Davis's shows so they could meet.

They arrived to find Miles standing idly offstage while the rest of the band—John Coltrane, Cannonball Adderly, Wynton Kelly, Philly Joe Jones, Paul Chambers—kept playing. He and Dorough were quietly introduced, and, foregoing cordialities, Davis took him gently by the wrist and whispered: "Bob, go up and sing 'Baltimore Oriole.'" He then led Dorough to the stage, and motioned for Coltrane, Adderly, and Kelly to step aside. Befuddled, all Dorough could do was look at Chambers and give him the song's key. "I don't remember much about it," he says. "I just felt weird. It was a jazz job of the highest order, and I didn't know what these guys were gonna think. I just said to Paul, 'Well, it's in F minor, just follow me.' I didn't know what to do but just sing it." When it was over, the band took a break and gathered at the bar for drinks. By then, Davis had disappeared.

That encounter led to a friendship of sorts. They'd attend the same parties, and if Miles saw a piano he'd pull Dorough aside and ask him to play. "That's how I introduced him to 'Nothing Like You,'" he says. "He was always getting me to sing something for him." Dorough would open for Miles at the Village Vanguard once they reunited in New York. He would spend evenings at Miles's home on 77th Street, listening to the rushes for *Sketches of Spain*, sprawled on the living-room floor, the casual intimacy of which he remembers as a "wondrous experience."

One morning in the summer of 1962, Dorough got a call from Davis, who asked if he would write a Christmas song for an upcoming Columbia Records project. It was a quick call, mostly with Miles's attorney, Harold Lovett. Dorough immediately began work on what would become "Blue Xmas," a hard bop number in which he transposes his interpretation of a Miles Davis attitude into the lyrics, aiming for a "very Dickensian 'Bah! Humbug!' sentiment."

They arranged the song with Gil Evans the night before recording, and even devoted some time to working on Dorough's "Nothing Like You." The musicians gathered at the studio the next day—Dorough, Willie Bobo, Wayne Shorter (his first time playing with Miles). Evans's charts arrived by messenger. Miles was in the booth, tied up on the phone. As Dorough wrote in his book on the experience,

Blue Xmas, "everything was going pretty smoothly, in that I was with some friends for the purpose of making music."

Then Dorough figured out what had been occupying Miles: He was desperate to find another piano player and had been calling around. Wynton Kelly was stuck in Philadelphia; Bill Evans was tied up with his own session. Writing about it later, Dorough recalls Miles driving in the dagger:

> I kept saying to Miles, "I can play it, man," and I was in place at the Steinway since nobody else was sitting there. That's how I did my vocals—seated at the piano. Miles would say, "Lay out." I had one delicious thought that I was being put in a class with Thelonious Monk. I'd once been present at Birdland when Miles kept turning to Monk saying, "Lay out." This came to be known as a texture called "strolling," where the horns and the bass and drums go without the piano chords.
>
> I said, "Miles! These tunes are too hard! I gotta play to help me stay in key." He'd say, "Just hit the first chord, Bob, then lay out." So that's how we did it.

The song required one take (afterwards, they moved on to "Nothing Like You," on which Dorough sang but was again discouraged from playing). When all was said and done, he would walk away with a standard musician's fee, with Davis listing himself first on the songwriting credits.

"We've all heard stories about Miles putting his own name on other cats' tunes," Dorough wrote. "To tell the truth, I stayed quiet about it and pretty much forgave him because of the magnitude of his talent. . . . My meeker, humble self rationalized that without Miles I wouldn't have a track on Columbia Records at all." And although Dorough actually owned copyrights to the song through the Library of Congress, "I just sat on the secret and let it ride."

Miles and Dorough would remain acquaintances, but their relationship would be lopsided at best. Bob would sometimes stop by Miles's home only to be turned away by a stranger; and on one occasion in the Village, Miles spotted Bob walking and flagged him down, but just to borrow twenty bucks ("Gotta see a man," he told him). Years later, at a musicians' hangout called Junior's, Dorough discovered Miles's rendition of "Devil May Care" on the jukebox. Miles had recorded the song just a couple of days after the "Blue Xmas" session, though Dorough never knew about it until he saw it on the Wurlitzer. He was shocked, but he was more bowled over by Gil Evans's arrangement. "I used to sashay into the bar . . . and go right up to the box with a quarter in my hand before ordering a beer. . . . I spent a lot of quarters on that." Miles would tip his hat again, in his own way, when "Nothing Like You" wound up on his 1967 record *Sorcerer*—a wispy, vocalese-bop intrusion on this otherwise atmospheric windup, its only connection being Evans's pianoless arrangement, its horn and bongo backbone. "I was dumbfounded," says Dorough. "Miles just dropped it in. Maybe he needed three more minutes, I don't know." Dorough would get royalties, but by then his relationship with Miles was all but dead.

Songs aside, Miles didn't do Dorough any favors with his brief mention of the "Blue Xmas" session in his autobiography, which amounts to a dismissal: "Then Columbia got the bright idea of making an album for Christmas, and they thought it would be hip if I had this silly singer named Bob Dorough on the album, with Gil arranging. . . . The less said about it, the better. . . ."

Miles Davis may be his own revisionist, but his dismissal cuts to the quick of Dorough's curious struggle as a jazz artist, which in turn leads to the curious issue of jazz's cult of high seriousness, the door through which most people first enter jazz.

The players who first guided my own fascination with jazz—Coltrane and Davis especially—were of that cult, masters of bebop's musical puzzle and arbiters of its detached cool. Charlie Parker was, in a sense, a transitional figure, a sanctified hunger artist who suffered famously but played with an untouchably pretty style and obvious wit. It's hard to say whether his vices handicapped his music, but it's clear that his sad backstory created an irresistible irony to how lovely that music was.

But to the extent that Parker introduced a bright complexity in jazz, so many of the trailblazing jazzmen who followed drew the music out to such depths of humorlessness that it remains stuck there. Coltrane, with his blitzkrieg solos, offered no musical levity to his addictions and suffering the way Parker did. No matter how brilliant, his sound is infused with moaning, low or high, always laced with the tragic. Miles, with his freaky, esoteric discipline and Prince of Darkness persona, flatly rejected ingratiating himself with an audience. Ornette Coleman, meanwhile, played with such abstract intensity that his music sometimes resembled a thesis.

To a greenhorn like myself, modern jazz is appealing for obvious reasons, not the least of which is the chance to bear witness to such profound talent. But jazz also appeals for many of the same reasons that a band like the Replacements did when I was younger: The music is mood-driven, often introspective, and speaks of suffering with beautiful flourishes. The rub is that jazz, by virtue of its difficulty, is exclusionary, a quality reinforced by the attitude of seriousness.

Dorough, of course, knows this peculiar form of exclusion—bebop's inner-sanctum politics—because he was there in the thick of it. Decoding the obtuse was a form of initiation. "It was supposed to be a revolutionary music," he says, "and its creators were trying to obfuscate the scene a little bit. They didn't want you to dig 'em. They say around Minton's Playhouse, where a lot of the fomenting took place, they had secrets, like knowing that 'Hot House' was really 'What

Is This Thing Called Love?' but unless you were an exceptional musician you wouldn't know what the hell they were playing. And you'd take your horn and sit down because you didn't understand it. So they were weeding out the lesser lights. It was a cutting session. We as students of the music, we were doing our best to be in on the secret. It was esoteric stuff, there was no doubt about it."

And while high seriousness developed naturally out of such complicated music, the posture of cool matured for a new purpose—mainly, the shirking of the traditional entertainer's role. Coolness on stage was a form of dignity, which young black players demanded not only through their technique, but also through their stage presence. Being funny, being lighthearted, being cordial all risked smacking of Stepin Fetchit.

That's a familiar line in jazz's sand: art vs. entertainment. It's a line that traces back to Louis Armstrong and his use of humor as a form of supplication. Beboppers rejected him for that easiness in his personality, the grin, his implicitly self-deprecating sense of humor, which they tagged to minstrelsy. But, as Ralph Ellison clarified when he wrote about this division in 1962, to dismiss Armstrong was to confuse politics with artistry.

"Louis always remained a consummate entertainer," Dorough says. "But it's true: Since his time, if you become a singer, it's different. It's commercial, it's troubadorish, it's clownish. That's why the beboppers wouldn't announce tunes or say anything to the audience. It was a political thing. So they'd just go on the stand and they'd nod at each other and go *dulitlitulitididididuh*—and when it was over they'd do another one. I'm a different kind of personality. I've just always felt that if I had a job, I had to say, 'Good evening.'"

So Dorough chats, introduces songs, tells a funny anecdote, hams it up. But does that mean that he lacks seriousness? In a narrow sense, yes. But he also exudes the tragic potential of the comedian, the offbeat wisdom of a trickster. I'd risk, too, that he often reflects the "crazy wisdom" of the Eastern holy fools. Tom Robbins, writing about the dour literature venerated by Western intellectuals, suggests that crazy wisdom might be an antidote to the "toxic contagions of sordid fiction" he finds so depressing. Robbins refers to those Tibetan mystics for whom folly and humor have as much spiritual potential as any Catholic tradition, who use playfulness to kick apart the wooden structures of conformity, clearing paths to enlightenment through a "wisdom that turns the tables on neurosis by lampooning it"—which, through a deceptively breezy approach to love and suffering, Dorough also does.

Much of his holy-fool effect relies on his voice. It flits and sidewinds through a ballad, but then dips into drunk-tank sourness in a song like "Small Day Tomorrow," dragging the syllables (*tah-maah-wrowww*) like he's having a slow-motion tantrum.

The voice, in turn, prods the lyrics, reams of which were written by Fran

Landesman, whom Dorough met while acting in St. Louis. Through dozens of songs, her hipster sentimentality juxtaposes elegantly with Dorough's glib delivery. Sentiments like "Yes, you showed me all the colors of the rainbow/But I didn't know the price I'd pay/Have mercy on me, babe. . . ." are trailed by something that wavers between a raspy croon and a yodel.

So really, the problem isn't that Dorough is inappropriately funny, or even silly. He's *strange*, sublimely so. Unintelligibility is easy to defend against, but strange gets under your skin. And artistic strangeness is rather difficult to achieve. In this case, being a jazz artist, it relies on musical prowess without taking the sentiment too seriously. The juxtaposition, when it works, works beautifully, as it does in "Whatever Happened to Love Songs?" The line I'm thinking of seems innocuous enough: "No magic left in the music/Now that my lover has gone." Reading it, you'd never guess how Dorough stretches that last vowel toward a high "A" just shy of the pitch. It is the opposite of crooning. It would make a balladeer wince. But it is lovely here—uncomfortable, intelligent. Granted, his style suits the giddy dangers of falling in love better than heartbreak's darker fallout; but no one does giddiness like this.

The story is that David McCall, a New York advertising executive, was at the end of his wits: His son simply could not grasp the multiplication tables, but knew every Rolling Stones lyric cold. McCall figured that if he could set the multiplication tables to rock, his boy would finally get it. He would fund the whole thing—costly, yes, but he was desperate.

He and his creative director, George Newall, auditioned dozens of Broadway songwriters. Newall, meanwhile, was going through a divorce and spending a lot of time at the Hickory House, listening to and hanging out with jazzmen he met there. He befriended the bassist Ben Tucker, who immediately recommended Dorough for the project. Newall had never heard of Dorough, but he was game.

"The other musicians all came up with something very simple," says Dorough, "you know, doggerel poetry and simple rhythms and melodies, as though children couldn't handle it. I thought he was going to give me a high-price jingle to write. But then he said, 'But don't write *down*.' That sent chills up my spine." Dorough left the meeting somewhat terrified, but thrilled. "Here was a chance to communicate with children—who didn't want simple stuff, who wanted *something*." He pored through books left over from a college course, studied for weeks before writing a single note. "I wanted to put the multiplication later," he says, "and first tell them something about the Trinity, the triangle. I dug up things from the Bible and philosophy. And I was a fan of Buckminster Fuller, who said, simply, that the triangle is stronger than the square or the rectangle, because you can't push a triangle over. It supports itself; there's nowhere to go."

"Three Is a Magic Number" was the result, the first song Dorough submitted for McCall's *Multiplication Rock* project. Ironically, it was never intended for television; it was only supposed to be a record. But it just so happened that Tom Yohe, the agency's art director, was in the room when McCall played the tape; he started sketching out what images the lyrics triggered. Those sketches evolved into a storyboard, and soon enough bulbs went off and wheels started spinning and both the song and storyboard were presented to McCall's biggest client, ABC. The network bought the project and commissioned the rest of *Multiplication Rock*, which included the songs "Three Is a Magic Number," "Figure Eight," and "My Hero, Zero." The group then tackled the eight parts of speech through *Grammar Rock*, which included the trumpeter Jack Sheldon singing "Conjunction Junction." Dorough put his touch on all of it, songs about science and history and civics. The show would be cancelled in 1985, but by then would have already imprinted in a million minds the basic lessons of education's three Rs through a simple musical principle—repetition. And, to boot, the songs easily hold their own against any of that era's pop music.

Dorough had no idea if the show was successful; it wasn't anything you could measure in sales. "I didn't know if anybody else was watching it," he says. "So I volunteered to do assembly programs. I took the Manhattan Yellow Pages and booked about ten recitals. I'd say, 'This is Bob Dorough. I'm with ABC Television and *Schoolhouse Rock!* We have a Christmas present for the kids....' ABC had nothing to do with it. I booked all these concerts myself. All I needed was a piano and a mike. I'd arrive at the school and the principal would say, 'Well, we never heard of you, but the kids seem excited.' And after getting up on stage, I'd go into 'Three Is a Magic Number,' and I would look out and see the kids. They'd be nudging each other: 'It's *him*.'

"Then I knew."

I saw Bob Dorough perform a few times before I got to know him, most recently in the sleepy lake town of Heber Springs, Arkansas, at a chamber music festival. His daughter, Aralee, is principal flutist with the Houston Symphony Orchestra, and had recently recorded an album with him, *The Houston Branch*. She'd been invited to Heber Springs to play chamber music and mentioned that her father was born in Arkansas, which inspired the festival organizers to invite him down as part of Arkansas Heritage Month. (He'd already been inducted into the Arkansas Jazz Hall of Fame.)

The turnout for his show was small, about twenty-five people. The intimacy worked and it didn't; the lo-fi dynamics were an injury. A good deal of Dorough's performance depends on the way his singing barges in on, ribs, and kneels before the music. Running his voice through what sounded like a tube amp made things a little rough.

But what the show lacked in hi-fi was overshadowed by intelligence. Dorough minded this classical context: New arrangements of his bebop songs were followed by a modern, contrapuntal duet for flute and oboe (featuring Aralee and her husband), followed by a piano/flute duet of "Yesterday" (an arrangement he'd written for Aralee as a child), and then an abstract version of "All the Things You Are." The songs were threaded together by the flute's touches. This was, after all, his daughter's occasion.

The second set opened with the *Schoolhouse Rock!* stuff (it usually does), and I got that slight nostalgic rush. So did the soundman, who was so moved he hooted. This material was really all I knew of Dorough's music then; seeing him perform it twice now, introduced the same way, as a singalong, and hearing a timid audience tip-toe through the multiplication bridge in "Three Is a Magic Number," I realized that he might actually be sick of having to work these songs into his set. So the nostalgia vanished, though I did my best to shout the numbers out.

We met up the next day, rising early. He seemed doleful—chuckling, and sweet, but also understated and careful. I ordered eggs. He ordered pancakes, said to the waitress: "But *done*, you know what I mean? And a side of bacon, just for atmosphere."

We talked about Sugar Ray and Los Angeles; he introduced me to a couple of theories on harmony. Thinking back on it now, his demeanor, I'm reminded of what Ellison wrote about Armstrong and the hard boppers:

> Certain older jazzmen possessed a clearer idea of the division between their identities as performers and as private individuals. Offstage and while playing in ensemble, they carried themselves like college professors or high church deacons; when soloing they donned the comic mask and went into frenzied pantomimes of hotness—even when playing "cool"—and when done, dropped the mask and returned to their chairs with dignity. Perhaps they realized that whatever his style, the performing artist remains an entertainer, even as Heifetz, Rubinstein or young Glenn Gould.

We talked about *Schoolhouse Rock!*, of course, and I asked him if he ever tired of playing it. "I'd be a poor musician if it wasn't for *Schoolhouse* and a few other songs," he said. "Theoretically, I make enough money to live on. I could just go to the mailbox every week. But I troubadour because I love to perform. And I'm a ham. I just feel I should get out there when I see the right opportunity and take a gig and work it."

He's played all over the planet; was there a kick to playing a quiet town like this one?

He chuckled: "I just go where there's a gig."

A jazzman steps out of the sideman's shade and sings, a persona for the public to consider. He makes an adequate living at it, but a better one helping other people make their own music. Still, those who hear him become members of a wildfire cult.

I'm one of them. It took some work. I didn't take him seriously at first; I didn't give him credit. I had to study a little—not just the music but the backstory, which, all things being equal, drives the music home. Charlie Parker's aura was generated by his music, but his legend owes something to his suffering. Bob's will owe something to his resilience and adaptability. His survivability. Maybe that sounds melodramatic, but it fits the cult of Dorough. Even Mort Fega, always crisply professional, gushed when he was asked for his impression of Bob: "I can't say enough nice things about him as a human being; and as nice as the things I might say about him as such, I'd say even nicer things about him as a musician—both a composer and a performer. Does that sound like a love affair?"

Or sentimental? Let it go. Loosen up. Shed the hairshirt of high seriousness. Crack apart the frigid attitudes by which you've approached jazz music. Listen to Bob Dorough, and listen again. After a while, the weird bliss gets through, and your prejudices begin to thaw. His selfless wit opens new paths to the jazz sublime, and you realize that, despite his obscurity, he is, in many respects, a genius.

I could go on. But I should probably just defer to that curmudgeonly hipster cousin of his whose line best describes what it's like to succumb to the Dorough effect: I was so much older then; I'm younger than that now.

Blues II

Hunting for Old Records:
A True Story

by R. Crumb

Portrait of the Artist as an Aging Lightnin' Hopkins Enthusiast

by Joe Sacco

His function is to help the listener wallow in his own bitterness and self-pity.

YEAH, WHEN TROUBLE GO WALKIN' OUT, YOU KNOW, BAD LUCK COME WALKIN' IN

IF IT AIN'T ONE THING, IT'S ANOTHER.

And though bitterness and self-pity are the purview of any worthwhile bluesman, perhaps only John Lee Hooker, whose discography is at least as tangled and extensive, ever rivaled Lightnin's ability to ceaselessly plumb the depths of human loneliness.

So what if Lightnin' did it over and over, so what if he once cut three albums in a single week, so what if he gave it away like candy to fawning, white, coffeehouse crowds?

The artist puts such considerations aside, losing himself in his own work.

Lightnin's words no longer register.

There is just an all-knowing moan accented by aching guitar flourishes —a sound bigger than Lightnin' Hopkins the man—to carry the artist through the night.

It's late, and finally the artist puts down his pen. He's pleased with the evening's work.

PERHAPS I'M NOT SUCH A FRAUD AFTER ALL.

PERHAPS I AM THE GENIUS THEY SAY I AM.

SAME TIME SAME PLACE TOMORROW NIGHT, LIGHTNIN'?

J. SACCO 6.05

Rockabilly
II

Carl Perkins

HOW A ONE-LEGGED CHICKEN LED THE WAY
TO ROCK & ROLL HEAVEN (an interview) by Joseph G. Tidwell III

===

*As a young man playing what he called "feel-good music," Carl
Perkins almost single-handedly ushered in rockabilly—a revolution in the American sound. But Perkins's career was challenged
by bad luck, personal tragedy, and bouts with drinking. In 1956,
for example, he was injured in a car crash on the way to* The Perry
Como Show—*an appearance that would have skyrocketed his
already promising career. In the time it took him to recover, he was
eclipsed by his friend Elvis Presley and a young Jerry Lee Lewis.
Still, he developed a loyal following. Other musicians spoke—and
speak—of his virtuosity and musical integrity in tones usually
reserved for Hank Williams or Blind Lemon Jefferson. Now, with
the recent release of an autobiography and an album—both titled*
Go Cat Go!, *after his signature shout—his accomplishments
promise to be re-evaluated by a new public.*

What pushed or pulled you toward music?

"Well, I was born in Lake County, Tennessee. All my early years I worked in the fields
picking cotton with black people. We were the only white family sharecroppin' on
this one farm. I remember that late in the evening when the sun was getting low, you
would hear these wonderful voices start to sing out. The music of these people would
be flooding the air after a while. To this day I can hear that music in my soul, the
rhythm, the feeling it gave me. I just knew one day—and I kept tellin' my brothers—

that I was gonna sing on the Grand Ole Opry. I knew I could do better. I felt music was the only way out of those Lake County cotton fields."

So is the old cotton land the foundation of the soul you put into your music?

"The foundation was a good momma and daddy. But at the time, I didn't know that the hard times would also help me in my later years. Those hard times made me look at music a different way. I sang country different from all the rest. More upbeat. I guess from that I came up with my own style of what was later called rockabilly. Kind of a combination of bluegrass, gospel, and blues, all mixed up."

Can you tell us about your first guitar?

"My daddy gave three dollars and a one-legged chicken for that guitar. He bought it from a black man named John Westbrook. John taught me some basics in the beginning. I'll never forget my little fingers bleeding 'cause the strings were so far from the neck. It should have been enough to discourage any youngster from wanting to learn to play the guitar. But there was just something inside my little soul that kept tellin' me to practice, practice, work, work. I knew this was something that could get me out of those cotton fields. That first guitar wasn't much and I lost my chicken, but I found my best friend musically I would ever have in my life."

Who was your musical inspiration?

"When I was growing up, I loved Bill Monroe. His influence was on all of us. I think the only thing he lacked was a drumbeat. That is, if he lacked anything. Some of those old Bill Monroe songs are so close to rockabilly it's scary."

How did you get picked up by Sun Records?

"I heard Elvis sing 'Blue Moon of Kentucky' one day. I told my brother I got to get to Sun Records in Memphis. Two weeks later I walked in the front door of Sun Records at 706 Union Avenue in Memphis. I explained what I was there for and the secretary told me that Sun was not listening to any more singers. As I was getting back in my car, I told my brother what she had said. Just about that time, a '54 light blue Cadillac pulled up and like to have tore the front bumper off my old car. I just felt that the man owned Sun. I got out and rushed over to him and introduced myself. It was Sam Phillips. I begged him to listen to just one song. Years later he told me he just didn't have the heart to tell me no. 'You looked like your world would have come to an end.' I guess that was true, it probably would have come to an end. We went in to Sun and I played him a couple of songs. He liked what he heard and sent me back to Jackson, Tennessee, and told me to write more songs and get back in touch with him."

Who was crazier, Sam Phillips or Jerry Lee?

"Well, hoss, let me just say, they were both unusual cats. They didn't believe in holding back in sayin' what was on their minds. Both were very talented and clashed a lot, butted heads. But Sam was very smart to be able to pick out as many artists as he did who became successful—Roy Orbison, Charlie Rich, Jerry Lee, Johnny Cash, Elvis, and me. All those started at Sun, and it did get a little crazy at times."

Can I get you to settle something once and for all? Was it the Million Dollar Quartet or the Million Dollar Trio [referring to a 1956 recording session made famous by a photograph of Elvis Presley, Johnny Cash, Carl Perkins, and Jerry Lee Lewis together at Sun Studio]? Had Johnny Cash really left the building?

"Yeah, John had left the Sun studio. And it was a trio. Jerry Lee, Elvis, and me. But John waited for the photographer to get there and then left before the recording was made."

What is your take on the Elvis phenomenon?

"I think God put him here to do exactly what he did. People ask me when I think this Elvis thing is gonna fizzle out. I tell 'em, It ain't. Why should it? He's in the pages of history. If they forget him, then they need to tell George Washington to move over, too."

How did it come about that Elvis did "Blue Suede Shoes"?

"My recording of 'Blue Suede Shoes' came out on January 2, 1956. On March 22, I was on my way to be on *The Perry Como Show*. I had *Ed Sullivan* booked the following Sunday. It never happened due to the accident. It was while I was in the hospital, and I didn't know this until after Elvis had passed away, that Elvis's people wanted him to record 'Blue Suede Shoes.' Elvis told them, 'I really wouldn't rather record it because Carl Perkins is my friend. I'll do it, but I want to wait.' See what a truly nice guy Elvis was? Had he jumped on that song when they wanted him to, I wouldn't have had a hit record. He waited till my song had sold over a million records and was starting to move back down the charts. Then he recorded it later. And when he did, it went right back to Number One. He had it on six different albums."

What did you think when you first heard Jimi Hendrix's version of "Blue Suede Shoes"?

"I had to think about it for a minute. I'm floored at the different people that wanted to do the song. I think he did a great job in his own style."

What is your favorite song?

"Well, there's so many. I guess I like that great song, 'How Great Thou Art.' There was a time in my younger rockabilly days when I didn't look past tomorrow. I thought Cadillacs and sharp clothes fell out of trees. Royalties and money comin' in from every which way. But I finally listened to the words of that song and came to understand the beauty and power of what it said."

You've played thousands of gigs in all sort of places. Do you have a memory of your absolute worst gig ever?

"Yeah—this woman came into this club and shot a man one night. We really didn't know what was going on at first, just heard all these loud bangs. It didn't take us long then to understand what it was. We all started scramblin' and duckin' for the door."

Why do you think rockabilly continues to be so popular in Europe, especially in Germany and Great Britain?

"Well, rockabilly releases the tension in people. You're not sad when you get into it. You're movin' with the music. It brings life instead of slowing down. Rockabilly is not the kind of music you sit and listen to. Something is gonna break if you don't get up and move. You pat your foot and pop your finger and become a part of the music. I think some of those countries don't have what we have here, the freedom may be in the music for them."

What is the story behind "My Old Friend" on your new album, *Go Cat Go!*?

"Paul McCartney called and asked me to come to a place where he was recording. Montserrat, an island in the British West Indies, I think. He was recording an album with Stevie Wonder and Ringo. I stayed eight days singing and recording and just havin' a ball. It's real beautiful down there. For an old country boy like me it was like going to heaven. Well, we worked hard for eight days straight. And, you know, I'm kinda sentimental, so I thought I would write Paul a song instead of getting emotional when I was leavin' the next morning. That night I sat on the balcony of my room looking out over that beautiful ocean. It came to me just how lucky I was to know and be with all these people. That's when this song came to me. Well, the next morning we all met in the studio and I told Paul I had written this little goodbye song. Well, I sang it and I thought I saw a tear roll down his cheek. Paul is such a sweet person. He said, 'Carl, I love that.' He asked if I would sing it again. I said, Sure. He called Linda in and they sat on the floor in front of me with their arms around each other. Now, Paul motioned for someone to turn on the recorder. I sang it again and, at the end, Paul was in tears. So, when we walked out of the studio, I could see Paul crying next to the pool. Then Linda put her arms around me and thanked me so much. She said Paul had been needing to let loose. Now, you got to remember this was back in February of 1981 and John Lennon was killed the prior December. Linda told me that Paul was finally getting to let it all out. To just cry it out. I said, Lord, Linda, I didn't mean to make him cry. She told me, 'He's been needing this.' Then she asked me how I knew. Knew what? I said. 'How did you know the last thing John said to Paul?' I told her I didn't know what she was talkin' about. Linda told me that Paul wanted to see John when they were in New York so they stopped by the Dakota for a visit. John walked them to the door as they were leaving and as he patted Paul on the shoulder, he remarked, 'Think about me every now and again, my old friend.' There I had put [that line] in this song not havin' any idea that this had happened earlier.

Paul McCartney has said to me several times that he thinks through my music, I'm his connection back to John Lennon."

Certainly "Give Me Back My Job" is the most ambitious song on *Go Cat Go!* what with six different guitarists playing on it and a Hall of Fame Quintet—yourself, Bono, Johnny Cash, Willie Nelson, and Tom Petty—sharing the solo singing. Was "Give Me Back My Job" done in a studio together, or did everyone send in their parts?

"It was like being in rock & roll heaven. Everybody was there together."

Are you sitting on a gold mine of Carl Perkins recordings that none of us have heard yet?

"I don't think Carl Perkins is sitting on a gold mine of nothin', really. I can say I've got a few old songs I need to record soon, though."

It'll be hard to top *Go Cat Go!* but are you planning another album?

Yeah—gospel. I've been wanting to do a religious album for a long time."

How and where did you and your wife Valda meet and fall in love?

"I never thought she would be my sweetheart. Valda was sweet and quiet and pretty. I would meet her at my cousin's house. Gosh, I don't know, she was just different from any girl I had ever known. She really made me feel comfortable. I knew there was something special about Val from the start. We went together for four or five years before we decided to get married. I think when it's true love, you got to go for it. Then we got married and started climbing that ladder of life together. People ask me all the time—Elvis, Jerry Lee, Charlie Rich, and others became big stars, what did you do? I tell them I went home to my wife and kids. Most of those people lost not only their families, but their lives along the way. I'm lucky enough to still have my family, thank God. And with Valda and the kids, Carl Perkins is a pretty happy old man."

Dale Hawkins

THAT'S GUITAR PLAYING! by Lauren Wilcox

──────

Spending time with Dale Hawkins, singer and songwriter of the 1957 hit "Susie Q," is a little like spending time inside a life-sized, long-exposure photograph: Certain details, appearing and reappearing in the same places, burn themselves into recognizable forms; others, whipping past, are inscrutable blurs. Hawkins is a tall man, angular and knobby, with a rubbery, animated face and a corona of wavy gray hair, which he wears wet-combed back in a modified pompadour. Now in his late sixties, he has a restless vitality. He hums, he croons snatches of old songs; he spins elliptical, looping narratives that emerge and recede and jump their tracks. He is constantly in motion, a gamboling, jointed motion, like a marionette—even his resting state is a fugue of low-grade popping-and-locking—and this contributes to an overall impression of the man first as a blur, then as an accumulation of images, and then as something more.

When I first got in touch with Dale, in early summer, he suggested that we meet for lunch in North Little Rock, Arkansas, where he lives, at the Red Lobster. But when he nosed his car into the parking lot, he looked a little peaked, and asked if we could just go get a cup of coffee. Smelling of cologne, he folded himself into the passenger seat of my truck. He was wearing a spotless pair of black, ostrich-skin cowboy boots, jeans, a black long-sleeved shirt, and a fat, gold ring with opal chips inlaid in stripes across the face. I asked him how his recent tour had gone, and he started to tell me, and then digressed into a point about a song called "My Babe," which was written by a songwriter he had known at Chess Records in the '50s, but which took the tune of an old gospel standard. Dale rapped the dashboard with the ring-wearing hand and sang a few bars of "My Babe" in a loud, golden twang, which filled the cab along with the cologne and the air-conditioning.

The framing facts of Dale's youth as he laid them out for me in the coffee shop barely deviate from the script for most musicians of that time, the ones who flooded into recording studios from hamlets all over the South in the years after Elvis cut "That's All Right" and "Blue Moon of Kentucky." "We were all raised the same way, taught the same things," Dale told me, "and poor." Born near the tiny town of Mangham, Louisiana, he left home at fifteen, doing a stint in the Navy and ending up in Shreveport working for Stanley Lewis at Stan's Record Shop, where he educated himself about music, helping customers who would sing him a little bit of a song they had heard on the radio and ask him to locate among the stacks of 45s.

"Susie Q," which took Dale five months to write, was cut in a radio station in Shreveport in the middle of the night. Accompanying Dale was a small cast of studio musicians that included the guitarist James Burton, who was fifteen years old. Dale was eighteen. "Susie Q" was released as an r&b single on Chess Records (Dale was the label's first white artist), and reached Number Seven on the r&b charts. When Chess "saw that white folks liked it too," Dale says, they rereleased it as a pop single, and it reached Number Thirty-One. He made the most of the attention he got from "Susie Q" and other releases, including a song called "La-Do-Dada." He appeared at record hops around the country, and by the end of the '50s, he was the host of *The Dale Hawkins Show*, out of Philadelphia, with guests like Dizzy Gillespie and the Isley Brothers. When the craze for rockabilly—what the writer Bill Millar calls a "mayfly era"—began to wane after a few years, Dale found work as a producer—in part, he said, to "quit the road" after his two sons were born.

Dale was quite successful as a producer, with hits like "Western Union" by the Five Americans, "Judy in Disguise" by John Fred & His Playboy Band, and several well-received albums by the Uniques. At one point, three songs he had produced made the Billboard Top 100 at the same time: "Do It Again a Little Bit Slower," by Jon & Robin, "Western Union," and "Sound of Love" by the Five Americans. Neither band had ever been in a studio before.

Along the way, two things happened. One was that Dale became addicted to the stimulant Benzedrine. The other was that "Susie Q," to which Dale had sold his share of the rights to Stan Lewis for two hundred dollars a few years before, had become a hit again for groups like Creedence Clearwater Revival and the Rolling Stones. It is hard to know, from the stories Dale tells and the way he tells them, what, exactly, persuaded him that he'd had enough of the music business, but in the early '80s he moved to Little Rock and entered a rehab program there.

For a while, he eschewed music altogether. An aptitude test administered in rehab suggested he might have a talent for motivational speaking, and for a couple of years he gave seminars for businessmen at insurance companies. He started Little Rock's first crisis center, with a suicide hotline for teenagers. In 1986,

Dale received an envelope in the mail from MCA, which had bought the entire catalog of Chess Records. The envelope held his share of this transaction, a check for sixty-four thousand dollars, after which he began to entertain thoughts of putting together his own studio and making music again.

After an hour or so at the coffee place, I had some of Dale's favorite stories written down on a legal pad, and a recording of him singing the guitar part of "Susie Q" ("Da, dee down down") over a coffee grinder roaring in the background. I did not have a sense of where the song had come from. Before I met Dale, it had seemed possible that "Susie Q" and its sly, almost sinister riff had been a fluke, an aberrant bit of rock & roll flotsam, pushed to the fore by something a little more forgiving than chance, by the pressure of a thousand artists in a thousand studios playing hopped-up, diced-up, mixed-up versions of the music they were raised on. But Dale Hawkins, circa 2005, did not seem like an aberration, or like what was left of one. He was sort of complicated and oblique, but he was genuine, and he seemed connected to music in a straightforward and intimate way that had nothing to do with the way his life had gone.

I asked if I could visit his studio, and he said, "Can you give me a couple of days? That place is a mess. I've been trying to find another place on the floor I can throw a piece of paper." When I laughed, he said, "Think I'm lyin'? Girl, I'll kiss your foot."

Dale's studio is in an unembellished one-story brick building that looks like it might have been a dentist's office. Reflective paper covers a picture window, which looks in on Dale's recording equipment in the front room. There are several arched windows, obscured by a particular vintage of burlappy, industrial-gauge curtain, and a front door that lets into a small foyer usually sealed off from the other rooms. The times I visited, I had to stand in the front yard and call Dale on his cellphone from my cellphone to let him know I was there.

The studio itself is a curious combination of works-in-progress and sentimental ephemera. It is filled with bristling banks of recording equipment, speakers, and drifts of paper and CDs. A Fender guitar is propped in the window, its back to the room, and the sofa is set up as a makeshift bed. A framed doily with HAWKINS crocheted into it is hung above the gold record for "Susie Q." Computers and computer parts are strewn about. Dale and his girlfriend, Flo, have six computers between them, most of which he built himself. At one point during one of my visits, a CD he was playing for me got stuck in the disc drive, and he pulled out a screwdriver and removed the side of the computer to retrieve it.

I liked the resourcefulness and practicality of this gesture; it seemed to embody a general principle of Dale's work. "I never was a great musician," Dale told me, "but I was good at writing, and I was good at putting music together." He has a tinkerer's appreciation for a well-crafted song, for how much music can do with so little. The songs he gravitates toward are more soapbox derby than Formula One, cog-and-piston-driven go-devils that do the job with punch and a minimum of fuss. Playing me a recording of one of his recent songs, "Boogie-Woogie Country Girl," he slapped his leg during a horn part and said, "We built this song on one chord. Hear that horn? That's a school teacher. I told him, 'Man, I want you to play me a fifth-grade solo. If I even *see* you moving your fingers, I'm gonna hit 'em.'"

Which is not to say his songs are easy. Nick Devlin, the guitarist on Dale's 1999 album, *Wildcat Tamer* (the one album Dale has released since setting up his studio), who has known Dale for almost twenty years, told me, "Dale's fond of making different guitar parts mesh together. He's a genius about it, really. He'll say, 'I want you to play decka decka decka,' and I'll think, *God*. But I'll go in there and play it, come out and listen to the playback, and it works. He can hear it all coming together. He'll err on the side of very, very simple, but there's sort of a sophistication about his thinking that you can't really get a grasp on. Sometimes I'll hear one guitar part against another guitar part and it's like world peace has been declared. It's that good freakin' news."

"Susie Q," of course, is a simple song. The riff, Dale said, is partly from the blues standard "Baby Please Don't Go," but instead of that blunt imperative, landing flat-footed at the end of the bar, there's just the name, guttering down the notes to a growl and hanging there, a pleading imperative in itself, cryptic and unanswered.

In Dale's hands, the riff and the chorus give the song something that in 1957 was just emerging in popular music, a funny frisson of desire, frank but illusory, that would become a hallmark of the age. Led Zeppelin's Jimmy Page said that the riff was what made him want to play rock & roll. John Fogerty and Creedence Clearwater Revival made "Susie Q" and variations of it into an era's worth of music. Jerry Wexler of Atlantic Records convinced me that Dale's sound was essential to the evolution of popular music. Rock & roll moved forward on the song's spare groove; the cowbell, the plain, dark, dirty lament. And then rock & roll moved on.

Why wasn't Dale a bigger star than he was? He always had the best bands, played with the best musicians—James Burton and Scotty Moore, who both played with Elvis; Roy Buchanan; Carl Adams, arguably one of rock's finest, who played his guitar upside-down and left-handed, with his pick taped to his hand because he'd had two fingers blown off by a shotgun. The music they made was called "rocka-billy," a label Dale still resists. In retrospect, his music does sound more raw, less varnished than the music of his peers. The songs I listened to in his studio—played fast and rowdy and sung with feeling—had hooks so catchy they were almost itchy. Dale recorded dozens, if not hundreds, of these songs, which were never released. Whether they would have matched the success of "Susie Q" is impossible to say.

To some extent, Chess Records and the music industry in the 1950s probably didn't know quite what to do with Dale's not-exactly-rockabilly, not-exactly-rock music; nor, perhaps, did it know what to do with Dale himself. As far as I could tell, he was impulsive, willful, and independent to a fault—all of his best stories start with him speeding off in a car—and while he was gregarious and hard-working, I could not imagine him having much truck with the finer points of self-promotion.

Yet there was more to it than that. *Wildcat Tamer*, Dale's first album in thirty years, which was given four stars by *Rolling Stone*, does not differ in major ways from his early work. And as we sat listening to his music, it was often hard to tell what was new and what was old. Even the new music he produces has an odd nostalgia to it. He told me that he recorded Kenny Brown, R.L. Burnside's guitarist, because he sang songs that were from what Dale called a "pre-blues era" on Beale Street. I asked him what that meant. "Kenny," Dale told me, "sang a song that said, 'She hit him with a singletree.' I said, 'Kenny, where'd you hear that?' A singletree is what we used to hook the mule up to, to pull the plow. He sang these hand-me-down songs. That was the reason I produced Kenny."

The more time I spent with Dale the more I began to think that maybe he *was* an aberration. He had devoted his whole life to an entirely singular vision of rock & roll, which had found its way into pop music in time to propel the entire genre forward. But as rock evolved, it expanded and warped and polyped and sub-genre'd. And the sound Dale responded to—the sound that was created when a person took the tune of an old gospel standard and sang about his girl—that sound became distorted beyond recognition, at least to him. To him, rock & roll was always the stripped-down, fired-up music he started making when he was fifteen and on his own. It had what Nick Devlin called a "thread of attitude," and it was partly about the blues and partly about rock, but it was also about making something your own when you didn't have anything else. "You take the talent to create away from a man," Dale told me, "and what have you got? You ain't got shit." That was the kind of music he made, and the kind he listened for in other people.

One of those people was a harmonica player named Little Cooper from Pine Bluff, Arkansas. Little Cooper, Dale said, cut an album in 1955 that was never released. Giving up the idea of making music for a living, Little Cooper moved up to Illinois shortly thereafter to work in a factory. A few years ago, after he retired, he showed up on Dale's doorstep—"He just found me," Dale said—with a sack full of old tapes. He had been writing music all these years, he told Dale, and he wanted to record some of it.

"We took down eleven sides in seven hours," Dale said. "His brother played piano and guitar. Little Cooper wore his harmonicas in a sling across his chest, like shotgun shells. They were beautiful people." He showed me a tea towel thumbtacked to the wall, embroidered with a harmonica, which Little Cooper's wife had sent Dale as a present after Little Cooper died.

Dale dug a CD out of a pile and fed it into his computer. Little Cooper's music ricocheted around the studio. Dale sang along. On one tune, Little Cooper and his brother are doing a swinging dance-hall kind of blues, the piano boogie-woogeying around the upper register. "East St. Looey," Little Cooper sings, and then the guitar comes in.

"Soop, dooey-ooh-wah," sang Dale, in my direction, trying to impress upon me the importance of the riff. "See that? You understand? I've got a guitar doing the horn part."

"Right," I said.

"*Right,*" Dale said with satisfaction, watching my face. "And that is very, very hard to do." He spread his arms, listening. He looked enormously pleased. "*That's* guitar playing," he said. "You ain't gonna hear that no more. When those boys finished, me and his wife were dancin' in the back of the room."

About a week later, Dale called me to ask if I wanted to drive down to Indianola, Mississippi, to attend the groundbreaking of the B.B. King Museum and to hang out with B.B., whom he had met back in the '50s at Stan's Record Shop. B.B. used to stop in at Stan's to make sure they were displaying his albums; once, Dale had accompanied B.B. to one of his shows in Shreveport. Dale told me he hadn't seen B.B. in almost fifty years. "We're just going to rub on each other's necks and catch up on old times," Dale said.

This would actually be our second attempt to see B.B. A couple weeks before, when the bluesman played a festival in Little Rock, Dale, Flo, and I tried to visit B.B. on his tour bus before the show. B.B., the guard told us, hadn't arrived yet, and he asked us to wait outside the gate. Dale had dressed up, in a suit jacket with a satin kerchief in the breast pocket, a different gold ring (this one with a gothic D on the face), and his cowboy boots. "I'm going to give him thirty minutes," he told us. About twenty seconds later, he said, "Let's get out of here."

The drive to Indianola, Mississippi, from Little Rock takes about three hours. The first hour is a meander through forested hills, and after that the road hits the flat griddle of the Delta and shoots to the horizon, through fields corrugated with rows of new cotton and corn. A lot of America's best music has come out of the area, which includes the birthplaces of Sam Cooke, Conway Twitty, John Lee Hooker, and Muddy Waters. From the highway, it is an empty, lonely stretch of land. Yellow cropdusters hotdog around the lowest level of the atmosphere. The bank sign in McGehee, Arkansas, said eighty-one degrees. It was shortly after eight in the morning.

Dale, who had come down the night before, had called and asked me to meet him in the parking lot of the Kroger where he was buying breakfast. He emerged from the store wearing a baseball cap that said FBI NEW ORLEANS, carrying a grocery bag and a cup of coffee for each of us. "Follow me," he said, hopping into his car. Dale's approach to traveling in unfamiliar areas is kind of like a scavenger hunt; he collects clues from passersby, tacking back and forth towards his destination. I followed him through a few lights and into the parking lot of a tire-repair place, where he sprang out of the car holding an entire chocolate cake aloft on one hand. "Want some cake, girl?" he murmured. One side of the cake had several chunks out of it. He handed it to me and headed into one of the mechanic's bays, shouting, "Hey, which way to the groundbreaking?"

At length, we found ourselves in a VIP parking lot surrounded by a chain-link fence. Dale had told me that he might play a couple songs with B.B. at that evening's show, and he had brought his guitar. We stood in the lot while he rifled through some papers, looking for the invitation to the ceremony. Some of the papers blew, one at a time, from the roof of his car.

I didn't know what to expect. Dale hadn't seen B.B. in fifty years, but I thought his name probably still held a certain cachet in the industry, and it seemed plausible that either Dale's or B.B.'s publicist had arranged, as Dale had said, for him to hang out with B.B. and perhaps to play with him. On the other hand, it seemed like a tall order. The ceremony we were about to attend was going to be hosted by former governors of Mississippi and various state officials, and mobbed by the press. There would be plenty of people interested in getting a piece of B.B. King.

A stretch limo pulled into the lot where we were standing. Dale didn't miss a beat. "Come on, girl," he said, and we slid inside. It discharged us at the vacant lot where the ceremony was being held, about a hundred and fifty feet from where we had parked.

I remember little about the actual ceremony, except that the sun bore down on my uncovered head so fiercely it was painful. The men onstage sweated through their suits. Dale's publicist, Del, a sunny woman in an orange hat, had secured him a place in the front row, next to an elaborately made-up woman of at least eighty, with fuchsia nails and a diamond ring on every finger, whom Dale introduced as "the first and only woman to play with Hank Williams," and who slipped her hand coyly into Dale's when the color guard marched past.

As soon as the final flashbulb had popped on the groundbreaking, Del grabbed Dale's arm and began to steer him towards B.B., in the middle of a crush of people in front of the stage. At the same time, B.B. King's people began to steer him toward a golf cart that was waiting to carry him to the reception. "Come on, if you want to," Dale hissed encouragingly at me over his shoulder. "And act official as hell."

When we were one handshake away from B.B., who was benevolently laying-on hands in a crowd ten deep, his escorts, like sheepdogs extracting an animal from the flock, plucked him from the crowd and deposited him in the golf cart. Dale's publicist, seizing the moment, lunged in front of the vehicle. "Mr. King, this is Dale Hawkins," she said in a rush. "He wrote 'Susie Q,' and worked at Stan's Record Shop in Shreveport."

It was difficult to see, from behind Dale, exactly what transpired between them at that moment, but after a pause, Dale poked his head into the cart, and B.B. slung his arm around Dale's neck. "All right, now," said B.B., his face unreadable behind his sunglasses. "How is Stan these days?" And then, spotting someone behind Dale, B.B. exclaimed, "Now that there is one of my most dedicated fans!" and the golf cart eased forward and was swallowed by the crowd.

Afterwards, Del made a valiant attempt to get Dale to the reception, saying that he might be able to play with B.B. that evening, or talk with him again. But Dale had had enough. "I've been doin' this my whole effin' life, Del, and I'm tired. If you only knew how tired I was." He pleaded with her in the emptying lot, and when she turned her back for a moment, he trotted briskly in the opposite direction.

On the way to the car, I asked Dale if he thought he would have more opportunities if he did more of the stuff his publicist wanted him to do. "That stuff just always embarrassed me, honey, I swear." He dropped his voice to a whisper: "But that was some good shit back there, wasn't it? Those cats at the magazine oughtta give you a raise."

I had expected him to be disappointed. But he was in a terrific mood. A few weeks before, when we had missed B.B. altogether at the festival in Little Rock, Dale had been just as buoyant: We were walking away from the guard and the gate when he grabbed Flo's hand and pulled her up the sidewalk in a little dance step. In the distance, B.B.'s opening act was wailing out a song about unrequited love.

"Hear that?" Dale asked us, cocking his head at the bass line. "That's Sly and the Family Stone. 'I want to thank you, for lettin' me, be myself,'" he sang. I didn't recognize it—the singer was singing some other lyrics—but about five minutes later, Sly's familiar melody came cranking through the trees. Dale reached back and goosed me on the arm.

"You see?" he said happily. "They finally got into it, after all that bullshit."

Playing

Notes From the Underground (Twang Tour)

WHEN IT'S JULY IN MEMPHIS, HOODOO HAPPENS
by Marty Stuart

July 4, 1997, P.M. Somewhere in Virginia.

The bulletin board in the front lounge of the tour bus reads: UNDERGROUND TWANG TOUR. TONIGHT: DUBLIN, VA. SHOWTIME: 8:15. Judging by the intensity of the rain that's pouring out of the black sky and the lightning that's flashing and occasionally smacking down, God has other plans. His big light show is going to lay waste to the fireworks spectacular that's planned to explode at the end of our Dublin show (if there is a show).

My band—the Rock and Roll Cowboys—and I are glued to the television in the bus as CNN shares live pictures from Mars.

"Where are we going after we leave here?" I ask the band. About seven years ago, I lost all sense of where I might be at any given moment. I'm told tomorrow's show is in Lula, Mississippi. We'll be performing at some cottonfield casino in a town off Highway 61, a few miles south of Memphis.

As we start discussing the joys of Memphis, the lightning stops, the rain ceases, and the clouds roll back. "Maybe it's a sign," I say. "Why don't we spend the day in Memphis?"

It's time for some fun. For the past ten weeks, we've been knocking off one-nighters like a golfer hitting buckets full of balls. The workload has severely out-weighed the fun factor. Memphis can't fix us, but it can help.

Memphis is one of my favorite towns. I've been lifted to the foot of the cross there, and I've stood close enough to the devil to smell his rotten breath. You have to enter Memphis with caution—or else it will slide right out from under you.

359

As word comes down that the Dublin show is on, we head for stage only after unanimously agreeing to visit Memphis. Just talking about it provides us with the spark we need for giving our rain-soaked Dublin fans a star-spangled show.

After the show, we vanish onto Interstate 81 South and I wish myself a happy Fourth of July. I also reflect on a show we played in Minnesota on a previous Fourth—we were the closing act for a wrestling match. I thank God for not having to do that again, and go to bed. The last thing I think about before falling asleep is how good it is going to be to wake up in Memphisto.

July 5, 1997, A.M. Downtown Memphis.

My bass player Steve Arnold—a Memphis native—and I try to come to life as we watch the new day unfold. Steve says, "It's good to be home." Home in Memphis for me is 706 Union Avenue. That's Sun Studio. Any time I'm in town, that's where I go. Going there gives me the same feeling as going to church. As we pull into the parking lot to set up camp, I am unaware until somebody inside tells me that it was forty-three years ago to the day that Elvis dropped by here and recorded "That's All Right."

The last time I was here was in early fall. The Cowboys and I had come to record some demos of songs I'd written. We were having fun and making music when a call came from Bill Monroe's manager. He'd called to tell me that Bill had just passed away and to ask if I would sing and play at the funeral. One minute we were playing in the same studio where Elvis had recorded Monroe's "Blue Moon of Kentucky," and a minute later I was leveled by sad news of that song's creator.

I called time-out and took a walk. Bill Monroe was my friend and one of the first musical inspirations of my life. When I was twelve, I saw him for the first time at one of his concerts, and after the show I asked him for his autograph. He handed me his mandolin pick and told me to use it. Every day I carried that pick with me to school. Later, I got a mandolin and listened to his records over and over and learned how to play using that very pick. Since then, he'd been a big part of my life, and not having him around was going to take some getting used to. When you lose somebody like Bill Monroe, your world shifts.

As I walked the back streets of Memphis looking for some peace, the only thing that came to me were some words for a song for him:

> I am a lonesome pilgrim far from home
> And what a journey I have known
> I might be tired and weary, but I am strong
> 'Cause pilgrims walk, but not alone.

I finished the song in about an hour, then took it back to Sun and played it for the band. We recorded it right there. I listened to the playback, then packed my mandolin and headed home to Nashville. As I was leaving Memphis that time, I thought, This town doesn't mind taking it away from you, but in the long run, it always gives you back a little more than it takes. This rumination drifted away when I heard Roger Miller come across the car radio. He sang "The Last Word in Lonesome Is Me" and then he too disappeared. The fluorescent lights on a billboard advertising Graceland were either blinking or winking at me. I made myself a promise: The next time I'm in Memphis, I'm going to Graceland to visit Elvis's gold lamé suit.

Any self-respecting son of the South knows that Elvis is, and will always be, our main cat. I always come back around to the sad feeling that he should still be here among us other than in spirit, and I'd be a liar if I said that I don't take pleasure in admiring his possessions. But what good are a king's possessions when he's not around to enjoy them?

Thanks to former Louisiana governor Huey P. Long, all of us Southern boys have the right to believe that every man's a king. I thought, Okay, if I'm a king, what are some of my possessions? I've had stars in the heavens, as well as children that aren't mine, named after me. Cats, horses, a parrot, a malt in a country music–themed restaurant in Hollywood, a Martin guitar, a street trolley in Nashville, and a country road in my hometown all bear my name. Treasures, no doubt, but then there are the more personal things, like my collection of country-music memorabilia that's touring across America this summer, and my dog, my house, my guitar, my jeep, and Geronimo's autograph. All mean a lot to me.

But one of my most treasured possessions is my bicycle. My friend and manager, Bonnie Garner, bought it for me as a birthday present last year. It's the first one I've had since I was a kid. I keep it underneath my bus, and I can't tell you the joy that it's brought me for the past year and a half.

I've ridden it—a Trek ten-speed—all over America's back streets, main roads, and town squares. It's my ticket to freedom. Today is no different. It's a perfect morning for a bike ride: There's not a cloud in the sky, the air is fresh, Memphis is barely awake, and I can't wait to tour the town.

I leave Sun Studio and cycle down Union Avenue in search of . . . nothing in particular. Before ten A.M., I tour Union, Madison, and Poplar Avenues, and Main Street. But no trip to Memphis is complete without a visit to the Peabody Hotel. So I scoot over there and have my bike valet-parked before I go inside to call Earl Scruggs for the King of Bluegrass Jimmy Martin's telephone number.

Jimmy left a panicky message on my code-a-phone yesterday. He said he needed some new white boots to replace the pair that he'd given me for my touring memorabilia exhibit. I can understand why they would be hard to replace. They are state-of-the-art white ankle boots made by Acme, with nylon zippers up the side. King Jimmy had them customized with gold tips and had an assortment of red-and-green rhinestones glued on the toes. His message said, "Me and Pat Boone always wore white on our feet. I'm concerned that my fans are upset with me for not wearing my white boots. Them light brown ones I've been a wearing ain't gittin' it! Now you've got to help me find another pair."

Anyone who knows anything about fashion knows that downtown Memphis is *the* place for flashy clothes. Let's say you have a red 1978 Fleetwood Cadillac with wide whitewall tires, gold-spoke wheels, a glow-in-the-dark hood ornament, and a neon-light package underneath the chassis to complement your customized license plates and tinted windows. If you need a suit, shoes, shades, hat, or other accessories to complete your ride, Main Street in Memphis is the place to shop.

Just a moment ago, I spotted a pair of white snakeskin ankle boots with Cuban heels on sale for $69.98 in the window of Discount Sammy's men's shop at 101 South Main. This might be what King Jimmy is looking for. But all I get is Jimmy's answering service.

I enjoy the living-room atmosphere of the Peabody lobby a little bit more before claiming my bicycle.

It hurts me to admit that my two-wheeler doesn't quite have the presence that the stretch limousine parked in front of me has. Although a bicycle is definitely not a star machine, it's a good way to gauge your charisma. You think you're a star? Get on a bicycle and see. The head bellman laughs when he sees whose bicycle it is. Then he tells the young man who delivers it not to accept my tip. He says, "Mr. Stuart has done hit on hard times. I remember when he used to pull in here in a car. He even had Jerry Lee Lewis bring him here one morning about three A.M. Then he got a bus. Then two buses. Now look at the boy—he's down to a bicycle. Let him keep that dollar. He might need something to eat." He tells me when I get something with a door on it to be sure to come back so he can open it for me, and to remember him on my way back up. I high-five the whole staff and take a left turn out of the parking lot toward Beale Street.

When I make Beale, I see B.B. King's nightclub and the Rum Boogie Cafe. I flash back on some reckless nights and unmentionable sights from days gone by. The smell of barbecue makes its way through the air. I notice the clock on the street reads 10:35 A.M. The shops begin opening slowly. I can sense the effects of last night all over everybody. I stop to admire my favorite folk artist Lamar Sorrento's painting of Slim Harpo in a store window. Music blasts from the restaurants and storefronts along the street. In the span of three minutes, I am serenaded by Robert Johnson, Sam and Dave, Ma Rainey, Elvis Presley, and B.B. King. It's a reminder of the difference in Memphis' music and Nashville's. In my star-making hometown of Nashville, we could and should serve up visitors with a twenty-four-hour-a-day smorgasbord of world-class music. Instead, our guests along Demonbreun Street are treated to karaoke cowboys and cowgirls singing along to pre-recorded, watered-down country music. In Memphis, you get the pure musical morphine.

This city hasn't had a hit in a while, but it will. Until that happens, Memphis' musical past is proof that pure soul will sustain you. It's better than money in the bank.

Along about where a historical landmark sign for Rufus Thomas stands, I think about Bonnie. She is thoroughly convinced that the month of July is a curse on her life. She can list a string of earth-shattering events reaching from now to deep in her past that have occurred in July. I know that if she had it her way, July would find itself in the trashcan alongside daylight savings time and taxes. I've tried to tell her to pray it away, will it beyond herself, and rise above it, but when it comes to July, Bonnie's a skeptic.

As I approach A. Schwab's department store, I remember from a previous visit that as you enter you'll find a section for magic potions to your left: oils, herbs, soaps, candles, and incenses to ward off bad luck, evil spirits, and dirty deeds. I decide to run in and buy Bonnie some lighthearted antidotes to July. I park my bicycle at the front door so I can keep my eyes on it while I fill my arms with spell-breaker soap, bottles of St. John the Revelator oil, court-case oil, Satan-Be-Gone oil, jinx-remover incense, a pair of pink fuzzy dice stuck on lucky eleven, and some anti-evil-deed incense guaranteed to stop any bad mojo that could be done against you by a hand with five fingers. I inquire about black cat bone, and the sales clerk tells me that she is currently sold out but does have black cat eye behind the cash register. It's then that I realize my enthusiasm has edged beyond novelty and touched on the outer realm of black magic and voodoo. I have no business there, so I back away as fast as my rock & roll Baptist soul can fly.

While still periodically checking on my wheels at the front door, I pay for my bag of fun, thank the nice clerk, and sign a couple of autographs. When I walk outside, I discover that in the few seconds my attention has wavered, somebody has stolen my bicycle. I think about going back inside to see if they have any bring-back-my-bicycle oil. There I stand in the middle of Beale Street, with a bag full of jinx removers and spell breakers, and somebody has hoodoo'd me out of my bike. A voice inside me says, Half of the thrill is the art of the deal. And in Memphis the most solid scams shift like the sand. When you forgot to look, my boy, you were took. And then the wisdom and words of the great bluesman, Sir Lightnin' Hopkins, come to mind: "Forget about it, 'cause rubber on a wheel is faster than rubber on a heel." I feel like a hick country boy in the middle of a marketplace in some third-world country who's just had his wallet lifted. I run around looking to see if anybody is riding my bike. I ask a woman sitting on a stool in front of a store across the street from Schwab's if she's seen anybody take a bike. She doesn't know what I'm talking about. I walk over to W.C. Handy's statue and start laughing. I remind myself that Memphis is all about magic and, of course, one of the greatest forms of magic is the disappearing act. Yeah, that's it. It wasn't stolen; it simply disappeared.

I walk up the street to the fire station. Fireman Steve Breault looks puzzled and says, "You're . . ." Before he can finish I say, "That's right. I'm the guy who just had his bicycle stolen on Beale Street." He laughs and says, "Welcome to Memphis!" He helps me locate a bike shop and offers me lunch before lending me his pickup truck to go buy another set of wheels. I drive out to the bike shop in his truck and buy another Trek ten-speed. When I return, I thank Steve for the fine Southern fire-department hospitality and then I take off on my new bike toward Sun Studio.

All of this commotion and I still make it back in time for a twelve o'clock haircut appointment with my bass player's personal barber, Robin Tucker. Her aunt used to do Priscilla Presley's hair. After the haircut, I drop a few quarters in the jukebox while having lunch at Taylor's Cafe and Gift Shop. Lamar Sorrento comes by with a painting to give me. He orders a glass of lemonade and by the time we've swapped some yarns I am out of quarters for the jukebox. I take that as a sign it's time to leave. I tip the waitress (who tells me I shouldn't eat things like the cheeseburger I just had), buy a couple of Johnny Cash records, and round up the Rock and Roll Cowboys. We board the bus for Graceland. The gold lamé suit is calling. Nobody in my band has ever been to Graceland. It seems an appropriate topping to an already full Memphis day.

We are given a private tour of the mansion, and, after a trip through the trophy room, every one of us bows in deference to Elvis. We all agree on two things: Elvis is still the King, and we still have a job to do tonight at the Lady Luck Casino in Lula, Mississippi.

Casinos are creeping like kudzu toward Memphis, but I know the city can handle anything that comes through its gates. As of now, the city is hanging on by its roots and looking for a hit. I hope when it's deal-cutting time, Memphis doesn't lose any more than a bicycle or two.

Lucinda Williams

TOUGH-LOVE SONGWRITER
(as told to) Marc Woodworth

▬▬▬
═══

*Lucinda Williams's laidback manner and languorous drawl sug-
gest she's got all the time in the world. If you didn't know her
songs—unflinching and precise accounts of heart-sore retrospec-
tion, self-destruction, and the insatiable desire that leads down the
dead-end avenues of the soul—you'd hardly guess that her vision
is often defined by an urgent darkness. When I ask her what scares
her, she gives two answers—death and flying—then calls one of
them "unoriginal" and the other "trivial." Abandoning any semblance of subtlety, I venture, "Then you're not haunted by inner
demons?" "Can't you see that in the songs?" she asks in response,
sounding a little disappointed. The signature blend of blues, rock,
and country that defines her most recent releases, Lucinda
Williams and Sweet Old World, is required listening. Once you
hear her songs, it's perfectly clear why she's become such a writer's
writer, a designation borne out by the fact that Tom Petty and
Mary Chapin Carpenter have covered her work, and that Bob
Dylan invited her to tour with him. Her forthcoming and long-
awaited album—the first since Sweet Old World in 1992—finds
the lanky, half-shy Ms. Williams exploring her characteristic
concerns—sex, death, and heartbreak.*

"I was always encouraged to be ambitious about whatever I chose to do and that's how I approach music. When I write a song, I can't do it halfway. I want it to have an edge, something more than the usual pop song. I appreciate a well-crafted hit with a great melody like Petula Clark's 'Downtown' or 'Monday Monday' by the Mamas and the Papas. Not every song has to be really deep, but I want to write something that goes beneath the surface. To work for me, a song has to look right when I read it on the page and feel good when I sing it.

My dad, Miller Williams, is a poet who was my mentor and critic, so I've always seen my work from a writer's perspective, not just a songwriter's perspective. When I first started writing, he'd look at my songs, give me his response, and tell me what I could do to make them better. He taught me to recognize what was and wasn't useful to a song and how revising a single word can change everything. I remember that he read the lyrics for 'He Never Got Enough Love' and suggested that 'faded blue dress' wasn't right. When I changed 'faded' to 'sad,' the song sounded much stronger to me. I learned from him that every word and line must have meaning and not to waste any words, to get right to the meat of the matter. I looked up to him and writer friends of his who would stay at our house: James Dickey, John Ciardi, John Clellan Holmes, and Charles Bukowski among them. I didn't realize at the time how lucky I was to be surrounded by these incredible minds, to be able to listen to them talk about poetry, to play for them, and hear their comments about my songs. I never felt self-conscious or intimidated by the fact that my father and his friends were poets. I wrote for fun the way most kids would be out playing ball.

Because of that creative environment at home, I've always felt I could try to write about anything. When I write, I don't think about whether or not the subject of the song is appropriate. It's not as if I sit down and say to myself, 'Now I'm going to take on the subject of death.' Issues like the ones raised by 'Pineola' and 'Sweet Old World' are just part of life.

'Pineola' is about the poet Frank Stanford, who committed suicide when he was still in his twenties. His death had a profound effect on me. It was so sudden and unexpected. I'd known someone else who'd killed himself but we weren't as close. Frank's death hit much closer to home. I had just gotten to know him. We'd hang out, drink coffee together, and talk. He was a great writer who had been one of my father's students in Fayetteville. I was staying at my folks' house when Frank killed himself. I'd just sat down on the couch when my father told me what had happened. That experience was very hard to write about. In fact, I write about experiences like that because they're so hard, because I need to deal with them. Songwriting is my main way of doing that. There are songs you feel you just have to get out. After I finish, I can move on. When I really start digging into my life and a song comes out, I feel an almost physical release—I know I've hit on something real when I get that feeling in the solar plexus. When I feel that, it's clear to me I've done something right and the song can convey my experience to a listener.

A song like 'Little Angel, Little Brother' took a long time not only because I was writing about my brother, who I really love, but also because I didn't want the song to tell anyone what to think about him. I make a conscious effort not to be polemical in my songs. In that one, I was trying to walk that tightrope between being personal and getting something more universal across. I have a new song called 'Drunken Angel' that, like 'Little Angel, Little Brother,' took a long time to write because I had to walk that same thin line. The song is about a self-destructive musician who was shot to death during a senseless argument. I try to look at him sympathetically but not in an overly romantic way. It's like the equivalent in songwriting of tough love, I guess. In my mind, he isn't a romantic figure, but in a song he could seem that way if I don't choose just the right words. With 'Drunken Angel,' I wanted to find a way to be true to my subject without romanticizing self-destruction. There are already enough songs that do that. I want what I write to be true to life rather than to repeat clichés and I want my songs to push people's buttons, to make them think.

I'll start any number of songs that I work on for a while before realizing there's nothing to do but abandon them. Some people say I'm a perfectionist. That comes into play when I'm trying to write but mostly I just think it's because I have high standards. I'm not the type to enjoy a success or relax and enjoy life all that much and there is a price to pay for being so serious all the time. The inner turmoil never really goes away. At least as a writer, though, I get something out of it. That's the irony: I write because I have these fears, but I'm not afraid to write about them. When I write, that's the only time I'm not afraid. That's one important reason why I do it. There's also a fine line between those who look down into the pit and those who jump in. I'm not on the self-destruct setting—I am able to control that tendency in myself—but writing about self-destructive people helps me understand the difference between looking and jumping. It's healthy for me to write about the darkness because it's there, it exists, and just about everybody has to deal with it.

I work on a J-curve: I won't write for months and months and then, all of a sudden, there's a rush of writing. Before that happens, I worry that I won't be able to write a song again. I've struggled a lot with a problem many of my friends, particularly women, talk about: the feeling that you can't create when you're content and in a relationship. That idea is, of course, total nonsense. To think that way is a copout, but it's a cop-out a lot of us use. If it's impossible to write and have a domestic life, then how do you explain all the novelists and poets over the centuries who were married, had children, and still produced great works of literature?

The real problem isn't necessarily that your partner is wrong for you, but that you don't know how to be with someone and still do your work. Before I understood that, I'd sabotage a relationship if it didn't live up to my overly romantic view of what being part of a couple meant: two people madly in love who live together, make love and art constantly, and inspire one another to do the best work they've ever done. When reality didn't live up to those unreasonable expectations, I'd go back to my little room alone and start writing wildly about how things didn't work out. After that phase, it's back to another relationship. It just becomes a vicious cycle.

I started playing guitar in 1965. That was the year a student of my dad's brought Bob Dylan's *Highway 61 Revisited* over to the house. I heard that record and said to myself, 'This is what I want to do right here.' We moved a year later to New Orleans when my dad got a position teaching at Loyola. The '60s in New Orleans was a special time. Like the Neil Young song says, 'All my changes were there.' I would hang out with friends and listen to Buffalo Springfield, Cream, and the Doors. That's when I first heard Leonard Cohen and Joni Mitchell. All my father's students were welcome any time of the day or night. They'd come over for dinner and hang around afterwards, drinking Jack Daniel's, talking about art and politics until three or four in the morning.

It's not surprising that I became a rebel, doing everything a restless kid could do during those years. Even though I grew up in a very supportive household, I still found something to rebel against. It runs in the family. My grandfather was a conscientious objector during World War I who was involved in the Southern Tenant Farmers Union scuffle. My dad worked for Civil Rights in the '50s and early '60s. George Haley—Alex Haley's brother—is my godfather. He and my dad were roommates in the South in the '50s. He's got some stories to tell about that.

My high school was overcrowded and understaffed—a typical inner-city public high school. I got kicked out a couple of times for trying to change things. The first time, I was expelled because I was handing out a list of grievances and demands we'd drawn up to present to the principal. When a black student and a white student would get into a fight, he would suspend the black kid while allowing the white kid to stay in school, that sort of thing. I was sent to the office for distributing these leaflets and while I was there the Pledge of Allegiance came over the intercom. Everybody was required to stand up and recite it. I refused and was sent home. My dad found an ACLU lawyer and I was eventually readmitted.

My father asked me not to do anything that would get me kicked out again but when I went back to school, there was a big demonstration going on. A group of black and white kids had boycotted classes and was marching around the school. SDS and the NAACP joined the march. At first, I just went up to my classroom to stay out of trouble, but when I looked out the window, I saw some of my friends calling for me to come down and join them. The students who were in the room with me were spitting on them. What was I supposed to do, stay up there with them? Hell, no. I went right down to join my friends. The feeling of adrenaline is hard to describe. We had the conviction that there was a real point to all of this and we felt an incredible sense of unity. You couldn't be on the other side. It didn't matter what the consequences were. I know it sounds corny now but that sense of purpose really did exist. The times were different then. Anyway, when the police came and started throwing everybody in paddy wagons, anyone who was involved in the demonstration got suspended.

My family was going to Mexico at the end of the year anyway and my father understood that things were too tumultuous at school so he told me to get my books and study at home. I actually read my books for the first time. I also sat in on some classes at Loyola before we left. When we got to Mexico City, I couldn't start classes because I didn't have the right papers. I spent the year I turned seventeen in Mexico City not going to school. I'd spend hours in my room just reading, playing my guitar, learning songs, and listening to records.

I also played my first shows when we lived in Mexico. I performed folk songs with a friend, Clark Jones, at different schools as part of a cultural exchange the State Department set up. At that time I wasn't writing a lot so we did songs by Bob Dylan and the Byrds, Joan Baez, and Peter, Paul, and Mary—lots of protest and traditional material.

After Mexico, we moved to Fayetteville, Arkansas, where I studied at the University of Arkansas for about a year. If I hadn't become a musician, I would have studied cultural anthropology. I was interested in other cultures because we traveled so much when I was growing up.

I think of myself as a Southerner and I'm very aware of the differences between home and other parts of the country. This is another world and I'm proud to be a part of it. I resent the negative stereotypes about the South and Southerners that are perpetuated by the media, the idea, for example, that everyone with a Southern accent is a dumb hick. The South I know has a rich cultural and artistic tradition. The fact that I'm from the South—I was born in Lake Charles and my mother's family is from Louisiana—shows in my writing. That I have roots here, that I can identify with a place so strongly, is important to me.

For all my fascination with particular places and cultures, my interest in anthropology didn't last long. When I was in school, I already felt the pull towards music as a vocation. My dad had some reservations about my decision to pursue music instead of finishing college. He wanted me to be able to support myself if music didn't work out, so I wouldn't have to go through what he went through trying to live as a poet. It was good advice, but I never did find anything to fall back on. It got to the point where I realized I had to make music work for me because there was nothing else I could do. I'd devoted everything to it. All those years of playing and singing started to pay off eventually, but it took a long time to happen.

Even though my choice to become a musician didn't make things easy, I had a lot of drive and good instincts. It's hard to say whether I created expectations for myself or whether they came from the family. I know that my father's example was important to me. My dad was so focused on his writing that he'd work amidst the most chaotic situations. It didn't matter what else was going on, he just wrote and wrote and wrote. Writing was at the center for him. I always admired him for that and wanted to be able to focus like he does.

I was so proud of him this January in Washington when I saw him read the inaugural poem. It was a fast and furious week. On Monday, my dad read his poem at the inauguration ceremony. Monday night they held one main ball and many smaller balls, including the one where I played. We were supposed to go on at 9:30, but we didn't play until twelve. I was supposed to perform an acoustic set with Charlie Sexton, because I couldn't bring the whole band, but it turned out Jessie Dayton, who I knew from Houston, was on the bill so his drummer and pedal steel player said they'd sit in with me. Once we went on, the chemistry was right, the place was packed, and everything came off well. My dad and mom were in the audience along with my godfather and his wife and my aunt and uncle. They were all feeling good because it was such a great day for my dad. Everything was right with the world.

After we played, the security people told me that President and Mrs. Clinton were on their way to our ball and that they wanted to see my dad and me backstage. Everyone was running around, all these volunteers and political wannabes. My boyfriend Richard was with me so a guard asked him to find my dad and bring him to meet the Clintons. When Richard stepped over the backstage barrier into the crowd, a Secret Service woman snapped at him, 'Where are you going? What are you doing?' These people don't fool around. He told her that he was on a mission for another guard to find Miller Williams, but she didn't believe him and pushed him backstage again. Nobody else went to get my dad so that plan fell through the cracks.

Meanwhile, I'm waiting at stage right for the Clintons to arrive. Billy Ray Cyrus is back there with me because he was scheduled to close the show. He's wearing holey jeans, a T-shirt with another shirt hanging out, and tennis shoes—his uniform. I had spent days in total anxiety worrying about what I was going to wear, noticing all these flaws about myself—my cuticles are raggedy, my eyebrows aren't right—and Billy Ray, bless his heart, is standing there like Andy Griffith, happy as can be.

Finally, the Clintons arrived at two o'clock in the morning. They went onstage, spoke for a few minutes, and did a signature dance. Afterwards, President Clinton came over, took my hand, and said, 'I know you're really proud of your dad.'

All the attention my dad got was amazing. He wasn't expecting the onslaught of reporters once it was announced that he was going to be the inaugural poet. The press, *The Today Show,* the calls never stopped from that day until the inauguration. Can you imagine sitting down to write an inaugural poem? Talk about writing on demand. Thank God I didn't have to come up with an inaugural song."

Guitar Lessons

LEARNING TO PLAY MUSIC IN THE MISSISSIPPI DELTA
by Steve Yarbrough

▬▬▬

One of the enduring memories of my childhood is the night I went to Carl Hamilton's house for my first guitar lesson. I was twelve years old. The Hamiltons' house was new and on a quiet street in a nice part of Indianola, Mississippi. They had a swimming pool out back—a rarity in town, and as sure a sign of affluence as Mrs. Hamilton's Cadillac, which stood parked out front in the driveway. The house had a big living room with polished wood floors and a fireplace and, off to one side, a smaller room with French doors where Mr. Hamilton kept all his musical equipment and gave lessons.

I sat on a love seat in the music room, my Sears acoustic archtop in a case at my feet, and listened for a few minutes while Mr. Hamilton played "Hambone" and "Wildwood Flower" on his electric guitar, a Gretsch Country Gentleman. He played in the Chet Atkins style—thumb thumping out muffled alternate bass; second and third fingers plucking melody on the treble. It's a style I never learned and one that seems sterile and predictable to me today, but that night it had the power to transform. For the first time in my life, I began to envision a future for myself that did not include driving a tractor in one-hundred-degree heat.

When he finished playing, Mr. Hamilton laid the Gretsch down. "I'm not going to teach you to play with a thumbpick," he said. "At least not right away." He reached into a bowl that stood on a nearby table and pulled out a thin, tortoise-shell flatpick. "You're gonna use one of these—it's a little bit easier to handle than a thumbpick. I want you to learn to hold it between your thumb and forefinger like this." He held the pick in the air, displaying the proper grip. "It'll turn on you if you're not careful, so you've got to hold it tight. But not too tight. Stay relaxed." He passed the pick to me—it was still warm from his touch—and told me to take out my guitar and let him tune it.

I handed him my guitar. Then, to my surprise, he handed me his. "Set that on your knee," he said, "and pick the little E-string—it's the one on the bottom of the guitar, but from now on we're gonna call it the first string."

I sat there with the imposing hollow-body balanced on my knee and picked each string as he directed, and he tuned my guitar to his. I felt a little thrill each time I plucked a string and sound came out of the Gibson amp that was sitting nearby. My father had promised that if and when I ever learned to play well, he would buy me an electric guitar and an amplifier, and by the time Mr. Hamilton had finished tuning my acoustic, I knew which electric guitar and amp I wanted.

As we exchanged instruments, I told Mr. Hamilton I liked his guitar. He said, "It's a good one—same kind as Chester A. plays." Every year or two, he said, Chet Atkins gave his guitar away and started using a new one. "I got my name on the waiting list for one of his," he said. "Maybe when I get it, I'll sell you mine."

"You know Chet Atkins?"

"Yeah, I know him. I did a little studio work a few years ago when we were living up in Memphis, and every now and then he'd come through there. He's as nice a fellow as you'd ever want to meet."

He picked up a red book that had been lying on the floor and handed it to me. The book was *Mel Bay's Guitar Primer*. I opened it to discover that the first few pages were devoted to such topics as "How to Hold the Guitar," "How to Hold the Pick," and "How to Tune the Guitar." Then it got really interesting. There was one song that consisted of a single whole note, played once per measure, for two complete pages. The title of the song was "The Choo Choo Train."

Evidently Mr. Hamilton noticed my dismay. He must have known that I had already begun to envision myself soloing on an electric guitar.

"It'll turn into fun one day," he assured me. "But first there'll be some hard work."

I went home that first night determined to work hard and learn to play the guitar well, but my resolve deserted me in a matter of days. The inarticulate, halting noises I made did not resemble music, and they gave me no pleasure. Practice quickly became tedious. It reminded me of so many other things I didn't enjoy: farm work, school, church.

In those first few weeks, I would go three or four days at a time without touching the guitar at all, without even looking at it, because until I started my lessons, playing it had been a dream, and now the dream was dead. When my father came home from the field, hot and tired, and saw me sitting around doing nothing, he'd bark at me to get the guitar out and go to work on it. "I'm spending money I ain't got on them lessons," he'd tell me. I'd get it out and pick "The Choo Choo Train" until Dad probably felt as if he were being tortured.

Whether or not Mr. Hamilton knew I wasn't practicing, I can't say. He drilled me four weeks in a row, without my showing any sign of progress.

"Just keep working at it," he'd say, with the big red Gretsch balanced on his knee, while I butchered "Mary Had a Little Lamb."

"Put in an hour a day going over your pieces," he said. "Playing 'em till you get 'em just right. It may not be too exciting when you're struggling at it, but it sure feels good when you succeed."

The problem was, I had already given up.

On the evening of my fifth lesson, as I sat knee to knee with him—staring glassy-eyed at the music stand on which *Mel Bay's Guitar Primer* rested, squeezing the neck of the guitar so tightly that my left hand cramped up, while my right hand slashed at the strings, missing them altogether at least half the time—he quietly reached over and shut the pages of the book. Then he laid his hand on the fretboard of my guitar, damping the strings.

I looked at him, my face burning, expecting a rebuke. But instead of telling me that I was lazy, which I already knew, or that I was hopeless, which I wanted badly to believe was not true, he smiled and said, "Hey, look at this."

He leaned forward, so that the neck of his Gretsch was just inches away. He began playing a guitar boogie—playing it slow, so that I could see how simple it was to make music out of wood and steel and a few tubes and diodes. I began to tap my toe.

"Try it," he said. "Lay your fingers on the strings."

I looked down at the fretboard and put my fingers right where they needed to be, then I looked down at my picking hand and struck the first note. In the space of a few moments, I did what I had thus far been unable to do: I began to play.

What led Carl Hamilton to throw away the book and teach me how to boogie? I feel fairly certain that he would not be able to say precisely what it was. But Mr. Hamilton must have realized that, for whatever reason, I simply couldn't do it his way. He might have put it down to impatience on my part, or laziness, or some blockage that existed somewhere between my brain and my hands. Whatever causes he assigned to my ineptness, he also recognized my need to make music.

Maybe he noticed the reverence with which I regarded his own playing. Maybe it was something that came into my voice, some note of longing, when I mentioned the musicians I loved—Bill Monroe, Roy Acuff, Jerry Garcia, and Indianola's own B.B. King.

Maybe when he looked at me he saw somebody who wanted to transcend his reality, if only for a few moments.

Maybe when he looked at me, Carl Hamilton saw, as I believe all good teachers do, a reflection of himself.

Within six months I was as much of a musician as I would ever be. I could listen to any song on the radio and play it back instantly. I could improvise credibly over the pentatonic scale; I was proficient at blues and country music, and I could play a fairly sharp Chuck Berry riff. Colors were forever beyond me—if I soloed in an original sounding way, it was accident rather than inspiration—but I sounded good enough to my father. Playing "Wildwood Flower" on the Sears archtop, the old Carter family tune that had been his mother's favorite song, I brought a tear to his eye.

A few days before Christmas, he and Mr. Hamilton drove over to Hearne's Music Store in Greenwood and checked out several electric guitars. Dad couldn't afford a Gretsch, and anyway, you couldn't buy one anywhere closer than Memphis; so he settled on a Fender Coronado II. He chose it, I suspect, because it was the least expensive guitar that Mr. Hamilton would countenance his buying. Fender quickly stopped making the model, which was never very popular. But its obvious drawbacks—it was an extremely thin hollow-body, not resonant enough to be a very good country guitar and overly susceptible to feedback if you tried to play high-volume rock & roll—meant nothing to me. I loved it as I have loved few things in my life; loved it, for all its deficiencies, much more than I've ever loved the Martin D-35 that I've played for the last fifteen years. I treasured it because I believed I had earned it. And, in retrospect, I can see that we were perfectly matched. It was a bottom-of-the-line Fender, and I was a bottom-of-the-line picker.

I played the Fender in the morning before I went to school and again in the afternoon when I got home. I liked to strum it while lying on the floor, the guitar resting on my stomach, and my eyes shut. I sometimes awoke in the middle of the night, and without even turning on the light, I would creep over to the corner where the guitar case rested and take the Fender out. You could hardly hear it when it wasn't plugged in, but I didn't care. I loved finding my way up and down the fretboard, loved the feel of the strings beneath my fingers.

In the fall of 1969, eighteen months after I took my first guitar lesson, I began to play in a country band with Carl Hamilton and Vardel Riggins, a local football coach. We were an unlikely combination. To begin with, our ages differed vastly. Mr. Hamilton was forty-one, Coach Riggins was twenty-five, and I was thirteen. Mr. Hamilton, the oldest, was also the smallest; he probably stood no more than five-four or five-five. Coach Riggins, a former college-football player, was six-four, and I was already six-one.

We had no bass player and no drummer. Mr. Hamilton played Atkins-style lead on the Gretsch, I played rhythm on the Fender, and Coach Riggins strummed a nylon-stringed guitar that you could hardly hear at all because it had no pickup in it, and we never tried to mike it.

I recently listened to a tape my father made of us sometime around the middle of 1970. Dad says the tape was made at a fish fry in Drew, Mississippi. I have no recollection of the event—I probably repressed it.

The truth is that we didn't sound too horrible. Mr. Hamilton's solos are clean if unexciting, the one exception coming when he puts down the Gretsch and plays "Salt Creek" on the banjo. He starts out playing Scruggs style, picking around the melody, then the second time through something happens and he starts to sound a lot like Bill Keith, picking one chromatic run after another. You can hear a couple of metal chairs scraping concrete as people whoop and stomp their feet. I play a nice T-Bone Walker riff on my own instrumental composition, which Mr. Hamilton dubbed "Steve's Twelve-Bar Blues in A." Coach Riggins, a Jim Reeves disciple, has a bad moment in the middle of "He'll Have to Go." When he sings the key line—"put your sweet lips a little closer to the phone"—he puts his own lips too close to the microphone, gets shocked, and says, "Bitch!" But for most of the set, his vocals are smooth and understated.

Among certain people—mostly, I suspect, among people who didn't really like music—we developed quite a following. Rotary Clubs and rest homes adored us. So did the individuals who planned retirement parties. It was as if they were saying to the new retiree, "Now that you've quit, you have to listen to this."

But we were serious and we were devoted. We practiced as many as five nights a week. At the time, I could not have imagined the toll this must have taken on the home lives of my two adult partners, but now that I'm a husband and a father I can imagine it all too well. The frown that almost always appeared on Mrs. Hamilton's face when she saw me downtown makes sense now. So does a brief encounter I had in Sunflower Food Store with Coach Riggins's young wife. My mother had sent me in to pick up some Wesson oil, and I was just about to pull it off the shelf when I sensed a presence behind me. Turning, I saw Mrs. Riggins. She was holding her baby, a little girl who must have been about a year old.

"She just went potty," Mrs. Riggins said. "Can you hold her for a minute?"

Evidently my face betrayed a lack of enthusiasm. Mrs. Riggins tossed her hair and stalked off down the aisle. "Never mind," she said over her shoulder. "You'd probably try to fingerpick her."

It ended as so many things do. One night Mr. Hamilton called me and said that Coach Riggins wouldn't be able to practice because his daughter was sick. We got together a few more times after that, but between each session, we had one or two cancelled meetings. One thing or another was always going wrong in Mr. Hamilton's life or Coach Riggins's. I suspect that the wives had put their heads together.

At the time, the demise of the band did not bother me much. I had gotten more interested in the harder brands of rock—I was listening, by then, to the likes of Led Zeppelin—and, in truth, I was a bit embarrassed about standing in the lobby at Care Inn, surrounded by people old enough to remember when Dixieland was new, and strumming chords while Coach Riggins sang "Release Me." I assumed that I'd have my own group soon, that I'd cut my first record long before I turned twenty. I imagined myself on stage at the Liberty Bowl in Memphis, a mountain of sound equipment behind me, sixty thousand scruffy-looking young folks—some from California—going crazy while I cut loose on one piercing solo after another. In this vision, my hair was long and stringy; I knew about dope; and I'd had sex with three different women.

As for Carl Hamilton, I believed he had long ago taught me all he could. But I was wrong.

Mr. Hamilton called one day about six months after we'd last played together and asked if I'd like to hear Chet Atkins perform with Floyd Cramer and Boots Randolph and several other Nashville pickers. I didn't particularly want to go, but I didn't want to hurt Mr. Hamilton's feelings either, so I said yes.

Mr. Hamilton picked me up on a Friday afternoon, and we headed for Memphis in Mrs. Hamilton's Cadillac. He joked that maybe we'd get backstage and he'd talk Chet into passing on his Gretsch. "If he does that," Mr. Hamilton said, "I'll just give you mine." We checked into a room at the Holiday Inn, then we went out to a nice restaurant where he bought me a steak dinner. Afterwards, we drove downtown to the new auditorium where the concert would be held.

We got there fairly early and parked on a street near the rear of the building. It was sheer luck that we were just getting out of the Cadillac as a limo pulled up next to us. Chet Atkins and another man, who, I would later learn, was Kenneth "Jethro" Burns—one half of the Homer and Jethro comedy team and perhaps the greatest mandolinist who ever lived—climbed out of the limo.

Chet was carrying a case that was much too small to contain the big Gretsch. It probably held one of the two classical guitars he would spend much of the evening playing; the Gretsch, I imagine, was already backstage. Jethro Burns carried an even smaller case. Since I didn't know who he was, I paid him no mind.

The great Chet Atkins was no more than six feet away. I looked at him, then at Mr. Hamilton, who was standing on the far side of the Cadillac, his keys dangling loosely from his hand. The expression I saw on his face is still hard to describe, though I've thought about it often in the last twenty-five years. His jaws had not exactly gone slack, but his mouth was slightly open, and his lips looked as if they were about to form the word *oh*. He glanced down at his keys as if they could unlock a door behind which might lie the answer to some particularly vexing question. He looked at me once more, then at Chet, who leaned back into the limo and said—to someone we could not see through the opaque windows—"Try the Black Label." He slammed the limo door, and he and Jethro Burns turned toward the auditorium. Chet grinned and said, very clearly, "Lord amighty."

What he was referring to I will never know, though I suspect it had something to do with the person who had remained in the limo. Chet was not looking at anyone when he said it. His eyes, if I recall right, were trained on the door at the rear of the auditorium.

But Carl Hamilton seized the moment. The last syllable of Chet's enigmatic utterance had scarcely faded when Mr. Hamilton stepped forward. He stood in front of the Cadillac, positioning himself directly before Chet Atkins and Jethro Burns, both of whom looked at him as if they thought he might be a crazy man, and he said, "Hey, Chet. You ready to give me your Gretsch?"

As I write what happened next, I am listening to a Jethro Burns CD, *Swing Low, Sweet Mandolin,* which was recently released on David Grisman's Acoustic Disc label. It's now one of my favorite records—relaxed and easy swing with tunes ranging all the way from Duke Ellington's "Solitude" to Hank Williams's "You Win Again."

That evening in Memphis, Jethro Burns stole the show from all the better known performers. Boots Randolph and Floyd Cramer and Chester A. himself hardly seemed to belong on the same stage with him. But Jethro Burns almost ruined the evening for Mr. Hamilton and, in a different way, for me.

Maybe the knowledge that in another hour or so his sense of humor would have to sparkle had left Jethro feeling sullen. Maybe the knowledge that he was a great musician who would never achieve the kind of acclaim he deserved, who would never be called by his name if someone really famous was walking along beside him, brought some hidden animosity to the surface. Maybe he didn't like the way Mr. Hamilton had blocked his path.

Because Jethro Burns glared at Mr. Hamilton and said something under his breath that I couldn't quite make out—but that Mr. Hamilton heard quite clearly—and in that moment Mr. Hamilton's face threatened collapse.

Almost simultaneously, Chet Atkins glanced at Mr. Hamilton, then at me, then at Jethro. His eyes were as fast as his fingers, but even more impressive was the speed with which he made a gesture that I will never forget.

"This is an old buddy of mine," he told Jethro.

Then he and Mr. Hamilton shook hands. "How you been?" Chet said.

Mr. Hamilton regarded him with gratitude, with admiration, maybe even with love. "Not too bad," he said.

"I'm gonna hang onto the old Gretsch a while longer," Chet said. "But when I get tired of her, your name's at the top of the list."

Mr. Hamilton and I stood there in the street and watched as Chet Atkins and Jethro Burns disappeared through the door to the auditorium.

For a while neither of us said anything. Then Mr. Hamilton put his arm around my shoulder.

"Jethro acts a little surly sometimes," he said. "But I never held it against him. He can flat-out pick the mandolin, and that makes up for a lot."

Classical/Avant-Garde

Moondog

THERE IS JAZZ, CLASSICAL, AVANT-GARDE—
AND MOONDOG
by Daniel Alarcón

The more you learn about Moondog's life, the more your own suffers by comparison. Whatever you might have done that you were proud of, those acts you had considered interesting or even brave—all those episodes in your life you were saving up, the anecdotes, the yarns to tell your wide-eyed grandkids: All this is so much hokum compared with the stories Moondog must have gathered up in his perplexing years on earth.

His biography, even when told in broad strokes, is startling. Born in 1916 in Kansas, Moondog spent much of his childhood in Wyoming, where his father was an Episcopalian minister, a missionary to the Native American tribes of the area. Moondog lost his sight at age sixteen in a dynamite accident. At the Iowa School for the Blind he received his first training in composition, then lived in Missouri to study braille. In 1936, the Hardin family moved to Arkansas, and Moondog spent a year studying at Arkansas College. They lived there for several years, in Moorefield, near Batesville, where Moondog was known for his long hair, his eccentric dress (even then, he was fond of capes), and his habit of walking alone along the train tracks between the two towns. He spent a year in Memphis as the private student of Burnet Tuthill, the director of the Memphis Conservatory. The following year, 1942, Moondog moved to New York and went directly to Carnegie Hall, and was in the front row the day Leonard Bernstein made his conducting debut. For a time, Moondog was the only person allowed to hear the New York Philharmonic rehearse; apparently the temperamental conductor Artur Rodzinski viewed the blind, bearded Moondog as a good-luck charm, an amulet.

Moondog set up shop on the corner of 54th Street and Sixth Avenue dressed as a Viking, with a horned helmet and spear, and stood there for the better part of three decades—day after day, whatever the weather, begging, making music, reading and selling his poetry.

If this were all, it would still qualify as an achievement: a feat of endurance, the mark of some kind of genius. In a city known for constantly remaking itself, Moondog, through sheer persistence, achieved such iconic status that the *New York Times* dedicated a two-column article to his mid-'60s costume change (new pants, same Viking helmet, same spear). When he died in 1999, the *Times* obituary called him a "landmark." But while most New Yorkers thought of him as nothing more than an eccentrically dressed homeless man, he was recording albums of inventive, experimental music for labels like Prestige, Capitol, and Columbia, compositions that included elements of Eastern melodic traditions, of jazz, avant-garde, and classical, along with a healthy dose of street noise: honks, whistles, traffic, surf, and everything else the grunting city had to offer. His admirers included Charlie Parker and Philip Glass. Janis Joplin covered a Moondog tune—without permission. In surely one of the odder pairings in contemporary music, Moondog teamed up with Julie Andrews to record an album of Mother Goose songs. He once shared a bill with Charles Mingus. When conventional instruments couldn't make the sounds he imagined, he invented his own: bizarre contraptions with names like the *trimba,* the *yukh,* the *oo.* His composition "Moondog Symphony" was used by Alan Freed, the legendary disc jockey credited with popularizing rock & roll. Freed was even known for a while as the "King of the Moondoggers" and his radio show was called "The Moondog Show"—that is, until our Moondog sued him and won. The story goes that Igor Stravinsky called the judge and spoke on Moondog's behalf: "Take care of this man," the famed Russian composer said. "He's a serious composer. Do him right."

When Moondog disappeared from the New York streets in 1974, many city residents probably assumed he had died. In fact, he had embarked on the next leg of his adventurous life. He left New York to play a date in Germany, and didn't come back for fifteen years. He made a home there, with a woman thirty-five years his junior named Ilona Goebel who managed his career, transcribed his music, and finally convinced him to abandon his Viking costume for more conventional attire. His compositions were performed all over Europe to wide acclaim, and he conducted orchestras in Germany and France. And Moondog continued to write music just as he had during his years on the streets, but now in the relative stability and comfort of the Goebel home. While his New York compositions were necessarily brief, never more than three or four minutes, now he had the tranquility to work on a larger scale. He immersed himself in many projects. Always grandiose, always ambitious, the former Viking of Sixth Avenue, who had described himself during his New York years as "a European in exile," wrote a series of eight canons called *Cosmos I* and *II* that would have required nine hours and a thousand players. He returned to New York in 1989, as an invited guest, and conducted the Brooklyn Philharmonic Orchestra. When he died, he left behind a musical legacy comprising dozens of albums, over three hundred compositions that include madrigals, organ and piano pieces, and over eighty symphonies.

It's wonderful now and then to stumble upon music that is unclassifiable. That borrows shamelessly, transforms mercilessly, mutating, mixing, fusing disparate genres until sparks fly and something unsettling happens. You can go on and on about this man's strange, fragmented life—on the streets of New York, in the concert halls of Europe, in recording studios everywhere, his glancing encounters with the musical royalty of his time—but this doesn't adequately address the disconcerting beauty of the music itself. Individual compositions have an impact, but what can you say about the collected compositions of Moondog? The syncopated madness of his rhythmic compositions; his distilled, stylized interpretations of free jazz; his urban tone poems, his spoken-word koans over lilting Eastern melodies—what would you call his *typical* composition?

If you take the man at his word, his musical project was the pursuit of correct counterpoint. Whatever he was creating rhythmically, in terms of harmony, he was a throwback. He saw himself as improving on Bach. Counterpoint, in the Moondog style, works this way: increasing complexity, layers upon layers, until you hear somewhere in the far distance a hint of a repeated theme—but here and now, on the surface, there is something new, there is texture, and intuitively you are aware that you've arrived at a new place. In the best work there is rising tension, even anxiety, a feeling that the music itself cannot withstand the weight of another voice, and yet there it is—and then another, and another.

And still counterpoint is, when coupled with strict tonality, somewhat rigid. In interviews, Moondog spoke often of "correct" counterpoint. He chided Haydn, Beethoven, and Bach for their "mistakes," and evinced a similar intolerance toward jazz musicians, and for the very idea of improvisations. No matter what you *think* you are hearing, Moondog is not a free spirit. All that seeming chaos, that street chatter, the honking horns, those unconventional sounds—none of it is left to chance. In interviews he comes off as a purist, even a control freak. Not exactly what you would expect from a man who named himself after a pet he was particularly fond of. Or from a man who dressed as a Viking and stood on New York's Sixth Avenue for nearly three decades. From a man who, given the choice between renting a room to live in or paying to have his music transcribed from braille into musical notation, more often than not, chose the latter.

Asked about his place in the avant-garde music scene in a 1998 interview, Moondog said, "I'm strictly tonal, so I feel kind of lonely."

And where was correct tonality being practiced these days?

"Pop music."

But there is nothing pop about Moondog, nothing pop about wearing Viking regalia for thirty years, nothing pop about a nine-hour canon for a thousand musicians. For all the rebellion his public persona implied, there was an asceticism to him as well: He was the monk of counterpoint, the man who eschewed comfort for music and brought a nearly fanatical dedication to the pursuit of "correct" harmony. In the process of looking for it, he made music of real beauty, and real character. And for this we can be grateful.

Still, there is the issue of categorization: where to place Moondog and his music? He belongs somewhere, within some tradition or within many. Or perhaps these are invented problems, issues only pertinent to those of us who rely on words to organize the world. When Moondog himself was asked if it bothered him when his music was put into categories, he had perhaps the best response: "It doesn't bother me where they put it, as long as they put it."

A Love Set to Music

by P. Revess

At the Young Composers' Concert

(a poem) by Donald Justice

―――――

Sewanee, Tennessee, Summer, 1996

The melancholy of these young composers
Impresses me. There will be time for joy.

Meanwhile, one can't help noticing the boy
Who bends down to his violin as if

To comfort it in its too early grief.
It is his composition, confused and sad,

Made out of feelings he has not yet had
But only caught somehow the rumor of

In the old scores—and that has been enough.
Merely mechanical, sure, all artifice—

But can that matter when it sounds like this?
What matters is the beauty of the attempt,

The world for him being so far mostly dreamt.
Not that a lot, to tell the truth, has passed,

Nothing to change our lives or that will last.
And not that we are awed exactly; still,

There is something to this beyond mere adult skill.
And if it moves but haltingly down its scales,

It is the more moving just because it fails;
And is the lovelier because we know

It has gone beyond itself, as great things go.

Playing II

The Song of a Sad Café

CAN YOU YEARN FOR A PLACE YOU'VE NEVER BEEN?
by Don Asher

Early in my musical career, I was discovering a kind of enchantment to darkened honky-tonks and nightclubs in the afternoon—places where I'd occasionally practice on the bar piano to escape my mother's home canasta games—a peculiarity of mood, light, and fragrance that I found myself irresistibly drawn to. In the case of Gabe's Silver Dollar in Worcester, Massachusetts (didn't every self-respecting blue-collar town in the '40s have one, along with a Valhalla—down a dingy flight of stone stairs—a Club Paradise, and, fronting on river or lake, a Jolly Roger?), it had to do with the sun beating ineffectually against dust-laden drapes, the gloom rarely penetrated—but when it was, a weak and murky light resulted that seemed to waver the way sunlight ripples across the bed of a pond. It had to do with the upright piano's dulled varnish gleaming in that ghostly radiance (the quality of light—ancient, cool, burdened—that you see in old Flemish paintings) and the hypnotic patterns of bentwood chairs systematically upended on Formica tables. Mostly it had to do with elusive, merging aromas of impregnated wood, rotting linoleum, the sawdusty urinous spilt smell of alehouse with its inseparable components of stale sweat, must, smoke, and dead air. (The dust and memories that collected in the folds of those moldy sun-faded drapes—you felt if they could be hauled outside, borne to the top of one of Worcester's more prominent hills, and shaken out, great clouds would plume and billow over the valleys like the smoke signals that majestically rose two centuries earlier from the hills named Pakachoag and Sagatabscot.) Paradoxically, that musty fragrance and pale transitory afternoon light conjured for me the sunny South, specifically Dixieland music, though

I'd never ventured south of Providence, Rhode Island. Can you yearn for a place you've never been? In high school, I was listening on 78s to the rollicking traditional bands blowing standards, the most earthy and evocative of which seemed to extol the charms of the South ("Basin Street Blues," "South Rampart Street Parade"), a repertoire that extended to up-tempo versions of the folk anthems— "Carry Me Back to Old Virginny," "My Old Kentucky Home," "Way Down Upon the Swanee River," many laced with lyrics (*'Tis summer, the darkies are gay*) whose broadcast would get you boycotted today. That rousing full-bore sound, clarinets wailing, sass and punch of brass—the fervid exhortations to *Look a-way, look a-way, Dixie Land!*—knocked me out and filled me with an inexplicable homestead longing for a life neither observed nor experienced, inducing memories without foundation.

> The moonlight on the bayou
> A creole tune that fills the air
> I dream about magnolias in June
> And soon I'm wishing that I was there

The music's spawning ground—its overflowing heart—was, of course, down yonder in New Orleans. My impassioned imagination effortlessly transformed the Silver Dollar and future reeking, smoke-filled dens into a class of storybook honky-tonks, replicas of the fabled river-town saloons, gangster-run speakeasies (offering, along with the music, bootleg gin, and whores in silk dresses), and funky-butt brothel parlors that were the mythical cradles of jazz.

I devoured biographies and memoirs of King Oliver, Satchmo, Jelly Roll, even Stephen Foster. I lifted their music off the turntable and airways, and plucked it painstakingly from sheet music. As I was the only one in our fledgling quartet who could read worth a lick—no major accomplishment: Felix, the most talented member, had been blind since birth—I got to pick out the music, run it through for the others, and sketch the rudimentary arrangements. So when we landed the gig, our first, at the Silver Dollar, the band library almost exclusively celebrated the South.

The 4 Sharps—formerly the Noteworthys or Noteworthies—both plural endings bothered the hell out of us—consisted of trumpet and vocals (Bobby), alto sax and clarinet (Felix), drums (Junior), and piano (me). Felix was the oldest, in his mid-thirties, and as I said, the most accomplished. We were lucky to have him; had he been able to read, we'd doubtless have lost him to one of the local commercial bands. The rest of us were recently out of high school, marking time and having fun while deciding whether to go to college or join the proletarian workforce. (We were pretty realistic kids; family pressures aside, a serious musical career did not appear a valid option at the time.) Felix's tone was honeyed, his phrasing and inventions assured;

small and lithe, delicately featured, he was a lure for the ladies until an intense new-comer appeared on the scene and wiped out the competition. Junior, a hulking, eerily silent kid, loosed his demons on his mother-of-pearl tubs; he was a thumper and a crasher, addicted to cowbell and tom-toms. Bobby's tone in the middle register (the only one he was conversant with) was dense and blatting like a frog in a drainpipe; he kept a mute in his horn at all times, at Gabe's insistence, to squelch the frog and mask the clams he hit every other bar. Grating tone and inconsistency aside, Bobby was a gifted *shpritzer*. He'd seize the mike at opportune moments and announce in a suave, silky voice, "Look who just walked in, folks—Rosemary Noonan, queen of the loom at Klevin-Schafft, and her devoted Larry. How about a welcoming hand for this incomparable duo...." Matching the gab was an uncanny eye for peccadilloes—guys or gals "tipping out" on their spouses. "See the cat holding the chair for his date?" he'd cue Junior and me. "I happen to know he's married. Watch, he's sliding the chair back, smooth as satin, big smile like it's the first time. Now dig he's bow-ing—*bowing*—ushering her onto the floor. I don't know what his old lady looks like, but four bits says that ain't her."

The Silver Dollar—I'm not sure what to call it, club, café, saloon, tavern; it was a dump—was located on Summer Street, a broad, grimy thoroughfare that housed, along with hole in the wall bars, cafeterias, trinket shops, and rubble-strewn lots, the Hotel Sincere three doorways down from us: a four-story red-brick building whose bricks pooched out at odd angles as if laid by a stoned mason. The marquee, extending to the curb, was fringed with dead lightbulbs, and taped to a top-floor cor-ner window early that summer was a hand-printed sign on what appeared to be butcher paper: HANGING ON. (Sometime in August it would vanish. Had the tenant moved, let go in one sense or another, taken the gas pipe?) Three blocks past the Sincere, two barred-window fortresses faced each other from opposite sides of a narrow sidestreet—the city jail and what was then called the insane asylum.

The bandstand, at one end of a stark low-ceilinged room, was flush with the floor and incongruously bordered on three sides by a three-foot-high white fence, the kind you'd normally expect to contain a lawn, garden, and cottage on a tree-shaded street. Striding one wall was a massive oaken bar that had spaced along its length fat jars of pickled pigs' feet, hard-boiled eggs, and sausages. Surrounding the dance floor small table candles in sooty glass chimneys flickered restlessly. You could order from the tables—few risked it—spaghetti and meatballs or spaghetti and sausage, heated endlessly on an iron stove behind the storeroom. These offerings justified one-third of the DINE & DANCE, LAGER sign scrawled in blue neon loops across the bug-spattered brick-and-plateglass facade.

Gabe, the proprietor, a sallow, skinny man with melancholy eyes and sunken cheeks, was reputed to have ties to the Worcester-Boston-Providence axis of La Cosa Nostra, but the place continued to slide downhill, and I never heard of any infusions of loot. Gabe was paying us low dollar and getting his money's worth. He knew a little about music and would wince dramatically when tempos wavered or one of us hit a clam. "Buckle down, guys. Try to find your way past the mud to the pearls." Periodically he'd exhort us, "Put some moxie in it—make 'em sweat, they'll drink more." One stormy slow-business night I had a bad cold and was working through a box of Kleenex at the base of the keyboard. I looked up from blowing my nose to find Gabe gazing sorrowfully down at me. "'S okay, kid, I feel like crying too." Gabe's accountant was Bobby's uncle, and the joint's tax returns, it was rumored, were complex. So that probably explains how we landed the gig in the first place and why Bobby's tenure, more so than ours, was reasonably secure.

Most of the regular patrons worked at the nearby Klevin-Schafft Knitting Mill. They jitterbugged and danced belly-to-belly through the blue smoke to our ragged sound, some of them really into it, seemingly unaware that we were pushing a resolutely Dixie repertoire. Until the night a stranger dropped in, a bald, wiry man whose manner and speech belied his attire—lumberjack shirt, bola tie, and dungarees. He sat at the bar, nursing a brew, listening, and toward the end of the set sauntered over to the white fence. "These tunes you're rendering"—slow, one-sided smile—"you may take that in the slaughterhouse sense if you like—went down with the *Monitor* and *Merrimack*. We are currently, I believe, residing in the industrial Northeast. Would it be too much to ask for a composition representative of the area?"

I could hear Felix chuckling behind me. I thought for half a minute. "How about 'Manhattan'?"

"Anything north of the Mason-Dixon would be welcome. Thank you."

Bobby didn't know the tune, but Felix did, and I sort of did. We played one chorus—not well. The stranger, who had been standing off to one side, head cocked, reached over the fence and dropped a quarter in the tip jar atop the piano; it rang hollowly. "A small contribution," he said, "toward bus fare back to Biloxi."

"What's the *Monitor* and *Merrimack*?" Junior said.

Bobby answered, "Our ships that got torpedoed in the Spanish-American War. Smarten up."

Later that night we woodshedded an addition to the band book, "Mississippi Mud," and, I won't lie to you, butchered it—Bobby, beered up, hogging the lead contrary to my instructions, Junior indiscriminately whanging his cowbell. A paunchy man, stained napkin tucked under his chin and tomato sauce at the corners of his mouth, stood unsteadily and bellowed at us, "There's such a thing as the quality of life!"

> Just as happy as a cow chewin' on a cud
>
> When the people beat their feet on the Mississippi Mud.

Halfway through the summer Gabe installed an attendant in the men's room. He was scarcely needed; it made no financial sense unless he was working solely for tips. But the joint had become a kind of repository for Gabe's down-and-out relatives: The dishwasher was a brother-in-law, one of the busboys a nephew. The attendant, Albert, was a cousin of Gabe's, a heavy, battered man in his mid-fifties with the ponderous movement, puffy ears, and banged-up nose of an ex-boxer. I asked the bartender, Louis, if this were so.

"I don't think so. He's just naturally kind of punch-drunk," Louis said. "But probably harmless." I had occasion to avail myself of Albert's services early on. He was hovering behind two patrons using adjacent urinals, armed with a stack of paper towels and a whisk broom, randomly brushing the back of a man's nylon jacket. He wore a short, too-tight red mess jacket, clip-on red bow tie, and black pants shiny with wear. A penciled sign taped to the mirror over the sink said:

MR. ALBERTO SALVO

ATTENDENT

(FASTEST BROOM IN THE EAST!)

While waiting for a urinal to free up, I introduced myself.

"I'm the piano player."

"How do," Albert Salvo said huskily, tucking the whisk broom in his left armpit and offering a hand; it was as soft and yielding as five pounds of butter. I was about to mention the misspelling on the sign, thought better of it, and pointed instead to the chipped shaving mug on a shelf adjacent to the sink mirror. A small square of cardboard attached to the mug by an elastic band said TIP. "You ought to prime it," I said.

Albert gazed at me, a dim uncomprehending smile softening the bulbous face. I took a dollar bill from my wallet, folded it lengthwise, and popped it in the mug. "Like so. Give folks a clue."

"Good idee!" Albert exclaimed. He hunched awkwardly and delivered a jab to my upper arm, rocking me back a foot. As I moved to reclaim my dollar bill, Albert's beefy mitt circled my wrist. "You'll be usin' the facilities in a minute, might as well leave it there."

"Good idea," I allowed. I stepped into a vacated urinal—the nylon-jacketed man hastily exiting, dodging Albert's fistful of paper towels—and soon felt the back and shoulders of my blazer being briskly brushed.

"Could you wait a minute until I—"

"Touch o' dandruff there, boss. Shows up real nasty on blue."

Back on the stand, I told the guys to cut down on the brew and avoid the men's if they could manage it.

Just a little bit south of North Carolina
You'll find Pa-ra-dise.

Around the first week of August, a small pale lady, neither young nor old, began dropping in. She roomed at the Hotel Sincere and was strolling by on a humid open-door night as we were closing the set with "Stars Fell on Alabama." Bobby liked to sing that tune in a simpering breathy voice, batting his eyes wildly on the lines "My heart beat like a hammer, my arms wound around you tight/And stars fell on Alabama last night." She slipped onto the end bar stool closest to the bandstand and listened intently. As we faded out on Bobby's vocal, she headed straight across the floor for us, oblivious to the perspiring dancers, her sandals shuffling through the thin sawdust.

"I was brought up in Phenix City so that song means a lot to me."

We stared at her. What was the connection with Phoenix? She had a soft bruised face—not bruised in the sense of, what, contusions, but a lived-in face; on the stolid side, but not unpretty.

I said, "Are we talking Arizona here?"

A tiny frown. "Phenix City, Alabama."

Now I caught a whisper of a regional accent, an upturn on *bama*. "Sorry, never heard of it."

"We are a small town on a rather large river. Do you know what stars falling on Alabama should sound like?"

Bobby snorted; I shook my head, waiting for the put-down of our version. "Consider the stars as toys—small as jacks—and you skip a handful across a frozen pond, across the whitest, clearest ice."

Okay, we had an odd, possibly nutcake, lady here.

"I thought your vocalist might have intended, in a not too subtle way, to treat slightingly . . . to mock my state."

"Not me," Bobby said. "I got nothing but respect for Alabama."

"Then I'll accept your denial in the proper spirit. Graciously, even gratefully."

In the coming weeks, I would hear her deliver such formal locutions—things you figured she must mean in a humorous vein—in a measured, leisurely manner, gaze solemn, straight-on, the light far back in wide-set gray eyes. But you'd wait in vain for a hint of a smile.

"Would you happen to know any other compositions from my neck of the woods, as it were?"

"Would we ever," Felix said.

> I'll be right there with bells
> When that old conductor yells
> All aboard! All aboard! All aboard for Alabam'!

She came in regularly after that, at odd hours, always solo. We wouldn't see her for a night or two, then there she'd be at the end of the bar nearest the music, a slight lady in skirt and blouse drinking a pink lady (that Louis had to look up in his mixologist's manual), sandals hooked over the rungs of the stool. Her name was Sally—she preferred Sal—and she had a part-time bookkeeping job in a chiropractor's office, we learned. During our breaks, she hung out with Felix, stepping inside the white fence to guide him to the bar where Louis, without being asked, would set in front of him a tall ginger ale, no ice. "I prefer not to drink when I'm driving," he told Sal early on. (We took turns driving Felix home; he lived with his brother and sister-in-law, one of whom would bring him to the gig.)

I heard her say to Felix the second or third night, "The sound you coax from your horn is pure molasses, it could be poured on pancakes."

"Oh boy, you're really pouring it on," Felix said with his sly, sad smile.

"Why would I lie to you? I reside at the Hotel Sincere."

And another night as I was sitting to their right at the bar: "It matters very little that you're unable to read music. I think you hear sounds in your head that become intensely focused and heightened so you're able to express yourself in a way that sighted musicians cannot. I'm certain this works to your advantage."

"If I had a choice, I'd swap the advantage for the sight," Felix said.

"I once read that sound pitched too low for the human ear can still make people sad. Do you think that's true?"

Felix scratched his nose, "I suppose I could answer that if I was a dog."

"You're trifling with me, but I don't particularly mind. Tell me something: What do you think of when you're playing? On the slower, romantic pieces I sometimes feel you've wished yourself into a veiled world—I'm allowing my imagination wide scope here—a place where you're walking with someone special in a soft spring rain. Holding hands perhaps, but not talking, for conversation would be an intrusion. . . ."

"What I'm thinking usually is. . . ." Felix made a sound in his throat like the start of a chuckle, paused for a sip of ginger ale, "is whether the soft cheese I left in the fridge two weeks ago is going moldy."

"You're mocking me again. Be serious."

"I am . . . partly. Well, most of the time I'm thinking of the chord progressions and the lyrics, if I can remember them."

"You have a gift beyond counting, Felix, you sparkle and shine," she said, unrelenting in her compliments. She ran a hand through his lank hair; something was developing here. "There are certain songs, again the leisurely, romantic ones, when your interpretation gives me goosebumps."

"You must chill easily," Felix said.

"Look who just blew in, folks, frivolous Sal, a peculiar sort of a gal. . . ." Bobby working the mike, lifting lyric fragments from a turn-of-the-century oldie. "Tad on the small side, at most a hundred-five soakin' wet, but a heart big and mellow, an all-round good fellow, that's our gal Sal. . . ."

She hadn't been feeling well and had missed most of a week. On her return, forever curious about aspects of the music, particularly our departures from the melody during the improvised or blowing choruses—what she called our "flights of fancy"—she posed this question to us, though as always directed primarily at Felix: "The main melody has vanished, gone with the wind, replaced by a second, ghost melody that bears little resemblance to the original. So where do the new notes come from?"

The question is unanswerable—some of us can do it better than others, some can't do it at all—and musicians often respond to the query in a carefree or frivolous way.

Felix said, "Hon, that's like asking where thirty-year-old memories come from."

I said, "I picture myself walking a horizontal black-and-white staircase that's always shifting. With every step I could fall between the cracks."

Junior said, "I don't need to worry about that stuff."

Felix added, "You have to get reckless. Mostly I just draw a deep breath"—drawing one—"hold my nose, jump off the board feet first, and hope the water's deep enough, but not too deep—"

Sal took his nose between thumb and forefinger and twisted. "You're mocking me again."

Felix said nasally, "You really like that word."

With impassioned hearts and minor skills, we continued to render our Deep South library for the Klevin-Schafft gang. And business kept slipping. Despite Felix's solitary sparkle and shine we never found our way past the mud to the pearls. But you can't always blame the band. The first television sets were creeping into mill-town households, draining live bodies from the saloons. The 4 Sharps' days were numbered.

Toward the end, Gabe discarded his brown suit and tie for an old wool cardigan. I passed him one night standing in back, arms folded across his chest, contemplating the sea of glimmering candles on vacant tables. He was murmuring —to me or to himself, I couldn't tell—"If we had a sprinkler system we could turn it on, and you know what? Nobody would get wet."

"All eyes front and center, folks—" Bobby spieled as Felix soloed on "When It's Sleepy Time Down South" and the *Monitor* and *Merrimack* mournfully sank. "Folks . . . ? I know you're out there, I can hear breathing. Marge and Tim—or is it Tom?—bless their swinging hearts, are really tearing it up. They'll be entering the jitterbug competition this Saturday night at the Middlesex County fair, and you better believe they'll be odds-on favorites. . . ."

Labor Day weekend, Gabe gently told us to pack it in. He had to stop the hemorrhaging somewhere, he said. The Music Mart had a sale on player pianos, and he'd decided to go that way; the picket fence would be dismantled. "Drop a coin in the slot, you never know where it'll take you," he said with a rueful smile. Shaking our hands, he wished us all the best. Between the lines I heard, "You gave it the old college try, guys, but if you ain't got it, you ain't got it."

Our final night, on an unavoidable trip to the men's room (cravenly some of us had been relieving ourselves in the weed-choked lot out back), I felt the inevitable brush on my shoulders. "Hear ya gonna be leavin' us. Still ain't licked that dandruff problem, boss. . . ."

I zipped up and reached for my wallet, a final contribution to the shaving mug. "No need to go in your pocket now—on the house. Compliments of Al Salvo. . . ." The Fastest Broom in the East bobbed, feinted with a left, and caught me with a right to the breadbasket.

I drove Felix home for the last time. Sal hadn't come in tonight.

"Another gig will turn up," I said halfheartedly, as I'd said to the other guys, though I'd pretty much made up my mind to go to college: Cornell was beckoning, my sole acceptance out of three applications. "If not, you'll connect with another group easy."

"We'll see," Felix said with a small smile.

A fat September moon rode the sky, and I thought of an old song lyric I had written about lovers leaving a country dance, walking hand-in-hand: " . . . and the moon, free to roam, followed us all the way home."

"Take care of Sal," I said as we pulled in front of his brother's house. They had grown really tight, dating on the band's off-nights.

"I think she may be dying."

In the streetlight's dim shine his face looked strangely serene. "What d'you mean?"

"Something in her gut. It's complicated." He folded his hands in his lap.

"I hope you're wrong." A shiver ran through me. I thought of the Hotel Sincere, the sign in the top-story window, HANGING ON, that had disappeared about the time she began showing up at Gabe's.

But Sal hardly seemed the kind who would flaunt. . . .

"Does she live on the top floor of the Sincere?" I said. "A corner room?"

"I don't know about corner. . . . Why?"

"Was that her sign in the window?"

"What sign?"

I lightly touched his shoulder. "It doesn't matter."

Three of the 4 Sharps scattered to the four winds. I majored in chemistry at Cornell (docilely following in the footsteps of my father and older brother), playing piano occasionally on weekends at frat-house parties and a downtown dive by the railroad tracks that summoned the Silver Dollar in all its pungent glory. Bobby phased out of the performing end of the music biz (wise choice), clerked in record stores, and worked summers in the Catskills as an assistant entertainment director; he eventually opened a talent agency in Albany. Junior dropped out of Holy Cross College and headed south—

> Creole babies with flashin' eyes
>
> Lazy rivers and azure skies

—banging his way all the way to Tallahassee, where, the last I heard (a lot of years ago), he was playing drums in a bowling alley cocktail lounge.

Felix and Sal got married that fall. I came back from Ithaca during Thanksgiving break and played solo for the reception held at the Italian-American Social Club. Sal looked demure and fragile in ivory satin and lace, Felix debonair in a tux with plaid cummerbund. I played "Stars Fell on Alabama" as they cut the white tiered cake, her hand guiding his on the silver blade, and thought of star-shaped jacks skipping across the whitest, clearest ice. She died almost two years to the day of the wedding.

Leap fifty years—over countless bar lines—to a chandeliered hotel dining room in San Francisco, where I'm currently employed. I had worked fitfully, unhappily, for a couple of years in small-town chemistry labs. On a gloomy winter afternoon, gagging on the toxic reek of benzyl mercaptan (think effluence of skunk), I jumped ship and circled back to the saloons, resuming my traversal of the horizontal black-and-white staircase, uphill (black keys), downdale (whites), ever-mindful of the cracks; picked up gigs in and around Worcester and began studying with the Boston-based virtuoso jazz pianist-arranger Jaki Byard (who came to a sad end in February '99); practiced, absorbed, expanded my repertoire, and embarked on a circuitous tour of gutbuckets, honky-tonks, subterranean holes-in-the-wall, taverns, halls, roadhouses, lounges, supper clubs, white-tablecloth restaurants (note the gradual escalation), banquet rooms, ballrooms, and country clubs that led to the chandeliered San Francisco dining room. . . .

The party being seated at a table close by the piano one recent night had a commanding presence: two men, thirty-five to forty, I guessed, tall and slim, elegantly attired in double-breasted blazers, and a dazzling woman who might have just stepped off the cover of *Harper's Bazaar*. They were African Americans, and I had just slipped effortlessly back into the old repertoire, picking my way through Hoagy Carmichael's loping, deeply grooved "Lazybones," whose lyric about a goof-off Negro "sleepin' in the noonday sun" no one has dared sing for many decades now. Good music is good music whatever the era or locale, I told myself; still, I experienced an anxious moment (segue to another song or keep swinging?), hoping they all had tin ears or were too young to know the tune. They appeared oblivious to the music; I kept on. The taller of the men leisurely spread his napkin across his lap, scanned the wine list, then turned to me with a courtly smile. "Surely, sir, that composition is not for our benefit. . . ."

The smile—his intent—was unclear. Unease must have shown on whitey's face. The smile brightened; he winked. "Relax, Mr. Piano Man, I'm putting you on."

The Silver Dollar has long since stopped rolling, but the call of the South lingers on, reverberating in my inner ear the way a siren's whoop and holler lingers, carried by the beaten air long after the excitement has ceased. I still hear—memory bestowing a patina of professionalism—the barrelhouse swagger of our up-tempo Dixie flag-wavers cutting through the smoke and babble, ringing the rafters (except the Silver Dollar had no rafters), Felix's fluid, high-register clari weaving choice filigree around Bobby's blunt (muted) lead, cowbell clanking, cymbals crashing; I can smell that stale-beer, smoke-choked, sawdusty, urinous, intoxicating smell as if it were last night, the storied fragrance of Mississippi Delta gutbuckets and cathouses that gave birth to the music, I can almost smell the *magnolias*....

Miss the moss-covered vines
The tall sugar pines
Where mockingbirds used to sing
And I'd love to see the lazy Mississippi a-hurryin' into spring.

The pipe dream followed me through middle age and beyond. Yet I was never tempted to follow Junior's lead and head south of the Mason-Dixon. The vision and longing were enough. I suppose I feared disenchantment, the South somehow coming up short—not wishing a stark perception of place to tarnish the sun-kissed melodies forever humming through my head.

Banjo

OBSESSION IS A GREAT SUBSTITUTE FOR TALENT
by **Steve Martin**

▬▬▬

The four-string banjo has four strings. The five-string banjo has five. The five-string banjo has a truncated string running halfway up the neck. It is called the fifth string and is rarely fretted. It creates a drone. Conventional history places the addition of the fifth string around 1855, but I saw a five-string banjo, by all rights an American instrument, in the Victoria and Albert Museum in London that dated back to the 1820s. The five-string is the banjo I'm interested in.

The four-string banjo is generally strummed, and the five-string banjo is generally picked. The four-string is associated with Dixieland music, and the five-string is associated with bluegrass or Appalachian music. Some five-string banjos are open-backed; some are closed in the back by a resonator. The resonator-backed banjos are louder and sharper than the open-backed. An open-backed banjo is softer and mellower. The five-string open-backed banjo is played in a style called "frailing." I have lost many games of Scrabble by using the word "frailing." It is not in the dictionary, but I assure you it's a word as valid as "oscillococcin-uin." Frailing is a combination of strumming and picking, sometimes called "drop-thumbing," or "clawhammer." The thumb drops from the fifth string to whatever string it chooses, while the forefinger plucks downward with the back of the fingernail, and the rest of the fingers strum across the strings. The style is highly rhythmic and strange. Even when I was immersed in learning the banjo, there were some frailing rhythms I could not duplicate or even fathom.

The resonator-backed banjo, or bluegrass banjo, is not strummed. It is picked by three fingers, usually at lightning speed. The style was formulated by Earl

Scruggs in the '30s. He is still the consummate *artiste* of the bluegrass banjo, because he understands that the player must always make music first, and show off second.

The sound I most like, of which Scruggs is a master, is that of a rolling, endlessly punctuating staccato that is at once continuous and broken.

I first heard Earl Scruggs on record in 1962 when I was seventeen years old. I was living in Orange County, California, about as far away from bluegrass country as one could get and not be in Taiwan. The sound hooked me, however, and I borrowed my girlfriend's father's four-string banjo in order to learn it. I did not know that I was one string away from nirvana.

Knowing nothing about music, I bought a chord book and meshed my fingers into the steel wires, using my right hand to place my left-hand fingers onto the frets. The first attempts I made sounded like a car being crushed in a metal compactor. I was so ignorant and untrained musically that when I finally learned to play several chords, I could not discern any difference between them.

I had a high-school friend named John McEuen, who was also interested in the banjo. He is now one of the finest banjo players in the world. It was at his house in 1964 that another friend, Dave, came over and played the banjo live. Dave sat in front of us and intoned "Flopped Eared Mule," a song whose high point came when the strings were struck behind the bridge, emulating the sound of a donkey's bray. Emulating the sound of a donkey's bray may not be your idea of music, but to us, Dave was Menuhin.

Dave showed us some simple picking patterns and wrote them down in impromptu hieroglyphs on a torn piece of paper. These patterns could be practiced not only on the banjo but also on your school desk and on the car steering wheel and on your pillow just before sleep.

I scraped together two hundred dollars and bought Dave's spare banjo from him. I still have it today, an open-backed frailing banjo, a Gibson RB-170. Its tones have mellowed nicely through the years.

The first song I ever learned was "Cripple Creek." The advantage of learning "Cripple Creek" was that it could be played over and over and over and over into the night, endlessly, forever. We could play it fast, then we could play it slow. We could modulate from fast to slow. We could play it quiet and then play it loud. It had lyrics that we could sing, and when we came to the end of a verse, the banjo would take over, and I would play it extra loud, believing the increased volume created excitement. Then, after hours of playing "Cripple Creek," we would look at each other and decide it was time to end it, and we would blunder to a coda, stop, and take a break. Then it would be time to play again, and someone would suggest "Cripple Creek," and the whole thing would start all over. To this day, I cannot stand to play "Cripple Creek." I can barely write its title.

Finally, I was ready to play for my high-school girlfriend, Linda. I put the banjo on my knee and played in all earnestness. She burst out laughing. The reason she burst out laughing was not my playing, but rather that my lips moved with each finger movement.

Worried that this involuntary twitch would signal the end of my embryonic two-chord career, I tortured myself trying to keep my lips still while playing.

Obsession is a great substitute for talent. I had several 33 rpm banjo records by the Dillards and Earl Scruggs. The Dillards boasted the fastest and most thrilling banjoist alive, Doug Dillard. They played live in Orange County in those days, and watching Doug Dillard was like watching God, if God were a finger-picking madman. Doug was rail thin, and when he grinned he looked like a piano keyboard stuck on the end of a reed. But the sound of the banjo accelerating from zero to sixty in a nanosecond, in a town that had heretofore heard only lazy folk guitar, made us freeze. Doug was generous, too, and he would teach us various licks (slang for finger and chord sequences). My obsession was such that I would hibernate in my bedroom and slow down the 33 rpm records to 16, and figure out the songs note by note. This process took days. I would have to down-tune the banjo until it was in the same key as the down-shifted recording, which caused the strings to become so slack that they would oscillate like a slow-motion jump rope. It also drove my parents crazy. Imagine the muffled sound of a banjo being clunked, insistently and arhythmically, through the paper-thin walls of a tract home, of a song being played so slowly that any melody was indecipherable. My understanding of how annoying this must have sounded led me to park my car on the street after dinner, close all the windows—even in the baking Southern California summer— and practice into the night. By the time I had closed myself in my '57 Chevy, however, I was getting somewhere, and I was entranced with the sounds I could make. One tone from one string could send me into ecstasy, and here I was, making thousands of notes in thousands of combinations. The songs that I worked on in the Chevy were "Doug's Tune," "Fireball Mail," "Earl's Breakdown," "Foggy Mountain Breakdown," and "Old Joe Clark." I'm sure if that car were unearthed today, my little tunes could be found trapped in the cellulose of its seat cushions.

My interest in the banjo was also heavily fueled by David Lindley. David played in a group at Disneyland called the Mad Mountain Ramblers. During my last two years of high school, I worked at Disneyland performing magic tricks in the magic shop. I arranged a deal with Patty, who worked there with me, where we would cover for each other when she wanted to sneak away to rendezvous with her boyfriend or when I wanted to sneak away to hear the Ramblers. In the summer nights at Disneyland, with the fairy lights in the trees, I would listen amazed as Lindley's authority over his instrument drove the music. I spoke with him once, and he explained the frustration of having his mind outpace his fingers' ability to move. I was still learning to put the fingerpicks on properly. He had an eccentricity of standing on his tiptoes as he played, which I copied for years afterward, thinking it was cool. I was also pleased to see that he moved his lips when he played. I intentionally redeveloped my old habit. Lindley later became a renowned rock & roll guitarist.

Some bluegrass instrumentals are called "breakdowns," which simply describes a song that is played very fast. When a song had the word "breakdown" in its title, it acquired a mystical *oomph* that sent the adrenaline rushing and the fingers pumping, whether they were quite ready to play that fast or not. It had the same cachet that the word "raptor" had after the movie *Jurassic Park* was released. Breakdowns were the meanest and baddest of the banjo tunes. Whenever I played a breakdown, I wanted everyone who was in listening distance to understand that this was something very special indeed. I would convey this by standing on my tiptoes and getting a very serious look on my face and moving my lips.

The Topanga Canyon Banjo and Fiddle Contest took place in the summertime in California, and the contest was held under trees in the dry forests of the Santa Monica mountains. Carrying my banjo in its case, I walked down the long road to the tree-shaded bowl and could hear the tinkling of dozens of banjos, all playing different tunes. As there were no seats, the audience spread themselves out on blankets. One could wander away from the contest itself and find, hidden away in the trees, an occasional clump of musicians, all whizzes compared with me, who had found one another and who expertly played the tunes I longed to know. The sound was so pure and exhilarating, it cleansed me. I had about three songs in my repertoire. I entered the contest in the beginner category and vaguely remember winning something, either first or second place. I have a clipping of me onstage that appeared in the local newspaper. Later that day, I heard the blues artist Taj Mahal, in the professional category, frail the song "Colored Aristocracy" so vibrantly that I actually wanted to *be* the song, to *be* the notes that wafted into the air under the broken sunlight filtering through the trees.

He won.

By the time I got to college, I had discovered another quality of the banjo, which came to dominate my initial desire for speed: melancholy. By then I had found recordings of artists both young and old, who wrung from the banjo an echoing sadness. The banjo had a lonesome sound, reminiscent to me of Scottish and Irish pipe music. One of my favorites was a song written and played by Dick Weissman called "Trail Ridge Road" (later, the title was changed to "Banjo Road," probably to avoid paying Dick royalties). I learned it the usual way, by slowing down the record. There are odd rhythmic passages that still elude me, but it is one of the few songs that I still play today. I had also become proficient enough to write my own songs. I went to Nashville with my soon-to-be manager, Bill McEuen, and the

Nitty Gritty Dirt Band, of which Bill's brother, and my old high-school friend, John, was now a member. Catching the coattails of the Dirt Band's recording time, I taped five original songs with the best bluegrass musicians around: Vassar Clements on fiddle, Junior Husky on bass, Jeff Hanna and John on guitar. Years later, I put the songs on the back of my last comedy album. I still take pride in these early efforts at creativity.

Some of the records I loved were *Livin' on the Mountain* by Bill Keith and Jim Rooney (Bill Keith stood banjo playing on its ear with his chromatic rendition of "Devil's Dream"); *Bluegrass Banjos on Fire* by Homer and the Barnstormers (because I have never heard of this group before or since, I believe they were created as a one-shot to satisfy the banjo-recording demand created by the popularity of "Foggy Mountain Breakdown," the theme song to *Bonnie and Clyde*); *New Dimensions in Banjo and Bluegrass* by Marshall Brickman and Eric Weissberg (Marshall Brickman is now a friend and the talented screenwriter who co-wrote *Annie Hall*); *Old Time Banjo Project,* an assemblage of various artists; and my favorites, *The Banjo Story* and *Five-String Banjo Greats,* available these days on one CD, under the title *Feuding Banjos.*

I played the banjo in my stand-up comedy act, largely using it as a prop, but sometimes played a full-out bluegrass song, which the audience tolerated. When I stopped performing live in 1981, I also stopped practicing consistently, though I would pick up the banjo periodically and get my thick fingers moving again. When Earl Scruggs asked me to play "Foggy Mountain Breakdown" on an anniversary album several years ago, I took up the banjo again and now practice every day.

Several months ago, I went out to the garage and sat in my Lexus and put in a CD of Bill Keith playing his whizbang version of "Auld Lang Syne." I plucked it out note by note on my banjo, just like the old days.

Nothing had changed but the price of the car.

The Most Human Sound

TWO STRANGERS WERE SHARING HER LAST
MOMENTS OF PEACE
by Rosanne Cash

━━━━

I eat no more than four oranges a year. They're either too tart or too bland.
Definitely too watery. But in the winter of 1981–1982, in the months of December
and January, I ate nearly a dozen oranges a day. I was heavily pregnant with my
second child and I lived in a big log house in the woods of Middle Tennessee with
my then-husband Rodney, my two-year-old daughter, and my six-year-old step-
daughter. It was one of the coldest winters on record in the South. The house
stayed warm until it got down to about fifteen degrees; below that, the beautiful
old virgin pine just could not hold the heat. For days on end, as the temperature
hovered around zero, and below, we all stayed close to the stone fireplace in the
great room. Rodney kept the fire going (a full-time job) and the little girls played
quietly with their dolls on a green turn-of-the-century Chinese rug that had been
rescued from an old brothel in Western Kentucky. I sat in a rocking chair next to
them, profile to the fire, a little melancholy, with a bag of oranges on my lap. I ate
my way though a new bag each day, tossing the peels in the flames as I rocked. The
bitter, wild aroma of singed oranges cut into the somber iciness of the room, and
soothed me. It was my personal statement against the chill. I spent many long
days like this.

In the first few days of January, three weeks before my due date, my old friend Randy
Scruggs called to ask Rodney and me to participate in a project he was doing with
his dad, Earl, and Tom T. Hall. They were making a record called *The Storyteller and
the Banjoman*. He invited us to come to his studio and sing on a couple of songs. It

was around Earl's birthday and there would be a lot of people there. I was past the point of maternal glow, way past being cooed at and patted, and lately inspired only expressions of shock and nervous retreat at this penultimate phase of gestation. But Randy was my dear friend, the record would be finished before I delivered my baby, and I really wanted to sing on it, so I decided to go. I didn't have a coat big enough to close around my belly, and that night turned out to be the coldest one yet of the relentless winter. The air was blue when we stepped outside. The thermometer in the carport registered eleven below zero, and sharp little ice crystals rose in gusts from the hard-packed snow in the driveway. I sulked as we started the long drive to the studio. Rodney, experienced with the consequences of unintentionally provoking a woman near the end of her third trimester, gave me a lot of room. It was a very quiet trip.

But it was a wonderful evening. We sang on three songs: "Shackles and Chains," "Roll in My Sweet Baby's Arms," and "Song of the South." Instead of being a sideshow freak, I was treated as a ripe little goddess, and it brought out the best in me. The company of friends and the balm of playing music was liberating, and I was fatigued, but content, when we left. The silence on our return had a decidedly different texture.

We drove, as if in a dream—past the empty country roads at the borders of wide fields enclosed by Civil War–era stone fences, past big, dark, and looming old estates and grand columned mansions that lonesomely adjoined lazy suburban tracts.

We had not seen another car for several miles when we made the turn onto the pike that began the final leg to our hidden house in its miniature valley surrounded by thick oaks and maples. Rodney drove very carefully as this road was used less than others, and it was still swathed in ice. I was drowsily contemplating having a few oranges by the fire before bed. Suddenly, flashing red lights appeared on the shoulder of the opposite side of the road about a hundred feet ahead. We slowed to a crawl and as we came upon the scene, we saw an ambulance, a car behind it, and, between the two, a man stretched out on his back on the frozen ground. The few people standing over him seemed in no hurry to get him into the ambulance.

"Oh, my God," we both said quietly when we realized the man was dead. Rodney glanced at me. I turned away, profoundly conscious of the baby inside me, reacting to a fierce, primal impulse to protect it from unexpected surges of my adrenaline—the heady, dangerous mix of the hormones of hysteria and fear. There was clearly no way we could help, so we drove on. A mile or so farther, we were astonished to see, striding toward us up the road, a sturdy-looking middle-aged woman with a tall walking stick. Her gait was so determined, and the stick planted so authoritatively with each step, I could practically hear the drumbeat behind her march. More astonishing still, she was dressed only in a skirt and a sweater: no coat, scarf, or gloves, and she was bare-legged. On her feet were awful brown oxford-type discount-store shoes, shaped carelessly from thin, cheap leather. Only sandals would have been more inappropriate in this weather.

Rodney stopped and rolled down his window. "Ma'am? Can we give you a ride somewhere?"

In a tight, high-pitched voice she said, "Are you sure you don't mind?" and then got into the back seat. She was pale and fair, and though her demeanor was reserved, even stiff, her eyes were darting about and she spoke quickly. "Oh, thank you so much! I'm just going back up the road a little bit. My neighbor there called and said someone had been hit by a car, and my husband was out takin' a walk and now I'm a little worried about him."

I didn't dare look at Rodney, but I could feel that we had both stopped breathing. My heart began to pound, and a queasy feeling rose in my abdomen. Rodney drove the car forward to a little cross street where he could turn around. Fortunately, we didn't have to say anything because the woman was chattering nervously.

"I told him it was too cold to go out walking, but he's stubborn. Said he had to have his evening constitutional no matter how cold it was. Now, are y'all sure you don't mind takin' me back up there?"

"No, ma'am, not at all," I said. "We saw some kind of disturbance back there, but I'm not sure what it was."

"Oh my Lord," she trilled, pleading and panicked. "Now, I don't want y'all to get hurt, too!"

I was struck as if by a two-by-four by that sentence. It still reverberates now, fifteen years later: the pitch of her voice, her self-effacing Southern politeness, the tears building behind the contained panic, the uncontrolled sense that danger newly pervaded the entire world. My heart broke for her. In about thirty seconds her entire life was going to detonate and two strangers were sharing her last moments of peace. But it was not my place to tell her.

It was several years later that a friend gave me a tape of Irish keening, which is the sound of women wailing at the graves of their loved ones—long, sustained, unbearably plaintive cries elevated by the deepest sorrow to an art form; the most human sound of the genesis of music. It sent chills down my back and brought tears to my eyes when I first heard it, and the first thing I thought of was her.

She got out of the car that night and a woman came up to her and put an arm around her shoulder and began to talk softly to her. We waited for a moment, then drove away slowly.

Through the closed car windows I could hear her screams: long, deep, circular cries, rising from the roots of her body, like a train whistle disappearing into an endless series of tunnels, like the wrenching Gaelic echoes that hang in the graveyard, like the hiss that escapes from the permanently shattered heart.

I had to borrow from my future that night in protection of my unborn baby. I drew from an unknown reserve of circumspection. "I will feel this later," I thought. And I was unyielding, my hands over my ears, my head bent to my chest.

And I paid, with interest.

On January 25th of that year, I gave birth, after only six hours of labor, to a gorgeous, nearly nine-pound baby girl with enormous bright blue eyes. She was healthy and strong and I felt proud that I had done my job so well. We named her Chelsea Jane, and I swaddled her warmly and took her home to the big log house. The girls welcomed their little sister and the temperature gradually eased back up into the thirties, where it belonged. My natural indifference to oranges returned abruptly, and the last few left in the bag shriveled and gathered mold before I finally threw them away. I kept the MAN KILLED BY CAR ON ICY ROAD newspaper clipping for a week or so longer, and then, that too, I threw away.

Contributors

▬▬▬

Daniel Alarcón is an associate editor of *Etiqueta Negra*, an award-winning monthly magazine based in his native Lima, Peru. He is the author of the story collection *War by Candlelight*, which was a finalist for the 2006 PEN/Hemingway Foundation Award, and the novel *Lost City Radio*, published in 2007. That same year, he was named one of *Granta* magazine's Best Young American Novelists.

Don Asher started playing jazz piano professionally at age fifteen in the dives and roadhouses of Central Massachusetts. In the early '60s, he was house pianist at the hungry i nightclub in San Francisco where he worked with such up-and-comers as Barbra Streisand, Woody Allen, Lenny Bruce, Bill Cosby, and Bob Newhart. Asher is the author of six novels. His nonfiction includes *Raise Up Off Me* and *Notes From a Battered Grand*. His short work has appeared in *Harper's*, *The Paris Review*, the *Washington Post*, and *San Francisco Magazine*, among others.

Chris Bachelder is the author of the novels *U.S.!*, *Bear v. Shark*, and *Lessons in Virtual Tour Photography* (an e-book). His stories and essays have appeared in *Harper's*, *The Believer*, *The Oxford American*, *New Stories From the South*, and elsewhere. He has an MFA in fiction writing from the University of Florida and is an assistant professor at the University of Massachusetts Amherst. He has also taught at Colorado College and New Mexico State University.

Mark Binelli is the author of the novel *Sacco and Vanzetti Must Die!* and a contributing editor at *Rolling Stone*. He lives in Manhattan.

Sven Birkerts is the author of eight books, including his memoir, *My Sky Blue Trades*, and the recent *The Art of Time in Memoir*. He edits the literary journal *AGNI* at Boston University and was recently named director of the Bennington Writing Seminars. His musical tastes run to folk and blues and he has played guitar at "the lowest-rank amateur" level for decades. He has also written about Lucinda Williams and Lightnin' Hopkins for *The Oxford American*.

Roy Blount, Jr., is the author of twenty-one books, most recently *Alphabet Juice*. Others include *Long Time Leaving: Dispatches From Up South*, which includes the "Gone Off Up North" columns he has been writing for *The Oxford American* since 1996; *Feet on the Street: Rambles Around New Orleans*; *Robert E. Lee*, a biography; *Be Sweet*, a memoir; and *Roy Blount's Book of Southern Humor*, an anthology which he edited. He is a panelist on NPR's *Wait, Wait . . . Don't Tell Me!*, a charter member of the Rock Bottom Remainders (a rock & roll band of authors), and a member of the Fellowship of Southern Writers. He has written profiles of Willie Nelson, Jerry Jeff Walker, and Loretta and Tammy and Dolly; performed songs of his own devising on *A Prairie Home Companion;* spoken out about the plight of the singing impaired; and collected 2,462 different songs about food.

Will Blythe grew up in North Carolina, lives in New York, and is the author of *To Hate Like This Is To Be Happy Forever*. He is also a frequent contributor to the *New York Times Book Review*.

In college, **William Bowers** fronted the Charleston, South Carolina, band Cluppy, which self-released its discs on the same day as Will Oldham's new works so they could take pictures of their albums sitting beside his at the shops. One reviewer observed that Bowers's vocals "strained the colander of aural bearability," so he became a music typist for the local free alt-weekly, from which he graduated to *The Oxford American, Magnet, No Depression, Paste*, the *Village Voice*, and *Pitchfork*. His poetry, fiction, essays, and book reviews have been published in *The Wallace Stevens Journal, Open City, Esquire*, and *People*, among others.

Wendy Brenner is the author of two books: *Phone Calls From the Dead* and *Large Animals in Everyday Life*, which won the Flannery O'Connor Award. She is the recipient of an NEA fellowship, Henfield Award, North Carolina Arts Council fellowship, and the AWP Intro Award for her short fiction. Her stories and essays have appeared in *Seventeen, Allure, Travel & Leisure, Story, Mississippi Review, New England Review*, and other magazines, and have been anthologized in *The Best American Magazine Writing* and *New Stories From the South*. She is a contributing writer for *The Oxford American* and teaches in the MFA program in creative writing at University of North Carolina Wilmington.

Kevin Brockmeier is the author of the novels *The Brief History of the Dead* and *The Truth About Celia*, the story collections *Things That Fall From the Sky* and *The View From the Seventh Layer*, and the children's novels *City of Names* and *Grooves: A Kind of Mystery*. He was awarded a Guggenheim fellowship and, in 2007, was named one of *Granta* magazine's Best Young American Novelists. Other than Iris DeMent's *My Life*, his favorite albums are *Astral Weeks* by Van Morrison and *Melody Mountain* by Susanna and the Magical Orchestra. He lives in Little Rock, Arkansas, where he was raised.

Ron Carlson is the author of nine books of fiction, most recently the novel *Five Skies*, which was selected by the *Los Angeles Times* as one of their favorite books of 2007. His new book on writing fiction, *Ron Carlson Writes a Story*, was also published in 2007. His stories have appeared in *Esquire, Harper's, The New Yorker, GQ, Epoch, The Oxford American*, and others, as well as *The Best American Short Stories, The O. Henry Prize Series, The Pushcart Prize*, and *The Norton Anthology of Short Fiction*, and dozens of other anthologies. A graduate of the University of Utah, Carlson is the director of the graduate program in fiction at the University of California, Irvine.

Rosanne Cash is a Grammy Award–winning singer and songwriter. Her fourteen albums, released over the last twenty-seven years, have charted eleven Number One singles. Her most recent album, *Black Cadillac*, was released in January 2006 and received a Grammy nomination for Best Contemporary Folk/Americana Album. Cash is the author of a book of stories (for adults), *Bodies of Water*, and the children's book *Penelope Jane: A Fairy's Tale*. Her essays and fiction have appeared in the *New York Times, Rolling Stone, The Oxford American, New York Magazine*, and other periodicals and collections. Cash lives in New York City with her husband, John Leventhal, and her children. She is signed to Manhattan Records and is currently working on her debut CD for the EMI-based label, as well as a book of nonfiction, to be published in 2008.

Billy Collins is the author of nine collections of poetry, including his most recent book, *Ballistics*. He served as United States Poet Laureate (2001–2003) and as New York State Poet Laureate (2004–2006).

It is safe to call **R. Crumb** the father of underground comix. His creations include *ZAP, Despair, Big Ass, Motor City Comics, Mr. Natural, Fritz the Cat, The People's Comics*, among many others. His books include *The Complete Crumb Comics, Crumb Sketchbook Vol. 10*, and *Your Vigor for Life Appalls Me*, a collection of his personal letters. He lives in France with his wife, Aline.

Lee Durkee was born in Hawaii, raised in South Mississippi, and now lives in Montpelier, Vermont. He has published stories in *Harper's, Zoetrope: All-Story,* and *Tin House,* and is the author of the novel *Rides of the Midway.* He is currently finishing up a play, a Shakespearian remix of the rap virtuoso Nas, *Ill Will: Hamlet Post'pocalypsed (a.k.a. KILL ALL VAMPIRES!).*

John T. Edge, a contributing editor at *Gourmet,* is a columnist for *US Airways Magazine,* the *Atlanta Journal-Constitution,* and *The Oxford American.* His work for *Saveur* and other magazines has been featured in every edition of the *Best Food Writing* compilation since 2001. His books include the James Beard Award–nominated cookbook *A Gracious Plenty: Recipes and Recollections from the American South* and *Southern Belly: The Ultimate Food Lover's Companion to the South.* He has also published a four-book series with Putnam on iconic American eats (*Fried Chicken, Apple Pie, Hamburgers & Fries,* and *Donuts*).

Beth Ann Fennelly received a 2003 NEA Award and a 2006 United States Artists Grant. She's published three books of poetry: *Open House,* which won the 2001 Kenyon Review Prize and the GLCA New Writers Award, *Tender Hooks,* and *Unmentionables.* She has three times been included in *The Best American Poetry* series and is a Pushcart Prize winner. Her book of essays, *Great With Child,* was published in 2006.

Carol Ann Fitzgerald is the managing editor of *The Oxford American.* Her fiction and nonfiction have appeared in *Ploughshares, The Gettysburg Review, The Oxford American,* and other publications. She lives in Conway, Arkansas.

David Gates is the author of the novels *Jernigan* and *Preston Falls* and the collection of short stories *The Wonders of the Invisible World.*

William Gay is the author of three novels and a collection of short stories, *I Hate to See That Evening Sun Go Down.* His novel *Twilight* was published in winter 2006. His fiction and essays have appeared in various magazines. He lives in rural Tennessee, where he is at work on a novel.

Robert Gordon is the author of five books and six films. Most recently, he was producer and director of *Respect Yourself: The Stax Records Story.* His other films include *William Eggleston's Stranded in Canton* and *Shakespeare Was a Big George Jones Fan: Cowboy Jack Clement's Home Movies.* His books include *It Came From Memphis* and *Can't Be Satisfied: The Life and Times of Muddy Waters.* His writing has earned him a Grammy nomination and, for a piece on Jeff Buckley that originally appeared in *The Oxford American,* an ASCAP Deems Taylor Award.

Tom Graves, a lifelong Memphian, is the former editor of the critically acclaimed *Rock & Roll Disc* magazine and now teaches English and creative writing at LeMoyne-Owen College in Memphis. He is the author of the biography *Crossroads: The Life and Afterlife of Blues Legend Robert Johnson*. He's written about music for *Rolling Stone, Musician*, the *New York Times Book Review, Washington Post Book World, American History*, and *The New Leader*. In 2003, he sold his beloved Les Paul guitar to a collector from Perth, Australia, to finance a trip to Dakar, Senegal, where he met his wife, Bintou.

Peter Guralnick is the author of the prize-winning, two-volume biography of Elvis Presley, *Last Train to Memphis* and *Careless Love*. Over the years his work has argued passionately and persuasively for the vitality of this country's intertwined black and white musical traditions, as well as for their integral place in mainstream culture. His other books include *Searching for Robert Johnson, Nighthawk Blues*, an acclaimed trilogy on American roots music: *Sweet Soul Music, Lost Highway*, and *Feel Like Going Home*, and the recent biography *Dream Boogie: The Triumph of Sam Cooke*.

Jack Hitt is a contributing writer for the *New York Times Magazine, Harper's*, and the radio program *This American Life*. Most recently, his work can be found in *Best American Travel Writing* and *Best American Science Writing*. Hitt won a Peabody Award in 2006 for the radio program *Habeas Schmabeas*. He is currently at work on a book about amateurs in America.

Bret Anthony Johnston is the editor of *Naming the World: And Other Exercises for the Creative Writer*, and the author of *Corpus Christi: Stories*. He is the director of creative writing at Harvard University.

Donald Justice (1925–2004) published fourteen volumes of poetry. His *Selected Poems* was recognized with a Pulitzer Prize in 1980. He also received the Bollingen Prize in 1991 and was a fellow and past chancellor of the Academy of American Poets and a member of the American Academy of Arts and Sciences. Justice was on faculty at the University of Iowa, Syracuse University, and for ten years until 1992, the University of Florida in Gainesville. His last book was *Collected Poems* (2004).

John Lewis is the arts and culture editor at *Baltimore Magazine* and a U.S. correspondent for *Vibrations*, the French music magazine.

Steve Martin has starred in such films as *Father of the Bride, Roxanne, Parenthood, L.A. Story, Pennies From Heaven*, and many others. He has also won Emmys for his television writing and two Grammys for his comedy albums. In addition to his bestselling novel, *The Pleasure of My Company,* and a collection of comic pieces, *Pure Drivel,* he has written a play, *Picasso at the Lapin Agile.* His latest book is his autobiography, *Born Standing Up.*

Robert Palmer (1945–1997), a musician, critic, and devotee of Dionysian ecstasy, was born in Little Rock, Arkansas. As a horn player (clarinet, saxophone, flute), he co-founded the seminal '60s band the Insect Trust, and jammed with Ornette Coleman, Bono, and the Rolling Stones. He cut his critical teeth writing for *Rolling Stone,* then wrote for the *New York Times* from 1976–1988. Best remembered for his book *Deep Blues,* Palmer also wrote *Rock & Roll: An Unruly History,* as well as books on Jerry Lee Lewis, Lieber and Stoller, and a monograph on Memphis and New Orleans music. He was equally at home rolling in the Delta dirt outside a juke joint, playing with Sufi mystics in Morocco, and hanging out at the Dakota with Yoko Ono. *Blues & Chaos,* an anthology of Palmer's writing edited by Anthony DeCurtis, will be published in 2009.

Michael Parker is the author of four novels and two collections of short fiction. His fiction and nonfiction have appeared recently in the *New York Times Magazine* and *Runner's World.* He teaches in the MFA writing program at the University of North Carolina Greensboro.

Michael Perry is a freelance writer and author of the memoirs *Population 485: Meeting Your Neighbors One Siren at a Time* and *Truck: A Love Story.* He is also the author of the essay collection *Off Main Street: Barnstormers, Prophets & Gatemouth's Gator.* Perry's essays and articles have appeared in *Esquire,* the *New York Times Magazine, Outside, Backpacker, Orion,* and *Salon,* and he is a contributing editor to *Men's Health.* He has written about music and musicians for publications ranging from *No Depression* to *Country Music Weekly,* and plonks away in 4/4 time with his band, The Long Beds. Perry lives in rural Wisconsin, where he remains active as a volunteer emergency medical responder.

Tom Piazza is the author of nine books, including the novels *City of Refuge* and *My Cold War,* and the short-story collection *Blues and Trouble,* which won the James Michener Award. About his fiction, Bob Dylan wrote, "Tom Piazza's writing pulsates with nervous electrical tension—reveals the emotions that we can't define." Also well-known as a music writer, Piazza won a 2004 Grammy Award for his album notes to *Martin Scorsese Presents the Blues: A Musical Journey,* and he is a three-time winner of the ASCAP Deems Taylor Award for Music Writing. He was *The Oxford American*'s "Southern Music" columnist from 1998–2001. His book *Why New Orleans Matters* received the 2006 Humanities Book of the Year Award from the Louisiana Endowment for the Humanities. He lives in New Orleans.

Mike Powell was an editor and staff writer at *Stylus* online magazine for three years. He has written for *Pitchfork*, the *Village Voice*, *Paper Thin Walls*, and a number of other publications. He has also created several blogs.

Ron Rash is the author of three novels, three books of poetry, and three collections of stories. His latest novel is *Serena*. He has won NEA fellowships in poetry and fiction, an O. Henry Award, the James Still Award from the Fellowship of Southern Writers, and is a 2008 PEN/Faulkner Award finalist. He grew up in Boiling Springs, North Carolina, hometown of Earl Scruggs, and now teaches at Western Carolina University.

P. Revess, also known as Michael Kupperman, is a cartoonist, illustrator, and writer who lives in New York City. His work has appeared in places ranging from *The New Yorker* to *Saturday Night Live*. He is currently working on an animated project for television.

Paul Reyes is *The Oxford American*'s editor-at-large. His writing has appeared in *Details*, *Esquire*, the *Los Angeles Times Book Review*, and *Slate*.

Mark Richard was born in Lake Charles, Louisiana, and grew up in Texas and Virginia. He is the author of two award-winning short-story collections, *The Ice at the Bottom of the World* and *Charity*; and the novel *Fishboy*. His journalism and short stories have appeared in *The New Yorker*, *Harper's*, *Esquire*, *GQ*, *The Paris Review*, *Spin*, *Vogue*, the *New York Times*, *The Oxford American*, and other publications. He is the recipient of the PEN/Ernest Hemingway Award, an NEA fellowship, a Whiting Writers' Award, a New York Foundation for the Arts fellowship, the Mary Francis Hobson Medal for Arts and Letters, and a National Magazine Award for Fiction.

Diane Roberts is a Florida native, educated at Florida State University and Oxford, England. She has taught at Oxford University and the University of Alabama, worked as a columnist and editorial board member at the *St. Petersburg Times*, made radio documentaries for the BBC, recorded more than two hundred commentaries for NPR, and written for the *New York Times*, the *Times of London*, the *Washington Post*, and *The Oxford American*. Her books include *Faulkner and Southern Womanhood*, *The Myth of Aunt Jemima*, and *Dream State*. In 2006, she got thrown back into the briar patch of Tallahassee, Florida, and is now a professor of creative writing at Florida State University.

John Fergus Ryan (1931–2003) was born in Shanghai, China, raised in Little Rock, Arkansas, and spent his later years in Memphis, Tennessee. His work appeared in

The Atlantic Monthly, Penthouse, Esquire, The Oxford American, and *Mayfair.* He was the author of two cult novels, *The Redneck Bride* and *The Little Brothers of Saint Mortimer.*

Joe Sacco is the cartoonist responsible for *Palestine* and *Safe Area Gorazde,* among other works of comics journalism. He once made a living as a poster artist in Berlin, chronicled in his widely panned book of music comics, *But I Like It.* His favorite Beatle is George.

John Ryan Seawright (1956–2001) was a fiction writer and essayist in Athens, Georgia, where he was considered a legend. He appeared in *Inside Out,* the 1987 documentary about the independent-music scene there, and frequently contributed to *Flagpole.*

Jeff Sharlet learned to love Al Green while living as an ambivalent member of a fundamentalist sect in Arlington, Virginia, a story recounted in his book *The Family: The Secret Fundamentalism at the Heart of American Power.* For Sharlet's first book, *Killing the Buddha: A Heretic's Bible,* he learned to belt the Who's "Baba O'Riley" while living in the South Carolina compound of the Baba lovers, a sect that reveres the late guru Meher Baba, for whom Pete Townshend wrote the song. Sharlet is currently working on a history of "If I Had a Hammer," which he learned to sing from a first-grade music teacher who didn't know it was written as a radical anthem. He's a contributing editor for *Rolling Stone,* where he does not write about music, and *Harper's,* from which his essay on the Dragons' album *Rock Like Fuck* was anthologized in *Best Music Writing 2004.*

Cynthia Shearer is the author of *The Wonder Book of the Air,* which won the 1997 Mississippi Institute of Arts and Letters Award for fiction, and *The Celestial Jukebox,* a fictional exploration of the effects of African immigration on the dying blues tradition in the Mississippi Delta. She was a recipient of an NEA fellowship in fiction in 2000, and a Pushcart Prize for essays in 2006. She lives in Fort Worth, Texas, and teaches writing at Texas Christian University.

A native of New Orleans, **Sheryl St. Germain** currently directs the MFA program in creative writing at Chatham University in Pittsburgh. Her work has received several awards, including two NEA fellowships, an NEH fellowship, the Dobie Paisano fellowship, and the William Faulkner Award for the personal essay. Her poetry books include *Making Bread at Midnight, How Heavy the Breath of God,* and *The Journals of Scheherazade.* She has also published *Je Suis Cadien,* a book of translations of the Cajun poet Jean Arceneaux, and a book of essays about growing up in New Orleans, *Swamp Songs: The Making of an Unruly Woman*. Her most recent book is *Let It Be a Dark Roux: New and Selected Poems*.

Susan Straight has published six novels, including *I Been in Sorrow's Kitchen and Licked Out All the Pots, Highwire Moon*, and *A Million Nightingales*. Her short fiction and essays have been published in *O. Henry Prize Stories 2007, Best American Short Stories 2003, McSweeney's, Zoetrope: All-Story, Harper's*, the *New York Times Magazine, WEST, Salon*, and *The Oxford American*, among others. She was born in Riverside, where she still lives with her three daughters, and sees that ex-husband of hers nearly every single day.

Marty Stuart is country music's Renaissance Man. He is a singer/songwriter, a musician, a producer, a writer of prose, and a photographer. He has scored six Top Ten hits, one platinum album, five gold albums, four Grammy Awards, and a Golden Globe nomination (for his film-score composition for *All the Pretty Horses*). He has also written about music and culture for such publications as *The Oxford American*, and his photographs have been exhibited in New Orleans and Nashville. In his songwriting, singing, playing, and producing, there is a storyteller at work—a man who listens to, and translates, the world he knows.

John Jeremiah Sullivan was born in Louisville, Kentucky, in 1974. He is a writer-at-large for GQ magazine, and his work has appeared in *Harper's, The Paris Review*, and *The Oxford American*. He is the winner of the 2003 National Magazine Award for Best Feature and the 2003 Media Eclipse Award for Best Feature, and the author of *Blood Horses: Notes of a Sportswriter's Son*.

Joseph G. Tidwell III was born and raised in and around Jackson, Mississippi. He is a self-taught writer of stage plays, movie scripts, novels, short stories, and poetry, and his work has been produced in Hollywood and other places around the country.

Nick Tosches is the author of the novel *In the Hand of Dante*, and many other books of fiction, nonfiction, and poetry. In 2006, *The Observer* declared *Hellfire*, his 1982 biography of Jerry Lee Lewis, the greatest music book ever written. His piece for *The Oxford American* was a part of his last, longest, and deepest exploration into the mysteries of American music. He is a contributing editor for *Vanity Fair* and spends most of his time in New York City.

Anthony Walton is the author of *Mississippi: An American Journey*, and co-editor, with Michael S. Harper, of *The Vintage Book of African American Poetry*. His articles, essays, and reviews have appeared in the *New York Times,* the *Washington Post, Harper's,* and *The Atlantic Monthly.* His poems have been published in *The New Yorker, The Kenyon Review, The Oxford American,* and *Notre Dame Review,* among others, and have been regularly anthologized. In 2005, he created, wrote, and presented the long-form radio documentary *Southern Road* for the BBC. He has taught at Notre Dame and Brown, and has been on the faculty at Bowdoin College since 1995.

Jerry Wexler, an inductee of the Rock and Roll Hall of Fame, began his career as a cub reporter for *Billboard,* where, among other achievements, he convinced the magazine to use the phrase "rhythm and blues" instead of "race records." He then became a partner at Atlantic Records, where he produced records by Ray Charles, Ruth Brown, Aretha Franklin, Wilson Pickett, Dusty Springfield, Willie Nelson, Otis Redding, the Rolling Stones, Led Zeppelin, Etta James, Carlos Santana, Esther Phillips, Percy Sledge, Solomon Burke, Dr. John, the Drifters, Big Joe Turner, Doug Sahm, and Bob Dylan, to name just a few. He is the author, with David Ritz, of *Rhythm & the Blues: A Life in American Music.*

Lauren Wilcox grew up in Durham, North Carolina. She has written for the *Washington Post* and *The Paris Review,* and was a former editor at *The Oxford American.*

Marc Woodworth is the author of *Bee Thousand* in Continuum's 33 1/3 series as well as *Arcade,* a volume of poetry. He is an editor at *Salmagundi* and lecturer at Skidmore College.

Elizabeth Wurtzel is the author of *Prozac Nation, Bitch: In Praise of Difficult Women,* and *More, Now, Again.* She is a graduate of Yale Law School, and lives in New York City.

Steve Yarbrough is the author of four novels, three short-story collections, and numerous essays and reviews. He is the James and Coke Hallowell Professor of Creative Writing at California State University, Fresno, where he directs the school's MFA program. Yarbrough plays a 1984 Martin D-35 and has recently taught himself to make noise on a 1961 Harmony Monterey mandolin.

Credits

Freight Micro and Freight Text were designed by Joshua Darden between 1998 and 2004, and interpret the traditional forms of Anglo-Dutch typography, which dates to the founding of the Oxford University Press in the early 1670s.

Further information about the face(s) can be found at the designer's website: http://www.joshuadarden.com.